Praise for *Atomic*

"Enthralling and riveting . . . [Greenspan] has brought together new material that rounds out Fuchs's life." —*The New York Times Book Review*

"Greenspan gives us fresh and fascinating insights into Fuchs's formative years." —*The Wall Street Journal*

"Spies make for enticing biographies. Well told, their stories combine the drama of a police procedural (how did they do it?) with the ambiguities of a psychological thriller (why did they do it?). Nancy Thorndike Greenspan seeks to answer both those questions in the very well told *Atomic Spy* . . . a deeply nuanced and sympathetic portrait of a scientist-spy with the best of intentions—an original addition to the shelf of Fuchs biographies." —*Nature*

"Nancy Thorndike Greenspan's biography offers a new look at Fuchs's story, all the more fascinating for its deviations from typical spy-movie script." —*The New Criterion*

"A detailed and authoritative yet equally interesting and readable study . . . From student to scientist to spy, Fuchs is portrayed as a careful and quiet yet passionate man who nevertheless persisted." —*Library Journal*

"This richly detailed work . . . blurs the lines between courage and treachery in thought-provoking ways." —*Publishers Weekly*

"Nancy Greenspan dives into the mysteries of the Klaus Fuchs espionage case and emerges with a classic Cold War biography of intrigue and torn loyalties. *Atomic Spy* is a mesmerizing morality tale, told with fresh sources and empathy."
 —Kai Bird, author of *The Good Spy: The Life and Death of Robert Ames* and coauthor of *American Prometheus: The Triumph and Tragedy of J. Robert Oppenheimer*

PENGUIN BOOKS

ATOMIC SPY

Nancy Thorndike Greenspan is the author of *The End of the Certain World* and the coauthor of four books with her late husband, child psychiatrist Stanley Greenspan. She lives in Bethesda, Maryland.

Also by Nancy Thorndike Greenspan

THE END OF THE CERTAIN WORLD:
The Life and Science of Max Born:
The Nobel Physicist Who Ignited the Quantum Revolution

ATOMIC SPY

THE DARK LIVES OF
KLAUS FUCHS

Nancy Thorndike Greenspan

PENGUIN BOOKS

PENGUIN BOOKS
An imprint of Penguin Random House LLC
penguinrandomhouse.com

First published in the United States of America by Viking,
an imprint of Penguin Random House LLC, 2020
Published in Penguin Books 2021

Grateful acknowledgment is made for permission to reprint the following:
Page 75: Photo courtesy of the Library and Archives of Canada, based on PA-143488.
Page 193: Photo courtesy of the Buneman family.
Page 245: Photo from Heritage Image Partnership Ltd. / Alamy Stock Photo.

Photo on page 17 by Ferdinand Urbahns; photo on page 127 is from Los Alamos National
Lab; and photo on page 329 is from the Library of Congress.

ISBN 9780593083406 (paperback)

THE LIBRARY OF CONGRESS HAS CATALOGED THE HARDCOVER EDITION AS FOLLOWS:
Names: Greenspan, Nancy Thorndike, author.
Title: Atomic Spy : The Dark Lives of Klaus Fuchs / Nancy Thorndike Greenspan.
Description: [New York, New York] : Viking, [2020] |
Includes bibliographical references and index. |
Identifiers: LCCN 2019053138 (print) | LCCN 2019053139 (ebook) |
ISBN 9780593083390 (hardcover) | ISBN 9780593083413 (ebook)
Subjects: LCSH: Fuchs, Klaus Emil Julius, 1911–1988. | Spies—Soviet Union—Biography. |
Spies—Great Britain—Biography. | Spies—United States—Biography. |
Espionage, Soviet—Great Britain—History—20th century. | Espionage, Soviet—United
States—History—20th century. | Physicists—Germany—Biography. |
Nuclear weapons—History—20th century.
Classification: LCC UB271.R9 F8355 2020 (print) |
LCC UB271.R9 (ebook) | DDC 327.1247041092 [B]—dc23

Printed in the United States of America
1st Printing

Book design by Daniel Lagin

To my husband, Stanley, who always believed that
the children and I could do what we set our minds to.
He led by example; he inspired us.

And to my friend Gustav Born, who generously allowed
me to write the biography of his father, Max Born,
the experience that led me down this path.

Contents

Prologue: Revelation, London, August 1949   1

I. RESISTANCE   17

    1. Beginnings, Leipzig 1930   19
    2. Loss, Kiel 1931   31
    3. Revolt, Kiel 1932   39
    4. Leader, Kiel 1933   49
    5. Underground, Berlin 1933   59
    6. Interlude, Paris 1933   71

II. RESCUE   75

    7. Safety, Bristol 1933   77
    8. War, Edinburgh 1937   87
    9. Internment, England 1940   101
    10. Internment, Canada 1940   113

III. RESEARCH   127

    11. Tube Alloys, Birmingham 1941   129
    12. Manhattan Project, New York 1943   143
    13. Trinity, Los Alamos 1944   155
    14. Director, Harwell 1946   175

IV. RECONNAISSANCE   193

15. Suspects, London, September 1949   195

16. Surveillance, Harwell, September 1949   211

17. Disposal, London, October 1949   221

18. Interrogation, London, November 1949   231

V. RESULTS   245

19. Disposal Again, London, January 1950   247

20. Confession, Harwell, January 1950   257

21. Arrest, London, February 1950   271

22. Trial, London, March 1950   285

23. The FBI, London, May 1950   299

24. Prison, Wormwood Scrubs, 1950 and On   313

VI. RETURN   329

25. East Germany, Berlin 1959   331

26. Expectations, Dresden 1960   341

Epilogue: Remembrances, Berlin, March 1989   351

Acknowledgments   355

Abbreviations   359

Notes   363

Bibliography   387

Index   391

ATOMIC SPY

Revelation, London, August 1949

ON SEPTEMBER 10, 1949, MICHAEL PERRIN'S PHONE RANG IN THE MIDDLE OF THE night. The message was simple, direct, and urgent: come to the American embassy.

Perrin, deputy director of Britain's longtime atomic energy program, jumped in a taxi for the five-mile trip south from Hampstead to 1 Grosvenor Square, where U.S. State Department officials hustled him into the communications room. There he learned the content of several coded telex messages from the Pentagon. The U.S. Air Force, using specially equipped planes, had detected radiation in the atmosphere. The only explanation could be the explosion of an atomic bomb. The United States needed an RAF plane to conduct additional tests to confirm the findings.

One week later, Perrin gathered with other experts for a meeting of Britain's Joint Intelligence Committee at the Ministry of Defense at Whitehall. To the surprise of many JIC members, the room was first cleared of secretaries and "anyone else who could not keep what was going to be said to himself," placing the meeting, as one observer described it, "under a melodramatic bond of secrecy."

A balding physicist with a serious countenance, Perrin somberly explained that the radiation detected was most likely the result of a Russian A-bomb test, most likely in the area of Lake Baikal. RAF airplanes outfitted with special filters had "obtained particles which have been definitely identified as plutonium," though he acknowledged that there was still some doubt about the specifics.

The committee approved Perrin and the director of MI6 to brief Prime Minister Clement Attlee at his country home, and the two men hastened up to Putney. But Attlee was already aware of these dire developments. He and President Harry Truman had been in contact by telegram.

Four years had passed since the American bombing of Hiroshima and Nagasaki, and the end of the war had brought a significant realignment of the world's major powers. Having sided with the Western democracies against the Nazis, the Soviet Union had emerged from the war—at least in the eyes of its former allies—as the greatest threat to the current peace. Joint Intelligence Committee papers had projected that the Russians would have a bomb by 1950 at the earliest, more reasonably in 1952. British military forecasting relied on these assessments. If the radiation was truly from a Russian test, how could this have happened so quickly? How could Soviet science have leaped so far ahead?

In classic understatement, one participant in the meeting noted the significance of the A-bomb test in his diary: "The [Joint Intelligence Committee] papers will, of course, have to be revised."

Not far from Buckingham Palace, in an unassuming office building of ordinary brick and limestone near Hyde Park Corner, a man sat examining top secret memos that might provide the answer to Russia's mysterious go-ahead. There was nothing about the man, Arthur Martin, to suggest international intrigue, even less so derring-do. The same was true of the building nestled in among the pubs and grocery shops of Curzon Street—except perhaps for some bricked-in windows. The gun ports on one side might strike an equally odd note for the careful observer. The bricks and the ports had been devised as last-ditch insurance against German paratroopers landing in Hyde Park during the war. The architectural anomalies made sense only if one knew that the unassuming building, Leconfield House, was the headquarters of MI5, the section of military intelligence tasked with hunting down spies on British soil.

The memos in Martin's care had originated across the Atlantic, where American and British code breakers toiling in Arlington, Virginia, had at long last made sense out of seeming nonsense. They had labored long and hard over a stack of coded messages sent between the Soviet consulate in New York and Moscow in 1944, back when the United States and the U.S.S.R. were closing in on German forces from opposite sides of Europe.

Now, five years later, the decoded threads revealed evidence of a wartime traitor. Urgency and dread pulsated through a telegraph from the British embassy in Washington:

> We have discovered Material, which, though fragmentary, appears to indicate that in 1944 a British or British-sponsored scientist working here on atomic energy or related subjects was providing Russians with policy information or documents.
>
> Agent's cover name was initially Rest subsequently changed to Charles. In July 1944 he had been working for 6 months.
>
> On one occasion he handed over through cut-out report described as M.S.M. -1(part 3) subject of which appears to be fluctuations in stream or ray. . . .
>
> My present opinion is that this will prove grave matter.

Again, British understatement held sway.

Arthur Martin was relatively new as an intelligence officer at MI5, but he had a history with signals intelligence and encryption. He had spent five years at the Government Communications Headquarters securing its systems and examining those of foreign powers. Just recently he had been made liaison between GCHQ and MI5's B Branch, counterespionage and counter-subversion, a division that was often the focus for high-profile action.

For decades, MI5 had bugged the British Communist Party headquarters, routinely opened the mail of its members, and kept an eye on fellow travelers. Since the war it had doubled its efforts. It worried as it looked to the East. Moscow's persistent pressure on Central and Eastern Europe had undermined nascent democratic governments. In March 1946, in a famous speech in Fulton, Missouri, Winston Churchill had described the Soviet menace with characteristically memorable prose: "From Stettin in the Baltic to Trieste in the Adriatic, an iron curtain has descended across the Continent."

A weakened postwar economy that included continued rationing for food and gas in particular, as well as an acute housing shortage, left Britain vulnerable to Soviet expansion and propaganda. The forced austerity of World War II and the Great Depression defeated Conservative governments and elevated left-wing ones to power, with Churchill sent back into the wilderness and Clement Attlee's Labour government in control.

Science was a bright spot, a positive side effect of weapons research that included development of the atomic bomb. The nuclear age could give Britain the capacity to develop new forms of power and medicine, and new weapons. Many of its top scientists, partnered with their American counterparts, had tirelessly slogged in the Manhattan Project, the joint U.S.-U.K. effort to build an atomic bomb, and now Britain wanted its own. Until the British achieved that milestone, the Americans had a monopoly—or so they had thought until they detected radiation in the atmosphere.

If Russia did have a bomb, and well ahead of schedule, it would shatter the West's atomic hegemony. What would this portend for the security of Europe, and in particular the security of England? Moscow was only fifteen hundred miles from London. One burdened soul later agonized that with sufficient bombs the Soviets could "blot this country out entirely."

Arthur Martin chased suspects through clues on paper: studying the messages, reviewing the files, and slowly filling in the pieces of the puzzle. The tighter the pieces fit, the clearer the patchwork scheme became, and the more effectively field agents could operate.

For this assignment, he had to penetrate the clues available in the decoded messages of the Russians and try to ferret out the traitor and what secrets he had betrayed. Hamstrung from lack of information, he could do little until the endless blocks of numbers in the coded messages yielded treasure. He waited.

In a move to lift the veil, British intelligence officers in Washington told Martin that they were keen to dig into the 1944–45 files on the Manhattan Project. Their information was still fragmentary, but using the specifics they had—a scientist, perhaps British or British sponsored, working in the United States on a project probably related to atomic energy in 1944—they thought they could link the clues and identify the scientist who had betrayed them. A week later, they cabled Martin that they had come up empty, and any notion of an easy solution had evaporated.

As the second week of the hunt rolled in, some light peeked through the clouds. The relentless chipping away of the code breakers in Arlington had extracted more information hidden in the blocks of numbers. The embassy sent Martin actual text from ten partially deciphered messages. But with the mixed bundle of fully deciphered sentences, partial ones, and large chunks of code that defied best efforts, he had plenty of head-scratching ahead. A message from New York to Moscow dated June 15, 1944, typified the decoded material he had in hand:

To VIKTOR.
[1 group unrecovered] received from REST the third part of
report MSN-12 Efferent Fluctuation in a Stream [STRUYA]
[37 groups unrecoverable]

Diffusion Method—work on his specialty. R. expressed
doubt about the possibility of remaining in the COUNTRY
[STRANA] without arousing suspicion. According to what
R. says, the ISLANDERS [OSTROVITYaNE] and TOWNS-
MEN [GOROZhANE] have finally fallen out as a result of
the delay in research work on diffusion. . . . *

*Only the latter part of the word has been recovered,
but "Diffusion" is probable from the context.

The code breakers had to turn seemingly random number blocks into
Russian words and then into English, with specific code names requiring
identifiers as well. Some of the identifiers were clear—"COUNTRY" was
the United States, "ISLANDERS" were the British, and "TOWNSMEN"
were the Americans. *R*, "REST," was the mystery.

Martin was different from most other officers in counterintelligence. He
didn't belong to the class of "gents" recruited from Oxbridge by way of
Eton or Harrow, the toffs who dominated the intelligence establishment.
His education was plebeian, and he belonged to no clubs. Baby-faced and a
heavy smoker, he kept a bottle of scotch in the desk drawer and drank it out of
a coffee cup when needed. But he was a dedicated professional and a lawyer
with meticulous focus, good intuition, and an analytical mind.

The director of B Branch, Dick White, had brought him in, and they
had a close relationship, both professionally and personally. Martin had
married White's secretary, Joan. Of course, in the symbiotic underworld of
spying, the connection didn't stop there. Before her marriage to Martin,
Joan had carried on an affair with White.

Scrutinizing the text of the ten new messages, Martin carefully extracted
and listed the certainties along with the uncertainties. He could document
that the spy called Rest was male, had been in the United States between
March 1944 and July 1944, had worked on an Anglo-American scientific
project, had contact with the report "MSN I-Efferent Fluctuations in the

Stream," and had a sister who probably lived in the United States. At least, the sister's time in the United States overlapped with his. In 1944, an unknown Soviet agent visited this woman in October and possibly again in November. The key uncertainties were the nationality of the scientist, his possible transfer back to the U.K., the location of his sister, and the nature of the scientific project he'd worked on.

The messages indicated that the British had considered transferring their researchers back to the U.K. because of tensions with the Americans. When confronted with this, the Americans countered that it would be a violation of the secret, scientific agreement that was part of the Atlantic Charter, signed by Churchill and Roosevelt. The messages didn't indicate a decision about the transfer. Had Rest been posted to another position in the United States or sent back to the U.K.? Martin was left hanging.

The British security officers in Washington worked closely with the FBI, the British shuttling between their embassy on Massachusetts Avenue and the FBI's Washington field office housed in the Old Post Office Building near the White House. They both concluded that Rest had most likely infiltrated the Manhattan Project on the atomic bomb.

MI5 and the FBI agreed on a concerted effort, to protect the top secret decoding project Venona, even if it slowed down the discovery of the spy. Initiated on February 1, 1943, and continuing for decades, Venona was run by the U.S. Army's Signal Intelligence Service (later absorbed into the National Security Agency) as a means of decrypting messages transmitted by Soviet intelligence agencies. The longer the Russians stayed in the dark about Venona and the extent of Venona's access, the longer Washington and London had an intelligence edge. Five-year-old messages could still betray valuable secrets.

Martin met with his counterparts in MI6, the military's division of foreign intelligence, to pinpoint the best entry into the maze of Rest's identity. On September 1, the embassy in Washington cabled him that the FBI had identified two possibilities. Following the trail of clues from the report "Efferent Fluctuation in a Stream" that Rest had handed over, they made a breakthrough.

That report had originated from the British scientific team. A particular physicist had written some papers for a research series, and his movements matched Rest's. The FBI offered up the name of one Karl Fuchs, a naturalized British subject of German origin. According to their information, he had arrived in New York on December 3, 1943, and had then been transferred to Oak Ridge, Tennessee, on August 14, 1944.

The Washington team requested all information on this man. Their main questions: Did he have a sister in the United States? And if so, where was she?

Martin now had a name to work with, except his request for a personal file on Karl Fuchs from MI5's Registry came back unfilled. But *Klaus* Fuchs, who had been a member of the British Mission on Atomic Energy in the United States, did have a file several inches thick, fattened with hundreds of documents.

The file followed the standard MI5 format. Every letter or memo, every set of notes from a meeting, a phone call, or report, was paginated and clipped in the file chronologically. An index at the front of the file, denoted as "Minute Sheets," briefly listed each document, its arrival date, and page number. Those privy to the file wrote comments to each other—called minutes—directly onto the index sheets. Plowing through it, Martin could follow the thread of confidential office dialogue to pry into the past interpretations and opinions of MI5 personnel.

MI5 quickly "Y-boxed" the file with a new sticker that overlaid its cluttered cover of stamps and file numbers. This new designation added security and meant that "this file when in transit must be in a closed envelope, addressed personally to the officer. HELD BY R5." A specific person, rather than the Registry, would hold it to ensure against peeks from curious personnel, mistakes in delivery, and leaks. In this case, that person was Arthur Martin. "Indoctrinating" officers—that is, granting access to the secrets in this file—had to be approved by him or the director general of MI5.

Klaus Fuchs's security file was one for Martin to ponder. Clearly, Fuchs had kept MI5 busy throughout his sixteen years in England and Scotland— no speedy thumb through here. The details in the hundreds of pages led to vague connections and baffling contradictions. In Martin's real-life game of whodunit, there was no answer card to correct a wrong guess.

Fuchs had been investigated at least seven times, an unusually high number. Few months passed between 1939 and 1949 without his folder landing on someone's desk for a review or approval. In Fuchs's case, there was a work permit in 1941, naturalization in 1942, an exit permit to the United States in 1943, and security clearance in 1946 for his employment at Harwell, the main nuclear research facility in Britain and center for all projects on atomic energy.

The last one was for a position as the head of the Theoretical Physics Division at Harwell. The letter requesting the security clearance explained that "there is, as far as we are aware, only one other person in this country who possesses qualifications and experience of Dr. Fuchs."

Clearances for top secret jobs and promotions required careful consideration and, on their own, would cause the formation of a security file. As Martin was about to discover, Fuchs's file had a different origin. MI5 had opened it within a year of his arrival in England.

Sitting in his office in Leconfield House, a supply of cigarettes within reach, Martin began his journey through Fuchs's refugee life in Britain— the file pages worn, rumpled, and faded after fifteen years of scrutiny by others. The first nine dispelled expectations of typical interoffice squabbles and dictates from those in charge. The naked condemnation contained in this initial information—together with its questionable reliability—was stunning.

The file began with a letter dated August 7, 1934. Four days before, twenty-two-year-old Klaus Fuchs, who was in Britain as a refugee from Nazi oppression, had gone to the German consulate in Bristol. He had been studying for a PhD in physics at the University of Bristol for about a year, and his German passport had expired in June. Staff at the consulate took his passport and forwarded it to the German embassy in London. The letter of August 7 was its response to Fuchs. For him to obtain a new passport, the police at his last place of residence in Germany had to certify that they had no objections.

Two months later, Fuchs submitted his request for a certificate to the police in Kiel, his last official residence. Within the week, the German embassy sent him a letter refusing him a new passport. It gave him no reason. Instead, it offered to issue him "a short-term certificate"—one way only—to return to Germany.

Fuchs knew that his life was endangered in Germany, and he couldn't go back.

But without a passport, he was stateless, stranded in Britain. It was a status becoming increasingly common to German refugees fleeing the Nazis and relatively easy to change. One simply applied to the Home Office to extend the time-limited residence permit.

Martin requested the Home Office's records on Fuchs, and they showed that year after year the government had rolled over his residence permits until 1938, when he gained permanent residence without a time limit. The only restriction imposed because of his statelessness was on travel outside the U.K. For this he needed official approval.

What Martin read next suggested more than a citizenship problem. At the time of the passport request in 1934, the German Foreign Office in Berlin had returned Fuchs's original letter to the consulate. On the back, the Gestapo in Kiel had scrawled a note. Translated, it read,

> The Student Klaus Fuchs, born 29.12.11 at Russelsheim was as per card presented here and dated 31.8.31 until 3.3.32 member of the Social-Democratic Party. Here he was excluded 1932. Fuchs joined then the Communist Party and worked for this Party as orator in the election-campaigns. Fuchs was leader of the Nazi commission of the Sea District, the task of which it was to break up the National-Socialist Party.

REVELATION, LONDON, AUGUST 1949

Under strict confidentiality, the consul had forwarded the denunciation to the chief constable of Bristol, who sent a report to the director general of MI5 and the Home Office:

> The above-named German subject landed at Folkestone on the 24th September, 1933, conditionally that he registered at once with the Police, and that he did not remain in the United Kingdom longer than three months. . . . Information has now been given to the Police by Mr. Carl Ludwig Herweg, Secretary to Mr. C. Hartley Hodder, German Consul . . . that Fuchs is a notorious Communist. . . . During his stay in this City Fuchs is not known to have engaged in any communist activity.

Disadvantaged by the fifteen-year gap since the incident, Martin didn't know how intelligence officers had weighed the chief constable's paraphrase of Fuchs as "a notorious Communist" against his observation that Fuchs's record in Bristol was unblemished.

He tracked the critiques through the file's pages and found that during the war, with Nazi atrocities emblazoning headlines, MI5 had treated this report from the Gestapo as highly suspect—most likely propaganda. For a start, the Nazis lumped all Jews, Social Democrats, and communists together. MI5 analysts awarded Fuchs the benefit of the doubt, especially given that the government wanted and needed his scientific expertise.

Martin skipped through the next eight years in the security file to find another troubling incident. Back in 1942, an MI5 informant had asked whether Klaus Fuchs was "identical with a certain CLAUS FUCHS." Claus Fuchs was a physicist of about thirty years old, had been interned in Canada, and in the camps became a close friend of a German communist named Hans Kahle, who was very active politically.

The question referred to the British internment of about thirty thousand "enemy aliens" at the outset of the war. Most of these—German and

Italian refugees who were not yet naturalized British citizens—were Jewish, like the vast majority of émigrés, although Fuchs and Kahle were not. Wary of the costs of corralling masses of scared and angry young men, the British had simply transferred several shiploads to Canada. The camps there were full-fledged prison compounds: barbed-wire fences, spotlights, and sentry towers. Some had volatile mixtures of Germans: Jews, Nazi POWs, and communists.

Was "Claus Fuchs" the same as Klaus Fuchs? The file gave Martin no immediate response, but digging through the minutes, he did find a later internal dispute that led to a conclusion: Klaus Fuchs had been shipped to Canada. Therefore, Klaus Fuchs and Claus Fuchs were probably "identical," and thus he was the friend of Hans Kahle, someone whose own security file included charges of being a Soviet agent.

The last document that drew Martin's attention originated from an MI5 informant who gathered gossip from communist groups in various British cities. The informant, "Kaspar," had heard that both Klaus and his brother, Gerhard, who now lived in Switzerland, had belonged to the German Communist Party. According to the rumor, Klaus never achieved any prominence in the party, but Gerhard was part of the "German Communist Apparat." Klaus had fled to Prague and was not involved in political activity there. In the U.K., he was part of "the usual Communist propaganda," according to Kaspar, but again not prominent. He concluded, "He bears a good personal reputation and is considered a decent fellow."

Was what Martin had extracted enough? Condemnation by the Nazis; a possible communist friend in an internment camp; and a report from Kaspar that stressed the actions of Gerhard and diminished those of Klaus. Did this give him an understanding of who Klaus Fuchs was? Most of the content argued and reargued Fuchs's reliability. Forms gave a basic timeline. There were no interviews of friends or colleagues. Voluminous though MI5's file was, Fuchs the person was a vague figure.

One thing was clear: during the war everyone knew that Fuchs could be a problem but hoped he wouldn't be. At a point when bombs pelted England, killing residents and burning cities, an MI5 officer had to decide about a work permit for Fuchs to do secret research. He called a colleague and asked if it was "really serious" if the research ended up with the Russians. Could they "employ someone else instead of FUCHS"? the other person responded. Notes on the conversation read, "I said I thought that was the crux of the matter, and that if the work could not be done properly without FUCHS, we should have to accept such risk as there might be." With devastation surrounding them, the British desperately looked to science for an edge to victory. After all, Hitler was still on their doorstep and could win. Fuchs received the permit.

Not all agreed with this rationale. One MI5 officer, a hardened veteran of the Battle of Dunkirk, asked "whether a man of this nature who has been described as clever and dangerous, should be in a position where he has access to information of the highest degree of secrecy and importance." To him, the evidence was enough to bar Fuchs from war research.

Martin read a particularly telling exchange from 1943 when Fuchs needed an exit permit to go to the United States with the British Mission on Atomic Energy. An MI5 officer wrote to Michael Perrin, already a highly respected scientist and administrator with the government's Department of Scientific and Industrial Research. DSIR was the official employer of the British team in the United States. Was Fuchs scheduled to stay in the United States? MI5 wanted to know. Perrin said no.

A month after the British mission's and Fuchs's arrival in the United States, Perrin reversed his reply because Professor Rudolf Peierls, a close colleague to Fuchs and a senior member of the British team, requested that Fuchs remain there. Knowing that some MI5 officers had "slight doubts" about Fuchs, Perrin wanted to ensure that there was no problem. "This is a very important matter vis-à-vis the Americans," he wrote, "and I want to be quite sure that we do not slip up in any way."

From the vantage point of 1949, Martin followed MI5's internal deliberations in the file, one that Perrin wasn't privy to:

[Fuchs is] rather safer in America than in this country . . .
away from his English friends. . . . [I]t would not be so easy for

FUCHS to make contact with Communists in America, and
that in any case he would probably be more roughly handled
were he found out.

Martin saw that the letter Perrin received from MI5 had said much
less. It read,

> It is considered that there would be no objection to this man
> remaining in the U.S.A. as he has never been very active politi-
> cally, and recent reports endorse the good opinion you have of
> his behaviour in this country.

And then came the caveat, which MI5 had added for Perrin's eyes only:

> It would not appear to be desirable to mention his proclivities in
> the U.S.A. and we do not think it at all likely that he will attempt
> to make political contacts in that country while he is there.

The restraint and composure of MI5's approval belied the serious consequences of a miscalculation. Then, and throughout the war years, the
agency's calm tone of denial covered a sea of doubt.

Fuchs's file was full of contradictions built on misinformation and misun-
derstanding that befuddled MI5's insight into what drove him. But even if
they had grasped the inner sense of justice that dictated his actions, they
might have been confused. He came from a world that had to be lived or
seen in deep relief to comprehend. For perspective, they might have harked
back to the sixteenth- and seventeenth-century religious turmoil of their
own ancestors whose beliefs were indestructible in the face of torture and
death. Those days of beheadings over faith and hiding holes for priests
were not so different from the turbulent times that shattered post–World
War I Germany. In this light, they might have understood that it wasn't

science that compelled Fuchs but an unwavering commitment to ideals that grew out of early years engulfed in political strife. That was the root of his story and of his being. That is what they needed to know, but didn't.

Clearly, what the Brits did know was that they were playing the odds, Russian roulette perhaps. And just as clearly, they intentionally failed to tell the Americans about the bullet in the chamber.

I

RESISTANCE

Nazi student group before the main building of the University of Kiel, 1938

CHAPTER 1

Beginnings, Leipzig 1930

WHO WAS THIS KLAUS FUCHS? COMMUNIST. PHYSICIST. POTENTIAL SPY. WHAT motivated him? Where did this amalgam of technical genius and ideology come from?

The last of those questions is the only one with a direct if simplistic answer. Klaus Fuchs came from Eisenach, Germany, a small town that pulsed with eight hundred years of history and culture. High above the Market Square that young Klaus crossed daily on his way to school was the Wartburg, an eleventh-century fortification. A symbol of protection and stability on a 1,350-foot rocky prominence, it had been Martin Luther's refuge from Charles V in 1521, when he translated the New Testament into German. In the center of the town was the birthplace of Johann Sebastian Bach.

Klaus's own birth, on December 29, 1911, was actually in Rüsselsheim, just south of Frankfurt, where his father, Emil, was the rector of the redbrick Lutheran church in the middle of town. From the family's thatched-roof cottage, Emil penned his weekly sermons as well as articles for its *Evangelical Community Newsletter.* On March 3, 1918, with the world war in its third year, he wrote one thanking God for Germany's new treaty with Russia that removed the Eastern threat. He awaited the collapse of England—a "robber nation," he called it—so that a free Germany with "a spiritual life of such power and purity, a state life of such justice," could emerge to create world peace. Like many Germans, he was still optimistic that the long war would soon end, with Germany victorious.

That summer, as fresh troops from America joined the battle and the Allies began turning back the last German offensives, the family moved to Eisenach. The church had assigned Emil a working-class parish drawn from the automobile industry there. He rented a house high on a hill over-looking the city—close to the Wartburg—with a garden and enough space for their goats.

Despite the humiliation of Germany's surrender six weeks before Klaus's seventh birthday, the kaiser's abdication, and the political and economic chaos that followed, the family still managed to enjoy their new home. The children celebrated holidays with friends; Emil wrote a play they performed at Christmas; little Klaus made a gizmo from a small piece of wood and gave a "serious" lesson to his class on his technique.

Klaus and his sister Kristel, two years younger, grew into playmates, exploring a fantasy world from a big gall at the base of a backyard tree that transformed into a horse (for her) or a camel (for him) and, on a sunny afternoon, offered a ride of imagination across the countryside. In quiet hours, he taught her to read. She watched as he built mazes and running wheels for his pet mice. His concern for animals led him to become a dedicated vegetarian at an early age. At twelve, he became so seriously anemic that his parents sent him to a clinic in Switzerland for a cure.

Emil transferred his older son, Gerhard, to the Odenwaldschule in August 1923. A sylvan oasis that combined theology, socialism, and educational reform, the boarding school was founded by an imposing tall, slim man with a full black beard and intense, deep-set piercing eyes named Paul Geheeb. Over time Geheeb and his wife became close to the whole Fuchs family, who one by one or in pairs escaped there for rest and recovery—especially Emil, who often sought respite from general life. Klaus loved his visits.

"But little by little," as Emil recalled, "political developments cast their shadows over cheerful work and family life."

All over Germany, angry and unemployed veterans rallied and sometimes rioted in the streets, protesting the ineffectual, socialist government that had replaced the empire and the supposed "stab in the back" by Jews and communists that the right wing said accounted for Germany's defeat, and after such sacrifice!

German soldiers had drowned in the mud and blood of the trenches, while civilians had suffered extreme privations. Especially during the so-called Turnip Winter of 1916–17, when there was little else to eat, Germans had made ersatz "coffee" out of tree bark and joked that they were forced to eat ersatz cats and mice. The Quakers set up feeding stations for the severely malnourished children. Emil wandered dead tired in villages, going to friends of a cousin to buy food for his family. He kept them fed, but he could do little about the lack of heating fuel during the bitter cold.

After Germany's humiliating surrender, the Allies' blockade continued in order to extend the suffering and force harsh treaty terms, including the payment of reparations that crippled the economy. The French occupied the Ruhr to carry off German coal, and then came three years of dizzying inflation: 1 million marks for a loaf of bread until the next week, when the price doubled or tripled, finally hitting 200 billion marks.

Paying the tuition for Gerhard at the Odenwaldschule worried Emil. A friend in London sent him five pounds—a windfall given the exchange rate—and rescued him financially. It allowed Emil to send twenty-five million marks as partial tuition payment. He ruminated, "But what is so much German money beside the five pounds? One feels how poor we have become."

Emil sermonized about spiritual life but lived a political one, which could be dangerous, especially in the unsettled days of Germany's first experiment with democracy, the Weimar Republic. The foreign minister was murdered, as were leftist leaders, and anyone such as Emil who was sympathetic to workers' rights was automatically a "red" and treated accordingly.

Lutheran ministers were a conservative lot, and Emil was one of the few to join the moderate left-wing Social Democrats, the largest political party in Germany. The local newspapers regularly published his opinions and letters—as well as others' dissents—as he pursued his passion for the rights of the working class.

Emil brewed his first political storm in the early 1920s with an article that condemned the murder of fifteen workers—supposed communists—by university students in a right-wing paramilitary group. As Emil later said, "the bourgeois world of Eisenach" was "completely inflamed." The local church council voted to remove him from his parish. His parishioners gathered three thousand signatures to save him.

The strength of Emil's convictions arose from his fundamental belief in God. For him, "the existing theology stood too far from practical life and life's need of men." In 1894, he had heard a liberal Lutheran minister lecture on the responsibility of religion to reach out to the working poor. He immediately rejected the conservative principles of his father, also a Lutheran minister, and four siblings. Throughout all the crises during the tumultuous era in which he lived, Emil exercised his ideals through this religiosity—something none of his children ever professed. He never looked back even in the face of desperation.

Emil's notoriety fell on his children. When the mother next door learned the family's politics, she forbade her children to play with them. Teachers, nervous from the political mood, lacked the will to protect them.

Of the four Fuchs children, Elisabeth, the oldest, was the least affected. She left for the Academy of Fine Arts in Leipzig in 1926. Gerhard, two years younger, and Kristel freely voiced their opinions and were hounded the most. Before transferring to the Odenwaldschule, Gerhard had stuck up for a Jewish boy bullied by a school gang. Emil found out that they were going after Gerhard too when the postman, stopping at the garden gate, urged him, "Pastor, hurry up. They'll beat up your boy."

Emil wanted Klaus, his second son and a "sensitive soul," to follow in the family tradition and become a Lutheran minister. Klaus had other ambitions. Having inherited his father's strong will, as well as a gift for mathematics, he won.

Since 1921, Klaus had attended Eisenach's Gymnasium, a 750-year-old school originally church sponsored with instruction in Latin that had educated Luther and Bach. By the time of Klaus's graduation, as a family friend later remembered, he was "known and famous" for his mathematics brilliance. His classmates vied for his help, especially in math. Even so, Klaus later said that he never had any friends there.

In 1927, Adolf Hitler, the hero of the right-wing veterans' groups and leader of the rapidly rising National Socialist Workers Party, spoke at Eisenach's Hotel Fürstenhof to a full house. The following year, the tenth anniversary of Germany's new, supposedly democratic order, the government announced an award of a special history book to the top student in each city. After the celebration at school, Klaus came home and told his father that he had won the prize for Eisenach. Pleased, Emil replied, "You can be proud of that!" "No," Klaus said, "I'm not. When the school celebration ended, the headmaster came past my bench and said, 'Klaus, come with me to my room for a moment.' There he gave me the book in private!" Emil saw his son's hurt. He guessed that the headmaster considered Emil's politics too well-known and provocative for a presentation to Klaus before the Gymnasium's conservative students.

Unlike his father and siblings, Klaus didn't engage in political discussions. Only once did he let politics provoke him. In 1929, at his school's celebration of the republic's constitution, students mocked the anniversary, hanging the republic's flag upside down and wearing the imperial badge. Goaded, Klaus pinned the badge of the republic to his lapel. A student ripped it off.

This was Klaus's last year at the Gymnasium. When he graduated, he came home and threw his books in a corner, angrily telling his father, "None of these masters ever gets to see me again!" There was one exception: Dr. Erich Koch, a young, exciting teacher of physics and mathematics.

Throughout his life Koch remained friends with the "quiet and pale" young man from the Gymnasium in Eisenach.

Klaus would later describe his childhood as "very happy." Certainly, at times it was. His kindly mother, Else, raised the children while Emil traveled to lecture on education and religion. "It was the power of my wife," Emil wrote, "who, though suffering from many attacks of melancholy, perhaps for that very reason spread a circle of quiet joy which one could not resist." When he was around, the rectory vibrated with evening discussion groups, formal instruction, and parties. A friend of Klaus's remembered dancing to folk music and singing socialist songs. Emil described a "big, lively house." His tempo ensured it.

Emil also had a tough side. Even he thought his political persona, with "hints and reminders and reprimands," was sometimes too severe. He never connected this insight to the family. A good friend of Klaus's later related that Klaus described his father as "a martinet," as illustrated by his demand for coffee and cake at exactly 4:00 p.m. each day. As an older man, Klaus wistfully said to his nephew, whom Emil had raised, "I'm jealous of you. You had his kind side." He didn't stop with that, adding, "There are some things I can't forgive him for." He didn't elaborate on the complex relationship.

It is unlikely that eighteen-year-old Klaus recognized May 12, 1930, for an especially consequential day when he took the train to Leipzig, filled out the registration card for enrollment at the university, and declared studies in mathematics and physics. His brother, Gerhard, who had been a law student at the university for the last two years, changed apartments so that the quiet, scholarly, and politically remote Klaus could live with him at Stieglitzstrasse 24. His sister Elisabeth lived close by while she studied at the Academy of Fine Arts. But the larger world, as well as Klaus's private one along with it, was shifting on its axis.

Leipzig was situated directly east of the center of Germany. It had grown from an important market town in the Middle Ages, with a confluence of three rivers and two important trading routes, into a large industrial one. Traditionally, the city enjoyed a strong economy and important cultural position. Along the way, it had attracted luminaries in the world of music. Eisenach's own J. S. Bach had composed some of his most important works during his quarter century in residence. Mozart, Liszt, and Mendelssohn also spent time there.

But Leipzig, like all of Germany, was now in the midst of change.

Emil had shaped his children with the ideals of the Social Democratic Party. The SPD, which had a plurality in Germany's parliamentary body, the Reichstag, had risen as a political force in the late nineteenth century, when two workers' rights parties merged to advance equality and support trade unions in a capitalist system. Within it, though, a militant faction influenced by the teachings of Marx and Engels stirred tensions.

At the war's end in 1918, fraught relationships forced a wrenching split in the fragile coalition. The moderates, Emil Fuchs's branch, believed in a democratic process with a platform of social equality. The radicals argued that capitalists would never willingly cede power and called for revolution. In the rupture, the moderates maintained the SPD name; the radicals ultimately became the Communist Party of Germany, the KPD. Immediately after the war, the radicals fought in the streets to establish worker councils mirroring those Russia had formed in its revolution a year before. The Social Democrats, who controlled the new government after the kaiser abdicated, crushed the revolt. Unforgivably, their militia tortured and murdered the revolt's two leaders, Rosa Luxemburg and Karl Liebknecht. From then on, the communists hated the Social Democrats, even when facing threats far greater than their differences.

In 1930, the year Klaus entered the university, the Nazis earned 18 percent of the vote in the elections for the Reichstag, a huge increase over the previous election, but still the combined percentages for the SPD and the KPD were almost 38 percent. Together the SPD and the KPD had power, but animosity and zealotry prevented them from using it.

By this time, the Great Depression that had begun with the Wall

Street crash of October 1929 had crossed the ocean and sent Germany's economy reeling all over again. The new hardship was another incitement for the generation of unemployed young men who had gone from fighting in the streets to saluting "Heil Hitler." But the belligerent and nationalistic ideas of the Nazis were not confined to the slums and the working-class districts. These same sentiments had infected many young people with the means to attend universities. Like their jackbooted colleagues in the streets, the right-wing students used violence to intimidate Jews and foreigners, especially to keep them from participating in the democratic process. They boycotted professors whose lectures didn't promote Nazi ideals, pressuring the rector to remove them. Some of the faculty—party members who actively pushed Nazi propaganda—abetted the students. Others simply went along. As one professor in Leipzig later said, "It was totally futile to be against the National Socialists at the university, as a significant part of the faculty tended to the ideas of the right-wing party or had no desire to burn their fingers with the visibly rising new power."

In February 1928, a couple of months before Gerhard had registered at the university, the yearly election for student council members took place. Elisabeth had watched it unfold. Candidates ran as independents or from student clubs, including political ones, and the results were astounding. Candidates from the Social Democratic Party drew 10 percent of the student vote. The total for the National Socialist candidates, along with a closely linked right-wing group, was 26 percent. A Nazi election placard had boldly predicted, "But we know, Leipzig will be ours."

Gerhard and Elisabeth soon joined the Socialist Student Union, an affiliate of the SPD and the main resistance to the Nazis on campus. Gerhard organized lectures and celebrations and set up a dorm for needy students. Finding some time for fun, he put on cabaret shows where the women vamped and the men strutted. He took his turn spoofing Charlie Chaplin or a Nazi with a swastika emblazoned on his "Brown Shirt," ogling the femme fatale. Given their father's beliefs, it was a comfortable political home, although limited. The heated political flyers and impassioned voices couldn't compensate for the paucity of members.

"To achieve something today without any political orientation," Gerhard told a friend, means not coming "to grips with the central problems of this time and society." Two days before Klaus arrived, Gerhard's group, the Socialist Student Union, petitioned the rector to remove Nazi propaganda. The petition accused the Nazi students of slinging "the worst outgrowths of the daily political struggle."

Klaus quickly joined the Socialist Student Union and followed Gerhard in joining the *Reichsbanner*, a paramilitary group closely allied with the Social Democrats. They were two of more than three million members nationally. In city streets throughout Germany, young men like them protested, marched, fought the Nazis and the communists to defend the republic, and suffered fatalities. Leipzig was no exception. When a group held a meeting in the evening, the opposition sometimes waited outside to attack. Klaus would later say that in Leipzig he learned more in the streets than in the classroom.

Nationally, the communists and the Social Democrats agreed on a united front against the Nazis in support of worker rights. But in Leipzig, the communist leaders verbally attacked SPD leaders, and even though the communist students disagreed, they stayed silent. The duplicity of the leaders and the cowardice of the students angered Klaus.

As roommates, Klaus and Gerhard filled hours analyzing the economic devastation of the Great Depression and the plight of the hard-pressed workers. Given the upheaval all around, academic work was almost an afterthought, but Klaus still managed to study. His physics professor was the young and brilliant Werner Heisenberg. But to Klaus's dismay and boredom, this legendary theorist lectured on the basics rather than his insights into quantum mechanics for which he would soon win the Nobel Prize.

At semester break in August 1930, Gerhard suffered an acute lung infection, and fearing that the industrial pollution in Eisenach would exacerbate his frequent and debilitating bouts of asthma, he stayed in Leipzig. Klaus traveled to Dresden with members of the Socialist Student Union, and thus both brothers missed the excitement in Eisenach when, at the end of the month, the dirigible *Graf Zeppelin* skimmed the town to celebrate a Nazi gathering in the marketplace.

The next day a meeting in the city's Wartburg Castle, famous for having sheltered a heretical Martin Luther, featured the fervent Nazi Hermann Göring. Meanwhile, at her school in Eisenach, Kristel, the youngest, listened to one particularly intolerant Nazi teacher. Overall Emil judged the local schools a "hair-raising" experience for his children, "almost driving them to despair."

But in September, the nation's attention shifted to Leipzig when three army officers accused of fomenting revolution on behalf of the National Socialists went on trial. These three had joined the Nazi Party, distributed their literature, and tried to recruit fellow officers—acts expressly forbidden by the army. It was a case of treason not seemingly widespread, but the government feared the efforts of these three junior officers might be merely the most visible evidence of a larger effort.

In the early morning chill of September 25, thousands of Nazis, young and old, waited for hours in front of the supreme court's grand imperial facade. At 9:00 a.m., an exceptional witness for the defense arrived. The crowd cheered and saluted, awed by the presence of Adolf Hitler as he strode up the magisterial steps, his right arm outstretched triumphantly in the fascist salute. They swarmed after him in an unruly throng. Police blocked their entrance to the court.

The Nazi Party's eightfold increase to 18 percent in the Reichstag just weeks before in the national elections made the National Socialists the second largest of a dozen or so political parties, lagging behind only the Social Democrats. Joseph Goebbels's well-targeted propaganda had glamorized Hitler's promises of the return to a glorious Germany. The farmer, the soldier, the lower middle class, and civil servants alike were enthralled.

For two hours, Hitler stood in the courtroom, testifying "that the German State and the German people should be imbued with a new spirit." He assured the court that his revolution for a renewed Germany was appropriately political—the Nazi Party planned to govern by winning elections. And when he laid out his plans to rip up treaties and exact reprisals for past mistakes, the courtroom erupted with shouts of "Bravo!" The judge directly requested Hitler to deny the use of violent means. Hitler did so emphatically, his denial ending his testimony in what became known as his "oath of legality."

The foreign press largely dismissed Hitler's performance, but the German public saw a patriotic, respectable, and credible leader. It was a clear turning point. Within days, Wilhelm Cuno, president of a shipping line and a former German chancellor, pledged to introduce Hitler to financiers and industrialists. This former corporal and failed artist was not only powerful; he was now respectable.

When classes in Leipzig resumed in October, Klaus found himself facing down the Nazis without Gerhard. His brother had withdrawn from the university and gone to Berlin to try to recover at the home of the family friend and minister Arthur Rackwitz.

On November 18, Klaus and his club distributed leaflets to protest the Nazis' "political radicalism." Leaflets, the primary voice of political groups at a university, could be lethal. When criticized, the Nazi students attacked, and this time a riot broke out.

Three days later, university officials called a student assembly. The Socialist Student Union presented a resolution expressing regret over the unrest, blaming the National Socialist students, and calling for "a decisive position against the terror of the NS students." It was signed "Klaus Fuchs, Vice-President." In six months, he had made the transition from quiet scholar to activist leader.

The Nazis delivered their response, also in a leaflet:

> The best should "prevail," the best will "prevail"! The German
> youth, student, and worker in a Front, in the Brown shirt, derided

and pursued—they carry on nevertheless. **Nothing can shake our advance!**

Four days later Klaus requested that the rector bring the resolution to the faculty senate for a hearing. Stressing the urgency of the problem, he wrote, "The great unrest in most of the various universities suggests that it is a deeper phenomenon that, in our opinion, must be fought as much as possible by the university."

In 1931, as Klaus struggled with the Nazis in Leipzig and Gerhard with asthma in Berlin, Emil Fuchs was called to a faculty appointment at the Pedagogical Academy in Kiel. Buoyed by his degrees in theology, he was to teach religious science, an opportunity he had long hoped for. Initially when the minister of education proposed to call him to the post, the idea met "a very passionate resistance of all ecclesiastical circles," Emil told a close friend and then jested, "That's how important I am, I say with a smile, that my name arouses horror everywhere."

Later, he reflected on the splintered destiny the move brought about, as he with his wife and daughter Elisabeth said goodbye to the clerical life in Eisenach. Parishioners and friends gathered at the train station with flowers and fond farewells, sadness and love flowing after their thirteen years there. "We did not know how heavy would be the fate that we traveled toward," he wrote. "Of the three of us, I alone am still alive."

CHAPTER 2

Loss, Kiel 1931

IN KIEL, EMIL AND ELSE FUCHS SETTLED INTO AN APARTMENT WITHIN AN EASY WALK of his Pedagogical Academy and the university. Else could rest a bit after the years of being a minister's wife and helping Emil with his congregation. Recovered, Gerhard was there to finish the remaining semesters before taking his law exams. So was Elisabeth, at twenty-three, her training in art almost complete. Klaus would transfer from Leipzig but not until the semester's end in August.

Kristel was at the Odenwaldschule, the boarding school that Gerhard had attended. Emil had written to Paul Geheeb when the political environment in Eisenach became intolerable for her. Kristel, he told him, was much like Gerhard and had difficulty keeping her opinions to herself. He thought she would flourish under the Geheebs' tutelage as Gerhard had. Soon after, Kristel traveled to the school, where she did indeed flourish.

The two daughters resembled their mother with thin angular faces, as did Gerhard, but Klaus was his father's son, an heir to the Fuchs full cheeks. Offset by wire-rim glasses and an increasingly high forehead, the cheeks gave him the look of a boyish intellectual, though with penetrating eyes. In terms of character, father and son appeared to be opposites—Emil energetic and Klaus reserved—but Klaus had his father's inner toughness. In hard times, they both collected themselves quickly and moved on.

An old and beautiful city on the southwest coast of the Baltic Sea, Kiel had evolved from a Viking colony on a small island in the fjord. At one point a haven for pirates, the island had been connected to the city when fill dirt was dumped into the narrow waterway. Automobiles and trams crossed the cobblestoned Market Square, vibrating the abutting city hall, church, and seventeenth-century houses and shops. Directly to the north was the *Schloss*, a castle originally part of the city's defenses.

The role of providing security along the Baltic had passed to Kiel's Imperial Naval Station, where in November 1918 a mutiny ignited the revolution that spread across the country and sent the kaiser into exile. In the early 1920s, restrictions in the Versailles Treaty all but closed the naval yard, and its garrison of thirty-five thousand men left the city. The vacuum sucked up much of its economic life and replaced it with unemployment and misery that made it fertile ground for radical ideas.

Gerhard Fuchs took little time to survey the political terrain in Kiel before forming a strategy based on the belief that only a united working class could stop Hitler. The communist and socialist clubs at the university, the Revolutionary Student Group and the Socialist Student Union, were moribund. In Leipzig, the SPD and the KPD had been too far apart, but in Kiel, with the university students at least, he saw the opportunity to form a coalition—which he did—the Free Socialist Student Group. The SPD leaders begrudgingly accepted this alignment. What they needed to unite *against* was becoming increasingly more obvious.

At the end of June, the *Kiel Daily News* reported on an attack during a lecture to a student club in the university auditorium. While Professor Walther Schücking spoke on the "organization of the World Court," a young man burst through the door and hurled a canister eight inches long. It bounced off a shoulder, landed on a table, rolled onto the floor, and exploded. Glass shards struck three people, one suffering deep cuts to the legs. An odor permeated the room—tear gas.

The culprit ran out and jumped on his bicycle, but the crowd caught up to him. He was a nineteen-year-old medical student and a member of the National Socialist Student League, that is, a Nazi.

A few days before, at the consecration of a memorial to students killed in World War I, a representative of the Nazi students provoked a less injurious but more telling incident. First, he made remarks approved by the university. At the end, he inserted the salutation "Heil." A chorus erupted with "Germany, Awaken" and "To Our Future." Then "Destruction to the Jews" rang out.

When brought before the University Senate, this student explained, "I regret that the idea of our movement finds so little understanding in the circles of professors that this 'Heil' has been felt as a provocation and not as a self-evident greeting to our dead." The senate was unsympathetic and reprimanded him. The university also withdrew its approval of the Nazi student group.

Less obvious was the fact that orchestrating these incidents was a practiced Nazi instigator and propagandist named Reinhard Sunkel. He carefully crafted statements for the press that minimized the offenses and claimed police bias against the Nazis. Three local newspapers always printed them.

Sunkel and his friend Joachim Haupt, hardened from service in a paramilitary group, had come to Kiel in 1926 specifically to infiltrate the student body and undermine the university. Within a couple of years, they had set up a Nazi student club (one of the first), launched a university newspaper with Sunkel as publisher, and connived to get Haupt on the student council. Haupt, a PhD student in philosophy, quickly became a board member and took over the organization, causing other organizations to withdraw in protest. Outside the university, the Nazis had already built up a small regional network in the area that Sunkel and Haupt could rely on.

They left the university and Kiel in the late 1920s—Haupt, with his new PhD, to teach in area institutions, and Sunkel to organize activities at the office for Nazi student groups in Berlin. Sunkel decided to return to Kiel in March 1931 to head the local Nazi Party—coinciding almost perfectly with the Fuchs family's arrival. In Sunkel, the Fuchs brothers would have a malicious and well-established opponent.

Klaus arrived in August and by the thirty-first had registered at the police station as a Social Democrat. Elisabeth and Gerhard had already done so. By the start of the winter semester on October 1, the two brothers had officially organized their coalition of socialist and communist students and applied to the university for approval of the new Free Socialist Student Group. Gerhard was the public face, and Klaus was the political leader. They were ready to combat Nazi students and their propaganda, with tactics that addressed substantive issues rather than old grievances and wounded national pride. Their first effort was to target the loss of students' economic rights.

The government funded and controlled the universities, hiring and firing professors (who were consequently government employees) and setting fees, a number of which it had increased for the fall semester. Gerhard requested the university's permission to lecture on this issue at the Seeburg, the student union, on November 6. An issue important to students, especially those with lower incomes, it avoided a direct attack on the right. Klaus and Gerhard wanted to test the Nazis and see how they would respond to their call for all students to protest. Their flyer began,

The fees are increased!

Protest with us against this university reaction, fight with us for our demands:
Sliding-scale fees according to income!
Scholarships for the working and middle class based on talent!

The full-page leaflet blamed the increases on capitalists whose wealth didn't support the government because they avoided paying taxes on income from their foreign businesses.

That fall, while Gerhard and Klaus organized, their mother fought a different and even more insidious opponent. Depression had been a recurring problem for her, but now, with the political climate weighing her down, the cloud just wouldn't lift. In September, the twenty-fifth anniversary of her wedding to Emil gave her a brief respite: the couple took a short trip; the children made special gifts for her. But her melancholy was stubborn and deep, and saying goodbye was continually on her mind. "What comes now, I can no longer bear with you," she told her husband.

On the evening of October 9, Klaus and Gerhard invited their father to hear the well-known sociologist and Social Democratic professor Alfred Meusel speak on the path of nationalism and fascism. Meusel gave a clear and distressing view of what was before them. The next morning Meusel's words occupied Emil's mind, and he gave less time to Else.

Elisabeth came running from the kitchen yelling, "Mother is on the floor! She's not moving." Doctors came, but they were helpless. Else had drunk hydrochloric acid, and nothing could be done. As the family watched Else die a torturous death, she called out, "Mother! I come!" She had witnessed her mother's suicide. Else's was the seventh suicide in a direct family line.

As her own mother's witness, Elisabeth drew a picture of the deathbed, one that gripped Emil as "powerful and shattering." The impression etched into Elisabeth was not lost on him.

Emil had immediately written to the Odenwaldschule, telling them that Else was terribly sick and that doctors feared for her weak heart. Kristel was on a school hike, however, and men on motorbikes were sent to search for her. She didn't arrive in Kiel until the thirteenth, unaware of the tragedy until she arrived.

The family held a quiet funeral for Else in Kiel. The family's death notice read, "We ask you to refrain from condolences. Even flowers are not in her nature. Whoever wants to commemorate her, befriend those who are in need."

Emil and the children moved to a new apartment and tried to resume their lives. Meanwhile, Gerhard and Klaus organized the socialist students; Elisabeth continued with her art; Emil taught and closely watched political developments at the Pedagogical Academy; Kristel returned to the Odenwaldschule. Klaus never spoke about his mother's death. His only acknowledgment was to write on administrative forms, on the line next to "Mother," "deceased, 10/10/31, age 60, cause: political reasons."

Gerhard held his lecture on November 6. No protests on the injustice of the fee increases followed. No outcries from other student groups arose. The university educated the children of the civil service and business classes. The working class was only 2.1 percent of the student body. It wasn't a large enough core group—even with Social Democrats from outside the working class—to galvanize the full, thirty-two-hundred-member student body.

But the Nazi students noticed and responded quickly. With the foundation provided by Sunkel and Haupt, they had largely controlled the political field, but now here were two newcomers, Gerhard and Klaus Fuchs, stirring up students.

In a letter printed in a local right-wing newspaper a week later, the Nazis touted their own demands over the last year for reduced fees and a sliding income scale. At the same time, they launched a bold new effort to recruit Nazi members from Marxist ranks. In Nazi vernacular, "Marxist" was a catchword that swept communists, Social Democrats, and Jews together and branded them as the cause of Germany's downfall. Gerhard and Klaus were ready to push back with the same belligerence. In their newsletter, *Red Students*, they declared, "Who has betrayed us? The Nazi fascists."

Over the next year as fees continued to rise, this pattern—a call to resist the increases, words between the two sides, defamatory rebukes— kept the university community on edge.

The two brothers never backed down. They had watched as their father *always* passionately spoke his mind and pushed his ideals. He believed, optimistically and doggedly, in the power of each person to change the world, a characteristic not lost on his children. For his own contribution, he co-founded a reform movement for adult education, participated in founding a group called the Religious Socialists, and became a Quaker and preached peace while also maintaining his Lutheran ministry and pricking the conservatism of the Lutheran Church.

The children differed from their father in style, motivation, and temperament but not in their single-mindedness. All four saw a world urgently in need of reform. Their perception of the woes of the working class and the success of the capitalists riding on its back shaped their lives and individual actions. For Klaus, this commitment to the idea of fairness would ultimately contribute to his sharing the West's nuclear secrets with Soviet Russia.

CHAPTER 3

Revolt, Kiel 1932

THE ADMINISTRATORS OF KIEL'S 250-YEAR-OLD UNIVERSITY STRAINED TO CHECK THE clash of ideologies, as well as the heightened, sometimes violent, passions of youth from left and right. They issued warnings, stipulated conditions, and called in offenders to threaten reprimands.

These officials were largely middle-aged university professors elected to their governing posts. The fifty-three-year-old rector, August Skalweit, ordinarily a professor of economics, had no experience controlling conflict. Neither he nor most of his colleagues were Nazis or Nazi sympathizers, but they were all acutely aware of the precarious political storm ahead of them, as were the rectors at Germany's several dozen other universities.

Matters came to a head in 1932, when a national election was so disruptive that it caused the student alliances to shift. Klaus later described this moment of realignment as "the decision that determined my whole life." It "created my whole future."

The seven-year term of Paul von Hindenburg as president of the Weimar Republic was coming to an end. The old general (a veteran of the Franco-Prussian War!) had been called out of retirement in 1914 to lead the German army. It was he who, when summoned to appear before a parliamentary commission to explain Germany's loss, refused to admit being bested on the battlefield and offered up instead the myth of the "stab in the back" by liberals on the home front. In 1925, he had been persuaded to come out of retirement for a second time to run for president.

In 1932, Hindenburg's opponents would include Adolf Hitler and Ernst Thälmann, head of the KPD, the Communist Party of Germany, who very much had become chair with the support of Joseph Stalin. The more moderately "left" SPD, the largest party, feared splitting the antifascist vote and allowing Hitler's election, and as a result decided not to run its own candidate, instead supporting Hindenburg.

But the KPD leadership made a much more Machiavellian calculation. Watching from Moscow as Hitler gained influence, Stalin and his Politburo saw an opportunity. If Hitler should come to power, they reasoned, he would never be able to sustain it, and when he faltered, the old order of the capitalists and the Social Democrats would collapse, opening the door for a Marxist-Leninist revolution in Germany.

This was the same all-or-nothing approach that the communists had relied on to seize power in Russia in 1918. When the German party leader Thälmann declaimed, "Socialists and fascists are twins," the Social Democrats hurled back, "Bolsheviks and fascists are brothers." The Social Democrats were closer to the truth, but the Fuchses were oblivious to the conniving of the Politburo.

For Klaus and Gerhard Fuchs, Hindenburg symbolized the very capitalist elite they railed against every day as they fought for the rights and the future of working-class students. In their minds, the SPD had acquiesced to the "bourgeois parties" and sold out, when a united working class was the only victorious counterforce to fascism.

The Fuchs brothers gave their support to Thälmann, becoming surrogate speakers for him in Kiel. Within a few weeks, the SPD banned their student members from participating in the Free Socialist Student Group at the university. The KPD happily took in the Fuchs brothers, as well as their sister Elisabeth.

At first, Klaus was ambivalent, but not because the communists called for revolution and demanded allegiance to the Soviet Union. It was memories of the conflict of loyalties he had witnessed in Leipzig when the communists and the Social Democrats agreed on a united front to support worker rights, and then the communists attacked the SPD.

Emil didn't follow them. At the war's end, having added the Quaker pacifist beliefs to his ministry in the Lutheran Church, he rejected the revolutionary cries of the communists. Although he respected his children's choice, it made him both uneasy and prophetic as he wrote to Paul Geheeb, his friend at the Odenwaldschule, "They are all—each in his own way—very one-sided and they are unbending in their character. They will not have it easy in life."

The election was a major event in Kiel, with politically sponsored speakers, musical entertainment, and film evenings from all parties drawing large crowds and predictable violence between the Nazis and the communists or *Reichsbanner* or both. Street fighting increased, and police remained on standby to intercede. In communist neighborhoods, the Nazis constantly pushed for a foothold as local Hitler Youth and the *Sturmabteilung*, or SA, marched through to rile up residents, start fights, and lure the young men with their displays of power. Somewhere during this time Klaus, the studious math prodigy, lost three front teeth, most likely in a brawl.

In an effort to keep the peace, the university banned political activities until after the elections. But Klaus transferred to the local youth KPD chapter, several hundred members strong, and took up leadership of the Red Spark, an agitprop troupe. Agitation and political theater—part entertainment, part hard-core political propaganda as typified by the plays of Bertolt Brecht—had been used successfully by the Bolsheviks during their 1917 revolution.

The troupe crisscrossed the countryside in flatbed trucks wooing voters. Usually from the truck platform or the sidewalk, they sang, danced, and acted out cabaret-style skits: serious drama à la Brecht, a contentious legal sketch on abortion, a spoof on the design of women's bathing suits, or daily political news with portrayals of Hitler. It was a mix of the group's ideas and those from headquarters in Berlin.

For Klaus and friends, it was hardly a carefree jaunt through the countryside. The farms, small towns, and seafaring villages around Kiel were mostly Protestant and vulnerable to a fascist message. As early as 1925, Nazi leaders had identified the farmers' vote in the northern part of Prussia as crucial for making "the sea-embraced Nordmark ours." Prominent Nazis came to speak. The rural crowds, often first-time voters, came out in droves to hear fervid orations filled with slogans and vague promises.

The Red Spark played in one town and their Nazi counterparts in another. Klaus's sometime girlfriend Lisa Attenberger—three years older than he, pretty, flirtatious, and sassy enough to more than offset his reserve— was part of the troupe. According to her, Klaus always cast himself against type in reactionary roles, including Hitler. Anticipating cudgels and knives in the sidewalk crowd, they brought along protection from their own paramilitary group, the Red Front. The Nazis did the same with the SA.

Klaus and his colleagues printed flyers in attic rooms that the KPD rented. They attended a required program on Marx, Engels, and Lenin but had little time for it. The politicking was all consuming, especially for Lisa, who was not a student and worked full-time.

One day, city authorities notified her to come in for an STD exam. Someone had reported that she "had many men in the booth." Apparently, the authorities had other motives, namely her relationship with Klaus. At the end of the exam, they asked if she had slept with him. She said she didn't remember.

Lisa wasn't Klaus's only interest—nor obviously he, hers. He had an unnamed "soul mate" someplace away from Kiel with whom he was in love—a person fighting for the cause with him—and then she left him. Years later, when he described this unidentified woman as very shrewd and unscrupulous, "the Beast and the Devil," he said, his feelings seemed still raw.

The presidential vote was held on March 13, 1932. That morning, the *Kieler Zeitung*, a mainstream newspaper that supported Hitler, ran the headline "Destroy the System: Vote Adolf Hitler."

By the end of the polling, no candidate had a majority, so a runoff was held on Sunday, April 10. Hindenburg won with 53 percent to Hitler's 36.8 percent. Thälmann, losing support in the second round, finished with 10 percent.

Although Hitler's total averaged below 50 percent in Kiel and its province of Schleswig-Holstein, seven of the twenty-four districts gave him an absolute majority in both rounds. The next day, the headline in the *Kieler Zeitung* read, "Heil Hitler," omitting from the front page that Hindenburg had actually won.

The Nazis had rolled up gains with a strong nationalist message. They sold the public racial prejudices, economic strength, dislike of foreigners, and rejection of the Versailles Treaty.

One week later, Klaus spoke at the Seeburg on the capitalist forces against socialism. Gerhard spoke on the "'fascization' of worker rights." Although students who were SPD members could no longer be officially part of the group, the lectures were open to all.

The Fuchses' new political alignment didn't change the political message much. Occasionally someone in the group lectured on the Soviet Union or included references in newsletters. Mostly they argued for opportunities for the working class or slammed the Nazis for a long list of wrongs: warmongering, terrorism, cowardice, and/or deception. On those occasions, the Nazis, as usual, went straight to the officials with complaints of horrible mistreatment.

Both sides attended the others' events and watched for an opening to provoke. At the end of April, Gerhard and Klaus called for a strike to challenge another university fee increase. The Nazis rejected their request to join in and belittled them in the press.

Meanwhile, the Nazis were raising funds for schools in territory ceded by Germany to Denmark as the result of a 1920 plebiscite. Gerhart attacked the Nazis' effort, condemning what underlay it, namely *Deutschtum*, the Nazi creed that demanded possession of all foreign lands with a German culture in order to create a pure, world-dominant Germany. This was the path to war, Gerhard charged.

At the end of May, the newly reelected president, Hindenburg, chose a new chancellor, Franz von Papen. A semi-closeted conservative and monarchist, he formed a cabinet of politically inexperienced businessmen and aristocrats who immediately set about trying to dismantle the Weimar Republic.

One of Papen's first actions would change the course of world history: he reversed the ban on the SA, and thus gave Hitler back his most effective weapon. According to newspapers sympathetic to the Nazis, it was to protect the public against the Marxist violence and *Reichsbanner* terror that filled the streets. In actuality, it gave free rein to Hitler's incitement to violence. After a row in the *Schloss* garden, next to the university, officials found a grenade. Unreported by the newspapers, the first murder in Kiel after the SA were set loose was a *Reichsbanner* man.

On the morning of June 23, 1932, around 11:00, the university inspector Karl Lichtenfeld passed the *Freitreppe*, the "Free Steps" that led down to the garden from the university's main building. Students milled peacefully around during their break, and two handed out flyers. When Lichtenfeld took one, he noted the title, "Prohibition," and that it was sponsored by the socialist students.

Seeing perhaps as many as fifty men clustered throughout the garden, he feared that the flyer's strident sentences such as "The Nazi leadership has to conceal the treason that it uses with its twelve million voters" could provoke riots. He quickly made a needed trip to the library and returned to find groups of nonstudents moving between three specific points around the grounds and bordering streets.

The bell for classes rang, and most students went in, leaving half a dozen or so that Lichtenfeld recognized as Nazis, along with a larger group gathered at either end of the path in front of the entrance. Among these Lichtenfeld spotted Gerhard, well-known and one of two students wearing the communist lapel pin with hammer and sickle.

Lichtenfeld, seeing no overt conflict but sensing tension between the Nazis and the communists, secured some of the doors at the top of the steps. Two policemen arrived and smoothly dispersed everyone—many departing on bicycles. The police maintained a double patrol around the building for the next few hours.

After this near confrontation, the Nazi students sent a complaint to the rector and to the newspapers, a ploy to aggravate university officials. They alleged being attacked and mistreated in "unspeakable ways" by socialist students and demanded protection.

At 3:30 that afternoon, the rector sent Gerhard a letter to revoke permission for a lecture at the Seeburg that evening. Gerhard searched for the rector to persuade him to change his mind, but his plea failed.

The university councillor Hoepner summoned Gerhard to his chamber the next afternoon, where he asked about the "incident." With an attitude Hoepner deemed disrespectful, Gerhard denied having amassed the fifty to sixty men at the garden but acknowledged that some were acquaintances of his.

The Nazis swiftly issued a "notice" clarifying their complaint against the socialist students and stressing a ban. At the end, they requested permission to wear brown uniforms with a shoulder strap and red swastika, which the Prussian government had barred.

At the University Senate meeting the next day, its members enacted more measures to keep the peace—police posts, protection for Nazi students, restrictions on the Seeburg. Gerhard received a reprimand for improper behavior against officials and students with different beliefs. The Nazis were denied permission to wear uniforms or armbands.

On July 1, a group calling itself "University of the KPD-Kiel"—with no individual's name attached—distributed a flyer at the *Freitreppe* that labeled the Nazi students "masters in the methods of the lowest, wickedest, and dirtiest slander." With more flyers, complaints, and wringing of hands, the university brought Gerhard up on disciplinary charges. The Nazis insisted on "immediate dispersal of the Red Student Group" and the members' expulsion.

The head of the Nazi students, Walther Essmann, wrote to the rector for a quick verdict, but the rector had already left for vacation.

On July 20, the focal point of German unrest, Adolf Hitler himself, came to Kiel. At 4:15 in the afternoon, forty thousand adoring followers rallied in and around the city's largest auditorium. Reinhard Sunkel, who had insinuated the Nazis into Kiel several years before, introduced him. Hitler's hour-long oration churned up the usual grievances—the 30 percent unemployment, the onerous provisions of the Versailles Treaty, and the violence in the streets that was eating away at Germany's social fabric. Then he spelled out a new future for the German nation: the importance of the farmers and working class as the fundamental basis for economic growth, coming together as the *Volk*, to bury class divisions. He fed his audience a simple word, *Volk*, that to his listeners embraced the pure and powerful tribe of German myth. The crowd went wild.

"With subhumanity," Hitler insisted, "there is no understanding—we will clean up with them!"

Evidently, with shades of the Valkyrie, he and his audience would choose who was to live and who was to die. Rarely at this point were Jews singled out and directly named unless the atmosphere welcomed it, but the Nazi point of view was already well established. The party platform from 1920 defined Jews not as "racial comrades" but rather as the root of Germany's and the world's problems.

At the end of the speech, there was a clash between the SA and the communists, which required a massive police contingent to break up.

That very same day, Chancellor Papen dismissed the Prussian cabinet in what became known as the *Preussenschlag.* Already in charge of the federal government, he used the pretext of the chaos in the streets to put himself in charge of the Prussian state government as well. Of course, the chaos he decried was largely his own doing, the result of his decision to legalize the SA.

When Klaus heard the news, he rushed to find his friends—communists, Social Democrats, and in particular the *Reichsbanner*. They had gathered spontaneously, eager to fight for the autonomy of the Prussian government. But they had to sit and do nothing. The Prussian president and other Social Democrats called for calm, deferring to a future decision by the *Reich* court, and otherwise putting up no resistance.

The broken spirit of the SPD members weighed heavily on Klaus. They had been forced to withdraw from the Free Socialist Student Group a few months before, and now their party sat passively in the face of Germany's destruction. Helpless, he watched as the SPD basically ceased to participate in political action. From then on, he knew that he and his like-minded comrades had to resist largely alone. The battle in the next Reichstag election set for July 31, a last-ditch effort to revive the dysfunctional parliamentary body, would have to come from them.

On Election Day in July, the National Socialists won 46 percent of the vote in Kiel. Nationally, they won 230 of the 608 seats in the Reichstag with 38 percent of the vote. The Nazis were now the largest party in the parliament, but it was still without a governing coalition.

When the winter semester began in October, so did the formal senate proceedings against Gerhard for disparaging *Deutschtum*, the Nazis' dream of a greater Germany. During the break, the university had collected about seventy-five pages of letters, sworn affidavits, minutes of meetings, and flyers. To the consternation of the Nazis, these showed no direct link from the offending flyer to Gerhard. And naturally he denied everything. That he was responsible or at least fundamentally involved was little in doubt, but no hard proof existed, so the university dropped the charges for lack of evidence. Although unstated, the tone of the official records was one of relief at the outcome.

By the time the senate decision came down on November 7, Gerhard had left Kiel for Berlin with his girlfriend, Karin, ostensibly to prepare for law exams at the University of Berlin, but he couldn't turn from the political crisis. The communist leadership named him editor of a bimonthly newsletter *Mahnruf* (Warning cry), with 140,000 subscribers. Emil wrote to Paul Geheeb, "Gerhard has the doggedness of the Fuchses and the certainty of his convictions."

With Gerhard gone from Kiel, Klaus would come into his own as a leader. The Nazis, and the rector, would see that he did not lack his brother's zeal. But where Gerhard had aggression, Klaus had steely, quiet determination. And while the Nazis hated Gerhard, Klaus they would try to kill.

CHAPTER 4

Leader, Kiel 1933

AS THE NEW LEADER OF THE FREE SOCIALIST STUDENT GROUP, KLAUS SHOWED THE sense of obligation, responsibility, and self-righteousness that some would later characterize as arrogance. At twenty-one, in his first solo conflict, he still maintained his quiet reserve, but he was uncompromising, was wary of being used, and, like his father, had an impulsive streak.

With the Nazi students having a new representative too, Werner Krugmann, the university councillor Hoepner used the moment to establish ground rules. He requested that Klaus come to his chambers at 1:00 p.m. on November 15. Krugmann was scheduled at 3:00 p.m. for the same day. None of the other university clubs received such a summons.

Klaus had already distributed a flyer for the lecture "Fighting the Suppression of the Socialists" that bore his name and official approval. Hoepner delivered a strong reprimand to him. He wanted "the dragged-out battle" between the socialist and the Nazi groups to stop. If not, he threatened "suspension of the guilty academic union and disciplinary punishment for the responsible official." The new orders limited attendance at an event to members of the political group. They required all announcements and advertisements on groups' bulletin boards to adhere to a 1929 regulation that ruled out politically volatile content. Klaus told Hoepner that "he would tell this to the members of [his group] but that he couldn't make assurances about anyone's behavior."

But Klaus's reserved and polite demeanor didn't stem from timidity. Three days after the meeting with Hoepner, he responded with his group's conclusion: "On the basis of the arguments presented, we cannot obey your order." He objected to the threats of "the most severe disciplinary action" to pressure him to agree to the restriction on the rights of the student body. "A factual intellectual debate is best suited to maintain 'quiet and order' at the university. Preventing such an argument would achieve the opposite result," he wrote to Hoepner. The order, he said, didn't hinder the Nazis at all, because they never held public meetings or debates or used the bulletin board to post events. They mostly complained. It restricted the socialist students only.

Klaus promptly posted his response on the group's bulletin board in direct violation of the new order. Authorities just as promptly confiscated it and warned him.

On November 22, Klaus and Councillor Hoepner met again, and when he emerged from the administrator's office, he found the Nazi leader, Werner Krugmann, and another Nazi member in the anteroom waiting for their own appointment. The three started a conversation, which led to a dialogue over the next several days in which they discussed how to respond to this suppression. They decided on yet another protest against fee increases. Klaus argued for an approach not limited to resolutions and flyers but one that "really mobilizes the student body to fight." Krugmann, the Nazi, fell back to a much less aggressive approach—flyers only—and then failed to respond to Klaus's letter arguing for more action.

Thrown into this curious dialogue was an election for student council representatives. Klaus and another group member were running, and Klaus decided to go after the Nazis. He remembered that with an earlier fee increase they had delayed action and then said it was too late to protest. He wanted to call out their duplicity, not hear another excuse. He released a one-page flyer advertising the group's candidates and their pledge to fight:

Against the University reaction!

For the Interests of underprivileged students!

Against the Education monopoly!

Then it described the agreement of the socialists and the Nazis to fight together, but pointed out,

> The NSDStB and the FrKSt [both Nazi groups] have perma-
> nently delayed an answer. No student would blame us if we are
> suspicious especially after the experience of last semester. All
> the more, the former leader of the NSDStB declared at the first
> exchange: "It is a brilliant university scandal."

We do not want a Scandal!

What we want is

A tough and untiring fight.

The single-spaced taunt of the unnamed Nazis Essmann and Krugmann urged students to fight. Students stood on corners around campus and in front of academic buildings handing out the message.

Writing about the flyer to Hoepner, Klaus stressed that everything in it was accurate and that Essmann had confronted him immediately upon reading the "scandal" comment. He also branded Essmann's comment about scandal as dangerous. He feared that the Nazis' intent was to weaken the university rather than support students. "I therefore thought it my duty to point out this danger to the student body."

Essmann, feeling besmirched, went to the rector, emphatically denied all, and threw in a few more grievances.

Years later, Klaus remarked that he "had violated some standard of decent behaviour" by not giving the Nazis an ultimatum before issuing the flyer. "I came to accept that in such a struggle of this kind are prejudices which are weaknesses and which you must fight against." But his prejudices and his sense of obligation at that age were integrated as a whole—"one-sided" and "unbending," as his father had said.

A few days later, Rector Skalweit dismissed Essmann's complaint on the grounds that Klaus was not "conscious" that his charge against Essmann was misleading.

Throughout the fights, meetings, and letter writing, Klaus continued his studies. A favorite professor, Abraham Fraenkel, who by the 1930s was a recognized expert on set theory, gave Klaus a strong base in logic and mathematical foundations. January 1933, appearing relatively calm, afforded opportunity for quiet scholarship. But this was to end.

Toward the end of the month, Rector Skalweit felt "a certain agitation within the student body." He saw it in the halls of the college buildings, with frequent stink bombs set off, and in the groups standing around. The students were generally edgy. Newspaper accounts of Papen's push to appoint Hitler as chancellor—the conservatives in the government were sure they could control him—excited those who hungered for the Nazis' vision of a new Germany and roiled the jittery nerves of everyone else.

In the meantime, Klaus continued the Tuesday night meetings in the Seeburg with such topics as "The National Question." The new rules required an admission ticket indicating the student's membership in the sponsoring club and a check on a list at the door. A guard, paid three reichsmarks by the university, stood on watch. No new protests or flyers appeared.

On January 30, 1933, Hindenburg doomed the Weimar Republic, as well as the millions of people who would die in the years of war and mass extermination to follow. He granted Papen's appeals and appointed Hitler chancellor.

On a cold, wintry night three days later, thousands of Kiel's citizens lined the streets for a torchlit victory parade led by hordes of brown-shirted men. For as far as one could see, they wound down Holstenstrasse into the old market square. Flames from the torches cast eerie shadows on the city hall, footsteps spiked the cobblestones echoing into the night, and the crowds cheered wildly and sang. Klaus presumably stayed away. It wasn't a safe place for a recognized communist.

On February 4, with President Hindenburg's approval, Hitler issued a decree that banned meetings and publications considered a public threat. It had swift ramifications for the state of Prussia, because at the same time Hermann Göring became Prussian minister of the interior, which gave him direct control of the police. The *Preussenschlag*, when Papen took over the state's government the previous summer, made this transition swift and efficient.

Göring quickly mobilized. He and Hitler had an urgent goal: to eradicate the only real organized opposition to a Nazi takeover, namely the communists. Within a few days, he had ordered the Prussian police, in collaboration with paramilitary groups, to suppress political meetings and marches and to fire on demonstrators at will. Then he created an auxiliary police force thousands strong drawn mainly from the ranks of the *Sturmabteilung*, primarily young and hefty thugs. Armed with pistols, rifles, and rubber truncheons, they were lawless police, beating and arresting anyone who criticized the Nazis.

Kiel's chief of police, Otto Graf zu Rantzau, soon became chief of the local Gestapo there, launching eviscerating raids on the communists in and around Kiel. For the time being he didn't bother students at the university.

It took the Nazi students five days after Hitler's ascent to petition Rector Skalweit. Some of their demands seemed trivial to Klaus next to the chaos in the country. Two alarmed him: recognition of the Nazi-backed student council as the representative of the student body and prohibition of Klaus's socialist club. As the Nazis well knew, the rector didn't have authority over these decisions. Part of their intent was to box him in.

The government then scheduled yet another round of elections for the Reichstag in March 1933. On Monday, February 6, consistent with university policy, the rector closed the Seeburg to all political events. In a tense meeting, the Nazis met with him to question the policy. Afterward, they hurried to the newspapers to give a grossly distorted version of the discussion that

the newspapers printed. The chain of events led to the University Senate's
sanctioning the rector. Emboldened, the Nazis incited a student demonstration against him.

On Friday afternoon, Nazi student leaders gathered a crowd in front of
the main university building. They called for a two-day strike and hurled
insults at university officials while their classmates, agitated and angry,
swarmed and cheered. A mob of storm troopers marched from the city center
as Klaus and other socialist students surged against them. A riot broke out.
Stink bombs flew through the air, fire hydrants spewed, and flyers inciting
hatred littered the ground. Seizing the moment, the storm troopers jumped
on Klaus and beat him. The Nazi crowd yelled, "Throw him in the fjord!"
They were out for blood. Police stood by and watched as they threw him into
the icy waters of Kiel's fjord, leaving him for dead. Miraculously, he survived, and when the crowd had gone, he swam to safety.

The rector shut down the university for three days. A crowd gathered
in front of the university the next day, and again a riot broke out. Police
quickly quelled it.

The Nazis' calls for a strike and their insults to the rector aggravated
a large segment of students. Their vocal opposition forced the Nazis to
cancel the strike and ask for mediation with the rector. The newspapers,
complicit with the Nazi students, persisted in goading Skalweit.

In a move not reported by the newspapers, on the following Monday
the socialist students filled the void left by the canceled Nazi protest with
their own illegal demonstration. According to Klaus, it was disciplined and
impressive. "We knew, however," he later remarked, "that these were the
last victories before a retreat."

During the riot, the police had stood about and passively watched the
SA's almost deadly attack on Klaus, and he complained to the rector about
their neglect. Resigned to the situation, the rector in his answer made it
clear that he could barely defend himself let alone defiant students.

Shortly after, Gerhard, in Kiel on a visit from Berlin, found out that
the Nazi student leadership had sentenced Klaus to death. Klaus and Elisabeth went into hiding. Gerhard headed for Berlin.

The direction of the country was clear, as was the fate of the communists. The February 9 edition of the *Kieler Zeitung* quoted Hitler as saying, "In ten years, no more communists in Germany!" But the Nazis weren't content to wait that long.

The morning of February 28 was dreary and stormy in Kiel. As Emil walked to his office, he saw people ignoring the rain and crowding around the cylindrical advertising columns on Holtenauer Strasse. Curious, he stopped to read the banner headlines. The night before, exactly four weeks after Hitler assumed power, the Reichstag had burned to the ground.

The Nazis, with almost complete control of the press, wasted no time blaming the communists and raising fears of a communist reign of terror. A Dutch communist, Marinus van der Lubbe, was implicated—convicted and executed—but he said he'd acted alone. Later information strongly suggested that the Nazis had set the bonfire themselves—or at least fanned the flames—as a "false flag" operation to justify a crackdown. According to Reuters, "Even anti-communist journals in France are skeptical of the Nazis' claims." More than seventy years later, the German government would give Van der Lubbe a posthumous pardon.

President Hindenburg was a sick and addled bystander, easily coerced by Chancellor Hitler to suspend all civil liberties in light of the crisis. The government justified the partial suspension of the constitution "as a defensive measure against communist acts of violence that endanger the state."

With no delay, the police, the nascent Gestapo, and the storm troopers spread out to neutralize opposition. The sinister thud of black boots falling on wooden stairs resonated in apartment buildings across Germany. Lists methodically drawn up over previous months made the kidnapping, torturing, and slaughtering of communists, Jews, and Social Democrats a matter of routine. The number one student on the list in Kiel was Klaus Fuchs.

At four o'clock on the fateful morning of the twenty-eighth, Klaus had caught the train to Berlin. The fact that he had slipped away just in time was purely by chance. As head of the socialist students, he had been called to a general meeting of representatives. Only in transit, when reading the newspaper, did he learn about the Reichstag fire. He coolly removed the small symbol of unity, the hammer and sickle party pin on his lapel, and dropped it in his pocket.

The next day, his girlfriend Lisa went to see Emil and help him figure out what to do. In mid-morning, a knock on the door interrupted them. The police entered and demanded that Emil tell them where Klaus was. Emil, understandably nervous, asked, "Why are you searching for him here? He's at his girlfriend's." The police knew that wasn't true. They told him that they had already checked there. What they didn't realize was that the young woman standing in front of them was that girlfriend. When they finally identified her, they demanded to know why she had not stated her name. Lisa met their anger with her usual sass: "How come? You didn't ask me." Fortunately, she was dealing with the local police, not the Gestapo.

The authorities searched the apartment and, finding no Klaus and no guns, settled for Emil's collection of books by Marx, Engels, Lenin, and Stalin, throwing them into a cart to haul away. Inexplicably, they showed no interest in the duplicating equipment sitting in Klaus's bedroom nor the fresh supply of propaganda flyers piled next to it. They overlooked the tiled heating stove too. It was stuffed with the files of the Free Socialist Student Group. At some point, someone had tried to burn them; their mass had suffocated the fire. The papers sat there, cold and intact. A few pages lingered in a corner of the room. Emil and Lisa systematically burned each sheet, fearful of a repeat search. Then, in vain, they made a list of Emil's remaining books.

Sometime later at the police station, Emil asked why they had searched his apartment. "It concerns your son Klaus," the officer told him. "We must have him. Where is he?"

Emil stayed in Kiel in his position at the academy and continued his pacifist resistance, courageously speaking at the funeral of a *Reichsbanner* member killed by the SS. Even though about half of the students at the academy were Nazis, they didn't boycott his classes as they did other socialist or Jewish professors. But the mood was shifting.

On March 4, 1933, the university swore in a new rector. It was a sober, almost funereal affair, the invitation to the faculty instructing, "Please wear dark suits."

On orders from the Prussian minister of education, the newly elected senate members reinstated the Nazi students who had been expelled or reprimanded in past years. The former rector Skalweit was posted to the University of Frankfurt at the end of the year. Professor Walther Schücking, the lecturer disrupted in 1931 by the tear gas bomb, was dismissed in November. In full circle, the newest rector, Karl Wolf, reported on these changes to Joachim Haupt. The same student who had come to Kiel in 1926 to Nazify the university was now deputy to the new minister of education in Berlin. Klaus's favorite math teacher, Professor Abraham Fraenkel, voluntarily resigned his position and left the university at the same time as Klaus in late February. He went to Israel, becoming a professor at Tel Aviv University, where he was recognized as a father of modern logic.

With the new regime firmly in command, the Nazi students proposed another list of four requests, this one respectfully submitted and with a new focus. Prior to March, the Nazi students had largely attacked the communists. Now it was the Jews. They argued that Jewish professors didn't understand Germany and German thought and that foreign Jews and communists would circulate antinationalist propaganda everywhere they settled. The four requests were (1) to enroll no new Jews; (2) to reduce the percentage of Jews enrolled to that corresponding to the German population [0.78 percent or a quota of twenty-seven Jewish students at Kiel]; (3) to carry out the same type of reduction in the teaching staff; and (4) to assure that all academic examinations have a German and objective composition.

Over time the students and administration ensured that the rest of the subhumanity, as Hitler had called them, was cleaned out.

Ironically, Kiel's first Nazi provocateurs, Reinhard Sunkel and Joachim

Haupt, had their own subhuman connection. Like Haupt, Sunkel became an assistant in the Prussian Ministry of Education. But when his Jewish great-grandmother was uncovered, he was expelled from the party. Haupt, besides working for Minister Bernhard Rust, became a *Sturmbannführer* in the SA and was close to its leader, Ernst Röhm. In 1934, when power struggles with the SS and the army led to the infamous "Night of the Long Knives," in which most of the SA leadership was brutally murdered, Haupt was spared the bloodbath because of a dental appointment. He was later discovered to be homosexual, imprisoned, then released, but expelled from the party. Eventually, he became a farmer. Sunkel committed suicide.

As for Kiel, which became a main U-boat base, Allied bombers—USAF B-17s and RAF Mosquitos—later laid it to waste.

Shortly before Klaus decamped to Berlin, Emil wrote to Paul Geheeb at the Odenwaldschule, where Kristel had returned. What "lay ahead" had arrived, and he was in a pensive mood. "All my children have the complete truthfulness and consequence of my wife and the passion of my commitment," he wrote. "But I hope that because they are beyond the most difficult period of their development, they can accomplish a great deal of good."

Except for Kristel, they cautiously made their way in the underground—Elisabeth in Kiel and Klaus and Gerhard in Berlin.

CHAPTER 5

Underground, Berlin 1933

WHEN KLAUS FUCHS STEPPED DOWN FROM THE TRAIN AT BERLIN'S MAIN STATION ON the morning of February 28, a transformed city awaited him. About a mile from where he stood, the ashes from the Reichstag fire still smoldered. Hitler promised that a new Germany would rise like the phoenix from the steaming rubble, a proud nation with a resurgence of the wealth, power, and purity of the *Volk*—and with no communists or Jews.

Hindenburg's decree in response to the Reichstag fire eradicated freedoms of opinion, of the press, of assembly and association; it erased rights to private communications through mail, telephone, or telegraph; it eliminated protections at home. House searches, confiscations, and arrests raged through the city. Police with German shepherds—eyes hungry, ears pricked, fangs temporarily muzzled—patrolled the streets.

German newspapers offered little real news; the government had muzzled the foreign press as well. Göring proudly boasted of the thousands jailed in the days after the fire, but under pain of expulsion no foreign reporter could describe their treatment or anything else that might be "malicious." Even those tortured in prison and released maintained silence. Otherwise, they as well as their families were promised further torture.

The new decree had ruled all communist meetings illegal; a week later, the party itself was banned. Despite this menace, Klaus made it to the now secret meeting of socialist students, where the leaders praised him for his work in Kiel. Afterward, they schooled him and the others on the new rules of underground resistance: small groups, oral messages, code names, and no lists. Don't write anything down, and don't sleep at home. Don't look back to check on being followed. Maybe wear a disguise. Inauspicious rules for a suddenly uncertain life, many of which the young resisters ignored until it was too late. But nothing could prepare them for the onslaught of brutality.

On February 24, days before the Reichstag fire, the SA had stormed KPD headquarters at the Karl-Liebknecht-Haus in downtown Berlin. The Nazi-controlled press assailed the building as a web of treachery and treason being readied for an imminent communist revolution. After the seizure, a large red flag with a black and bold swastika on a circle of white fluttered from the roof of the massive five-story building. It was repurposed as headquarters of the political section of the Berlin Police and renamed the Horst-Wessel-Haus, after the SA leader murdered by the KPD in 1930 and turned into a Nazi martyr by Hitler's propaganda minister Joseph Goebbels. Its basement, once described as a labyrinth of communist intrigue, became a detention and torture facility for Jews and dissidents.

At this point MI5 entered, when Captain Guy Liddell, one of its officers in Soviet counterespionage, arrived. But this was Neville Chamberlain's England that Liddell represented, a country whose royals and upper classes had strong family, social, and business ties with Germany and who were then arguably more concerned about communists than about fascists.

Liddell, who spoke fluent German and knew the country well—as a youth, he had been a promising cellist and studied there—was in Berlin not to investigate abuses by the SA but to explore the left-wing documents they had seized. He toured the building and heard from a Nazi official that none of the stories in the press about it were true. There were no underground passages. The "secret" trapdoors and staircases were in plain sight and used for office mobility.

During Liddell's ten-day stay, a who's who of Nazi officialdom welcomed him: Putzi Hanfstaengl, foreign press liaison; Rudolf Diels, chief of the political section of the Berlin Police (soon, the first Gestapo chief); and Joachim von Ribbentrop, foreign policy adviser (later minister of foreign affairs). Liddell reported back to London, "Those in authority are persuaded that they have saved Europe from the menace of Communism. They are proud of what they have done, and anxious to convince the outside world that their action was fully justified."

Liddell himself was not convinced. MI5 knew from intelligence sources that Moscow had instructed the KPD to do nothing that would provoke the Nazis to eliminate it. A communist street demonstration was plausible, he thought, but not more. It appeared to him, as to many others, that the Nazis had outmaneuvered the KPD and manufactured the fire in the Reichstag as an excuse to crack down and eliminate opposition.

Liddell's specific interest lay in files on the Communist International. How did the Comintern operate in Western Europe and the colonies? One of Berlin's police officials was dubious Liddell would learn much from the SA's haul. The communists had prepared for suppression over the previous year during Papen's chancellorship and destroyed documents. Liddell wasn't ready to concede that point. In his report "The Liquidation of Communism, Left-Wing Socialism, and Pacifism in Germany," he advised MI5 to keep "constant personal contact. . . . In their present mood, the German Police are extremely ready to help us in any way they can."

Klaus had no footprint in Berlin; he was largely unrecognized, but his name was known. The police president in Kiel had sent an alert to the Gestapo in Berlin. His name was on their wanted list, and they had an idea of where to find him.

Klaus had an aunt in Berlin, Frau Rossmann, who lived with her husband in the wealthy suburb of Zehlendorf. The Gestapo paid her a visit, and she dutifully handed them an address that Klaus had left with her after he arrived in the city. The address was a fake. Klaus and Gerhard both knew that their father's conservative family wasn't dependable.

Ten

Ten miles and a world away, Klaus and Gerhard were hiding out with Emil's close friend Arthur Rackwitz, the minister who had taken in Gerhard after his asthma attack in Leipzig. Like Emil, Rackwitz was a Lutheran minister, a Social Democrat, and a pacifist. Early on he had heard Emil give a lecture that drew him into the Religious Socialists, a group Emil had co-founded. Unlike Emil, when the SPD slanted toward establishment politics, he turned to the communists.

Rackwitz's combined rectory and church was a large stone edifice in Neukölln, a working-class district on the south side of the city. The blocks of five-story apartment buildings with flat, plain stuccoed facades and small shops tucked into the first floors hugged narrow cobblestoned streets. The underground Communist Youth organization headquartered there filled the neighborhood with young, bold resistance fighters. It was one of many such in an outer "red" ring around the city. These suburbs had given the communists a plurality in Berlin in national elections.

The church's bell tower rising far above the neighborhood was a beacon for the oppressed. It harbored not only the likes of Klaus and Gerhard but the families of those in concentration camps. Gestapo agents knew Rackwitz's politics, obvious from his being a minister in Neukölln. They transcribed his Sunday sermons but initially left him—and his rectory's dispossessed—alone.

The Nazis' lethal attack on the communist headquarters at the end of February, the Reichstag fire, and the myth of a communist revolution served the Nazis' campaign narrative for the Reichstag election on March 5. The party of Hitler desperately wanted an outright majority to prove their supremacy, but 50.1 percent was not an easy goal with six major parties fielding candidates.

Hitler's simple and fiery message—short on details, long on emotion—spewed from the radio, and listeners heard what they wanted to hear: "The night of the awakening nation," "Economic flowering," "Save the soul."

The demonized opposition, figuratively—sometimes literally—bound and gagged, could do little.

Under gray and rainy skies, March 5 was a quiet Sunday and a quiet Election Day for Berlin. The press reported little opposition. No hammer and sickle flags in working-class districts; a sole Weimar flag forcibly removed by Göring's special auxiliary police; communist "sandwich-board men" carrying posters around a few working-class polling places; Social Democrats standing outside some taverns. Trucks and motorcycles sped around the city carrying gangs of auxiliary police armed with truncheons and revolvers, sometimes rifles. They arrested 341 people. In Neukölln and other red neighborhoods, police and the auxiliary force patrolled with carbines slung over their shoulders. The Fuchses presumably isolated themselves in Arthur Rackwitz's rectory with like-minded friends, of which there were many.

It was a certainty that the Nazi Party and Hitler would prevail. The celebration began early. In mid-afternoon, twenty thousand *Stahlhelme* marched onto Unter den Linden through the Brandenburg Gate, ecstatic throngs cheering and saluting in the drizzle, to honor President Hindenburg.

When the polls closed at 6:00 p.m., the Nazis had received only 43.4 percent of the forty million votes cast. A great disappointment to their claims of legitimacy, but with the 8 percent for their coalition partner, the German National People's Party, they crossed the magic line of majority anyway.

The primary source of the increase of 5.6 million votes for the Nazis over the previous November was new voters rather than a shift from other parties. "It is these hitherto neutral and politically inexperienced people who have made this election such a success for the Nazis," wrote one reporter. Promises of economic gain and fears of an "indescribably horrible Bolshevik revolution" lured the dazzled "non-voters" to the polls.

Beyond Berlin, where many read only nationalist propaganda newspapers, there was relief. "Yes," one German said, "the old order is back again, and we were in dire need of it." Beggars vanished; work camps took shape; the youth had jobs for the first time. An American Quaker traveling through

Germany in the summer of 1933 who knew the country and the language summed up what he saw and felt:

> For in the last analysis the Hitler achievement is one of mass morale. He has been working a field left very much to weeds by our great industrial organizers, and there is evidence that he has discovered how to achieve results. The question as to the efficiency of his methods or of their ethical defense is an entirely separate one.

The Nazis and their supporters hailed their victory as a "revolution." The press qualified it as "so-called." To those who risked death to fight it, it was all too real.

The Nazis' brutality quickly devastated the top and mid-level ranks of the communists. Bruised and battered bodies, dumped wherever, piled up around Berlin. One newspaper noted, "Few passers-by in Berlin have failed to see something of these things." The auxiliary police dragged victims from their homes and tortured them in their private barracks. They stripped them and horsewhipped them, broke their fingers, left them for dead, men and women, young and old. The Gestapo found Ernst Thälmann, arrested and tortured him, threw him in a concentration camp, and eventually murdered him.

The communist leadership had already set up bases in neighboring countries. Those who could escaped: a sailboat to Denmark, a hike through secluded fields into France, or a climb over the mountains and forests into Czechoslovakia.

The mid-level staff who stayed in Germany struggled to evade the Gestapo. The meager circle coordinated with Moscow and gained information deemed valuable for the anticipated Nazi collapse. Those in the underground, most in their twenties like Klaus and Gerhard and committed to the fight, threaded their way through the Gestapo's traps until caught. As MI5's Guy Liddell predicted, the communist counterrevolution failed to materialize.

In Kiel, Emil saw left-wing leaders attacked, killed, or beaten and sent to concentration camps "without bourgeois Germany and its leading churchmen 'noticing' it." Warned that Nazi students planned to attack him, he moved up the coast to a lighthouse until the director of his academy, a swastika now hanging from the window, dismissed him.

Emil had little to fall back on because, like most Germans, he had seen his savings evaporate amid the economic crises of the Weimar era. He hoped for a visa that would enable him to relocate to Birmingham, England, to teach at the Woodbrooke Quaker Centre. Not wanting to leave Elisabeth in Kiel, he asked her to go with him, but she refused, feeling a need to stay and share her friends' difficulties. He continued to press, and seeing his anxiety, she finally agreed to meet him there. He then packed up and went to his sister's in Berlin. The city was being torn apart, but a patina of old-fashioned normalcy covered the wealthier areas, such as Zehlendorf, where he found refuge. Over the weeks, Berlin's decadent, self-indulgent, and socialist underbelly had evaporated, and the horrors on the streets weren't so obvious. The relieved, "good" citizens went about their lives; the "bad" citizens silently disappeared.

The election and tensions of life in the underground, along with a bout of asthma, had left Gerhard drained and sick in body and mind. Desperately needing a refuge, he and his girlfriend, Karin, made the daylong train ride southeast to the Riesengebirge, a low mountain range between Bohemia and Silesia. The waterfalls, glaciers, and fresh air promised peace and a cure.

But Karin, just twenty and almost four years younger than Gerhard, was quickly summoned by her concerned parents back home to Greifswald and away from Gerhard.

He returned alone to Berlin to take control of the Red Student Group's activities in Berlin and to the north. Before the "coup d'état," as they put it, the Gestapo estimated that the RSG, of which Gerhard and Klaus had folded one of its branches into their Free Socialist Student Group in Kiel, had 500 members in twenty groups throughout Germany; 150 were in Berlin. It was funded largely by the KPD, although the group wasn't specifically for communists. Now it drew from the Berlin underground, teeming with brash and zealous young men and women, leftist students who risked their lives to contest the Nazi takeover.

A few other groups, like *Der Rote Stoßtrupp* (the Red Shock Squad), filled with the radical fringe of the SPD, were relatively large. Most, though, were small cells of maybe a dozen students. Klaus's girlfriend Lisa, who had come to be with him, joined one of these groups. The students—now *former* students if they were Jewish—flung aside the historic enmities between the old-line leaders of the SPD and the KPD, whom the Nazis had largely eliminated. Gerhard's job was to recruit such idealistic and impassioned students, and the most fertile ground was the University of Berlin, where Klaus had registered to study math and physics as an excuse for being in Berlin if the Gestapo grabbed him. The party ordered Klaus not to take the courses or to be in a group because the Nazi students had infiltrated everything.

Gerhard relied on his brother to be his liaison with Germany's renowned technical university, the Technische Hochschule, in the affluent neighborhood of Charlottenburg to the west. Known as the TH, this institution epitomized the Nazis' dream university. It had had no official socialist student organization since the early 1920s, mainly because such a group could never have survived. It did have an informal but dedicated group of fifteen to twenty communist students, the Red Students' Club, but soon after the Reichstag fire, at the beginning of March, the TH expelled most of them. The vast majority of the thirty-five hundred future engineers and scientists were rabid fascists. With blind allegiance, they eagerly denounced communists and Jews, teachers and students. The Nazis used it as a backdrop for their performances. The May edition of the student newsletter declared,

German Students! For more than a decade, the German youth
have fought a state that, born from treason and cowardice, brought

our *Volk* to a time of decay in our political, economic, and cultural lives. Today, the bearers of that state lie defeated on the ground. The German youth have won. . . . Heil Hitler!

This was dangerous territory for someone trying to infiltrate for the resistance. Klaus described life as "cautiously living illegally." His challenge was how to recruit students without getting caught.

For those on the streets who carried or distributed antifascist literature, avoiding capture for three months was considered success. If arrested with literature considered subversive, a student without a police record might get a beating and a term of a year or two in a concentration camp—the harshness dependent on the brutality of the guards. For someone with Klaus's record, arrest meant torture. Later, it could bring charges of high treason and a possible death sentence, usually by beheading, guillotine-style. For protection, everyone had a code name. Gerhard's was Hans; Klaus's didn't survive. Since most of the students knew one another's real names, under torture the code names were quickly cracked.

Klaus found a few communist students at the TH whom he could deploy to recruit others. These students would ask seemingly harmless questions in seminars to stimulate conversation. If another student followed up after class, the recruiter would have a cautious discussion, then introduce the prospect to Klaus.

Meeting became an art, with Klaus seeing not more than two cell members together at various local taverns. He spoke in a low voice and kept an eye open for eavesdroppers. Everyone knew that Nazi block watchers hung around to question tavern owners about suspicious discussions. Whatever Klaus learned, he channeled back to Gerhard, who passed it on in weekly meetings with a KPD functionary or used it for political reports in newsletters and flyers.

Since newsletters and flyers were the weapons (not guns and knives), jobs ranged from writing articles—if the person had a typewriter and a safe apartment—to producing literature, distributing it, or carrying materials and instructions to liaisons. Klaus supplied students with flyers to place surreptitiously on tables in common areas or leave on a street corner. The resisters believed deeply as an act of faith that even in the face of overwhelming might, their messages would awaken people to rise up.

In mid-April, Emil traveled to Frankfurt for a meeting of Quakers and found "a gathering of deeply shocked people." From there, he visited friends in Eisenach. One day, strolling down the street, he saw Frau von Bardeleben, a member of his former parish, and they chatted. Seeing the swastika on her lapel, he asked if she had joined the party. She answered, "Certainly, these people just want what you've always said in your sermons." Provoked, he described how the government had fired him in Kiel. She asked if he believed the communists had started the Reichstag fire. The word of a criminal, who started the fire and confessed to be a communist, he said, shouldn't condemn a whole party. He was just being objective. He made the analogy to a state representative from Cologne who was mistreated by the SA. Their actions shouldn't condemn all SA.

They parted amicably, and she invited him to visit, which—wisely—he did not. Instead, he went back to Berlin, and she reported him to the police.

Wary of the police but needing a visa for Birmingham, Emil went to the Quaker Center for advice. A director, an American named Gilbert MacMaster, suggested he apply for his travel documents in Kiel, but Emil hesitated out of fear. A week later, MacMaster heard that Klaus wanted to speak with him. Emil had been arrested for spreading atrocity tales that harmed the welfare of the government. Clutching the New Testament, he was taken from his sister's house to the infamous redbrick Alexanderplatz police station known as the Rote Burg, or red fortress.

MacMaster and two other Quakers set out to see him. His cell was too small for visitors, so they saw him in an official's office. He seemed healthy; he hadn't been beaten. His main request was a copy of the English version of *The Journal of George Fox*, founder of the Society of Friends, which they sent the next day along with other books.

Emil felt desperate: "The whole horror of what lived in me had happened." As always in times of anguish, he heard Christ's voice in the solitude. And then he wondered, "Why did so very many, very clever and orthodox theological thinkers, scholars, pastors and leaders of churches not recognize evil?" His answer: "They were worshippers of nation and lovers of armies first, and afterwards Christians." For five weeks the police moved Emil from prison to prison, then suddenly released him. Through the efforts of a close friend of Rackwitz's, he would remain free until his trial date. The guards set him out on the sidewalk together with a heavy sack of his books and other personal possessions. With no money or idea where he was, he wandered around for a few minutes until he collapsed. A stranger found him a taxi that took him to his sister's house in Zehlendorf.

After recovering, Emil traveled to Kiel to clean out his apartment. He was there when through the door rushed Elisabeth and her boyfriend, Guschi Kittowski. They had sailed to Copenhagen in the family's collapsible boat and returned when she heard Emil was in prison.

The young couple hid with friends until midsummer, when the police swept up Elisabeth and Guschi in a "cleansing" that targeted university students. The court sent Guschi to a new concentration camp in Moorlager, a bitter, windy place along the river Ems off the coast of the North Sea.

Elisabeth languished in the women's jail in Kiel, marching around a courtyard a few minutes a day. The police made no formal charges because they had no evidence of specific activities. Emil was allowed to visit once a month, and he brought her paper and pencils for drawing. Emil's Quaker friend Gilbert MacMaster tried to visit but was turned away. If she cleared up the issue of why she had returned, the police told him, they would release her.

In Berlin, Emil saw Klaus and Gerhard regularly. One of them would phone his sister's and, assuming there were listeners on the line, ask vaguely, "Herr Professor, do you want to go for a walk?" They would meet in a pre-arranged spot close by at Lake Wannsee.

Emil bought a small piece of land from a friend in Bad Freienwalde, a spa town northeast of Berlin near the Polish border, as well as a one-room cabin—located elsewhere—from his sister's husband. Klaus and Gerhard disassembled it, loaded the parts onto a truck, and drove it to Emil's recently acquired parcel.

Gerhard reassembled the shack by himself; while in Berlin the police closed in on Klaus. In mid-July, Klaus fled the city, just hours before the Gestapo had planned to grab him. He said goodbye to his father on the porch of an inn in Zehlendorf, boarded a train, and began his long journey into exile.

CHAPTER 6

Interlude, Paris 1933

KLAUS RODE THE TRAIN TO AACHEN, THE WESTERNMOST CITY IN GERMANY, ITS OUT-skirts abutting both Belgium and the Netherlands. Border crossings meant thorough checks of passports and visas, so Klaus climbed down from the train, crossed into Belgium on foot, and headed to Paris.

It was a well-worn trek for those escaping Germany. As arranged with his father, he sent a postcard from Paris signed "Dr. Dietrich." A relieved Emil received it ten days after his departure.

The twenty-one-year-old, hunted at home, arrived in the City of Light with no prospects of an education, no facility with French, no money or job or place to go, separated from his family. It was an unnerving future. When he had to fill out alien registration forms later, he gave his address in Paris as 70, Boulevard Ornano, a highly styled Beaux Arts apartment building in Montmartre. That he ever lived there is doubtful.

He had come to Paris rather than Prague or some other city full of refugees in order to attend the World Congress of Youth Against War and Fascism, to be held in September. A KPD delegate, he had come early because of his flight from the Gestapo. About eighty other young Germans, many forced to hitchhike, would come later.

The city swirled with peace and antifascist activists that summer. In June, Paris had hosted the World Committee Against War and Fascism. The novelists Henri Barbusse and Romain Rolland attended as members of the executive committee. On that board but not in attendance were intellectuals ranging from Albert Einstein to Upton Sinclair.

The influence of communism and Soviet Russia was not obvious, but many well-known communists in exile swirled about the city too, setting up the Communist International headquarters in Paris. Georgi Dimitrov, a high-level functionary in the Comintern, initially had the controlling hand in the congresses. Implicated in the Reichstag fire, he was arrested in Berlin by the Nazis, cutting short his tenure. With Dimitrov removed, the titular direction belonged to the charismatic figure Willi Münzenberg. With a genius for propaganda, he had spearheaded the 1932 congress in Amsterdam, using prominent intellectuals to advertise, and had drawn in two thousand activists against fascism. He had also created dozens of front organizations and established a successful publishing group in Berlin for the KPD. One of its newspapers was *Mahnruf*, which Gerhard had run.

The real direction fell to Dimitrov's assistant Grete Keilson. A long-time party member, she had earlier been the assistant to the KPD leader Ernst Thälmann. Her husband, Max, an artist, created the graphics for the party's propaganda posters in the Berlin headquarters. As Grete organized the first congress in Paris, Max awaited trial in Germany for the Reichstag fire as well. The Nazis released him in July, and he made it to Paris around the same time as Klaus.

Klaus spent his Parisian summer working with Grete on the youth congress. Once limited to fighting students in Kiel or hiding in the underground in Berlin, Klaus now had entrée to some of the most influential left-wing intellectuals, as well as communist leaders, outside Moscow. He had been a communist revolutionary for all of eighteen months.

Emil's trial took place on September 22 at the special court of Thuringia in Weimar, a short distance from Eisenach. Crowded into the courtroom

were about fifty members of the press, many of Emil's friends from Eisenach, and four representatives from the Quakers.

There was only one state witness, Frau von Bardeleben, described by
one of Emil's friends as "probably the most unhappy person in the court."
Emil's attorney put her through a long cross-examination. The issue was
whether Emil thought the communists had set fire to the Reichstag. She
repeated their conversation. In his defense, Emil explained that he neither
subscribed to nor recognized the communists or the Nazis because of their
use of force. In emphasizing his objectivity to the court, he offered the
example of the politician from Cologne brutalized by the SA, asking, should
that condemn all the SA?

Emil's attorney demanded that the judge read the statement by this
politician in which he described the SA's vicious mistreatment. (From Paris,
Klaus had contacted the man and gained the statement.) The judge read the
document, but when it described the man being dragged through the streets
and badly beaten, he whispered inaudibly. In his closing statement, Emil's
"very brave" attorney read the entire letter in a loud voice so that all could
here. The Nazis never allowed this attorney to defend a political case again,
but in receiving such punishment, he was fortunate. As Emil rightly said, "A
year later, such words would have meant the concentration camp."

The state's attorney brushed aside defense claims of brutality and vio-
lations of due process and demanded a sentence of eight months. Emil had
disrespected the government and violated the law of March 21. After half
an hour's deliberation, the panel of three judges agreed on his guilt and
imposed a sentence of one month and court costs. Having spent five weeks
in prison already, Emil was immediately set free. He celebrated with friends
at the home of a friend in Weimar and returned to Freienwalde to spend
the winter.

By the time the World Congress of Youth Against War and Fascism convened in Paris, at the end of Klaus's two-month stay, he was living in poverty
at the Quaker Bureau, his life unsettled and unsure and miserable. His

father contacted a relative who had worked for a family in Bristol, Ronald and Jessie Gunn. They kindly plucked him from the bleakness with an invitation to attend the university there. The party had expectations of him to finish his education outside Germany. This was paramount so that after victory he could return as one of the architects of its future.

On Friday, September 22, at the Palais de la Mutualité, Henri Barbusse convened the congress, addressing the audience of 1,092 men and women, most in their twenties and representing forty countries, as "the shock brigade of contemporary humanity, the masters of tomorrow."

Those in a hall "ablaze with color" beheld flowing banners, an exhibition of books illegal in fascist countries, and most inspiring, as the whole congress rose to greet them, the entry of the German delegation. Someone in the audience described them as "the living incarnation of the struggle, . . . who in spite of tremendous terror, had illegally, amidst the greatest odds, smuggled themselves over the fascist frontiers." As they walked in, "the 'International' surged over the hall, when defiantly, with hands raised, they gave us the imperishable 'Red Front' salute of the fighting German youth." Presumably Klaus walked with that group.

The congress had a goal: to "examine the uncertain and often terrible situation of the youth in capitalist countries and in colonial countries; and deal with the life, the work, and the hopes of youth in the Soviet Union, socialist countries and the sole hope of peace in the world."

At the congress's close on the twenty-fourth, the 1,092 cheered a call to arms: "We will win because we will fight for the world we want to conquer!" It was bold, it was revolutionary, it was inspiring for the young believers. That it wasn't exactly a peaceful message didn't seem to matter.

Whether Klaus stayed to cheer is not known. What is known is that he had to get to the French coast that very day to catch a ferry for England.

II

RESCUE

A guard tower outside of Camp L in Quebec, 1940

CHAPTER 7

Safety, Bristol 1933

ARRIVING AT THE PORT OF FOLKESTONE, TWENTY-ONE-YEAR-OLD KLAUS FUCHS descended the gangplank and entered the two-story Italianate custom-house, one of thirty-one hundred German refugees to enter Britain that year. When the immigration officer questioned him as to his reason for entry, he handed him a letter that outlined an offer to study theoretical physics at the University of Bristol. It detailed free board and room from his sponsor Ronald Gunn, as well as payment of university fees by his father.

Despite being "white-faced, half-starved and with a dirty bag of linen," Klaus was deemed a refugee of "good class," and the officer granted him a landing permit with triple conditions: no employment without government permission, a time limit of three months, and registration as an alien in Bristol.

Permit in hand, Klaus followed the hall to the back of the building and climbed onto the train to London. There he changed to one heading south-west to Bristol, an industrial city of about 350,000 on the banks of the river Avon. The photograph on Klaus's registration card stamped two weeks later in Somerset shows him wearing a serious expression and a roomy suit jacket, still pale and thin, but he could breathe in freedom. He could also continue his work in opposition to the Nazi regime. Shortly thereafter, he made contact with KPD émigrés in London.

Ronald Gunn, his sponsor, had easily obtained the letter that Klaus presented at the customs office. Although official forms listed Gunn's occupation as a commercial clerk at the Imperial Tobacco Company, this prosaic description obscured family ties and inherited wealth. He was the great-great-grandson of Henry Overton Wills I, who had co-founded Imperial Tobacco, the largest of its kind in Britain. Gunn's cousin Henry H. Wills had endowed the eponymous, state-of-the-art physics laboratory. Set high upon one of Bristol's many hills, its crenelated tower beckoned scientists, whether esteemed or striving.

The difference in the social stratum between Klaus and the Gunns didn't preclude a kinship. Jessie Gunn, Ronald's wife, was a Quaker and shared several acquaintances with Emil Fuchs in the British Society of Friends. Ronald was at least a communist sympathizer and had traveled with Jessie to Russia in 1932. His and Klaus's worldviews encompassed the same attitude toward social problems and found solutions in the Russian socialist system.

Klaus's academic life began almost overnight when Gunn brought him to the physics department to meet its new director, Nevill Mott. Mott was twenty-eight, energetic, and an exceptionally capable scientist, having studied the mysteries of quantum physics with Max Born in Göttingen, Germany. Consequently, he spoke German, which was most helpful to Klaus, who spoke no English.

Klaus wanted to finish his bachelor's degree in mathematics, but Bristol didn't offer such a concentration, so he shifted to physics. Given the mathematical foundations of general relativity and quantum theory, it wasn't a great leap. The real challenge was absorbing information from lectures given in English. After a frustrated Klaus attended a few, Mott suggested that he earn his "B.Sc. by research," not course work. He rapidly advanced to a PhD.

Events in Germany had kept Klaus from math and science for the past year, but as Mott's assistant he dived in and, in 1935, published his first article,

"A Quantum Mechanical Investigation of Cohesive Forces of Metallic Copper Metals," in the *Proceedings of the Royal Society of London.* The research reflected Mott's interest in the properties of metals, for which he later won a Nobel Prize.

It was with another article written a year later that Fuchs made his first major mark in research. This work, which changed the fundamental understanding of the electrical conductivity of thin metallic film, served as a foundation for the development of microelectronics after the war. The results of the work—continually cited to this day—couldn't be fully appreciated in 1936, but Fuchs's singular intellectual abilities could.

Klaus received letters from home but few details. The Nazis controlled the information flow, causing one family friend to warn another, "Be careful what you write to Emil in Germany."

In the spring of 1934, the Gunns invited Klaus to go with them on a month's holiday to France and Switzerland. For Klaus, it became an opportunity to see Gerhard, whose underground work had moved from organizing students in Berlin to liaising with party officials in Paris and organizing émigré resistance in Prague. Gerhard had become adept at slipping over various borders and easily met up with Klaus. He shared the woes. Gerhard, Emil, Elisabeth, and her boyfriend, Guschi, lived together poverty-stricken in Berlin. Gerhard looked for a carpentry job, Guschi, for one as a locksmith, but his time in prison blocked opportunities. Elisabeth's art flourished but earned no money. Shares of IG Farben inherited from Emil's father-in-law offered some promise. With them, Gerhard and Guschi hoped to buy a couple of cars for a rental business and a taxi service, which they eventually did.

His children's desire for a business relieved Emil. He assumed they had left their perilous underground life. They were just as committed though. Emil was the odd man out. Early on, the family had agreed to share only as much as was necessary. His children had no need to share with each other.

The underground wove their lives and secrets together. They told him little, in part not to worry him and in part because he tended to speak loosely.

Kristel was the only one seemingly out of harm's way. The government had granted her a visa for Switzerland to study psychology. Because of their prison sentences, Emil, Elisabeth, and Guschi had lost their passports and were trapped in Germany.

Gerhard's news for Klaus offered little optimism, although Emil never lost hope. He persistently applied to the German government for a passport to go to Britain or the United States.

It was fortunate that Klaus made the trip with the Gunns in the spring. His German passport expired in June, and after a back-and-forth with the German consul in Bristol, he learned that the German government would not renew it. Instead, it offered him a one-way temporary pass to travel home. As a political refugee from Nazi oppression, he knew this option was meaningless. Returning meant certain arrest and torture—maybe death.

In October 1934, Klaus's stateless condition became a crisis. Refugees could not stay in England without Documents of Identity. The government issued them only for travel outside the country, not for residence within it. Without either a passport or these documents, he had to return to Germany.

Despondent, Klaus waited for deportation orders, but the angels of good fortune struck again. After four days, the Home Office offered a reprieve: Registering with the police would be sufficient, although there was a complication. To reregister required permission from the Home Office, and it needed an official ID paper such as his expired German passport. Klaus had sent this document to the German consul. He wrote and asked to have it sent back to him, and surprisingly the German consul complied without ado. By year's end, Klaus received his registration card, a welcomed Christmas present. The only restriction was foreign travel, which required permission.

Unknown to Klaus, the police president in Kiel, with whom he was well acquainted, had sent information on Klaus's life there to the German consul, and it reached the chief constable in Bristol. The chief constable relayed it to MI5 with a note summarily categorizing Klaus as "a notorious Communist" but also stating that he was "not known to have engaged in any Communist activity" in Bristol. In a routine gesture that would have much greater significance years later, MI5 opened a security file on him.

Contrary to the chief constable's belief, Klaus was engaging in communist activity in Bristol, although quietly. Students and faculty often gathered to discuss politics, and the majority view was far to the left. Klaus didn't participate, but he did leave propaganda pamphlets around the department. He also belonged to the university's Socialist Society. Its chair later described admiringly how at one meeting Klaus had a slip of paper with a message from "a Continental socialist" predicting a verdict in the trial on the Reichstag fire. A couple of days later, a main defendant, Georgi Dimitrov, was released. The chairman figured that Klaus had very good sources. He did. There was a small British network—émigré friends from the Berlin underground—and he was a part of it.

Otherwise, Klaus wasn't so different from many of his fellow students and faculty members. With Hitler and Mussolini ascending and with fascist stirrings in Spain, the youth especially reacted against a world tilting to evil. Bread lines, unemployment, and persistent economic anxiety lured tens of thousands to the ideals of communism. People simply wanted basic security with food, shelter, and education, something better than what they saw as the capitalist misery that robbed them relentlessly. Studying Marx and Lenin—an opportunity Klaus took in Bristol—was not extraordinary, as was obvious from a new endeavor.

In 1934, Klaus helped Ronald Gunn start a branch of the Society for Cultural Relations Between the Peoples of the British Commonwealth and the U.S.S.R., more succinctly the SCR. Gunn was chairman; its secretary was the wife of Ronald Gurney, a lecturer in the physics department. Although Klaus was never an official member, he regularly went to meetings. With 110 members (one of the more active branches) its inaugural year was sufficiently successful to receive praise in the SCR's annual report. Nevill Mott was listed among the 110. Gunn often held meetings at his new "concrete House," a marvel of engineering and something that drew neighbors' interest.

The SCR grew out of august origins. Virginia Woolf was a co-founder in 1924; John Maynard Keynes was its chair in 1936. Its list of vice presidents was a who's who of British intelligentsia, the likes of E. M. Forster, the dean of Canterbury, Aldous and Julian Huxley, H. G. Wells, and Bertrand Russell. The future Nobel physicist Patrick Blackett was on the executive committee. Headquartered in Bloomsbury two blocks from the British Museum, the group had thirteen hundred members, excluding branches such as Bristol. Membership offered opportunities to tour Russia—the Leningrad Music Festival, the Moscow Theatre Festival—and tickets to Soviet art exhibits, lectures, and ballet imported to London. The 1934–35 annual report heralded "the great improvement in Anglo-Soviet relations" marked by the visit of Anthony Eden, then an undersecretary in the Foreign Office, to Moscow. It was the first official visit since Lenin seized control of the Russian Revolution in 1917.

MI5 considered the SCR a communist front, although some of its officers thought it "mild" in that it offered a discussion on both sides and was cultural in nature, not political. It exemplified the successful style of the maestro of propaganda Willi Münzenberg (a probable acquaintance of Klaus's in Paris), the nondoctrinaire sort that created the desire among left-leaning British, such as Nevill Mott, to travel to Russia.

In 1934, Nevill Mott and his wife made the journey, as guests at the Mendeleev Congress in Leningrad. A few years earlier, friends had developed a "gloomy impression" of the Soviet experiment owing to the bad harvests and the problematic five-year economic plan that had caused severe deprivations. But now the Motts saw eager and healthy-looking workers with clothes that were neat and clean, goods available in shops, new paint on the palaces, even better roads. There was every evidence of a good, decent life, and apparently without unemployment—a radical improvement over tsarist days or the chaos and dislocation that had prevailed since the revolution. When Mott asked people about the standard of living, especially the cheaply built housing for workers coming to the new factories, they expressed little concern about the shoddy construction. They all seemed committed to the larger goal, which was "building the Soviet State."

But Mott also knew that the new Russia displayed to him was hardly a "worker's paradise." He asked a guide about kulaks, the prosperous, landowning peasants persecuted for their resistance to collectivization. He wanted to know how many had been banished, and he was told, "Half a million and that wasn't many was it." Mott was impressed that this man didn't cover up the facts. As he later wrote, the guide "wanted to believe in it." In truth, millions were exiled to Siberia, with thousands simply shot in their villages.

In Leningrad, Mott also saw the physicist Rudi Peierls and his wife, Genia, who lived in a nice, new apartment. It had a beautiful bathroom, but water only in the evenings.

Disagreement over just how much the Soviet reality matched socialist ideals—and how much Stalin's effort to "build the Soviet State" was an authoritarian betrayal of those ideals—would animate debates among left-wing sympathizers in the West for decades to come. But nonideological progress in physics continued.

By the fall of 1936, only three years after his arrival in Britain, Klaus had finished his undergraduate degree, received approval to do a PhD, and submitted his dissertation, titled "A Quantum Mechanical Investigation of the Cohesive Forces of Copper, the Elastic Constants, and the Specific Heat of Monovalent Metals." The award of the degree was just a few months away. He had also published three articles in the *Proceedings of the Royal Society* in addition to his groundbreaking article on electrical conductivity.

Also in 1936, in August, Kristel arrived on her way to Swarthmore, the

Quaker college in Pennsylvania where a friend of her father's had arranged a scholarship. She brought Klaus another update on the family, and again it was not good.

It began with Karin, who had returned to Berlin, married Gerhard, and become an underground recruiter, code-named Johanna, in Gerhard's student network. In 1935, the Gestapo penetrated the cell, arrested her, and let her suffer for months behind bars without a specific charge. She was pregnant, and very sick throughout her term, eventually giving birth to her son Jürgen in prison. Quakers in London tried to get her out, but couldn't.

According to the Gestapo report, they arrested Gerhard as well but for some reason released him. Soon after, as he walked down the street, a friend coming toward him signaled that the Gestapo were behind him. Gerhard escaped them, Guschi drove him to Dresden, and he made it over the Czech border. He was now penniless and soon became desperately ill with TB, ending up in a sanatorium. With Gestapo agents in Czechoslovakia stalking émigrés and kidnapping them, communicating with him directly was dangerous, so Emil used back channels to send him funds, selling subscriptions to his interpretation of the Bible in Switzerland and smuggling in copies. The money went into a Swiss fund for Gerhard. Emil knew that if caught, he would be charged with high treason.

Guschi, now Elisabeth's husband, had been arrested in mid-January 1936. The Gestapo probably would have arrested Elisabeth too, but she was in the hospital, their son, Klauslein, being cared for in a children's home.

The Gestapo had figured out that the rental car business—four cars and a gas station in Neukölln—Guschi and Gerhard had set up was being used to provide transport for the resistance. Working as a liaison between the underground in Berlin and resources in Denmark, and with Elisabeth and Klauslein in tow, Guschi would bring material to an uncle who lived in a fishing town close to Kiel. From there, the uncle organized the boats that carried literature back and forth to Denmark, a printing haven for the communists.

Guschi and Gerhard also used the cars to transport those fleeing the Nazis—communists, Jews, Social Democrats, anyone hunted—to the border of Czechoslovakia or to the Baltic Sea for transit to Denmark. The Gestapo rolled up the whole operation, then tortured and killed Guschi's invalid uncle.

Guschi was in prison awaiting sentencing. Karin had been imprisoned for more than a year with no trial; Elisabeth was about to be released from the hospital to the care of Emil's sister in Zehlendorf. Only Emil was at liberty, living in their Berlin apartment looked after by someone Kristel had hired. He was "closely watched."

By the beginning of 1937, Mott had three or four German refugees in the department and insufficient funds to keep them all. While Klaus waited to hear how Mott would resolve the situation, he joined a local relief committee organized to support the Republicans in the Spanish Civil War, and he attended the SCR, the Russian cultural group. The January 23 front-page headline in the *Bristol Evening Post* read, "Moscow Trial: 17 Plead Guilty, Charges of Conspiracy with German General Staff; Officials Accused of Anti-Stalin Conspiracy." This was one of the infamous "show trials" that Stalin used to justify liquidating most of the old-line Bolsheviks who had led the revolution, as well as current members of the army—anyone who might pose a threat as an alternative to his increasingly brutal and unpopular leadership.

The SCR-Bristol branch discussed whether the evidence against the "traitors" was really true. When transcripts of the trials became available, the group decided to reenact them. As in Kiel with the agitprop performances, Klaus played the adversarial role of the vengeful prosecutor Andrei Vishinsky with zeal, as he had done with Hitler. Klaus's venomous attack on the accused impressed Mott as a clear sign of "where his [Klaus's] sympathies lay and always remembered it." He knew nothing of Klaus's earlier thespian pursuits. In this case, though, Klaus might not have considered Vishinsky a bad guy. Generally, Klaus judged most Western news on Russia as mere propaganda to destroy communism.

Whether the performance was a deciding factor or not, Mott chose not to fund Klaus in Bristol, but he did find him a position at the University of Edinburgh with Max Born, Mott's former mentor at the University of Göttingen in Germany. He told Born that he was sending Klaus because Klaus "needed a change." Born later heard that Mott's real reason was Klaus's communist activities, a claim Mott denied. Whatever the reason, Mott remained Klaus's friend and supporter.

CHAPTER 8

War, Edinburgh 1937

PROFESSOR MAX BORN, CHAIR OF THE DEPARTMENT OF NATURAL PHILOSOPHY—
as the Scots called theoretical physics—walked to his office on the first
morning back from his holiday, the first morning of the fall semester at the
University of Edinburgh. He descended the stairs to the basement and
strode along the hall of the former University Infirmary, the troughs on
either side of the concrete floor a reminder of bodies on pushcarts. Off the
hall was his office, a large and dark room that held his desk and chair, a
couch, and a circular table and a rectangular one with chairs that had sat
depressingly empty for the last year.

Born had come to Edinburgh via a temporary position at the University of Cambridge and a years-long one at the University of Göttingen in
Germany. Before the Nazis stripped him of his position, he drew a constel-
lation of young academic superstars from Europe and America. About a
dozen would go on to win Nobel prizes, as did Born himself. One, Werner
Heisenberg, who would serve prominently in Germany's effort to build an
atomic bomb, had already received the prize for work he and Born had
collaborated on.

This morning something new warmed the dampness and cold of the coming bleak winter. At the table Born saw the eager faces of his first two graduate students. Both German PhDs in physics, they were relieved to have secured a position with him. The tall, blond, robust one, Walter Kellermann, the son of a rabbi, was an experimental physicist. The other, Klaus Fuchs, the son of a Lutheran minister, was a theoretician. Born later described Klaus as "weak in appearance but with a powerful brain, taciturn, with a veiled expression which disclosed nothing of his thoughts." Born's daughter Irene was softer in her comments but more prosaic, describing him as appearing to need a warm coat and a good meal.

Fuchs was not only a theoretical physicist but one whose fundamentals were rooted in mathematics, as were Born's. Born and Fuchs came to physics for different reasons, but their path led through the works of such mathematicians as Euclid, Lagrange, and Gauss.

Fuchs and Kellermann, a gift for Born, rescued his scientific soul. Fuchs, especially, lifted a depression that he had carried inside for some time.

At the outset, Born gave them a piece of advice: do not speak German in public. Separately, he told Fuchs to stop all political activity. He wanted none of the communist propaganda that had caused Mott consternation.

Refugee aid organizations had sterner recommendations: no political discussion in public; no description of the plight of Jews in Germany; no talk of the Nazis' real motives. They didn't want refugees to be seen as warmongers. Negative feelings toward refugees, and Germans in particular, had already surfaced in Britain.

Max and Hedi Born lived in a row house built entirely of stone, inside and out, that mirrored the city's stolid facade—short on whimsy, long on steadiness. Born's home was his favored setting for work, and Klaus joined him there regularly. Throughout the day, as he had with assistants in Göttingen, Born handed an idea to Klaus with a "Machen Sie das" (Do this). At the end of the day, Klaus often stayed for dinner and then played skat, a card game for three. He became part of the family fabric. When Hedi became a Quaker, Klaus did too, although he later remarked that his association was mainly to aid in contact with his father. He was an atheist, and although a pacifist at heart, he willingly joined the communists to drive out the Nazis. In doing so, he embraced their call for revolution.

Once a month or so, Born, an accomplished pianist, gathered together friends who made an informal chamber group. He invited Klaus to be second violin, even though Klaus was self-taught and didn't play that well. Klaus also played the viola in a quartet with physicists and mathematicians, with Kellermann playing second violin. In both groups, others noted that Klaus routinely lost his place in the music.

Kellermann and Fuchs were much more proficient in their work. They attended math and physics seminars, some given by guest lecturers drawn from Born's connections in Germany, some from his friends in the German émigré community. They began research projects and did some teaching, though Klaus less so. His German accent, stronger than Walter's, didn't resonate well with the Scottish ear. To bolster their credentials and guard against chaotic times, Born told them to apply to the university for a doctorate of science degree. Kellermann didn't have the required publications to qualify. Fuchs had amassed many from his work with Mott and Born and earned the degree. Around the same time, the Carnegie Trust awarded him a fellowship in mathematics to study (1) quantum theory, (2) statistical methods, and (3) theory of atomic nuclei. Born frequently described Fuchs by using some variant of the phrase "the best of his age group," favorably comparing him to his *Wunderkinder*, all those future Nobel Prize winners he taught in Germany.

At the end of December 1937, the relative tranquility of academic life was shattered when Klaus learned that Gerhard was seriously ill in a sanatorium near Prague. It wasn't only TB. He had had a mental collapse. Klaus continued to send Gerhard half of his twelve-pound monthly income from the university. Now he asked the British government for permission to travel to visit his brother, which it granted. Czechoslovakia, though, refused him a visa. He couldn't turn to his father, who was barely surviving under the Nazis, so he wrote a letter to the Geheebs in Switzerland, close friends to Gerhard since the Odenwaldschule days:

> Dear Frau Geheeb, I have received bad news about Gerhard and would like to turn to you with a request. Gerhard has had a complete nervous breakdown and at the moment is at an institution in Prague. . . . It seems urgent that he get out of Czechoslovakia into better air and a less stressful political atmosphere so that he really gets cured. I would be very grateful if you could procure the possibility for him to go to Switzerland. The greatest difficulty is surely the passport question.
>
> I have written to Father very cautiously that Gerhard is down with his nerves. Because he cannot do anything from Germany, it is unnecessary to worry him with the stress.

There was more behind the letter. Nazi Germany had its eye on Czechoslovakia. As part of Hitler's drive to annex foreign lands with a German culture, he demanded the Sudetenland, a section in the country that was majority German-speaking. Gerhard wasn't in that region, but would the Nazis stop at some invisible line?

Unknown to Klaus, Elisabeth was in the thick of dangerous intrigues in Berlin. Her husband, Guschi, had been sentenced to seven years in prison, which he was serving on a ship that dredged the Elbe River. Through secret communication with Elisabeth, he had plotted an escape with another inmate. On the specified day, Elisabeth swam the Elbe to meet him, and he didn't show up. Frantic, she returned to Berlin and told Emil she feared that the Gestapo had discovered the plan. She then ran off.

Emil heard a whistle outside—a signal—and looked out to see Guschi with old friend Arthur Rackwitz. Guschi told Emil that guards had arrested his escape partner. Guschi, who thrived in uncertain worlds, knew he couldn't wait. He watched a man go into a hut on the bank and come out in work-man's overalls. Guschi sidled in, exchanged his prison uniform for the man's civilian clothes, and casually walked out. Using money Elisabeth had passed to him earlier, he took a taxi to Berlin but knew he wouldn't survive there as a marked man. He waited for Elisabeth until morning, but when she failed to return, he took off for Prague without her.

To all appearances, Klaus had heeded Born's warning against communist activities. In reality, he had strengthened ties with German communist friends in London. An acquaintance from his days in Berlin, Jürgen Kuczynski, arrived in the English capital in July 1936, and he quickly became the polit-ical organizer of the secret German Communist Party in Britain. Driven and extremely capable, Kuczynski took the thirty to forty longtime KPD members there and formed a disciplined, effective, and tightly knit group to produce propaganda material for the German underground. Klaus was one of them. He acted as a conduit, arranging to send the material via coal ships from eastern Scotland.

Thirty-two-year-old Kuczynski had studied statistics at a German university, been a postgraduate fellow at the Brookings Institution in Wash-ington, D.C., and headed the economics department at the American Feder-ation of Labor. With excellent English, he crisscrossed Britain to publicize a new socialist-oriented publishing enterprise, the Left Book Club, lectur-ing to economically deprived workers. It was a perfect cover for his clan-destine activities. Klaus's occasional trips to London and Kuczynski's lecture tours gave the two men opportunities to stay in touch.

The Borns knew Klaus was a communist, and Kellermann suspected that his colleague had activist friends, although he had no direct evidence. The Born children and cousins braved Klaus's long discourses on Marxism on their Sunday walks over the rolling Pentland Hills, as well as on outings to the movies to see his favorite, Bette Davis. On walks in the Pentland Hills with members of the physics music quartet, politics never arose.

To most he seemed to be just one of many leftist graduate assistants, many of whom had been galvanized by the Spanish Civil War, where the main international aid for the Republicans came from communists.

Walter and Klaus rented rooms in town houses some three hundred feet apart on Marchmont Road, an area just south of the city's large swath of parkland called the Meadows. Walter lived with his mother, who had escaped from Berlin, his father having died a few years before. Klaus lived in a miserable studio, one room in a dark and dank basement with a bed, two chairs, a desk, and no kitchen. One wall held a bookshelf with volumes from the Left Book Club but no propaganda leaflets, communist texts, or Marxist screeds. His landlady fed him breakfast; Walter's mother washed his socks. The two physicists became good friends and often shared the twenty-minute walk to Born's institute.

Afternoons often found them sitting in one or the other's room talking politics. Walter listened to Klaus argue that the appeasement policy of Britain's Chamberlain government concealed its real goal, which was "to turn German aggression towards Russia." (Many Britons, especially those in the upper class, did consider Russia the enemy more than Germany.) Given the nonintervention of England and France in the Spanish Civil War, Klaus called Kellermann's contention that they would stand up to Hitler "starry-eyed" and cited Chamberlain's calmly sitting by as the *Wehrmacht* marched into Austria in March 1938.

And then, on September 30, 1938, Chamberlain had committed the cardinal sin of appeasement by handing Hitler the Sudetenland, confirming Klaus's worst fears for Europe, and for his brother.

Gerhard was still in Prague, but by March 15, 1939, when the Nazis swallowed the whole country, he had escaped, thanks to Quakers who had wangled a British visa for him to enter Switzerland the month before. In July, he flew to England with plans to visit Klaus in Edinburgh and then travel to join Kristel in the United States. Customs authorities refused him permission to land, though, because of his active case of TB, and he returned to Switzerland.

Elisabeth's needs were just as dire. She had never joined Guschi, who remained unaccounted for in Czechoslovakia. After he left Berlin, she had roamed Germany's eastern border, then returned to the capital, where she spent her days painting and playing with her son. Sometimes, though, demons came, and episodes of madness descended. One night in the summer of 1939 while with Emil visiting friends in the country, she knelt beside her father's bed, fraught with visions of Guschi tortured by the Gestapo. Friends from Berlin came to bring little Klaus back to the city.

Elisabeth calmed herself enough to travel with Emil to the Quaker Yearly Meeting in Bad Pyrmont. During the few days there, she seemed stable; she chatted and helped in the kitchen. The day before leaving, she gathered with others in front of an open window for a photograph. She smiled gaily, her eyes bright and clear.

On the morning of August 7, 1939, at the meeting's end, she and Emil walked to the train station to depart for Berlin. Sensing that Elisabeth was unsettled, he held her hand as they climbed onto the train. As it started to roll, he dropped her hand to steady himself, and she dashed from his side. When he looked around, the train door was open. She had jumped. He found her at the bottom of a ravine with her head smashed.

A few months later, Emil wrote to friends that the weeks since "had exceeded any misery or hardship I've ever been through. To this day, I do not know how to carry on without her." But as with all the tragedies in his life—and he had more than most people could bear—he relied on God. "However, it has worked so far and has to work out further. God has helped and will help, and the love of many friends has carried me. . . . She was on the peak of her talent and her last paintings are the most beautiful. But that was probably the seeking of life further after this life." Years later, Klaus saved this letter of his father's out of hundreds.

Within a week, Klaus began to receive condolences. He said little. On official forms, as he had done in relation to his mother's suicide, he entered Elisabeth's cause of death as "political reasons."

On September 1, 1939, Germany attacked Poland. This onslaught, the first example of the German tactic of *Blitzkrieg,* quickly overwhelmed the country's defenses.

Two days later, on Sunday morning, the Borns invited Fuchs and a few others over for cakes and tea. They were in the sitting room when the air raid siren sounded. Everyone jumped up to stand in doorways or scoot under tables. It was a false alarm—friendly aircraft mistaken for the enemy. It was also one of the last times they would gather for cakes, soon to be a scarce pleasure. That day, over the wireless, Neville Chamberlain pronounced, "This country is at war with Germany."

Britain's declaration of war left Fuchs unconvinced. A war against fascism? he asked Walter Kellermann rhetorically. "No," he answered, rather a war along old-fashioned nationalist lines. The British would fight for the survival of Britain, but not to defeat Hitler and defend democracy. He explained that his barometer was the British press. Except for Churchill's speeches warning of Hitler's aggression, he read little that showed awareness of Germany's true intent. Indeed, throughout the 1930s, the *Daily Mirror,* the *Daily Mail,* the *Evening News,* and others had supported Chamberlain's appeasement in the face of Hitler's aggressions.

A twist on this argument explained Klaus's rationalization of the stunning nonaggression pact between Germany and Russia signed a month before. In this pact, the two countries agreed not to attack each other or support another country that was their enemy. Klaus argued that Chamberlain's goal all along had been to provoke a fight between Germany and Russia (with Russia the presumed loser). With many in the British government more sympathetic to the Nazis than to the communists, Stalin's sudden shift was merely pragmatic. Russia needed time to build its defenses.

There was substance to Klaus's arguments. Russia had been in disarray from the time of World War I and the civil war that followed the revolution, as well as the years of famine and forced collectivization. Still, it was a jolt to idealistic Westerners who saw the Communist Party as leading the way to a new era in human development. For years, the party, and especially Germans like Klaus, had worked night and day to destroy the Nazis and fascism, not to join hands with them.

Officially, the Communist Party pivoted its propaganda to decry an imperialist war. At the same time, tripping over contradictions, the British Communist Party issued manifestos and declarations that supported Britain's new war footing. The government watched carefully for any call to resist it. There was none.

In July 1939, Klaus had applied to become a naturalized British citizen, but he was too late. Once the war started, the government stopped processing applications. In a quick reversal, his category switched from refugee to "enemy alien." Along with seventy-three thousand others—mostly German Jews—he was ordered to stand in court before a judge to determine if he was a danger to the country.

Facing uncertainty and fear, the government convened 120 tribunals throughout the country to classify refugees. *A* was for those most likely to undermine the country, and they were immediately interned; *B* was for those whose allegiances were uncertain, and they had their movements restricted; and *C* was for those who were religious or political refugees, and they had few restrictions imposed.

On November 2, 1939, on orders of the secretary of state for Scotland, Klaus walked with Max Born to the Edinburgh Sheriff Court in the center of the city. To this home of justice, its neo-Georgian facade embodying the values of the Scottish Enlightenment, he was to bring a statement from a British subject to attest to his character and the oppression in Germany. He had letters from Paul Sturge, general secretary of the Friends Service Council in London, and Born, whose own naturalization papers had come through just days before the war started.

The courtroom held friendly faces. Walter Kellermann, accompanied by his mother, was there for his hearing. Besides police officers and officials from the British Home Office, representatives from Edinburgh's Refugee Committee and Jewish Committee stood ready to assist if needed. The head of the Jewish Committee, Kellermann's reference, graciously supported Fuchs as well.

It was over in a matter of minutes. Those in attendance vouched for Klaus, a persecuted Social Democrat; the clerk took notes in shorthand; and the one-man tribunal, Chairman Simpson, ordered that as a "Refugee from Nazi oppression" Fuchs be granted "Exemption from Internment." Klaus became a category C refugee with minimal restrictions on travel and movement; Kellermann earned the same.

They walked back to Born's department to continue their research and teaching. Fuchs had a new grant in mathematics from the Carnegie Trust. With that funding, he worked on quantum dynamics and statistical mechanics with Born. Probably on his own, he explored the theory of atomic nuclei.

Some of Klaus's friends were less fortunate. A tribunal classified Jürgen Kuczynski, the energy behind London's small group of German communists, in category A as a serious security risk. He was interned, but his connections ensured that it wasn't for long. Members of Parliament, the dean of Canterbury (first cousin to the queen), and all manner of British elite pressured the Home Office to release him. Within a few months, he was free.

A steady state of anxiety prevailed as the world watched Hitler overrun all countries in his path. In the early hours of May 10, 1940, from the ground, in gliders, with parachutes, German troops attacked Belgium and the Netherlands. Bombs shattered the rest. That evening, Winston Churchill replaced Neville Chamberlain as prime minister.

The Borns had invited Kellermann and Fuchs over to play bridge. By the time of the party, the Belgians were only twenty-four hours away from surrender. The Dutch fell quickly thereafter.

At its closest point, Britain is about twenty miles from the French coast. Within a matter of hours, Prime Minister Churchill ordered Sir John Anderson, the home secretary, to intern every male enemy alien between sixteen and sixty from the vulnerable eastern coast "in view of the imminent risk of invasion."

Anderson, a thoughtful and serious public servant, didn't support internment. His report "Control of Aliens," prepared two weeks earlier, argued for individual examination. He maintained that the government's prior steps were adequate: registration for entry by immigrants; examination of the 73,353 aliens by tribunals; declaration of the eastern coast as a protected area that restricted aliens. Germans who were known or suspected Nazis had been encouraged to return home. Those who didn't were interned. Anderson had concluded, "Obviously, no decision that a purely arbitrary proportion of Germans and Austrians should be interned could be justified. Nor would the internment of an arbitrary proportion without regard to the characters and circumstances of the individuals have any value for security purposes."

Addressing a large-scale internment similar to that in the previous war, Anderson asserted, would waste manpower, not guarantee the safety of vulnerable points, and rile public opinion. But therein was the problem. He knew that headlines such as "Collar the Lot" whipped up substantial public sentiment and "easily excited" negative feelings against refugees.

Anderson lost the argument; the military prevailed. On May 11, he had to issue orders to the chief constables to intern the "enemy aliens" along the eastern coast. "All male Germans and Austrians, including refugees, 'rounded up' and interned," Hedi Born wrote with alarm in her diary. The order affirmed Max Born's belief in the ferocity of ideologies. He wrote to Hedi, "Fanaticism versus fanaticism, belief versus belief, the distortion and repression of truth is raised to a political art."

On Whitsunday, the twelfth, morning until night, constables rapped on doors up and down the coast from Nairn to Hampshire. Friendly, even apologetic, police told three thousand refugees to pack a suitcase with enough to last for two weeks and come along. Because of its location, those in Edinburgh, including Fuchs and Kellermann, were among the first to be affected by the day-old edict.

It became evident very quickly that a fifth column, foreign collaborators inside a country under attack, had conspired in the annihilation of the Netherlands, so the pressure on Home Secretary Anderson didn't stop. Churchill and others in the War Cabinet wanted to know the possibility of a German fifth column in Britain. Anderson met with the Dutch and learned that the Nazis had been able to set up agents there thanks to the Dutch having an open border with Germany, a right of free access guaranteed by treaty. The fifth column required no subterfuge. According to the Dutch, there was "no evidence that such assistance had been given by the refugee element."

The situation in Britain simply wasn't analogous to that in the Netherlands. Anderson, convinced by the "very strong and obvious objections to wholesale measures of internment," recommended that the government not implement a general one.

The War Cabinet met at 10 Downing Street the next day and took up the question. There was only one vote in the room that counted: Churchill insisted on stiffer measures. By the end of the summer, the government had put about twenty-seven thousand men and women into camps. Interestingly, Jürgen Kuczynski, Fuchs's London friend, wasn't among them. His earlier release was permanent.

In the eyes of officials in Whitehall, Fuchs, Kellermann, and thousands of other internees were no longer refugees from Nazi oppression but likely Nazi saboteurs. The government, in its muddled thinking about the dangers of a fifth column, had gathered up those most likely to be threatened by Nazis: Jewish refugees. Many in the War Cabinet and the security services felt that if there were an invasion, "a considerable number of enemy aliens, who might now be genuinely well-disposed to this country, would, by virtue of their nationality, help the enemy. On this view, even enemy aliens who were refugees from the Nazi regime presented a potential danger."

On the night of May 12, Fuchs and Kellermann found each other at Donaldson's School, where the local police had deposited them along with scores of others. Empty because of a holiday, the school had transformed itself overnight into a miserable military transit camp. According to Born, Klaus went to the authorities, demanded urgent supplies for the internees, and helped to locate them. A few days later, after the military worked out a makeshift arrangement for their next camp, the police crammed the detainees onto a train and took them away. They had no idea where they were going.

CHAPTER 9

Internment, England 1940

THE BRITISH GOVERNMENT'S CONVERSION TO AN INTERNMENT POLICY TOOK ONE DAY. It had no official plans, procedures, or supplies, just precedent from the internment of enemy aliens during World War I twenty-five years earlier. Neither the government nor the refugees knew what to expect.

The transport train from Edinburgh carried the internees south and several hours later stopped in Huyton, a small town outside Liverpool on the west coast. Klaus and Walter disembarked to a shocking reality. Before them were two twelve-foot-high barbed-wire fences that encircled a "camp." Soldiers patrolled a narrow footpath between the fences while others, armed with rifles and fixed bayonets, stood on guard inside. Just a few days before, the camp had been a newly built housing estate—long lines of small, brick, single-family row houses for the working class. Half of it, separated by barbed-wire fences, was still ordinary housing. From one spot, the young men penned inside could see children laughing, riding their bikes, and staring at the "enemy aliens."

Guard towers that loomed over the camp were added quickly, and searchlights illuminated both sides of the fences. One internee called these towers "wooden shooting platforms" because "whoever enters the illuminated area is shot."

Threatened by Nazi aggression, British authorities were not afraid to employ methods that might appear reminiscent of Nazi Germany. Certainly, conditions were primitive. Each man filled a sack with straw to serve as a mattress. Each man had two blankets, a plate, and an enamel mug, but no towels and little soap and toilet paper. Suitcases doubled as chairs. Each man was allowed one bath a month, but the shortage of coal meant no hot water. Klaus and Walter's good fortune was to be among the first arrivals, which earned them a strip of floor in a row house that would ultimately accommodate twelve to sixteen men. Those who came later subsisted in tents that, after a hard rain, filled with oozing mud.

Klaus and Walter shared a room with blackout curtains and no furniture other than their straw mattresses on the floor. Two other men soon arrived to share their floor, veterans of the Spanish Civil War who had been sponsored in England by a Czech refugee organization. They were in fact German communists who, like Gerhard, had fled to Czechoslovakia because of the Nazis. Although nothing was said, Walter sensed that Klaus already knew them.

The military staff was overwhelmed as more refugees arrived at the camp daily. In the chaos, an internee by the name of Hans Kahle stepped forward. An early escapee from Nazi Germany, the forty-one-year-old soldier had commanded a battalion in the Spanish Civil War and, after many close calls, made his way to England in 1939. Local police had picked him up working on a farm in the countryside around Cambridge. He arrived in Huyton with a group of refugee scholars from the university. He exuded charisma and a sense of authority. His ability to take charge impressed another internee from Cambridge who wrote,

> He never raised his voice; he just took charge. People were split
> up in groups of twenty or so, each group allocated to one house
> and told whom to send off to find straw pallets, . . . whom to dis
> patch to check out cooking and washing facilities—things just
> fell into place.

Kahle and Klaus may have met before, in Paris in 1933, or still earlier in Berlin, and if not on the Continent, then in London through Jürgen Kuczynski. There Kahle had worked with Kuczynski to lead the group of communist émigrés who supported the German resistance. With veterans of the Spanish Civil War, with Czech roommates, with Kahle, with the shadow of Gerhard, Huyton wove together so many threads from Klaus's former life. Internees later described Klaus's voicing the communist line and hanging around with "a prominent German Communist" who was part of the Czech group. Walter Kellermann sought his social connections elsewhere.

Conditions at Huyton were stark and depressing for the twenty-three hundred imprisoned men. In the first weeks, three men were shipped to a "psychiatric asylum." Another hanged himself. As dirty and hungry as everyone else, Klaus shared the deprivation and powerlessness and despair.

The depressing physical environment was made even worse by the government's ban on newspapers, magazines, and radios, as well as ordinary mail. Within the camp, the rumor mill had the Germans surrounding Paris and Italy declaring war on Great Britain. The men had no idea what was true, but they wondered and worried if England was going to be the next to fall.

With no communication in or out, the men also worried about their families' lack of information on their whereabouts. Finally, the camp commander allowed them to send a letter or two a week on special spongy paper invented to foil the use of invisible ink. Censorship delayed the delivery and receipt of mail by weeks.

In the mess tent, five hundred men at a time ate either "awful tasting" porridge or herring or "indescribable rotten stuff, ½ potato, 6 bitter beans, a little meat." Two weeks into internment, one desperate sixteen-year-old cried out in his diary,

> Today again we got scarcely anything to eat. I can't stand it anymore! I'm terribly weak and have a headache from sheer hunger most of the time. What will happen now! We're wasting away in this mass imprisonment. I keep asking myself—why is all this happening.

The government later admitted to "occasional considerable temporary shortages."

In their haste to create a system for internment, the government had mindlessly thrown together an explosive mixture of Jews, dangerous Nazi POWs, and communists. The POWs' treatment, especially regarding adequate food, adhered to the Geneva Convention. Otherwise, the guards treated everyone the same—as though they were all enemies of the country. When the POWs sadistically taunted the refugees, especially the Jews, the guards did nothing, even though the guards knew who were refugees and who were captured enemy soldiers.

The residents of Huyton, however, didn't know. Newspapers had whipped up scares of fifth columnists with little distinction between Nazis and those who had fled them. When the refugees walked from the train through the town to the camp, some residents lined up on the side of the street to spit and jeer at them, assuming the worst. Given their own hatred of and persecution by the Nazis, the refugees were utterly confused.

Internment deepened Klaus's suspicions regarding Britain's true motives. He told Kellermann that the government's decision to intern antifascists to appease the right-wing press confirmed its real goal: "not to establish freedom and democracy, but to continue to attempt shameful compromises with the Nazis."

As the government came to grips with the almost daily "kaleidoscopic changes" in internment policy, the refugees experienced the impact. Fuchs and Kellermann heard that about a thousand of them were to be shipped to the Isle of Man, a rugged hunk of rock in the middle of the Irish Sea. In the early morning dew of June 14, about three weeks after their arrival in Huyton, the men ate breakfast, assembled for roll call, and marched through the town—displayed "like animals in a zoo," one of them wrote—to take a special train to the Liverpool docks. There, armed soldiers loaded them onto excursion steamers, and they began the four-hour voyage out into a calm sea. Soon the British coast faded behind them. Just one month earlier, Fuchs and Kellermann had been at the Borns' home, enjoying an evening of bridge.

The Isle of Man was a favorite resort equidistant from England, Scotland, and Northern Ireland. Its capital, Douglas, on the southeast shore, had a broad promenade framed on one side by a long sandy beach and on the other by scores of Victorian-style hotels and boardinghouses. Normally, thousands of holiday seekers jammed the area, but the outbreak of war had canceled the vacation season for the foreseeable future. As in the last war, the British government requisitioned much of the island for a string of internment camps and forced out the owners of the boardinghouses. Workers had grappled with pneumatic drills to tear up the concrete on the sidewalks and install metal posts for a high barbed-wire fence.

The refugees came ashore loaded with suitcases, boxes, even violins, and walked down the promenade enclosed by the new fence. A newspaper reported, "One ingenious fellow had casters fitted to his suitcase so that it could be wheeled along quite easily!" Crowds of townspeople pressed against the fence to get a look. A statement by the island's governor marked them as "military prisoners of war." A local newspaper labeled the bunch "ragged creatures." The refugees referred to themselves as "His Majesty's loyal enemy aliens."

Fuchs and Kellermann were assigned to Central Camp in Douglas: a block of white boardinghouses—seventeen in all—encircled by barbed wire, the six at the front of the block offered a prime sea view. Within a few days, another seventeen houses from the block next door were incorporated into Central Camp, in all a total of two thousand internees. Eventually, the island held about thirty thousand enemy aliens, men and women, in ten different camps.

Central Camp was different from Huyton. Food was as scarce and hunger constant—they called the mess "Starvation Hall"—but the military commander gave the men much greater autonomy. Like Fuchs and Kellermann, many of the internees had entered England on student visas and were highly intelligent. The commander gave them the use of a few rooms for lectures, given mostly in German. The attendees brought chairs. The impressive range of subjects included literature, physics, theology, and philosophy. Fuchs gave a seminar on vector analysis.

With a nod to democracy, each of the thirty-four boardinghouses in Central Camp elected a housefather. Fuchs represented his. Together they formed a "parliament" with a speaker and a deputy speaker to bring complaints to the commander. They assailed members of Parliament, refugee organizations, and trade unions with letters arguing for an end to internment.

By now these men had been out of touch with the world for more than a month. They didn't know the government's plans; they didn't know if their families were safe, had money, or had been rounded up. They did know that the British had made them sitting ducks if the Nazis crossed the channel. They had heard that the French had put Jewish refugees in camps and delivered them to the Gestapo. Would the British make them part of a settlement or prisoner exchange? Terrifying rumors swarmed.

On June 30, German troops stormed and occupied the Channel Islands just off the coast of Brittany—perfect stepping-stones to the British naval base at Plymouth. With limited resources, the British government struggled to mount defenses for the anticipated German onslaught: repelling ground troops; withstanding high-intensity bombing forays; preparing civilian evacuation routes that left roads clear for troops; safeguarding children, some already sent to the country. The *Blitzkrieg* of Poland left no illusions about Germany's intent to annihilate anyone who stood in its way, or about the difficulty of stopping it.

These dangers did not make the government any more sympathetic to refugees who might pose a threat. Two weeks after the men arrived in Douglas, officials finalized plans to ship thousands of those under age thirty to more remote locations. The Canadian government had agreed to take seven thousand men: three thousand German POWs and four thousand internees who were, as the lord president of the council exclaimed to the Canadians, "the most dangerous characters among the Germans and Italians." Another ten thousand were to go to Australia and New Zealand.

John Anderson stressed undertaking a careful selection—do not mix Jews with fascists, do not include the aged or infirm—but his was a lone voice. The anti-immigrant and anti-Semitic factions thought that, "in principle, all alien internees were dangerous" and better "out of the country." The pragmatists insisted that when the ships were ready to sail, those in charge should simply fill them up. Vetting to select "the most dangerous" or separate out political or religious persuasions was too cumbersome and time consuming. Take advantage of the Canadian quota, they argued, and fill the berths with whoever was at hand. Their argument won. No one told the Canadian government that the British had replaced the "most dangerous" with ordinary refugees. Likewise, the refugees had no idea of their new status.

The substitution solved a couple of problems for the British. There would be no young, angry, energetic men making trouble in cramped boardinghouses on the Isle of Man or in camps such as Huyton. And there would be fewer mouths to feed.

On July 2, the day before he shipped out, Fuchs wrote to Max Born:

Dear Professor Born,

I can only write a few words before we are leaving, since I have been running about all morning and there's not much time left. It looks as if we are leaving Britain altogether, but as yet we do not know definitely.

I have little hope to see Edinburgh again, and must try to express a few rushed words of all I owe you during the time I have been with you. I think you will understand without my saying very much about it.

I find it hard to cut away from a country which I have learned to love, especially at such a time, and until the last moment I

hoped that [it] might not be necessary. But there is no point in
deluding myself.

Hoping to see you and your family again in better times.

Yours ever, Klaus Fuchs

At nine o'clock that night, Fuchs, Kellermann, and nine hundred others
marched to Douglas harbor, boarded a ship, and waited until 5:00 a.m. to
steam to Liverpool. Among them was Hans Kahle, who, being over thirty,
was outside the targeted age range but included because he was on a list of
sixteen "Active Nazi Sympathizers." He was also classified as a "trouble-
maker." The latter label might have fit, but certainly not that of Nazi. Once
again the government was jumbling Nazis, Jews, and communists together in
its overheated search for "fifth columnists."

Once in Liverpool, Fuchs's cohort of nine hundred, along with four
hundred more directly from Huyton, were crammed into a large, dirty
warehouse along the dock. They sat on their suitcases until mid-afternoon,
when their ship was ready for boarding. They walked along a pier lined with
rifle-toting soldiers and went up the gangplank to the SS *Ettrick*, a "big white
ship" designed to accommodate 1,150 troops in hammocks and 400 passengers in cabins. A week before, as France capitulated to the Germans, the ship
had evacuated Allied troops from Bayonne.

The thirteen hundred refugees boarded and wound down the stairs
deep into the ship's bowels, where some were quartered in two low-ceilinged
decks filled with long, rectangular dining tables. Others settled in the
luggage hold at the very bottom. Each deck was about sixty by ninety feet
and had a large central hold of fifteen by fifteen feet. The portholes had
been nailed shut, and a nauseating stench of rotten food hit the men immediately, made worse by the hot and sweaty refugees themselves. A few naked
lightbulbs hung from the rafters and lit up the depressing site. The doorway
through which they had entered was the only exit back to the upper decks. It
was big enough for one person to fit through single file, and its door was covered with barbed wire.

When the guards distributed life belts and hammocks, the latter to be hung above the tables, there were not enough to go around, which started a ruckus. The unfortunate had to sleep on the floor, on or under the dining tables, wherever they could find space. A shortage of blankets caused another to-do.

By 5:00 p.m. the transport was under way and, according to the rumor mill, en route to Canada. Two destroyers escorted the *Ettrick* out into the ocean. When they dropped back, the captain took a northerly route, zig-zagging to evade U-boats.

At 8:00 that night the men were fed, thirty hours since their last meal. After the prisoners cleaned up the dishes, the guard padlocked the door.

A few of the men kept diaries, the pages filling with the physical and psychological torment that began on the first night. One described the discomfort and claustrophobia:

> There is no way out of this trap; the barbed-wire door has been closed and a sentinel guards it. We are truly caught. We are sitting, lying, standing shoulder to shoulder, arm to arm, leg to leg. Some tread on us, some stumble and fall on us. . . . But mind your head when you stand up for hundreds of hammocks have been strung from the low ceiling.

The refugees didn't even have use of the entire space. Down the middle of each deck was a wall reinforced with heavy barbed wire and, beyond it, eight hundred war-hardened German POWs, the allotment of "the most dangerous," as well as four hundred Italian civilians. Rumor was that the captured soldiers had been part of the original assault troops on Holland and Belgium.

Kellermann claimed a place to sleep under a table but lost track of Klaus, who, it seems, had made his bed—literally and figuratively—with the communists on a different deck. It didn't matter; the same squalid conditions, with everyone packed in like cattle, prevailed.

Then seasickness added to their miseries. Vomit streamed down from those swinging in the hammocks. Kellermann's fortuitous place under the table saved him from the torrent but not from the indescribable stench. No lavatory was accessible until the guards unlocked the barbed-wire door at 6:00 a.m.

The second night, the crew handed out buckets; five sat on steps near the door. It was only a slight improvement. Finally, the colonel was persuaded to let one man at a time go to the lav during the night.

Over the next few days, stomachs settled down, and a routine developed. The men gained permission to take saltwater showers and to go in shifts of three hundred to the upper deck for a two-hour respite from the "stinking hole." Some played chess or skat. Twice a day they ate meals that were woefully inadequate. As one diarist put it, "The whip of hunger is once more beating us down into animals. We cheat each other, steal, and fight to fill our bellies."

The Nazis goaded, yelling that they were about to win the war, that the refugees would soon be forced to return to Germany. At night, from the other side of the partition, they sang songs "filled with bestial cruelty, lust for blood, and racism"; the refugees responded with "My bonnie lies over the ocean." The guards threatened to shoot if the uproar didn't cease.

Early one morning, diarrhea hit almost all the men at the same time. The lav became hideous. As one refugee memorialized it,

A sight worse than anything I have ever seen confronts me there. The pissoirs are choked and filled with vomit and shit. Shit and vomit everywhere. On the walls, on the doors, on the handles, simply everywhere. Here the portholes are open, but each one is occupied by someone whose body is thrown into violent spasm at intervals. All this is accompanied by groans.... My only thought is to get into a cubicle as fast as I can. I sit down, however much shit there is on the seat. Christ!

Suffice it to say that there is no [toilet] paper and the drainage system had broken down. . . . This trip is turning into a nightmare. Never have I seen such conditions—people are desperate with pain and grief.

The refugee doctors in the group thought it must be food poisoning from the tinned food. Others suspected that the commander had intentionally added a laxative to the food.

A detachment of volunteers, manning buckets and mops and stripped naked except for the crew's gum boots, waded into the ankle-deep waste and for four hours scrubbed the eight washbasins and four toilet stalls, cleaning out the toilets with their bare hands. There were no rubber gloves.

Accenting the blur of brown excretions in the lav were splotches of bright red. One distraught internee had cut his wrists.

Memories differ on who among them had volunteered to clean up. The divergence arose out of the cliques—the intellectuals, gangsters, musicians, and communists—that camp life fostered. The disagreement was mainly between the communists with Kahle's leadership and the Cambridge group, a subset of the intellectuals, with Count von Lingen's.

An alias adopted to reduce attention, Lingen, a student at Corpus Christi College, was officially Prince Friedrich of Prussia, son of the crown prince and grandson of Kaiser Wilhelm II. He wasn't an intellectual or particularly bright, but he embodied a calm and respected authority.

For sure, Kahle had secured power hoses, Lysol, and bottles of paregoric, an antidiarrheal and morphine derivative. But the Cambridge group took credit for the real cleanup.

According to Klaus, the communists did the hard work, scrubbing. Klaus insisted that Lingen's crew had kept only their own "corner" of the deck clean, ignoring the needs of the less educated Jewish emigrants surrounding them. In fact, both teams scrubbed and scoured in alternating shifts. But the ordeal lived on in Klaus's mind as the epitome of class struggle.

On the third day out, the refugees learned that U-boats had torpedoed the British transport ship *Arandora Star*, which had left Liverpool twenty-four hours ahead of them. It, too, had been bound for Canada carrying

German and Italian civilians and POWs. Given the timing of the attack, the government knew of the tragedy before the *Ettrick* left port. Its sole effort to protect the second ship from a similar fate was to not announce its departure the next day.

The BBC had reported that all on the *Arandora Star* were lost. (Later reports showed that half the passengers survived.) The father of one of the refugees aboard the *Ettrick* heard that news and believed his son to be on the *Arandora Star.* In despair, he committed suicide.

For the rest of the crossing, the men crowded below deck listened to the vibrations of the engines and wondered what their fate would be.

On the seventh day, July 10, someone saw two birds. The next day they saw "a long dark shape on the horizon" and presumed it was Newfoundland.

The northerly route, and the zigzagging to evade U-boats, had lengthened the trip from four days to ten. As one internee summed it up, "It was the longest 10 days of my life."

CHAPTER 10

Internment, Canada 1940

THE ST. LAWRENCE NARROWED, AND THE SCENT OF PINE AND SPRUCE WAFTED ACROSS the ship's bow. Klaus Fuchs, along with the other thirteen hundred emaciated enemy aliens packed together on the ship's deck, looked out on the verdant riverbank. After ten days of living hell crossing the Atlantic, this seemed like a vision of heaven. One internee estimated that given the bagginess of his clothes and the protrusion of his ribs, he had probably lost ten pounds on the trip. Now church bells pealed in the distance, and the earth smelled sweet.

On this sunny Saturday, July 13, 1940, roll call began on the upper deck at ten o'clock, and the sun's heat was welcome. As they came into a harbor at last, tugboats guided them past the bustling shoreline. At 1:30 p.m., the ship reached its dock. Looming high above, majestic and bold, was the Château Frontenac. They had reached their destination—Quebec. The rumor had been true.

By 4:00 p.m., the men had stood for six hours in the sunshine that had gone from welcome to searing. After a long while, soldiers gave them their first drink of water—lukewarm but delicious. Bathroom facilities became accessible too, but internees doubled up with hunger pains received no solace. Some simply lay down on the deck until the colonel ordered the sentries to use bayonets, if necessary, to get them up. The officer viciously kicked a few to make his point.

The Nazi POWs occupied another part of the deck and disembarked first. It was 7:30 before the refugees began to wind down the gangplank onto a pier lined with well-armed soldiers. The men walked past them and climbed onto buses where three guards made sure that these "dangerous men"—so beaten down that they could barely climb into their seats— caused no trouble. As motorcycle police escorted the buses up through the neighborhoods terraced into the city heights, little boys derisively gave the Nazi salute, women stood on corners shaking their fists at them, some spat and yelled—much the same scene as when they had left Huyton.

The buses reached the heights of the city and drove through the gates of the massive citadel onto the Plains of Abraham, where in 1759 British forces defeated the French for control of Canada. At the top, in an area known as Cove Fields, a camp nested within double rows of barbed wire and sentry posts with machine guns stretched out before them. Beyond that, in the distance, the unattainable and wild freedom of the St. Lawrence River.

When war broke out in 1939, the Canadian military had hastily constructed the camp as a temporary site for troops waiting to ship out to the European front. Newly outfitted as a prison compound, it would now hold 793 category B and C internees, about 60 percent of them Jewish, intermingled with about 90 pro-Nazi internees. Cove Fields had become Camp L.

After leaving the buses and being hustled into one of the dull-gray wooden huts, the men heard the sergeant major bark the first order: strip naked for inspection for venereal disease. Soldiers took their clothes—the stained and filthy ones they hadn't changed in the ten days on board—and emptied out their pockets to facilitate a search for sharp objects. Naked, starving, and vulnerable, surrounded by soldiers who spoke only French, the internees stood helpless as the soldiers returned some of the belongings to the internees' bags and put the more valuable ones in their own pockets. Precious watches, fountain pens, lighters, cigarettes, small amounts of British pounds—everything the internees had in this new world—vanished.

The inspectors found two hundred cases of dysentery and a few of typhus. Klaus's inspection report noted his "three false teeth in front" but no other health problems. He was, however, extremely thin. At five feet ten, he weighed 126 pounds.

At one o'clock that morning, the lucky ones, those who had left the ship in the first group, were fed. It had been seventeen hours since their last meal, the hours meticulously counted by the starving men. The unlucky ones waited another two hours to get their slice of bread and slab of gelatinous meat called bully beef. The one glass of water was a lifesaver, a memory to be relished years later.

In each hut that first night, one hundred men slept in bunk beds crowded into a room designed to accommodate fewer than eighty. Barbed wire covered every window. As on the *Ettrick*, the door was locked, and there was no bathroom in the hut. In an emergency, the distressed refugee switched the lights on and off for a guard to escort him to the latrine.

The next day a couple hundred POWs in Nazi uniforms strutted into the camp. Pondering whether the Canadians realized the impact on them, one Jewish refugee thought, "Surely not—they think we're one and the same—all GERMANS." Early in the morning a few days later, the POWs marched out of the camp, singing as they left.

Nazis in the camp—internees and POWs alike—agitated the refugees, but no fights broke out. The men did hear that a guard shot a young man in the leg who had been trying to climb out of a barbed-wire-covered window. Rumors spread: he was relieving himself through the window; he was trying to escape; he had gone crazy. He was taken to a hospital in Quebec and expected to recover. Inexplicably, he died the next day. A report attributed the death to "shock" rather than the gunshot wound. The fact is, the boy had suffered beatings in a German concentration camp and went berserk on seeing the barbed wire and the watchtowers. When a guard put him in an isolation cell, he tried to escape.

ATOMIC SPY

As on the Isle of Man, the huts elected "fathers." Fuchs and Kellermann were selected from their respective huts, Fuchs entrenched in the communist group and Kellermann with his new friends. The leaders of the *Ettrick*'s lavatory cleanup brigades, Hans Kahle and Count von Lingen, were also elected. The camp commander, Major C. W. Wiggs, appointed Lingen camp leader— the internee who was to bring the commander complaints, then take instructions back to the other hut fathers.

Kahle and Klaus fumed at Wiggs that the son of the former German crown prince should represent refugees. Wiggs made no change. The majority of refugees admired both Lingen and Kahle for their singular abilities and protective air of authority. Klaus saw the prince as nothing more than a capitalistic predator.

Tall, blond, blue-eyed, polite, and immaculately groomed, even on the *Ettrick*, the twenty-eight-year-old Count von Lingen was the great-great-grandson of Queen Victoria—and every inch a Hohenzollern. Fearing negative publicity, the British government had refused to give him special treatment and, instead, swept him up along with the other thirty German students at Cambridge. The queen's granddaughter Princess Alice was wife of the governor-general, the king's representative in Canada, and lived in Ottawa. Lingen called her "Aunt Alice." After learning Lingen's identity, the Canadian authorities treated him carefully.

The exiled prince used the familial connection to benefit his fellow internees where he could. The few times he was allowed to attend a party at Aunt Alice's residence, he looted the ashtrays for cigarette butts—gold in the camp—for the experts there to tear them apart to get at the tobacco and re-roll. After he requested recreational equipment, her aide arrived with boxes full.

The polar opposite of the kaiser's grandson in the political scheme of things, forty-one-year-old Hans Kahle was a military man and the son of one. He had fought in World War I as a teenager and then the Spanish Civil War, where he commanded the Austro-German battalion in the XI International and became friends with Ernest Hemingway. The rumor in Camp L was that Hemingway had modeled General Hans, a minor but praised character in *For Whom the Bell Tolls*, on Kahle. True or not, the celebrity gave Kahle added panache as well as the rank of general among the internees, even though he was only a colonel.

Internees uniformly found Klaus quiet, introverted, and intellectual, not one to show off his abilities. He attracted a group of "young chaps" around him, but he wasn't universally liked. One friend thought his shyness sometimes caused him to be abrupt. Others found his "fanatical" expression of Marxist views aggravating. The camp's intelligence officer considered him Kahle's deputy. For Klaus, it appeared that Kahle had replaced Gerhard in the role of older brother, showing the way.

At the first council meeting, the hut fathers confronted the unsettling question of why the Canadians treated them as dangerous. They composed a letter stating that they were loyal to the Crown, not fifth columnists, and delivered it to Major Wiggs, who believed them. He had already formed his own opinion, remarking sardonically, "I never knew so many Jews were Nazis."

The Canadian government's official answer explained the "why" in simple terms: They had agreed to take three thousand German POWs and four thousand German internees described as "so dangerous, in attitude and design, that their presence in England at a time of threatened invasion was a menace to the safety of the nation." The refugees were stunned to discover that they were not only considered part of the four thousand but also, inexplicably, branded as POWs.

The council deluged officials in Ottawa and in England—the War Office, the Home Office, members of Parliament—protesting the repulsive Nazi POW label. There was no reply.

Within the camp, Lingen as internee leader used "old-fashioned diplomacy" and a deferential attitude to deal with the issue. Meanwhile, the communists and young Jews who had suffered under Gestapo sadism demanded a more confrontational approach.

Kahle and Klaus assembled a "refugee" committee around the issue of

the POW label. They were part of the leadership—Klaus, the secretary—
the core of which was Jewish. Klaus now had authority to act. Later, in
describing the committee, he used a telling "we":

> In contrast to the camp administration under a Hohenzollern
> prince, which was set up by the Canadian authorities, we organized
> the overwhelming majority of the camp in a refugee committee.

Rather than just preach to friends about communism, Klaus Fuchs had
once again become an active resister.

It was a deft move that gained Kahle's communist group a larger base of
support. While everyone resented the POW status, with its locked hut doors,
machine guns, and POW uniforms, the Jews had an overriding fear that they
might become tokens in a prisoner exchange. One young Jewish refugee
wrote, "So, the English are in the position now to turn us over to Hitler in
return for English prisoners of war. This is the prospect for us refugees from
Nazi Oppression!" Their label could determine whether they survived.

Mail was the first battle in the war over the POW designation. Canadian authorities prominently placed the words "Prisoners of War Mail" in
large, heavy type on envelopes for the refugees' use. Postcards read the
same. Incensed by the mischaracterization, the refugees threatened to
smash up the camp. After weeks and weeks, they needed to contact their
families. They agonized over the decision to use the stationery. Ultimately,
they united against it.

The hut-father council, working to find a solution, proposed crossing
out "POW Mail" and inserting "Civilian Internee Mail." Major Wiggs
approved the change, and after modifying the stationery by hand, the refugees wrote home that they were safe.

Days later, sacks of letters appeared. The censors in Ottawa had rejected
all mail with the cross outs. Some refugees gave in and wrote to their families
on the POW paper. Others protested by sending the POW postcard with only
their name and status in Canada. The Kahle-Fuchs faction had a mail strike

for a couple of weeks but finally wrote one letter to their families about the POW classification and vowed not to write again until it changed.

When the internees at long last received letters from England—twenty-five hundred arrived at once—the news was mixed. The *Blitzkrieg* and the U-boats' relentless attacks on the navy threatened their families and England. However, headlines from the sinking of the *Arandora Star* had created pressure to release the civilian internees. Ones such as "Friendly Aliens, Grave Injustice" championed the men's cause. A few outraged members of Parliament examined government officials on deportation decisions during Question Time in the House of Commons. The government either dissembled or had no answers. Home Secretary John Anderson, who had argued against internment, was the exception. He spoke forthrightly:

> I am not here to deny that most regrettable and deplorable things have happened in connection with the internment camps. I regret them deeply. They have been due partly to the inevitable haste with which the policy of internment had to be carried out. They were due, however, in some cases to mistakes of individuals, stupidity, muddling. These things all relate to the past. So far as we can remedy mistakes, we shall remedy them.

Parliamentary pressure caused the government to issue a white paper at the beginning of August 1940 that detailed eighteen classes of category C internees who were eligible for release. Included in the list was a class for scientists who could aid in the war effort.

Watching the shifting policy from Edinburgh, Max Born, a prodigious and persistent letter writer, waged his own campaigns. He had already pushed prestigious academic friends in the United States, including Albert Einstein and the mathematician John von Neumann, to send reading material to Fuchs and Kellermann in Canada. In a letter to von Neumann, he wrote of Fuchs as "really a rare personality and it would be a shame to let him go down after he has suffered by Nazi persecution more than any of us." His friends did comply, and Born's former students eventually received physics books and journals, but with the initial ban on mail and difficulty with delivery it took weeks.

Then Born pressured the Royal Society, Britain's august national academy of science, to recommend Fuchs and Kellermann for release to the Home Office. It included them on its list for the government to consider.

With time, physical conditions in the camp improved. The bountiful Canadian fields and farms provided three hearty meals a day. The internees had won the heart and hand of the corpulent Major Wiggs, whom they nicknamed Piggy-Wiggy after Dickens's Pickwick.

But boredom was still a problem. The internees' only assigned task was to clear space for exercise in the rocky field surrounding the huts. Otherwise, their day began at the 6:30 a.m. reveille and continued with the prescribed activities—meals, inspections, and so on—until 11:00 p.m. Initially, guards removed all reading material; newspapers and magazines were banned. This in a population crowded with intellectual firepower. As Major Wiggs exclaimed, "Some of the brainiest people in Canada are in this camp."

From within the barbed wire, the world would gain a future Nobelist in biochemistry (Max Perutz), developers of the steady state theory of the universe, engineers, industrialists, journalists, painters, architects, and professors. Many a name later bore a "Sir" before it. By September, they had resolved the boredom by founding a university and cultural center, a grander version of the institutions they had founded on the Isle of Man. The list of classes ran from bookbinding and bricklaying, to preparing for British matriculation exams, to high-level university subjects. Fuchs, whose pupil Perutz remembered his "remarkable ability to explain difficult concepts lucidly," taught theoretical physics and mathematics.

The sympathetic major Wiggs brought in a piano, and musicians, many professional, gave inspiring concerts in the mess hall or outside. Staging and lighting gradually appeared. The Quebecois listened to the performances from Battlefields Park, a broad swath of grass and rolling hills that commemorates the surrender of the French Marquis de Montcalm to the British General James Wolfe in 1759.

Through the layers of barbed wire, internees could watch tennis players, picnickers, and strollers enjoy the freedom denied to them. Knowing that these outsiders could see in as well, they used the opportunity to advertise who they were. A sign in English and in French, crafted from rugs and sackcloth and hung on the wall of a hut, read, "We are refugees from Nazi Oppression."

News of the white paper and the decision to release some category C refugees reached Canada by the end of August, but the debunking of past "news" made the men afraid to think of freedom. And something closer to home occupied them.

As icy winds and rain already howled across the St. Lawrence River, fierce enough to keep them huddled in their uninsulated huts, a new rumor circulated: they were to be moved to another camp. Huts at Camp L couldn't protect them from the impending frigid winter air. And in fact, thirty pro-Nazi Germans left for a different camp the next day.

Within two weeks, the director of internment operations requested the hut fathers draw up a list of the internees, noting professions and trades, religion, and original tribunal category of each man. A week later he wanted a count of Jews and Gentiles. This raised the inevitable and polarizing question: What are the definitions of "Gentile" and "Jew"? "The term 'Jew,'" the hut fathers were told, "means a person of Jewish faith or race."

The hut fathers called a special meeting to give a count: "498 Jews, 121 persons of Jewish descent, and 141 persons of non-Jewish descent (Aryan)." That same day the guards hung prison numbers on the internees, took their photographs, then fingerprinted one finger. One internee described it as "very Dachau-like." The parsing of "Gentile," "Aryan," and "Jew" provoked other parallels—the fatal racial divisions in Hitler's Nuremberg Laws.

On September 27, the internees learned that they would be split up on racial grounds and sent to new camps: the 141 Gentiles to an "Aryan camp," the rest to a "Jewish camp." Complaints from Orthodox Jews about working on the Sabbath or having pork sausage as a staple on the menu had persuaded the authorities to create a kosher camp.

To soften reactions, the authorities described the new Jewish camp as a model with every amenity.

Lingen, Kahle, Fuchs, and others drafted a protest to Major Wiggs:

> [We] should like to protest with all emphasis against a separation based on racial grounds. It is true that the majority among the refugees are Jews. But by no means all. Many of the others are persons who, though no longer of Jewish faith, are Jewish or partially Jewish by descent and had to leave Germany because of racial persecution. What is still more important, many others are refugees from Nazi Germany on political grounds.

The internees thought of separation in terms of Nazi versus anti-Nazi, not race or religion. New friendships among the Jews (confessing and nonconfessing), Protestants, and Catholics had eliminated religious boundaries. A primary worry was the makeup of the alternative Aryan camp. Would it be a "Nazi camp," one filled with pro-Nazi Germans?

Major Wiggs wrote a letter to the director of internment operations supporting the refugees' position. The director would not alter the decision.

Canadian officials knew the total number of Gentiles—141—but not the names. When surveyed, only 80 identified themselves. Major Wiggs wanted the missing 61 names, who happened to be the political refugees. As one refugee noted, it boiled down to "where Kahle and his group were sent."

Schemes floated up to fill the "Aryan" quota. Jews who wanted to stay with close Gentile friends considered losing a Jewish parent and becoming "½ Jews"; Gentiles who wanted to go to the Jewish camp suddenly discovered Jewish grandmothers in the family tree.

Jews who considered racial separation anathema didn't care who the sixty-one were. They wanted to thwart the government's intent. Kahle used the refugee committee to do so. Unusually direct for him, Klaus later declared, "I was especially responsible for the review of the refugees in the camp." He craftily kept Kahle's group out of the "Aryan camp."

Major Wiggs sent off the final list of names for the two camps on October 8 and informed Lingen that he was one of a hundred going to the Aryan camp.

On the morning of October 15, the "kosher" group said sad goodbyes to the others and walked to the train station in the pouring rain, wearing the hated POW uniforms: blue trousers with a red stripe down the sides and a blue jacket with a large red circle on the back they likened to a bull's-eye target. On either side soldiers with bayonets guarded them. At 8:30 a.m., the train departed with 618 men eagerly awaiting the model camp promised them.

The train traveled for a few hours through dense forests and by rippling lakes and reached the end of the line at 1:30 p.m. The men looked out the windows and saw two huge, seemingly abandoned brick buildings surrounded by a barbed-wire fence. Disembarking, they traipsed through the mud and rain into the larger of the two. They found dust and soot covering six stinky indoor latrines, five cold-water taps, and six lights with bare bulbs. The empty buildings were part of a railroad depot near Sherbrooke and Newington, small towns south of Quebec. To the men, Camp N, as it was called, was "worse than imagination could have invented:"

> Train tracks criss-cross the stone floor, which is covered with a
> layer of foul-smelling mud. There are several large pits in the
> floor, half filled with stagnant water. . . . Everywhere puddles of
> rainwater have collected. It has either blown in through the bro-
> ken windowpanes or leaked through the roof.

As the refugees would find, the "worse" was yet to come. When they objected to the putrid dump and their treatment, the commandant threatened to shut the doors, turn off the lights, turn off the heat, and cut off rations; if that didn't work, he would request that Ottawa transfer them to a Nazi camp. The sergeant major, a bull of a man with "malicious eyes and a hateful glean," yelled at those he called "dirty Jews." Sadistic guards shoved anyone who didn't obey into an isolation cell, cold, dark, and cramped, six feet by four feet, with a sack of straw, no light except a window, and a pail for waste. An internee equated them to Nazis, "brutal men without heart and some who delight in malice and bad treatment."

Camp life continued nonetheless, with hut fathers, who included Fuchs and Kellermann, and with Kahle named as camp leader. Regular mail, magazines, and newspapers arrived. The men organized to make the camp habitable. They slept, ate, cleaned, and built the facilities they needed.

The word "release" was in the air, Canadian and British newspapers having quoted politicians who dared to utter it. By November 1940, the Germans were no longer on Britain's doorstep. The government had withstood the *Blitzkrieg*. It could now address the "vocal element"—the internees and their supporters in the Commons. "The rough and ready measures adapted in the early summer," it said, "had been justified by the danger during that period, but we can afford to take a less stringent line." The government's emissary for a "less stringent line" was Alexander Paterson, His Majesty's commissioner of prisons in Britain and a true social reformer, the perfect ambassador.

Paterson arrived at Camp N in mid-November's frigid weather wearing a tweed suit, a hat, and no overcoat. The refugees judged him "our savior, our messiah." For three days he sat in a makeshift office high up in a loft interviewing 350 internees in category C, Fuchs and Kellermann among them. Days later, a mere 11 names appeared on a list for release for home. Kahle and 10 others left the camp, no other information given. In a few more days, a camp official posted another list with 156 more to leave in mid-December. This one included Fuchs and Kellermann.

The night of December 15 was a time for parties and farewells for the chosen 156. The next morning, they began a twenty-eight-hour train ride to Halifax. Just before Christmas, they boarded the *Thysville*, along with Kahle and his group of 10, and feasted on hors d'oeuvres, soup, fish, chicken, and special Christmas pudding. One of the internees thought it the best dinner he had ever eaten. They sailed the next day in a convoy.

With the Battle of the Atlantic in full force, they crisscrossed toward Iceland to avoid U-boats. Unlike during the trip over, they "traveled like grown-ups," staying in cabins, sleeping on clean sheets, eating good food, and all without guards. But they slept in their clothes and wore life belts. The sea was choppy, breakers washed over the bow, and U-boats were still an invisible threat.

Seventeen days later, on January 11, 1941, they cut through a minefield near the Irish coast and reached the Liverpool harbor around 9:00 p.m. Air raid sirens screamed, delaying their disembarkation. With its access to the Atlantic and its war construction, Liverpool was under constant threat from German bombers. Just two weeks earlier, 350 people had died in a *Luftwaffe* raid.

After the all clear, the returning detainees descended the gangplank, where soldiers again waited with bayonets. Dismayed, the captain explained to the commander of the detachment that these were not dangerous men. The troops removed the bayonets.

Immigration officers processed Fuchs and Kellermann at Huyton Camp and gave them ration books and train tickets to Edinburgh. The government had granted them permission to reside in the protected coastal area. By the thirteenth, they were home. It had been a very long eight months, and a critical period in Klaus's life, especially the close camaraderie with Kahle. How much of a difference Kahle made in his allegiance to communism is not known. But it certainly would have reinforced a commitment to the cause.

III

RESEARCH

Main Gate at Los Alamos, 1940s

CHAPTER 11

Tube Alloys, Birmingham 1941

JANUARYS IN EDINBURGH ARE BLUSTERY AND GRAY. THE COLD, RAW AIR FROM THE English Channel blankets the city of stone and seeps into the bones. When Klaus and Walter arrived at Waverley Station in January 1941, the weather was typically bleak, the chill cutting deep, though still mild compared with Canada. The city was relatively quiet, the sky free from planes and falling bombs.

Max Born was surprised and delighted to see his former associates. Neither one talked much about the camps, but Born knew it had been rough. What he did not know was the effect of those camps on Klaus, one that had drawn him much closer to his communist friends.

Born wanted Kellermann and Fuchs—especially Fuchs—to stay in Edinburgh to continue their studies and research, but that would require that he find funding for them. The university had no money or grants; fellowships from foundations, the Carnegie Trust for one, no longer offered enemy aliens research support, although Born hoped that Fuchs could be an exception. An obvious employer, the British government, restricted enemy aliens from working on confidential weapons research. Klaus had reapplied for naturalization to reverse that problem, but it wasn't always a remedy and would take time. Teaching was a possibility. British physicists' work on weapons research had created a shortage of math and science teachers in secondary schools and colleges.

Kellermann received an offer from a college in Southampton, located on the south coast and a prime bombing target for the *Luftwaffe*. He gladly accepted the appointment despite the risk.

Although Klaus was primarily a researcher—since returning, he had already written two papers that Born judged "excellent"—he did apply for one teaching job that didn't work out. Another possibility, though, hovered in the background.

While Klaus was in Canada, Rudi Peierls at the University of Birmingham had written to Born asking if Klaus would be available for a teaching position with him. Peierls was a highly respected physicist, a German émigré, and a good friend of Born's. He had first met Fuchs years earlier in Bristol with Nevill Mott, and then again when he gave a seminar in Born's department. He respected Klaus as a scientist and had used some of his results in his own research. Ultimately, the uncertainty of internment had led Peierls to hire someone else. Even so, he asked Born to let him know if Fuchs needed funding.

In March, Born approached Peierls, who had nothing immediate to offer. Then things changed. By the beginning of May, Peierls was a consultant to the Air Ministry and needed a good physicist. Fuchs's status of "enemy alien" constrained Peierls from specifying the nature of the job other than "theoretical work involving mathematical problems of considerable difficulty." Still, Fuchs was his choice, and he wrote to Born about the position. He included a detailed letter to Fuchs, giving Born the option of not passing it on "if you think he ought not to take the job." His hesitation wasn't in deference to Born, who he knew couldn't keep Fuchs. Mott and Peierls were good friends. Had Peierls heard something from Mott about Fuchs's politics that could lead to a problem with government clearance? He didn't elaborate.

During this period, some of Fuchs's friends from the camps visited Edinburgh a time or two, reasons unidentified. Kuczynski, an outsider to that particular group, also made the trip. In April 1941, Fuchs returned the favor by traveling to London to attend a party probably held at the Free German League of Culture. Established in 1939 by Jürgen Kuczynski and a number of other German émigrés, it was antifascist, with a strong communist strain of the German type moderated by influence from the Social Democrats.

Bringing German art, literature, lectures, and social events to area refugees, the league occupied a large brick four-story semidetached Victorian house on Upper Park Road in Belsize Park, London. Before the league took it over in 1940, Kuczynski and his wife had lived there. Unlike many of its neighbors, it had made it through the *Blitz* unscathed. In this warm and comfortable setting—it had rooms for lectures, exhibits, and meetings, a café and a restaurant, a library and an office—Klaus could easily see friends from the Berlin underground and from internment, Kuczynski and Kahle among them. Old associations and memories were everywhere. One of the main organizers of the league was Alfred Meusel, the professor whose lecture Emil, Gerhard, and Klaus had heard in Kiel the night before Else committed suicide. The world of German communists in London was small and close.

Details are vague, but another attendee at the April party might have been Simon Kremer, officially the secretary to the Soviet military attaché in London. According to MI5 files, he was also an agent for the GRU, the arm of Soviet security concerned with external espionage, as was Kahle. About Kuczynski, MI5 wasn't sure.

Klaus always avowed that he asked Kuczynski for a contact—who turned out to be Kremer—but the truth of who initiated the encounter may have been someplace in the middle. Kremer might have met Klaus there or at some other function to observe him, with Klaus not knowing who he was. Kahle would certainly have been very involved in the plans. Whether Kahle and Klaus had ever discussed such a possibility while in the camps is unknown, but even if not, it couldn't have been far from Kahle's thoughts.

As much as Kuczynski, Kahle galvanized the German Communist Party in Britain, just as he had taken charge in the camps and embodied General Hans for Ernest Hemingway.

Klaus found himself at London's King's Cross rail station at 11:45 on the night of April 15, having missed his train back to Edinburgh by fifteen minutes. Still required to check travel plans with the police, he notified them and was told to take the next train at 4:30 a.m., which he did. In spring 1941, neither the police nor MI5 had reason to take note of him.

Once Klaus was back in Edinburgh, Born passed the letter from Peierls on to him, and the discussion moved quickly. By May 22, Fuchs had visited Birmingham, accepted the offer, and received a provisional work permit, renewable monthly to work on the "undisclosed" research. Given that the Air Ministry banned enemy aliens from its payroll, Peierls had to finagle a salary scheme for his new recruit. The "undisclosed" research with which Peierls had become involved would ultimately bring World War II to a dramatic close and heighten the tensions of the cold war to follow.

In March 1940, Peierls and the Austrian refugee Otto Frisch, also in Birmingham at the time, wrote a memo that redefined the feasibility of an atomic bomb, contradicting the assumptions of a panel of eminent British scientists. It came about, in part, because as German refugees they were excluded from wartime weapons research and had time to indulge their curiosity.

Both men were brilliant physicists. Frisch had the benefit of a distinguished scientific lineage. His aunt, the Austrian physicist Lise Meitner, had spent thirty-one years in Berlin working with the German chemist Otto Hahn, before having to escape to Sweden in 1938 because she was Jewish. In their last four years together, they had bombarded uranium with neutrons. Hahn continued with his bombardments after Meitner's departure and a few months later obtained results that would only in retrospect be understood as showing that the atomic nucleus had been split. Hahn, not quite understanding what he had, immediately wrote to Meitner.

Meitner along with Frisch, who happened to be visiting, worked out the physics, ascertaining that the uranium atom had split and, in doing so, had produced two different and smaller nuclei. In the beginning of 1939, shortly after Hahn published his groundbreaking article, they published theirs, explaining why the uranium nucleus had split and ejected neutrons and released massive amounts of energy—nuclear fission.

Splitting one nucleus did not create an atomic bomb. Scientists needed to split many nuclei very quickly to release enough energy for an explosion, and the most abundant type of uranium atom, the isotope U-238, couldn't do that. They needed an atom that could split and eject enough neutrons at the right energy to hit another atom, which would then split and continue the process, a chain reaction, to create an explosion and release massive amounts of energy. They identified a uranium isotope that could do that.

All elements have isotopes (that is, an atom with the same number of protons in the nucleus but a different number of neutrons), and they soon realized that a particular uranium isotope, U-235, was fissile, meaning it could create a chain reaction. The problem is that U-235 constitutes a very small percentage of natural uranium, 0.714 percent. With that low density, chain reactions fizzle out before reaching the critical stage for a nuclear explosion. British physicists, therefore, had assumed that vast amounts of U-235 were necessary for a bomb, which would make one difficult to create during wartime.

The key insight in Peierls's and Frisch's memo was that a sustained chain reaction could result from a relatively small amount of U-235.

In the spring of 1940, Peierls and Frisch kept their idea secret, giving their only extra copy of the memo to the head of the theoretical physics department at Birmingham. He, in turn, alerted a top science adviser to the government who shared it with a few more. They realized that the Peierls-Frisch memo necessitated a second examination of the feasibility of an atomic bomb.

Days later, *The New York Times* ran the article "Vast Power Source in Atomic Energy Opened by Science." It painted a rosy, perhaps cavalier, picture of the probability of exploiting the potential power in U-235, saying, "All that is necessary to liberate its energy is to keep it in contact with a constant flow of cold water." Already General Electric, it reported, had "separated a relatively large sample of the U-235." The article offered no rationale of the method or proof of this claim—nor in fact was it true.

One detail in the article drew special attention, especially from German refugees. The newspaper had a report, supposedly leaked "through highly reliable channels," that the German government had ordered its scientists and engineers to devote all resources to the work of extracting U-235 from uranium. This information compelled a noted émigré chemist at Oxford's Clarendon Laboratory, Francis Simon, to write to Churchill's chief science adviser urging him to expend more research resources on U-235. The outcome was a blithe memo from the adviser to Churchill unequivocally stating that there was no danger of U-235 becoming operational for some years.

In spite of this memo, Churchill agreed to create the so-called MAUD Committee. Government regulations excluded enemy aliens, in this case Peierls and Frisch, from belonging, but the Nobel laureate G. P. Thomson, the chair of the new committee, knew them as "reliable" physicists and wanted their contributions. He explained to the government that "the initial stage of the work will be on a laboratory scale"; that is, the small-scale nature of the research meant they wouldn't run afoul of regulations, and they could be included in the first stage of the investigation. Thomson anticipated problems with the next stage, saying, "If and when it is found that there is a real promise of success, it would be necessary to work on a much larger scale and I think that then the question of the collaboration of PEIERLS and FRISCH would need to be reviewed."

Thomson created a technical panel and put Peierls and Frisch on it. With their naturalization a year later, they became full members, Peierls as the leading mathematical physicist.

Born and Fuchs had not needed Peierls to identify the nature of the project Fuchs would be working on. Both knew that Peierls was involved in atomic research. Appealing to Fuchs's ideological leanings, Born had tried to dissuade him from taking the job. He described the discussion to his son, Gustav, a couple of years later:

> When Fuchs went to Birmingham to join the uranium people, I had a serious talk with him. I told him that if they succeeded it would mean a new concentration of power in the hands of a few, and very likely the wrong ones, capitalists and nationalists; I warned him who confessed to be a communist that the result of this work would mean a strengthening of capitalism. He answered that it had to be done as they knew that the Germans [were doing] it.

For Fuchs, the top consideration was to destroy the Nazis by any means necessary. He later wrote down his own thoughts on the question of building a bomb:

> And so all illusion of a neutral or value-free science died overnight with the serious question that also required me to make a personal decision in 1941, as I received the invitation to collaborate on the English atom bomb project: "Would the power be used for good or evil? How great is the danger of Hitler's fascism? How great are the dangers of this frightening weapon in a world torn apart?"

On May 31, 1941, he arrived in Birmingham to begin his position with Peierls.

Rudi and Genia Peierls lived in the well-to-do suburb of Edgbaston on the southwest side of Birmingham, a pleasant, relatively quiet area compared with the rest of the city, one of the country's main manufacturing hubs. In wartime, this meant that the city's industrial might was focused on weapons, supplies, and the famed Spitfire fighter plane, which made Birmingham a prime target for German bombers. By the end of May, when Fuchs arrived, the deadliest raids were over, but not all. He wrote to Born to describe a bomb that blew out windows at the university.

The Peierlses' white house, neo-classically themed, had plenty of space, and Klaus became their lodger. They found him pleasant, courteous, and even-tempered. "Rather silent" unless asked a question, said Peierls, and then he gave a "full and articulate answer." Genia found him less garrulous and called him "Penny in the Slot" Fuchs. "You put your penny in and get a word back."

Russian-born, Genia had a degree in physics and an outsized personality often labeled effusive and loud, but she was equally warm and caring. The Peierlses, along with other physicists, had shipped their two children to the safety of Canada. Klaus helped to fill up the house. He became almost a surrogate child as Genia sewed on buttons for him and cared for him when he was sick.

Peierls was enthusiastic about Fuchs from the start. On the day the young man arrived, Peierls wrote to Otto Frisch, "I must not tell him anything yet about the purpose of the work, but even so, this is a great help." In fact, Fuchs far exceeded expectations.

Within the first week, Fuchs had recalculated how the neutrons ejected by the atoms would scatter, creating more hits than previously assumed, and theorized a reduction of the required critical mass—the amount of U-235 needed for a sustained chain reaction—by a factor of four. Two months later, the two men were fleshing out the theoretical properties of different methods to separate the fissile material U-235 from the more abundant uranium isotope U-238. Even though Fuchs was ill in June and later too—at least one of his problems was an eye infection—they made rapid progress. For Peierls, he was the perfect fit, "quick on the uptake, flexible, and willing to look at new problems." Peierls didn't think he could have made a better choice.

By August, Klaus was well enough to travel to London again to meet up with Simon Kremer, the Russian official whom he had met in the spring with Kuczynski and Kahle. Klaus called Kremer "Alexander," and they met in the evening, mostly on weekends, and only a few times. The exchange of papers, wrapped in packing paper or in an envelope, happened quickly at a crowded bus stop or on a dark, quiet residential street where Kremer arrived on foot. Klaus handed over only what he himself produced. Until he had signed the Official Secrets Act, a document that restricts communication of confidential government information, he was restricted from classified research, and although Peierls was loose with that restriction, some material was kept from him.

Fuchs was fully committed to supporting British efforts toward inventing an atomic bomb before Hitler did. He was equally committed to supporting Russia and communism.

By this time, the German-Soviet pact had disintegrated as almost four million German soldiers attacked Russia on June 22, 1941, in Operation Barbarossa. Russia became a strong ally of England and France and, much to the German military's surprise, did not crumble under the onslaught as had every other nation. But successful Russian resistance wasn't a certainty. Stalin pleaded for England to divide German forces by opening up a second front. The Allies didn't listen. Those such as Fuchs saw this rebuff as a desire for the two armies to destroy each other.

In October, Fuchs received his work permit from the Alien War Service Department, and he was able to become an official government employee. He didn't have access to secret research, but it didn't matter. He didn't really need that for the most part. His research with Peierls created many of the secrets.

The MAUD Report, initiated the year before by Peierls and Frisch's memo, was issued in September 1941 after a few months of wrangling. It confirmed that an atomic bomb was feasible, and it ignited the government's major push to build one. The code name for the project was the purposefully nondescript Tube Alloys.

The British shared the report with the Americans, and it gave them the same sense of urgency. Here was a report by respected scientists predicting that with a method called gaseous diffusion, U-235 could be separated out from U-238, increasing its density and enabling a runaway chain reaction. They could build an atomic bomb and affect the outcome of the war. Until this time, the Americans had made the same assumptions as the British and did little research, but on reading the MAUD Report, they sought out President Roosevelt to create a partnership on the bomb with the British. He authorized a letter to Churchill, who greeted the proposal with little enthusiasm. Churchill saw the British superiority in this field as leverage to use over America and was uncertain about how much help and information to give them. From that time on, the Americans went forward on their own.

Gaseous diffusion, already used for other purposes by this time, required filtering uranium gas through a series of porous barriers to separate U-235 from U-238. U-235, the lighter of the two molecules, would pass through the filter more rapidly than U-238 and enrich the gas with U-235. The lighter isotope would be only marginally more abundant in a sample of gas that had passed through one or even several such filters, and successive passes, on the order of thousands of interdependent ones, were needed to enrich the gas sufficiently to create a chain reaction.

The basic concept was somewhat straightforward; the details were devilish. Multiple problems had to be worked out: the types of pumps used to circulate the gas; pressure ratios between the various spaces so as to maintain a steady state; leakages and impurities in the metals; the design of the semiporous membrane used as a filter so that it didn't clog or tear; prevention of the corrosive gas creating rust. The person who ran many of the experiments to address these problems was Francis Simon at Oxford, the chemist who had warned Churchill of the need for research on U-235. Well before Fuchs arrived in Birmingham, Simon had conceived of using the diffusion approach.

In Birmingham, Peierls and Fuchs focused on the theoretical calculations. When Simon asked if it was better to use a continuous or discontin-
uous pump, they measured the effects of the different assumptions. Letters,
memos, and exhaustive research papers constantly flowed between them
and others in their labs and departments, delivering the calculations, offering opinions and insights, and raising objections—all bound by the Official
Secrets Act except, as yet, Fuchs. Peierls, and now Fuchs, were part of a
network of top physicists. They plowed through the research and calculations with a group at the university and at Peierls's home. At night Fuchs
often toiled away in his room.

Their work was so extensive that later in November 1943 the Peierls,
Fuchs, and Simon collaboration resulted in an application for a patent on
their design for gaseous diffusion, "Cascade of Cascades," the repetitive filtering method to enrich the uranium gas.

Hanging over their efforts was the question of what the Germans were
doing. Fuchs and Peierls examined German science journals looking for
clues—studying lists of lectures and articles for changes in locations or
research interests; listening for rumors on the top physicist Werner Heisenberg's activities; asking colleagues to read particular articles perhaps relevant
to the development of a bomb. The investigation was ongoing, inconclusive,
and, as Peierls later said, ultimately "in vain." It didn't answer whether German scientists had shifted their focus to developing an atomic bomb.

In the first part of 1942, Kremer was recalled to Russia, and Klaus had no
contact, so Kuczynski made another introduction for him. This time it was
a young woman, code name Sonya, who in real life was Ursula Kuczynski,
one of Jürgen's five sisters. Under various pseudonyms, she had been a stel-
lar operative for the Russians since the early 1930s. Jürgen made the contact hastily without notifying Moscow Center, but they went along.

Sonya and Klaus first met at a café across from the train station in
Birmingham. After that they met on a country road near Banbury, seemingly two young lovers walking arm in arm down a rural lane. The transfer

took two minutes; they spent half an hour walking so as not to attract attention. The meeting times, mostly on weekend afternoons, depended on the train schedules. Sonya had a regular arrangement to pass the material to another agent for submission to Moscow.

Fuchs didn't limit himself to the environs of the Peierlses' home in Edgbaston or meetings with Sonya. The city of Birmingham had something to offer—a branch of London's Free German League of Culture that he frequented. Kuczynski turned up in Birmingham several times as well for various events. Any meetings between them aren't recorded, but given the involvement of both in the KPD, it's highly probable. Czech friends from internment brought him to their special club too. The spirit of the internment brotherhood and the British KPD quietly permeated his life in Birmingham.

On June 18, 1942, Fuchs signed the Official Secrets Act. Peierls immediately sent memos to the staff that Fuchs now had authority to discuss "matters of relevance" with the Birmingham team and others in the Tube Alloys work. A month later, Fuchs became a naturalized British citizen and swore an oath of allegiance to the Crown.

An in-depth review by MI5 had preceded this new status. Fuchs's security file, holding evidence from the Gestapo that damned him as a "notorious Communist," created consternation among the MI5 officers. Any information from the Gestapo, though, raised suspicions of reliability. MI5 officers questioned employing him on sensitive war research, but with pressure from the research community and the obvious need for scientific talent, they decided that they had to take the risk.

Throughout the early war years, Churchill had used all his wiles to persuade Roosevelt to enter the war, but in spite of them, he only gained arms through the Lend Lease program in return. When the Russians didn't collapse from the German onslaught in June 1941, Churchill and Roosevelt realized that the world order might change—and Churchill saw an opportunity to pull the United States into the war. The two leaders met in Newfoundland to sign the Atlantic Charter, a joint declaration mainly on the postwar international system, stating principles on trade, territorial acquisition, self-determination, and freedom of the seas, as well as economic welfare standards. Churchill wanted the agreement to create public support to propel the Americans into the war.

News of the charter didn't move the Americans to enter in, but the Japanese attack on Pearl Harbor, on December 7, 1941, did.

With the Americans' burgeoning commitment to atomic research, large resources, and no significant worry of being invaded or bombed, some in England recognized that in time they could lose their lead and be left in the Americans' backwash. Sir John Anderson, who had realized the errors of internment and now, as lord president of the council, was running the country's domestic agenda, sent a memo to Churchill urging cooperation with the Americans:

> We must . . . face the fact that the pioneer work done in this country is a dwindling asset and that, unless we capitalise it quickly, we shall be outstripped. We now have a real contribution to make to a "merger." Soon we shall have little or none.

The British establishment had debated whether it had the resources to undertake the necessary infrastructure for an atomic research program by itself. A gaseous diffusion plant was a huge structure and would be visible and within reach of the *Luftwaffe* any place in Britain. Only a physical plant, however, would offer the answer to the essential question: Could the design yield sufficient U-235 to create a chain reaction in an atomic bomb? Geographically, America would be much safer, but if the two countries worked together, would it be a loose collaboration or a joint project?

The British and Americans reached consensus on a mutual effort to build an atomic bomb in August 1943, when the two countries signed the top secret Quebec Agreement, which was not made known even to the U.S.

Congress. There were five basic statements, the first of which was not to use it against each other. Two others required mutual consent: for using the bomb on a third party and for giving information to a third party. One recognized "the heavy burden of production falling upon the United States" and, as a result, gave it decision-making power over which industrial or commercial advantages would be shared with Great Britain. The last determined the nature of the collaboration, in particular the "interchange of information," which specified that it be kept "in the same sections of the field."

This agreement was consonant with the order of General Leslie Groves, head of the U.S. project, to compartmentalize information. Information in a specific research area was shared within that area only. John Anderson understood General Groves's goal:

> He looks on co-operation as a means of speeding up the American full-scale effort. He sees no need nor obligation for reciprocity in the sense of giving us information which might be of help to us.

As Rudi Peierls summed up, the agreement didn't specify mutual trust.

CHAPTER 12

Manhattan Project, New York 1943

ON DECEMBER 3, 1943, THREE MEMBERS OF THE FORTY TO FIFTY IN THE BRITISH SCI-entific mission—the physicists Rudi Peierls and Klaus Fuchs, along with the chemist Frank Kearton—arrived at the port of Norfolk, Virginia. Their trip across the Atlantic on the troopship *Andes*—an ocean liner built in 1939 and, when war broke out, immediately refitted to carry four thousand troops—was uneventful. The threat of U-boats was not nearly as bad as when Fuchs had crossed on the *Ettrick* three and a half years before.

The three men took the train to Washington, D.C., some hours away, met with their new boss, General Leslie Groves, filled in paperwork, and headed to New York City. So began their sojourn in America—working for what the United States officially named the Manhattan Engineer District, a frenzied drive to beat the Germans to an atomic bomb.

The Army Corps of Engineers, in the person of General Groves, con-trolled the project. An engineer educated at West Point, he was very intel-ligent, bullish, determined, decisive, and always right. His physique, thick and powerful, matched his personality. He had complete command.

The East Coast headquarters of the corps was at 270 Broadway in New York City. Its location supplied the "Manhattan" part of the project title.

Footsteps away on the same block, the Woolworth Building housed the Kellex Corporation, designers of the U.S. gaseous diffusion plant. A fifteen-minute walk from there was 43 Exchange Place in the financial district and the office of the British Supply Mission shared by Peierls and Fuchs. Kearton, liaison between the diffusion research in the United States and that in England, worked from there too. Tony Skyrme, a newly minted Cambridge graduate, soon joined them to assist with calculations. Proximity created a pressured and close work environment. The geographic outlier was a group of physicists at Columbia University, on the Upper West Side, who mostly consulted with Fuchs.

Meetings between the British team and Kellex began immediately on December 7. General Groves had been assured by the British representatives in the United States, as an Army Corps of Engineers memo on the eighth stated, that "all these people have been cleared by the British Security." U.K. officials had run a "special clearance" on those working in the United States. Accordingly, they received "District Identification Cards" that gave their British affiliation and allowed them access to facilities in the District. They needed special permission to access "particular classified information or restricted areas." In fact, the latter permission was hardly special—just a sheet of onionskin paper containing name, rank, name of facility to visit, and date. Permission was granted automatically; otherwise, British personnel threatened to "take it to the White House."

The engineers at Kellex had developed a preliminary design of the diffusion plan, ordered components, and begun the site preparation for construction in Oak Ridge, Tennessee. With the British team's more sophisticated design too late to be useful, its role became one of calculating how the plant's thousands of components and stages would respond to small changes. Fuchs took up the task, and January 5, 1944, saw his first report, MSN-1 "Stability of Plant with Reset Controls." More followed quickly.

Between his arrival and the first report, Fuchs went to his sister Kristel's house in Cambridge, Massachusetts, for Christmas. It had been seven years since they had seen each other in Bristol, and her life had changed dramatically. She was now married with two children and chose to be called Christel, the baptismal spelling of her name.

While at Swarthmore, she had a scholarship covering the tuition, as well as free room and board with a wealthy, somewhat demanding woman who lived on the Main Line. She went to classes, struggled to learn English and adjust to a new educational system and culture, and worked afternoons in a tearoom.

In 1938, her student visa was to expire, and replacing it with a permanent one required applying while outside the United States. The U.S. embassy in Cuba had a reputation for expediting the process, although it wasn't guaranteed. She was afraid of arriving there, being denied a visa, then facing a one-way trip back to Germany.

But she made the trip and returned to Swarthmore by the first week in June without incident and, with the new visa, as a happy young lady. And a fortunate one. An intensive refugee crisis in the United States began that June. The 1924 Immigration Act allowed a total of 150,000 visas per annum apportioned among countries: the count for Germany was 27,370. In November 1938, after *Kristallnacht*, when Nazis burned down synagogues and assaulted Jews, a Gallup poll asked Americans if the United States should take in more Jewish exiles. A resounding 72 percent said no. In 1939, the waiting list was about 310,000. The allotted number of visas didn't change.

Christel never received her degree. In October 1938, she married Bob Heinemann, who had graduated from Swarthmore in the spring and enrolled as a graduate student at Harvard. From Cambridge, she worked tirelessly, and futilely, to bring Gerhard and Elisabeth along with Elisabeth's son and husband to the United States.

On February 5, 1944, a wintry Saturday afternoon in Manhattan, Klaus made another journey, one that would change the course of his life and, some might say, the course of history. As darkness fell, he reached the appointed place on Henry Street set up before he'd left Birmingham. This was the Sabbath, in the heart of a Jewish neighborhood on the Lower East Side, and the sidewalks were deserted.

But then, across from a fenced excavation site, he saw a short, full-faced man wearing a dark suit and an overcoat. He wore gloves as well, but he carried an additional pair.

Dressed in tweeds, Klaus carried a book and a green tennis ball. He crossed the street, and the man asked him, "What is the way to China town?" He had a strong Philadelphia accent.

Klaus responded, "I think China town closes at 5 o'clock."

This, their first encounter, went exactly as planned, except that the man from Philadelphia was to carry a single glove, not a pair. And Klaus wanted to be called by his name and drop his code name, Rest. The other man went by "Raymond."

Slowly, they turned and walked together down the street. Sensing Klaus's reserve, Raymond chatted about himself until Klaus seemed to relax. They took the subway and then a taxi uptown and ended up at a restaurant on Third Avenue. The conversation over dinner was sparse. Klaus was still uneasy, and he didn't consider a restaurant a safe meeting spot. He could have been followed from work.

After dinner, they strolled, and Klaus explained his assignment on isotope separation. Besides the work in Manhattan, research was taking place in Berkeley, California, and at a place simply referred to as Camp Y, possibly in New Mexico. Researchers in England were carrying out preparatory work, and the United States was in charge of production. The work in the United States was done in "water-tight compartments" for security so that no one knew the full scope of the project. Klaus told Raymond that results were expected in 1945, but he was doubtful.

Before going their separate ways, the two men agreed to rules for future meetings: no restaurants, no place twice, as brief as possible. The overriding rule was caution. Accordingly, for this first meeting, Klaus had brought no materials. But both understood that in the future he would furnish Raymond with everything he could.

Prior to this rendezvous, Raymond had been told almost nothing about Rest (name used in Russian messages), except that he was a scientist. He began his report with the basics: "He is a member of a British mission to the U.S. working under the direct control of the U.S. Army. . . . The work resolves itself mainly into a separation of the isotopes . . . with the diffusion method. . . . He is most likely a very brilliant man to have such a position at his age (he looks about 30)." Raymond reassured his superiors: "He obviously has worked with our people before and he is fully aware of what he is doing. Also, he is apparently one of us in spirit." Raymond's estimate shaved Klaus's age by a couple of years.

Raymond handed off his report to "John," an operative at the Russian consulate in New York. Its next stop would be the KGB's Moscow Center.

The KGB knew a lot about Klaus. Staff in Moscow had received a lengthy brief from the GRU on its history with Klaus in London, attesting to his credentials and values: Klaus believed in communism, his motives were ideological, and he worked on war research. On handing him over to the KGB, the GRU advised that he took no pay but sometimes accepted monetary gifts.

The memo from the KGB's Moscow Center to its staff at the consulate in New York exuded excitement. Pressures on them had mounted owing to their failure to infiltrate U.S. war research. Now they had something. The memo proclaimed, "As an agent, 'Rest' is a major figure with considerable opportunities and experience in agent work."

But there were also reservations. "Be very cautious when working with Rest," Moscow Center advised. The threat of U.S. counterintelligence was ever present. Surprisingly, there was another potential hazard—the GRU itself. In the opinion of the KGB, its spying partner, which had handed over Rest, was "not known for its discretion."

For the next several months, meeting once a month—sometimes more—and always at night, Klaus and Raymond hopscotched from the Queensboro Bridge to Greenwich Village, to the Grand Concourse in the Bronx, to Queens Boulevard in Long Island City. Along jammed streets, in dark alleys, and in dimly lit cafés, they had fleeting encounters where

Klaus handed over handwritten documents. He knew that the copies typed
at work were numbered and couldn't be used because each one was distributed to a specific person. But the typists gave the original, longhand drafts
back to him, and these he handed to Raymond. Anything else of importance he put in writing. He could tell that Raymond had some scientific
background, but he didn't think he would grasp the complexities of the
research.

Raymond had his own drill. Within half an hour of the rendezvous, he
met his controller on a nearby street corner and transferred the folder.
Once, his curiosity gnawing, he opened the folder. He saw page upon page
of mathematical equations.

One day, Klaus asked about the reaction to his material. Raymond said
it was "completely satisfactory" but that Moscow Center wanted more: a
detailed description of the "whole set-up"—that is, production plans and
drawings. Obviously aggravated, Klaus replied that he had handed that
over in England. His research in America was different, and it would be
dangerous for him to carry that kind of material. But finally, he agreed.

Raymond was pleased with the material he was able to supply to Moscow Center, but unexpectedly, they chastised him. Why had he, "Goose"—
his code name in the messages to his superiors—not provided "precise"
information on Rest himself: place of employment, address, meeting
arrangements, his impression of Rest. And they admonished him about the
lack of a backup if contact were lost.

Early on, the two men had fabricated a detailed cover story for their
friendship—a symphony concert at Carnegie Hall where they had sat next
to each other, chatted, and become friends. With this prop they sometimes
relaxed their taboo on dining to enjoy a rapport filled with office news.

One night, Klaus described his supervisor's visit to Camp Y to consult
on developing a large-scale "launch" of a bomb. Another time, he told Raymond about a "definite break" between the British and the Americans. The
British wanted to build their own diffusion plant in England to separate
isotopes, a direct breach of an agreement.

The work of the British team in New York was self-limiting and, by

May, coming to an end. This led Klaus to warn Raymond that his next assignment—England or Camp Y in New Mexico—was uncertain. He might be leaving for England in six weeks.

Peierls had already left for Camp Y, a.k.a. Los Alamos, New Mexico, and the site of the construction of the atomic bomb. The Theoretical Division needed mathematical physicists to accelerate the delivery of a plutonium bomb.

The scientists and engineers at Los Alamos had developed a bomb using the fissile material U-235 with a simple gun-type device, where a projectile of a subcritical mass of fissile material meets another subcritical mass to create a critical mass and start a chain reaction. But enriching uranium with U-235 was a lengthy process. An alternate fuel existed: plutonium, an element that could also sustain a chain reaction. Researchers had determined that sufficient quantities of plutonium were quicker and easier to obtain. Trace quantities appear in U-238, and a few years before, scientists had discovered that they could produce more through neutron capture by U-238, which would subsequently decay to plutonium's fissile isotope PU-239.

It wasn't to be an easy solution, though. In April, they realized that their simple, gun-type device worked well for a U-235 bomb but wasn't suitable for plutonium. Because plutonium's rate of spontaneous fission was too fast, plutonium fuel in a gun-type bomb would fission before reaching a critical mass and create an abbreviated explosion, that is, a "fizzle." A plutonium bomb required a completely new—and unexplored—approach.

A weighty question confronted Robert Oppenheimer. Should he make an abrupt shift from a dependable gun-type bomb with a limited fuel supply to one clouded by uncertainties but with more readily available fuel? The outcome of the project—and perhaps of the war—could depend on that decision. Oppenheimer anxiously mulled it over for a few months. With input from Peierls and others, he became convinced that they must start over and design a plutonium bomb.

A far lesser, but still important, uncertainty was the placement of Fuchs

and Skyrme. Tube Alloys administrators in London and Peierls in Los Alamos debated whether they were to go home to design a now viable gaseous
diffusion plant or go out west to Camp Y to design a bomb. Peierls had
requested that both of them go west.

As officials pondered Fuchs's fate in the first weeks of June, Allied
troops landed on and secured the beaches of Normandy. Victory over the
Germans now seemed within reach—unless, of course, the Germans had
an atomic bomb being readied to drop on England.

The decision to transfer Skyrme to New Mexico came quickly, but
Fuchs's deployment remained a subject of debate. Kearton wanted Fuchs
back in the U.K. to push forward the work on diffusion. Peierls could go
along if the diffusion work was really a serious effort, but he and Hans
Bethe, the head of the theoretical physics division at Camp Y, doubted that
it was, and thought that Fuchs would be more valuable at Camp Y. Bethe
was an esteemed physicist and later Nobel laureate, a German refugee who
knew the British team well. His journey to America wove through England:
first Cambridge, then Manchester, where he had lived with the Peierlses,
and finally Bristol, where he first met Fuchs. Bethe had overlapped with
Gerhard Fuchs too at the Odenwaldschule.

A month into the deliberations, those in charge tilted cautiously in
favor of bringing Fuchs back to England. But Kearton hesitated, fearing
that the Americans would interpret Fuchs's transfer home as a slight, a lack
of commitment to the war effort. Fuchs, too, favored returning. Without
identifying the location of Camp Y, Peierls had told him its purpose. Fuchs
felt he could make a "special contribution" in the U.K. At Camp Y, he saw
himself as one of many and not able to make a significant difference. He
stated his preference, but he didn't argue it.

The dithering left Fuchs restless and bored, living alone in an apartment on the West Side and rarely socializing. He did receive one dinner
invitation, though, from Maria Goeppert Mayer, a scientist on the Manhattan Project team at Columbia University and a future Nobelist. She was
an old friend of the physicist Edward Teller, who met Fuchs while en route

to Los Alamos in early 1944. Teller wrote to Maria that Fuchs was a very nice man and someone she would find interesting:

> He was a student of Born and you remember that he has worked on Joe's [Maria's husband] theory of condensation.... In talking, his spontaneous emission is very low but his induced emission is quite satisfactory.

In mid-June, Fuchs sent Peierls his latest report, MSN-12 "Fluctuations and the Efficiency of a Diffusion Plant—Part III," which outlined a theory with "just tolerable" conditions for bypasses in the diffusion process. After he finished a couple of other reports, he complained to Peierls that being "practically out of work, I have tried to comfort myself by considering what we have done during the last months." That resulted in a dense, single-spaced four-page report in which Fuchs succinctly summarized their work:

> In the diffusion plant for the production of the isotope uranium 235, the [gas] uranium hexafluoride passes through several thousand states which are all interdependent on each other. Conventional measures of pressure and flow control are completely inadequate to control such a complicated system, and I developed the theory of the control system of such a plant, which was further amplified by the research group at Kellex and applied to the operation of the diffusion plant. Also, I developed the theory of the effect of the remaining pressure and flow fluctuations on the performance of the diffusion plant and advised Kellex on steps that could be taken to minimize losses of performance.

Out of the British mission's seventeen reports, Fuchs wrote ten, the remainder from Peierls and Skyrme. The Americans had much to thank the British team for, especially Fuchs.

At the end of July 1944, Klaus made two more trips. The first was to Washington, D.C., to see the director of the British mission and resolve the issue of where he would work next. When he left, the decision was for him to go to London.

He then traveled to Massachusetts to say goodbye to Christel, leaving her with instructions in case Raymond (whom he referred to by another name) visited her. Fuchs was vague about where he was going.

As Oppenheimer moved decisively to support plutonium and the design of a new triggering device, Fuchs's instructions changed: he was now going to be deployed to Los Alamos.

When Fuchs's British employer, the Department of Scientific and Industrial Research, initially proposed to send him to America in 1943, MI5 had queried whether his appointment was short-term or permanent. DSIR answered that it was the former. Once he was in the United States, Peierls quickly requested an extension, and DSIR forwarded it to MI5, which reconsidered Fuchs's security clearance. It returned a qualified endorsement for Fuchs to stay: DSIR should not mention Fuchs's "proclivities" to officials there.

No one revisited this topic with regard to Camp Y. Neither Peierls nor Bethe was aware of the questions about Fuchs's loyalties.

On August 5, Klaus and Raymond were to meet in Brooklyn in front of the Bell Cinema, near the Brooklyn Museum of Art. Raymond stood around and waited. No Klaus. They always set a backup date, but Raymond had to be someplace else. He did show up for the next date, but he stood there alone. In short order, Moscow Center's fear had come true.

Unknown to Raymond, Fuchs was on his way to Camp Y. On the eleventh, he took the train to Chicago and then boarded another to New Mexico.

Raymond plotted with his controller to figure out how to recover what was one of the KGB's most valuable assets—if not the most valuable. The plan they came up with—sending Raymond to Klaus's apartment—violated all the rules, but this was no time for scruples. John found Klaus's address, and Raymond bought a book to use as a guise for his visit. He inscribed Klaus's real name and address in it and set out for 128 West Seventy-seventh Street.

West Seventy-seventh was a quiet, narrow street lined with trees and brownstones. Raymond easily gained entry to number 128. As he searched for Klaus's apartment along a corridor, an old woman stuck her head out from her apartment. He queried her, and then the janitor who happened by, as to the whereabouts of his friend. Raymond wanted to return a book, he explained. From them, he learned that Klaus had left . . . to go "somewhere on a boat." Not good news.

The next discussion between Raymond and his controller was more fraught. They posited various schemes and agreed on contacting Klaus's sister, who lived somewhere in the Boston area. When Raymond located her at 144 Lakeview Avenue in Cambridge and knocked on the door, a cleaning lady answered and said that the family was on vacation. Raymond asked about the wife's brother and heard that he had visited to say goodbye.

The next cable to Moscow Center read, "Contact with 'Rest' has been lost."

CHAPTER 13

Trinity, Los Alamos 1944

THE TRIP TO THE SOUTHWEST, THREE DAYS LONG AND DULL, TRANSPORTED KLAUS TO a new world. He stepped off the train in Lamy, the nearest main line rail station to Santa Fe and a hot, dry desert town with little more than a hotel and lunchroom and a few run-down adobe houses. All around, rugged mountains sprouted prickly green tufts of sagebrush. The air was thin at the sixty-five-hundred-foot elevation, the sun strong. Left far behind was the humidity of New York, crowded with 7.5 million people.

A car met him and carried him fifteen miles north to East Palace Avenue, Santa Fe. They stopped at a long, low-slung, centuries-old adobe building in the middle of town. There was no sign, just a plain, nondescript door and the number 109. It was a magical door, beyond which physicists lost their identity and became "engineers"; driver's licenses showed a number only (no name); and banking was done in Albuquerque. All mail came to one address, box 1663 in Santa Fe. Guards, invisible in civvies, hung around day and night. Just as Peierls and Fuchs had researched the whereabouts of German physicists (that produced little information), Groves wanted no telltale signs to alert curious Germans to the whereabouts of his own scientists.

On hand to greet Klaus was Dorothy McKibbin, the indispensable gatekeeper for the Hill, as Los Alamos was called. Besides running the registration office and handing out security badges, she organized deliveries, helped plan parties, and basically mothered anyone who needed it, including Fuchs, whom she found to be polite and gentle—as well as "attractive." From her, Fuchs received a white badge indicating almost unlimited access to the secrets of Los Alamos. Without a badge from Dorothy, there was no access to the Hill.

The research site was still forty-five miles away, including a ten-mile detour around a rickety bridge. As Fuchs's driver went north, about two miles from the center of town off to the west was another guarded site that no one talked about: a Japanese American internment camp with a twelve-foot-high barbed-wire fence, searchlights, sentry towers, and well-armed guards, very similar to where Klaus had been interned in Canada. Intermittently, it housed German and Italian POWs.

After Fuchs and his driver crossed the Rio Grande, they reached the Pajarito Plateau, where high mesas, striated pink and white, rose before them. These high, flat-topped hills with steep sides had formed out of the fire and smoke of volcanoes that exploded into the sky a million years ago, prefiguring the kind of combustion these men were exploring. The blistering, roaring eruptions had spewed so violently that jetsam covered the earth in a five-hundred-mile radius. The vestiges of ash, pumice, and lava flows created the soft, porous rock out of which erosion created a labyrinth of deep canyons setting these stark and stunning formations in relief.

From the canyon floor, the car slowly climbed another two thousand feet, following the curves of the switchbacks, most not more than one lane wide, that edged a precipitous drop, no guardrails in sight. At the top, a white clapboard hut appeared, the Los Alamos Main Gate on the east side of the mesa. After the guards checked Fuchs's pass, the car headed down the dirt road through a chain-link fence topped with barbed wire, stands of piñon and juniper trees on either side. Two miles farther, they stopped at another security gate that marked the entrance to the town, and after another check of credentials they drove past rustic log cabins and a lodge with a pond in front, eventually reaching the housing office, where Fuchs picked up the keys for his bachelor room in the "Big House."

This two-storied lodge and the log cabins around it were relics of the Los Alamos Ranch School that had educated a diverse collection of wealthy young men ranging from William S. Burroughs to Gore Vidal to Arthur Wood, a future president of Sears, Roebuck. Familiar with the location and its inaccessibility, Oppenheimer had identified the school as a potential site for the nuclear research facility, and the government purchased it in 1942. The Big House, formerly a dormitory, became the residence for single men.

Fuchs's next-door neighbor there was Richard Feynman—six and a half years younger and a rising star in the physics firmament. He wasn't a bachelor, but his wife suffered from tuberculosis and was in a sanitarium in nearby Albuquerque.

After Fuchs bought a very beat-up Buick of the fifty-dollar type in Santa Fe, he regularly lent it to Feynman so that he could visit his wife. The two men became good friends, and Fuchs watched out for him. One night when Feynman passed out from too much alcohol, Fuchs carried him back to the Big House.

Evenings when they were free, they pondered politics, Los Alamos security, and what constituted an acceptable exchange of information with foreign scientists. They even bantered about which of them was more likely to be a spy. It was the kind of game that the spirited Feynman in particular enjoyed. They mutually agreed that Feynman, who later gained fame for his humor, his bongo playing, and his popular books—as well as his contribution to physics—was the more likely one.

Feynman ran computations with a new IBM machine using punch cards and quickly advanced to become a group leader. Fuchs worked in the Theoretical Division in group T-1 under Rudi Peierls. Bethe assigned this group exclusively to handle the theoretical problems of Division X, the explosion group. Group T-1 did the calculations for and design of the lenses, a key component of the implosion mechanism that was the triggering device for the plutonium bomb.

Implosion was a completely different type of trigger design from the gun type for the U-235 bomb. Most simply, thirty-two lenses made of explosive material, surrounded a core of plutonium. Detonating the lenses compressed or crushed the plutonium core to start a chain reaction. To work, the pressure from the exploding lenses had to be sufficiently power-ful, completely symmetrical, and perfectly timed. The firing mechanism, shape, and speed had to be so exact that the lenses exploded simultane-ously down to a tolerance of one-millionth of a second. Otherwise, some of the plutonium would squirt away from the whole, creating a jet. The optics group at Los Alamos developed X-ray cameras that could take microsec-ond exposures to assess the symmetry. Fuchs made or reviewed the theo-retical calculations supporting many of the components in the mechanism, especially the lenses, creating the theory to eliminate jets.

Oppenheimer had originally designated the Hungarian physicist Edward Teller to head group T-1, but the assignment didn't measure up to Teller's sense of his own worth. Teller, who would later become highly con-troversial for his testimony before Congress questioning Oppenheimer's loyalty, as well as for his backing of what others saw as extreme uses of technology, thought that he, rather than Hans Bethe, deserved to direct the whole Theoretical Division.

Teller was a brilliant physicist; he was also loud, assertive, and not widely liked. When he refused to head the implosion group, Oppenheimer acquiesced in his wish for a separate team to work on the more powerful hydrogen bomb, also called a fusion bomb. Theoretically, it worked by taking the energy from a fission bomb and using it to fuse small atomic nuclei together. Many more years would be needed to make it operational, and in 1944 it wasn't clear it would ever work.

Teller, like Fuchs, was among the many leading physicists who had come under the tutelage of Max Born. Teller had been his assistant in the early 1930s, and Born had helped him escape Germany then. Oppenheimer had received his PhD under Born, around the same time as Maria Goeppert Mayer, the Columbia University physicist who had invited Fuchs to dinner in New York.

In the mid-1920s, at the height of the quantum revolution partly led by

Born, a program of the Rockefeller Foundation had academically cross-fertilized the physics world, sending the best young physicists to study in a foreign country—the Americans to Germany, the Germans to Denmark, and on and on. Teller and Peierls had studied together at the University of Leipzig—just before Klaus Fuchs arrived there—under Werner Heisenberg, another former assistant to Born. This new generation of physicists had played together, gotten drunk together in bars, pubs, and *Kneipen*, and studied together. The best minds in physics had all been intellectual intimates until the Nazis ripped them apart.

Ironically, the historical development of physics in Germany and the Eastern European countries opened the theoretical area more readily to Jews than the experimental one. When these young Jewish scholars fled, the Germans forced an extraordinary scientific shift to Britain and America. This interwoven but partitioned world fostered a respect by those in America for their German rivals, one that pushed them to work all out to win the race.

General Groves, with a thoroughly military mind-set, had no interest in camaraderie and the free flow of information. He wanted Los Alamos to run as an army base with scientists in uniform and all groups compartmentalized and isolated. He might not have said as much to Oppenheimer, but Groves's insistence on maintaining tight controls was directed not just against the Germans but also against America's allies. The pioneering work of British scientists might have been instrumental in getting the Manhattan Project going, but he didn't want the British to build their own bomb using his information.

Oppenheimer, as thoroughly academic as Groves was military, refused to go along. Success, he told Groves, required a combination of the spirit of collaboration and a constant exchange of ideas. To Groves's credit, Oppenheimer prevailed; one physicist deemed Los Alamos a "scientific paradise." With weekly coordinating meetings and colloquiums, Oppenheimer created what the scientists thought was a perfect research environment, enriched by the exciting and uncompetitive free flow of ideas. Although it wasn't so free. The United States kept a list of which British personnel went to the colloquiums or coordinating committee meetings in order to forestall any attempts by the British to claim a patent on an invention that arose by way of meetings there.

Fuchs's first invitation to a colloquium came in October. The topic was "on preparing shaped masses of high explosives for implosion spheres." Although Fuchs was one of eleven British scientists—along with Peierls, Skyrme, and Frisch—with blanket permission to access all reports (except those specifically limited), as well as any area of the laboratory, it was December before he began attending Oppenheimer's meetings on a semi-regular basis.

Weekly meetings of the Theoretical Division's working groups were different. Hans Bethe handled those. Whenever he asked for a liaison to a group, Fuchs raised his hand. Bethe considered him vital to the project.

Fuchs regularly attended the weekly working group that designed the lenses. Their design was one of his main theoretical challenges. He was the only physicist to take an interest; he said little but dutifully took notes.

On October 24, 1944, Raymond knocked on the door of 144 Lakeview Avenue in Cambridge around 10:00 a.m. This was his third try to make contact with Christel Fuchs Heinemann.

When she opened the door, Raymond introduced himself as a friend of her brother's, and they exchanged code words as Klaus had informed her to do. He had brought candy for her children and a book, Hersey's *Bell for Adano*, for her. She had not heard from Klaus, she told him. She thought he had most likely gone to England.

Undeterred, Raymond returned the next week on Thursday. Again, he brought candy for the children and the book *Some of My Best Friends Are Soldiers* for her. She had very good news for him: Klaus had traveled to Chicago for business and called her. He told her that he was working in New Mexico—he didn't specify where—and that he would visit her for two weeks at Christmas. Overjoyed, Raymond stayed for lunch. He said that he would visit again in three or four weeks.

A month later, Raymond was there again. Christel had heard nothing more from Klaus, but she expected to see him over the holidays. On the previous phone call, her brother had said that he might have to go to New York for a few days. Raymond took that as a message that Klaus wanted to see him, and he wrote a note to Klaus for her to give him. On it was a name and phone number for Klaus to call when he arrived.

The scientists on the Hill worked day and night. Whenever an idea hit them, they could stride through a security gate into the Tech Area, which was isolated from the small town by another fence topped by barbed wire, and enter one of the barracks-like buildings. Fuchs's office was in Building E, confusingly referred to as the "T-Building," *T* for "Theoretical," also the location of Oppenheimer's office. Fuchs shared room E-118 with Tony Skyrme. Peierls was next door in E-119. Johnny von Neumann was a member of T-1 and a few offices away. An extraordinary collection of intellect, but that was true for every floor in T-Building. Feynman, leader of group IV, and Victor Frederick "Viki" Weisskopf, leader of group III, were one floor up.

Weisskopf was yet another of Born's former students and had overlapped with Teller. He and Teller never got on, but they did have a deep, unknown connection. They both adored Maria Goeppert Mayer, the former Born student now at Columbia, their whole lives. When Teller later learned that Weisskopf was equally smitten, he said with surprise, "That's the only thing I know that Weisskopf and I ever agreed on." T-Building held more than simply atomic secrets.

The scientists were sworn to silence about the project; not even their spouses could know. Guards allowed only those with the appropriate badge into the Tech Area. Everything that happened inside this fence stayed inside. Patrols in jeeps and on horseback wore a track outside the main perimeter of the base to ensure that it did. Others on horseback rode into the mountains and camped out looking for spies.

The secrecy, as well as the pressure to accomplish what some considered the impossible, created a constant tension. Social life, as much as time allowed, helped to dissipate it.

Administrators encouraged their cooped-up researchers to make the most of their splendid isolation. The denizens of Los Alamos hiked or rode horses through the pristine forests; they fished in the streams of the Jemez Mountains; they skied; they visited nearby pueblos for the festivities and beautiful pottery. The fresh air and the remarkable beauty rejuvenated tired minds. It only took gazing at the red glow of the Sangre de Cristo Mountains at sunset to appreciate the mysterious wonderment of the universe, despite their efforts to redirect some of its most basic principles.

The British team was particularly close knit. Klaus often joined the Peierlses and friends on excursions into the mountains, taking risks and dealing with the challenges. Genia remembered him climbing over extremely dangerous cliffs to test himself. Risk-taking was a central feature of his personality, as was control. The group's explosives expert had cleared an overgrown slope with dynamite and fitted it out with a tow rope. They called it Sawyer Hill. One afternoon, as he was learning to ski, Klaus severely damaged his ankle. Genia watched as he skied down with great control in spite of the pain.

He dated a couple of the grade school teachers at the facility, later admitting that with one he almost formed a relationship. At that time in his life, though, he wasn't quite capable of a long-term commitment.

Otherwise, filling the few down hours meant chess, bridge, charades, hobbies, music, and lively parties at Fuller Lodge. Fuchs was noted as a skilled dancer, and one with very good rhythm—at one party leading the conga line through the commissary. He also had a reputation for consuming large quantities of alcohol at parties. Genia's impression was that he could drink a whole bottle of vodka in one gulp. How much it affected him wasn't clear. Rudi Peierls's memory wasn't consistent, on one occasion saying he never saw Klaus drunk, on another remembering that he sometimes had "a little more than he could stand."

Klaus sometimes supplied what he and others drank, volunteering to

drive to Santa Fe for liquor. Everyone on the Hill was entitled to one shopping day a month in Santa Fe. Exiting involved a stop at the gate to let the
guards inspect the car; drivers and passengers were not searched. In Santa
Fe, some of the British mission thought that GII (security) men kept an eye
on them; others thought they were left alone. For sure, GII watched the
American scientists closely.

At first the army didn't want anyone to leave the Hill, but by 1944 the
officers realized that the scientists worked so hard that they had to get away.
Klaus asked for leave at Christmas to see Christel in Massachusetts. The
travel time was three days out and three days back. But Klaus's Christmas
leave was canceled and rescheduled for February.

Klaus arrived in Cambridge in February and quickly used the contact number that Raymond had left with Christel. Raymond didn't call first, fearing
that the phone could be bugged, but merely showed up at 144 Lakeview on
the morning of Monday, February 19.

This time when Christel answered the door, she asked him to return
on Wednesday because her husband was home. Raymond could see Klaus
sitting in the parlor. Raymond couldn't stay in the area until Wednesday,
so he called the house an hour later. A man answered the phone, whom he
took to be Christel's husband, and he pretended to have a wrong number.
He took the train home to Philadelphia and returned to Cambridge on
Wednesday.

This time, Raymond and Rest were reunited, and they went into Boston so Klaus could buy presents for friends at Los Alamos.

They talked while traveling into and out of the city, Klaus explaining
that he had to report on every person he met outside work hours at Los
Alamos, even those outside his own field. On Monday, he hadn't wanted to
introduce his brother-in-law to Raymond. He also said that he had checked
carefully, and he wasn't being watched.

They were back at Christel's by 1:00. After lunch, the two men went upstairs to Klaus's room, where he described Los Alamos and the setup for developing the bomb. They agreed on plans for Raymond to visit Santa Fe on the first Saturday in June. Klaus had already thought through how they should proceed, telling Raymond to set his watch by the large clock on San Francisco Street, handing him a map and a bus schedule, and detailing the passwords and signs if a substitute had to come. He then gave Raymond several pages of notes he had written from memory while at Christel's: principles of the A-bomb construction, dimensions of the bomb, and the possibility of a plutonium bomb. That information centered on the trigger for the plutonium bomb, implosion—the types of explosives, their timed sequencing, and the properties of plutonium, all still being worked out.

On orders from Moscow Center, Raymond delicately tried to offer Fuchs fifteen hundred dollars. The gesture met with a cold response. Fuchs said he made all the money he needed. He did have a request, though. When Russian soldiers entered Kiel and Berlin, he wanted them to go through the Gestapo files and destroy any information on him. They must stay out of the hands of the British. The only reason he could do this research was that the British didn't know about his communist past.

For many, Fuchs remained an enigma, or a cipher. One of the wives admitted not recalling what he looked like each time she met him; another said that he faded into the background. Colleagues noted his reserve, but also his generosity with his time. As Edward Teller wrote,

> He was willing to help with any project, whether it was to discuss a colleague's problem and suggest possible new approaches or to act as a chauffeur for wives whose husbands had no time for that. His services earned him a fond spot in many hearts.

Teller's wife, Mici, was one of those wives. She and Fuchs enjoyed each other's company. Fuchs was everyone's favorite babysitter. Even animals seemed to love him.

The detonation of a bomb using U-235 was sufficiently straightforward not to require testing. With the complex plutonium bomb, only a test would prove it viable, although there were constraints on testing either bomb. Sufficient U-235 existed for only one bomb, and only enough plutonium for two. In the spring of 1945, Oppenheimer set July 16 as the test date for the plutonium bomb, nicknamed the Gadget. But then the pace of events began to accelerate, bringing radical change.

In April, German strength began to collapse, the concentration camps were liberated, and Hitler and Mussolini died. On May 7, Germany surrendered unconditionally, and the next day, V-E Day—for Victory in Europe—jubilation overtook every street corner in America and Britain.

For many scientists, the end of the war suggested that the creation of an atomic bomb should end as well. Given the horrific devastation, most of them had rationalized their participation in creating it only because of the urgent need to rid the world of Hitler and the Nazis. That goal had now prevailed, but the government wanted to press on as eagerly as before. As early as September 1944, with the tide of war in Europe turning sharply in the Allies' favor, Churchill and Roosevelt had secretly agreed that "when a 'bomb' is finally available, it might perhaps, after mature consideration, be used against the Japanese."

But also in April 1945, Franklin Roosevelt died, altering the equation even more. Fuchs later wrote that he experienced the shock of FDR's death deeply. Fuchs, along with many other physicists, viewed Roosevelt as a moral voice who would make just decisions. Whether Roosevelt would have ordered the bombing of Japan with atomic weapons can never be known. But there is compelling evidence that his attitude toward Russia was less bellicose than that of others in power, including Churchill. He was also willing to consider international control of atomic weapons.

Not so his successor, Harry S. Truman. Thirty years after Truman approved dropping the atomic bombs on Japan and obliterating two cities, Fuchs, in a lecture to students, condemned him as "ruthless."

On June 2, 1945, Fuchs used a shopping day for a trip into Santa Fe. This was the day for his meeting with Raymond, arranged a few months before in Cambridge. At the center of the trove of documents Fuchs had brought with him were plans for the plutonium bomb that was to be tested on July 16. These were meaningless without a high level of precise detail, so before this rendezvous Klaus had copied specifications including a sketch with all the important dimensions. Leaving Los Alamos, he stopped at the security gate per protocol, climbed out of the car, and waited while the guards searched the vehicle, then waved him on. The plans for the atomic bomb were in his pocket.

He arrived in Santa Fe two to three minutes after the appointed time of 4:00 p.m., picked up Raymond on Alameda, a graveled street next to the Castillo Street Bridge, then drove on a little farther to a side road where they parked. As they talked, Klaus made clear that even though everyone at Los Alamos was working without a break, he himself putting in eighteen to twenty hours a day, he thought the bomb would not be ready to use against the Japanese. At the very last moment, when dropping Raymond off in Santa Fe, Fuchs handed over "a considerable packet of information." Making the transfer at the last minute was a precaution against being stopped by security personnel.

Monday, July 16, at 2:00 a.m. was zero hour for testing the Gadget. The site chosen was about 230 miles due south of Los Alamos, in the flat, scorching desert near the small town of Alamogordo. The conquistadors had named it Jornada del Muerto, "journey of the dead." The U.S. government used it as a bombing range. In the spring of 1945, crews had constructed a hundred-foot steel tower to hold the bomb, a base camp, and observation bunkers 5.6 miles away. Oppenheimer, who had a mystical streak, called the test Trinity.

Key scientists went to the site a few days before the test to assemble the bomb. On Sunday, the fifteenth, late in the afternoon, buses left the Los Alamos mesa carrying other senior scientists south, some to the site and some to a hill twenty miles away. Peierls and Fuchs were in the second group. They all received welders' goggles to protect their eyes from the flash, and they were instructed not to look directly at it. Unofficial groups drove to various mountain ranges east and south of Albuquerque with sleeping bags and food. Most who stayed behind knew what was about to happen. Everyone was anxious and distracted. For a time, there had been concern that the nuclear detonation would ignite the atmosphere and destroy the planet. Certainly, they were entering unknown territory.

As darkness fell, Don Hornig, the young physical chemist who had designed the ignition switches for the lenses, sat alone on a platform at the top of the hundred-foot tower, on hand to babysit and to make last-minute adjustments if needed. The fully armed Gadget hung just below him, its plutonium core inserted along with the detonators. Then, shortly after midnight, a violent storm moved in, and the wind, rain, and lightning whipped around him. Those at the base camp and the few on the ground at the tower wondered if they should go ahead. Hornig agonized over a lightning bolt striking the tower.

As the storm raged unabated, the detonation time was rolled back to 4:00 a.m., then later to 5:30, the last possible minute before the sky would brighten. The scientists wanted to capture the explosion on film, and the appropriate photographs required darkness.

The countdown started at 5:10. Quite unintentionally, there was Russian radio interference. The base camp used the frequency of a radio station that was off the air at night. It picked up a close frequency, and in the background a Tchaikovsky waltz accompanied the countdown.

At 5:29:45, for all those watching from the north on crests near Albuquerque, it was as if the sun had risen in the south. Dorothy McKibbin, the guardian of the gate in Santa Fe, experienced "an unholy light like no one has ever seen before." She also remembered the solemnity. "There was no celebration at the Test site or on the Hill. The men had done the job their government had asked them to do. They were relieved that it had been successful. They were not elated. It had been too terrible a sight for that emotion." According to the wife of the physicist Martin Deutsch, those returning from Alamogordo were "bedraggled and depressed; they had been through hell." This appraisal might have reflected her husband's condition especially. He had hoped from the start that the task would prove impossible. One exception to the funereal mood was the irrepressible Richard Feynman, who played the bongos as he sat on the hood of a jeep.

The government explained to the public, who obviously noticed the weird phenomenon, that an ammunition dump had exploded in that area of Alamogordo.

The next day a petition circulated at Los Alamos requesting that President Truman not approve "the use of atomic bombs in this war unless the terms which will be imposed upon Japan have been made public in detail and Japan knowing these terms has refused to surrender." They didn't know that Truman and Churchill had already settled questions about Japan soon after Germany's defeat. It was to be Hiroshima and Nagasaki.

Whatever warning the Japanese people received was too little and too late. In July, the U.S. Army Air Forces did drop leaflets warning of bombings and devastation. Those concerned firebombings, not atomic bombs. Leaflets did rain down on Nagasaki to warn of an atomic bomb. They fell on scorched earth. The army had dropped the plutonium bomb on the city the day before.

The military argued that dropping the bomb on Japan was the only way to avoid having to invade the Japanese homeland, and thus it would save hundreds of thousands of American lives and end the war in the Pacific quickly. There was another factor. At a dinner party in Los Alamos some time earlier, the physicist Joseph Rotblat, a Polish émigré who would later win the Nobel Peace Prize, supposedly heard General Groves say that for the United States to become militarily dominant, it was necessary to intimidate the Russians, and the atomic bomb would do that.

President Truman was to meet with Winston Churchill and Joseph Stalin at Potsdam, Germany, the day after Trinity. He wanted to dangle "the new weapon" in front of Stalin, and with the successful test he could and did. Stalin had little reaction. Of course, neither Truman nor anyone else there appreciated that Stalin knew almost as much about the bomb and the Trinity test as they did. Scanning the documents that Fuchs handed to Raymond in Santa Fe two months earlier, he would have seen the detailed drawing of the plutonium bomb.

According to an agreement with the Allies, three months after the fighting in Europe was over, the Russians were to launch a new offensive against Japan, which they did against Japanese forces in Manchuria on August 9. The Russians had additional plans to invade Hokkaido, the second-largest island in the Japanese archipelago, but Stalin aborted them. It is thought that the bombing of Hiroshima and Nagasaki caused Stalin not to risk a confrontation with the United States.

After learning of the massive destruction and loss of life caused by the U-235 bomb on Hiroshima on August 6 and the plutonium bomb on Nagasaki on August 9, scientists now intensely and openly debated the control of the atomic bomb, their ambivalence long dammed up by the need for secrecy and for simply getting the job done. Military or civilian? National or international? For some time, many had debated among themselves. A consensus arose that effective international control required the Russians to have full information. Some argued that if Washington didn't see this, they, the scientists, had their own obligation to provide it. Fuchs was one of the few scientists who didn't join in this discussion.

To shape the answer to the question on national control, the U.S. Congress proposed a bill, May-Johnson, that allowed the potential for military control. At congressional hearings, heated testimony by dismayed scientists stymied a vote. An alternative bill proposed by Senator Brien McMahon called for greater civilian control. At the same time, it included stringent restrictions on the release of nuclear information, even to the British. With a Russian defector having exposed a network of spies in Canada only a couple of months before, the already vigilant American security apparatus became even more restrictive.

Scientists gravely cautioned their governments about the potential devastation of an arms race if the Russians weren't full partners in developing and enforcing restrictions on nuclear weapons, which meant that first they had to be partners in sharing information. The British scientists at Los Alamos wrote a memorandum to their government stating, "We have recently had many discussions with our American colleagues, and practically all of us, Americans and British, are in agreement as to the gravity of the problems involved in controlling the use of atomic bombs." They reasoned that in wartime "belligerents" wouldn't keep any treaty against the use of atomic weapons. The scientists' advice to obstruct an arms race or a full-out nuclear war was to enforce "1) international supervision of materials and facilities, and 2) free movement of scientific information and personnel among all countries."

Fuchs was a signatory. He revealed no other opinions at the time. He had earnestly engaged in the development of the bomb for the purpose of stopping the Nazis, as had many if not most of the British and American scientists. He had advised Raymond that it probably wouldn't be ready to use against the Japanese. With preparations for the test advancing, it was an opinion seemingly based more on hope than reality. His father's stance on pacifism and his own early disgust with killing animals and so becoming a vegetarian argue for a turn to pacifism, but it wasn't an issue he discussed.

Scientists at the California Institute of Technology, where Oppenheimer had taught, signed "An Open Letter to the President and the Congress of the United States of America" that echoed the proposals in the British memo. Oppenheimer was one of ninety-five signatories. Hans Bethe drafted a separate declaration that began, "We, a group of the scientists who have proposed and developed the atomic bomb, feel that we cannot escape the responsibility for its consequences." He argued that military bases could no longer protect the United States. The solution was either for the U.S. populace to disperse from large cities or for a world authority to control atomic weapons.

The national versus international discussion was ultimately decided at the newly formed United Nations. In 1946, the United States proposed that an international authority control all aspects of nuclear energy. Once such an authority was established, the United States agreed to destroy its nuclear weapons. The Russians wanted the United States to destroy its weapons before international control was established. Issues over inspection also arose. There was no agreement.

With the formal signing of Japan's surrender on September 2, 1945, World War II was completely over, and the British mission in Los Alamos was ready to go home.

On September 19, Fuchs drove down to Santa Fe to pick up a carload of alcohol for a farewell party. This coincided perfectly with the arrangement he and Raymond had worked out. Never meeting at the same place twice, they rendezvoused on the outskirts of Santa Fe, near a church on Bishops Lodge Road. This time, Fuchs was very late, and Raymond became extremely nervous.

He showed up after twenty minutes. His first remark was "Well, were you impressed?" Raymond responded that he was both impressed and hor-rified. Klaus told him that the "test shot had far exceeded expectations but that these had been purposely toned down because the results of the cal-culations showed them to be so incredible." Explaining his tardiness, he described driving more slowly than usual because of all the glass bottles of liquor he'd purchased in Santa Fe. There had also been friends there with him, and it had taken time to break away.

Fuchs later related that he gave Raymond documents he had written on the side of the road, stopping in the desert on his way from Los Alamos to Santa Fe, a distance of about forty miles. In a curious mix of realities, he added that the spot where he pulled over was twenty miles from Alamogordo, the Trinity site, and that he could see the results of the test. Alamogordo is approximately two hundred miles due south of Santa Fe. More confusing, Raymond later said that Fuchs "dropped off" people in Santa Fe. If so, how did he stop on his way to write down his notes? Did lapses in both their memories account for the twists in the stories?

Whatever the incongruities, what Fuchs provided was another mother lode for Raymond. What had been theory in June was reality in September. He now knew the construction details and the results, the blast waves, the rates of U.S. production of U-235 and plutonium and the size of the bombs (allowing calculations of the production of bombs), and where errors might occur. He also had some early information about a hydrogen bomb.

Before parting, they set up two other meetings. Fuchs, expecting to be transferred to England at the end of the year, said he would probably visit his sister in November or December. Raymond would keep in touch with her to know when. They also set up contact in London: Mornington Crescent tube station at 8:00 p.m. every first Saturday of the month after his return until someone managed to connect with him.

On Saturday, the twenty-second, the members of the British mission pooled their ration books and hosted a lavish farewell celebration at Fuller Lodge, with dinner and dancing. The British "stiff upper lip" gave way to skits and frivolity. Fuchs danced the night away.

A few members of the British mission were to stay on, Fuchs among them. Before the Peierlses left in December, Klaus took a trip to Mexico with them and Mici Teller, as a stand-in for Edward, who was busy consulting on Senator McMahon's bill for the control of atomic energy. Other than the earlier visit to his sister in Cambridge in February, and a conference in Montreal, this was Fuchs's only time away from New Mexico that year. The foursome had a relaxed trip, seeing a bullfight and viewing decorative arts in Mexico City, their only difficulties being episodic car problems and convincing hotels that they needed three rooms rather than one with two double beds.

When Raymond met with his contact in New York, he learned that he shouldn't meet with Fuchs again but should visit Christel, tell her that

Klaus should leave materials for him and that he would come for them. A sign in her window would let him know that Klaus wasn't there, avoiding any ties in case the FBI was watching Gold.

By now, caution was very much in order. In September, a Russian file clerk named Igor Gouzenko defected from the Russian embassy in Ottawa with a pile of documents exposing a Canadian spy ring. In the United States, Elizabeth Bentley, an American agent for the Russians, defected and began to name names. In January 1946, the KGB would order all agents connected to "Enormous," its code name for the American atomic bomb project, to suspend activity.

Raymond did make one more visit to Cambridge. In April 1946, he knocked on Christel's door and learned that Klaus had returned to England and hadn't left any materials for him. Strangely, Klaus was still at Los Alamos. Either Christel didn't want to be bothered by Raymond anymore, or somehow Klaus had slipped a message to her. Raymond had no more contact with either of them.

During Fuchs's twenty-two-month stay at Los Alamos, he produced more than fifty scientific reports. He summed up his work as a member of the "Implosion Group" for his personnel form in Los Alamos:

> I developed the theory of the jets observed in non-lens implosions, the elimination of which is necessary in order to make the type of implosion workable. I directed the work on the theory of the hydrodynamical processes in the initiator for the implosion bomb, and worked on other implosion problems.

The theories on the jets, hydrodynamics, and the initiator were of fundamental importance in the development of the atomic bomb. As with his time in New York, Fuchs had strongly served America's interests. He had also repeatedly betrayed its most vital national security secrets.

CHAPTER 14

Director, Harwell 1946

THE WAR'S END BROUGHT SWEEPING CHANGE FOR THE BRITISH ISLES. NOT TWO months after Germany's surrender in May 1945, the government called new elections, the first in ten years. Fuchs, who was still in America, gave Max Born his proxy vote for the Labour Party, Born's choice as well. In a landslide, voters sent the indefatigable Winston Churchill, savior of king and country, back into retirement. The detritus from the war years—food shortages, strict rationing, and lack of housing—was too strong a reminder of the misery of the 1930s depression under Churchill's Conservatives. Even Born's district in Edinburgh, always Tory by a large margin, swung left. The people's choice was the quiet, contemplative leader of the Labour Party, Clement Attlee, who had been deputy prime minister in the coalition government during the war.

The election took place during the Potsdam Conference, where Truman, Churchill, and Stalin met to discuss the shape of postwar Europe. Midway, Attlee arrived to take Churchill's chair at the table. Tellingly, the only veteran leader in the triumvirate was Stalin.

After six uncertain years, British scientists were eager to bring the benefit of the research they had conducted back to their home country.

In two world wars, Britain's victory had depended on the newly emerging global power of the United States. The Soviet Union, having shown its strength in defeating the Nazis in the East, was now challenging the old order in Europe by retaining control over the lands it had occupied. The Atlantic Charter, initiated and signed by Churchill and Roosevelt in 1941, had advocated decolonization. The new United Nations reinforced that dictate by guaranteeing an international platform for emerging nations, put to the test by India's declaration of independence in 1947.

Britannia still ruled many a wave, but the lands they washed upon were breaking free, and Britain's stature was declining. Having an atomic weapon would free the U.K. from being dependent on the vicissitudes of the Americans for protection. It would also secure British authority and influence in the evolving new world.

As the British mission straggled home from America, the government requisitioned a surplus Royal Air Force base near the village of Harwell as a research facility. Appointed director of the Atomic Energy Research Establishment—the official name with Harwell the colloquial one—was the eminent physicist John Cockcroft, very much in the reserved and thoughtful mold of so many other British men of science. Fuchs was one of his first recruits.

During his two years on the Manhattan Project, Fuchs's brilliance had matured. While still at Los Alamos, the young German was named to head the Theoretical Physics Division of the British nuclear research effort. He accepted the offer but requested that it be a temporary one. He didn't explain why he wished to maintain this flexibility. Perhaps he wanted the option of a more traditional academic career, or perhaps he thought of his long ago promise to return to Germany and help build a new country. Many of his refugee friends in London made the trip back during 1945 and 1946.

While details were being worked out, Rudi Peierls, who had returned to the University of Birmingham, advised Fuchs, still in the United States, on staff possibilities and the scope of the division.

"Harwell" was a new word in everyone's lexicon. Curious, Peierls visited it and sent "Klaus" his impressions. With an informality and comfort emulating the Americans, they now used first names in the salutations of letters, especially with colleagues who had shared the Los Alamos years. No more of the stiff British and Continental tradition of "Dear Fuchs," "Dear Bethe," "Dear Frisch," and so on.

> The location of the place is very nice. It is about 15 miles almost due south of Oxford with lovely country around, but few amenities other than those provided by the place itself. Such buildings as are there now are all still the permanent buildings of the [RAF] and they are very nice. For instance, the Skinners' house is a lovely house, although not quite of the standard of their house in Bristol. The officers' mess has lots of clubrooms which compare very favorably indeed with Fuller's or the Big House [at Los Alamos], both in space and standard.

Throughout the war, bombers took off from three runways, casting silhouettes on the town of Harwell a couple of miles away, rattling its thatched-roof houses. Prior to that, cherry orchards and cornfields had interlaced green meadows, horses and sheep grazing on the undulating hills of the chalk downs. Millennia ago, the Druids offered prayers and sacrifices in mystical rituals. One of their legacies was the "White Horse," a sleek minimalist graphic dug into the earth and outlined in white on the top of a chalk down. The graceful beauty of its striding form flowed seamlessly from the Iron Age into the Atomic.

The similarities with Los Alamos were obvious: isolated and self-contained, with older buildings reuseable for laboratories, atomic piles, housing, and dining, and a secluded setting for top secret research. For Director Cockcroft, other characteristics were useful: a runway on which his five children could ride their bikes, and the Downs where he could stroll along the pre-Roman road that ran along the crest.

At the request of a U.S. government eager to retain his services, Fuchs remained at Los Alamos for six months after the British mission departed. He compared the density of the ball of fire for the Trinity, Hiroshima, and Nagasaki explosions, examined the blast wave, optical data, and blast measurements at Trinity, and calculated the effect of the A-bomb on ships. When Hans Bethe stepped down from the Theoretical Division, he inherited the production of his volume on blast waves, the pressure emanating from the bomb's core that toppled buildings and bent steel.

Also while still in New Mexico, Fuchs advised the British when conflicts with the Americans arose. Acknowledging their past cooperation, the U.K., Canada, and the United States were trying to reach a cooperative agreement to formulate rules for declassifying some of the wartime research. At the same time, the McMahon Bill to oversee and restrict the availability of future atomic research gained momentum in Congress.

On Sunday, June 16, Fuchs set out for Washington, D.C., to see British officials. Afterward he visited Christel in Cambridge, where he showed slides he had taken of the Trinity test—the expansion of the ball of fire from six milliseconds to thirty seconds as it ascended into the sky, its skirt of dust on the ground, its radioactive glow. He borrowed a car from a friend, and the two drove to Cornell to see Hans Bethe. Then it was home to England.

Administrators preferred that he travel on the *Queen Mary*, a two-week ocean voyage, but Harwell was impatient. He flew by bomber from Montreal on June 28 and, as requested, arrived in Harwell on July 1 to attend Cockcroft's steering committee meeting at 9:30 a.m.

One of his first "duty calls" as division director was to Oscar Buneman and his wife, Mary. They had moved back from Berkeley, California, and the component of the Manhattan Project there a few weeks before. Klaus found them unpacking boxes in the run-down, semidetached home assigned to them.

Oscar was a theoretical physicist who worked under Fuchs and was almost Fuchs's doppelgänger: a German physicist who grew up in a non-Jewish, socialist family, was sent to jail by the Nazis for distributing anti-Nazi flyers, and left Germany in the early 1930s. He gained entrance to Britain as a political refugee to finish his studies. Mary was a pretty, vivacious hostess who developed a sweet spot for Fuchs, whom she had met in 1944, in New York, as she and Oscar traveled to Berkeley. At that time, he had been a pale, quiet man in a somber suit. Now she hardly recognized the confident and keen Fuchs, his pallid complexion bronzed by the New Mexico sun, his clothes more stylish—so changed. She also noticed that he walked with a new air of authority.

Now thirty-four and a naturalized British citizen, Fuchs was widely recognized as one of the top atomic physicists in the world. The refugee years, internment, poverty, and lower-status jobs faded as the auspicious future offered at Harwell lay before him.

Even so, one administrative matter still needed sorting out. The war's end had strengthened the government's attitude on security. In the fall of 1946, the "Standard Conditions of Government Contracts" was revised to stipulate that hiring naturalized citizens for classified work now required a more extensive background check by MI5. Straightaway, the counterspies opened an investigation on Fuchs. They were already mindful of their long-standing hesitancy over his past—in particular, the 1934 statement by the Gestapo on his communist activities and his friendship with Hans Kahle during internment. Peierls faced the same scrutiny. He had visited Russia in 1937, after all, and still had a Russian wife.

After heated wrangling within MI5 on past and present governmental attitudes toward security, the deputy director ordered mail inspections on both men, but they discovered nothing untoward. In early 1947, MI5 sent their security files back to the Registry in the basement of Leconfield House.

If MI5 had done more than a mail inspection—surveillance, bugs, or phone taps—it would have come up with nothing. Fuchs didn't follow through with the arrangement he and Raymond had made back in Santa Fe for contact in London. The risks were simply too great. For almost a year, tales of Russian spies had rocked three countries: in September 1945, in Canada, the defection of the Russian cipher clerk Igor Gouzenko; in November 1945, in the United States, the defection of American spy, Elizabeth Bentley; and in March 1946, in Britain, the arrest of the physicist Alan Nunn May for passing nuclear secrets, implicated by Gouzenko's documents. With the security agencies on high alert, Fuchs waited a full year before making contact in England, which was almost two years after his last meeting with Raymond.

By the summer of 1947, when Fuchs felt that it was reasonably safe to make contact, both his former liaison Jürgen Kuczynski and Hans Kahle had left for Germany. He managed to connect with Johanna Klopstech, an old friend probably going back to the Berlin underground days and someone he had worked with in the KPD ranks in London. On July 19, 1947, they walked through three-hundred-year-old Richmond Park, a famous red deer habitat established by King Charles I. Under the ancient, spreading oaks, on the sunny summer afternoon, Johanna gave Klaus the date, location, and signals for a rendezvous with a new agent.

The location was the Nags Head pub across from the Wood Green tube station, a distant suburb of London. On September 27, 1947, at 8:00 p.m., Fuchs was to meet his new handler, "Eugene." To be sure there was no surveillance, Eugene checked out the location a few days before. To reach Wood Green, both men traveled in the opposite direction, then doubled back by bus and underground. As the fog rolled in, Eugene exited the tube station a few minutes early and waited by a bus stop reading a newspaper. He kept an eye out for the man who could be Fuchs. He saw someone tall and thin, with "his head held high," come around the corner and go into the pub. Surely it was Fuchs. He continued to watch for anyone who could be following him, and once assured that he was not being watched, he opened the door to meet the aromas of beer and tobacco in the pub.

Klaus was on a stool at the bar, drinking a beer and reading a newspaper as prescribed; Eugene carried the agreed-upon red book. He sat farther down the bar and ordered a beer. They exchanged the conversational passwords. Soon, Klaus finished his beer and left, and after a minute Eugene followed, barely having enough time to enjoy the warmth of the pub. When Eugene caught up with the slow-walking Klaus, they exchanged names and started to get to know each other. Klaus handed Eugene some documents on the production of plutonium, and Eugene handed him cigarette paper (easily swallowed if necessary) with a list of questions, which Klaus read, memorized quickly, and handed back.

At this meeting, Eugene offered him two hundred pounds as gratitude and as extra cash because Moscow knew he was now financially responsible for his father, his brother in Switzerland, and his nephew. Klaus would accept only a hundred pounds and later said he took it to prove his "loyalty." Other than travel money early on, it was the only money he ever accepted.

They then set up the next meeting. This would be their routine: about every three to four months, 8:00 p.m., second Saturday of the month. If one of them missed a meeting, the backup was a month later. Throughout, Klaus never asked Eugene for his real name or any personal information.

MI5 had undertaken its security review of Fuchs without appreciating the expanding scope of the research at Harwell. The public objective, and what MI5 knew, was to harness nuclear energy for domestic use. Harwell had an in-house pile (or nuclear reactor) to experiment with producing plutonium for this purpose. This pile had another use as well: plutonium harvested for energy production could just as well be harvested for use in an atomic bomb. Prime Minister Attlee kept this program a deep secret for years.

The British thought they had secured access to American scientific technology through the 1943 Quebec Agreement. Signed by Churchill and Roosevelt, it promised that the two countries would share in "full and effective cooperation." Under Oppenheimer at Los Alamos, research conducted with this open-access policy created an atomic bomb against high odds. The British scientists, instrumental in the ultimate success, had paid for the access by waiving all patent rights.

But the U.S. Army now had another objective—to preserve its monopoly on atomic energy. And with the war over and Roosevelt dead, the U.S. government easily relegated the Quebec Agreement to the past. It ordered a report on the extent of the British physicists' knowledge, the September 1945 report concluding,

> The extent of the technical knowledge of the Project by British personnel cannot readily be determined. . . . It is safer to assume, and more nearly correct, that everything which is common knowledge in this laboratory is known also to the British. . . . This full knowledge of the local project cannot be doubted [because the British mission had] general access to (1) the Document Room, (2) the various local sites, and (3) the organized meetings of the local project.

In August 1946, Congress enacted the McMahon Bill to reshape the future. A colleague in the United States wrote to Fuchs of the demise of the collaboration between the allies:

> As a result of the passage of the McMahon Bill, there has been a considerable tightening up of all access to information relating to Atomic Energy. For instance, the few people remaining at Los Alamos will only be allowed access to the material previously

available to them, but they are not to be allowed access to new material. This, of course, is not really serious at present, but it indicates the way things are developing.

The new U.S. policy meant that the British scientific program would require more effort than appreciated at first. Nonetheless, buoyed by wartime wisdom and peacetime enthusiasm, the British moved forward on their own to initiate what would prove to be a huge industrial endeavor: reactors, diffusion plants, and high-speed centrifuges and compressors. Harwell was one of three main divisions in the section for atomic energy under the Ministry of Supply.

Fuchs's Theoretical Division with its fifteen to twenty physicists was integral to the success of the overall effort. They solved whatever theoretical problems arose, worked on the diffusion plant under construction, and pursued fundamental research on nuclear reactors for the peaceful use of atomic energy. He committed himself to running the division.

As he had done at Los Alamos, he took a personal hand in every dimension—"ubiquitous," one person labeled him—from committees for the design of the Windscale Piles, to the diffusion plant, to nuclear power. Construction of the actual bomb was assigned to another division in the Ministry of Supply, and Fuchs was the only Harwell scientist deeply involved with that effort. He kept his ties to American scientists as well, through declassification conferences for which he was a "responsible reviewer," making the initial determination on what research from the Manhattan Project to declassify, a job involving no review of current research.

But when he traveled to the United States for a declassification conference in 1947, new information was part of his mission. Someone had asked him to glean what he could about American progress on reactors and bombs. He brought back invaluable intelligence for the British—and for the Russians: the latest developments in producing the hydrogen bomb.

Fuchs's approach to running the division earned mixed reviews. One physicist in the division, Derek Behrens (Mary Buneman's cousin), saw him as encouraging researchers to develop their ideas rather than simply carrying out specific tasks, the same sort of "curiosity-oriented research" Oppenheimer had promoted at Los Alamos. Another one, Brian Flowers, who eventually took over the Theoretical Division, turned Behrens's opinion upside down: "very authoritarian over silly things; bit of a megalomaniac. He took interesting problems for himself, he thought he alone could do something. He thought he was better." Rudi Peierls, observing from Birmingham, saw a director who energetically intervened if a staff member was treated unfairly or, on the other hand, not working efficiently.

As far as we know, Oscar Buneman never recorded his judgment, but Mary did. She saw none of the "opinionated conceit" noticed by colleagues like Flowers.

But all of the disparate assessments had some element of truth. Fuchs was kind and unselfish with friends and colleagues. At the same time, with ideas, he could be rigid and intellectually arrogant, and in this context generosity did not always hold. Rudi advised him to be less aggressive and more polite in his critiques.

In 1948, Rudi Peierls and John Cockcroft weighed in on Fuchs as a researcher by proposing him for membership in the Olympus of British science, the Royal Society. They cited his contributions to quantum theory as well as his pioneering work on atomic energy, stating, "There is hardly a theoretical problem in the atomic energy field in which our knowledge has not been widened considerably by his work, or by work done under his guidance and inspiration."

In May 1948, three junior researchers at Harwell were fired because of links to the Communist Party. At the same time, Klaus missed his first meeting with Eugene, who had sat on a bar stool, sweaty and anxious, waiting. He missed the backup a month later too. Moscow Center attributed it to the firings and alerted London that Fuchs could be under surveillance and might even have been interrogated. Rather than possibly lose him, Moscow began plans to "remove" him to Russia to do research there.

He did arrive for the meeting that October and excused his absences by citing the need to be at Harwell, where the work had focused on readying the launch of a new reactor. He missed another too, and Eugene suffered again. Eugene decided to try a new system for rescheduling a meeting. He identified a house in Kew on a corner across from Kew Gardens where Klaus was to throw a copy of the magazine *Men Only* over a fence between the second and third of four trees. On the tenth page, he would mark a new date for a meeting if an interruption had occurred. Klaus tried it out once to make sure it worked. He never used it, because Eugene decided it was too risky. The owner of the house belonged to another network, and it was against the rules to mix separate networks.

Geographic remoteness, along with the gas rationing that lingered into peacetime, meant that those living and working at Harwell played out their life's dramas largely within the enclosure. Squabbles, promotions or being passed over, and suspected affairs buzzed around the place as the pressures mounted. Relief valves for the increasingly close community were the drama society, band, orchestra, and choir, which made the most of the exceptional degree of musicality among the physicists. The wives, largely minding children, hanging out the wash, and finagling to stretch ration coupons, organized dances, plays, musical events, and "beer nights." Brushing aside Mary's nudge for him to play the violin, Klaus confined his rhythm to the dance floor.

But unlike his remoteness at Los Alamos, where he was mostly a social tagalong, at Harwell he made friends. He often stopped by the Bunemans' for a drink and sometimes stayed for dinner, expressing great fondness for Mary's cooking. The younger Buneman son, Micky, remembered him as "kind, generous, quiet, tall, slim, underfed and very intellectual." Mary remembered a hesitant Klaus, reluctant to leave, stifling yawns, then admitting, "I had better be getting along."

Mary's cousin Derek Behrens, who was more like a brother to her, would often stop by as well. The two men became good friends, so much so that Klaus served as best man at Derek's wedding.

In 1945, when friends had gone to Europe to scour for scientists and secret facilities, Klaus asked them to search the concentration camps for his father and his nephew and namesake. As he left Los Alamos in 1946, he learned they were alive, both living in Frankfurt in the American military zone. He wrote to officials in London about their coming to England. He hadn't seen his father in thirteen years, and he had never met the boy.

For non-Jewish nationals to exit Germany was almost impossible. The Allied military governments examined everyone for a Nazi stain, and Emil's file stated that he had belonged to an organization that assisted Nazi families. What it was and what he had done weren't clear, although the military government later wrote that it had wrongly classified him. Nevertheless, correcting the record so that he could gain permission to leave was a Herculean task.

Klaus made up some work-related justification for a trip to Germany in May 1947. The British were wary that the Russians might kidnap a top scientist, so he traveled under the assumed name of Strauss. He reported back that his father wasn't in Frankfurt, seeming to imply that he didn't see him. He didn't report that he saw his brother in a TB sanatorium in Switzerland, or that he met Emil while his father was in Bad Pyrmont for a Quaker meeting. Emil remembered Klaus dressed in an American army uniform—the reason for the uniform or its origins unspecified. But with Pyrmont only about fifteen miles from the East German border, maybe it was a safety precaution on Klaus's part. Perhaps he wasn't supposed to be there.

Surviving the war—evading the Gestapo, dodging bombs in Berlin, and eking out a living by selling (illegally) his interpretation of the Bible—had taken all of Emil's grit. With no other family around, he and his six-year-old grandson stayed with friends. Given that his friends were often targeted and arrested by the Gestapo, they had moved every few months.

When the bombs fell on Berlin, the diminutive sixty-six-year-old pastor had to prod the robust and resistant boy to the basement shelter.

Eager to find safety, in 1944, Emil answered a newspaper ad for free room and board in an Austrian village.

Gortipohl, five hundred miles to the south of Berlin, sat nestled in a long valley dotted with hamlets and surrounded by ten-thousand-foot alpine peaks. With the local men at the front, the old farmers needed field hands, so grandfather and grandson made their way. While Emil traveled back and forth to Berlin, the boisterous, by now ten-year-old herded cows on the mountainside during the summer and attended a one-room school during the winter while also tending a small plot of potatoes.

It was a harsh life, and the isolated location, which should have suggested safety, actually presented a danger. Gortipohl was only twenty kilometers from the border with Switzerland, and the underground resistance led by a shoemaker from a nearby village smuggled Jews and political victims across the border. Young Klaus climbed up the mountainside with food for those hiding and waiting in a cattle hut. Twice he guided a family to the border when the regular smuggler didn't show up.

In the spring of 1945, German soldiers rolled in to wipe up resisters and blow the dam of a large reservoir, assuring a flooded valley to block a thrust by Allied troops. The resistance stripped out the explosives, though, allowing French Moroccan troops to invade. Capping the final moments of his wartime experience, young Klaus escorted a Nazi official at gunpoint to the resistance leaders.

The boy and his grandfather survived, but with most rail lines nonfunctional it took them six arduous months—including thirty-six hours crammed in a cattle wagon—to make their way to Frankfurt. What they found was a city of skeletal buildings, mountains of rubble, and little food, shelter, or clothing.

Emil suffered from exhaustion and starvation, and his friends feared that if he couldn't get away from Germany for a rest, "it will be the end." Nevertheless, he found a niche lecturing to labor unions on religion while he persistently applied for visas to visit Gerhard, still in a TB clinic in

Switzerland, and Klaus, now working in England. As was his wont, he succeeded with both, spending a couple of weeks with Gerhard and four months with Klaus in the fall of 1947, much of the time teaching at a Quaker center near Birmingham.

Emil's ultimate objective was America: to lecture and to see Christel and her three children. Unfortunately, the U.S. stance in 1948 was "Immigration for Germans is not yet open." A special U.S. education program provided a visa for Emil only, but he refused to leave young Klaus behind. Eventually, they both received visas, and, in 1948, the two traveled to England and then to New York, with Klaus paying all their travel expenses.

Before Emil left, the University of Leipzig in the Russian zone had offered him a position as a professor of religion, but he declined, saying that he wasn't willing to separate from his children, all of whom lived outside Germany. The success of his lecture tour made Emil contemplate trying to immigrate to the United States with his grandson. He told friends that Klaus was thinking of it too, to be near Christel and her children.

But during Emil's visit with his daughter at Christmas, a letter arrived from Leipzig, saying that the university wanted him anyway. Here was an opportunity to do reconciliation work through religious teachings in the Russian zone. He told friends that he would never be satisfied if he didn't grab the offer. By mid-June, Emil had firmed up plans to become professor of Christian ethics and the sociology of religion in Leipzig.

In Cambridge, Massachusetts, he had watched as Christel sat despondent for long periods gazing out of the window. Eventually, her husband committed her to a psychiatric hospital for what Emil described as a "nervous breakdown." He worried that his being there had awakened painful memories of the prewar and war years. She hadn't suffered as the other family members had, but she had the frustration of failure when she had tried to save them.

From 1947 to 1949, Klaus and Eugene met about six times. During that period, Klaus handed Eugene ninety documents on such highly sensitive areas as the theory behind the hydrogen bomb, the plans for an isotope separation plant, and the blueprints for nuclear reactors. Most of the time their meetings were short, with little time to talk. One cool and cloudy Saturday in February 1949, they sat on a bench in Putney Bridge Park near the Spotted Horse pub—keeping a stranger's distance between them— and chatted a bit about personal matters. Usually Moscow Center had more questions for Eugene to ask than time allowed—nothing but business. But Eugene wanted more and initiated the conversation.

When he asked Klaus why he had never married, Fuchs told him, "I think about it from time to time. But you know I'm walking through a minefield. One false move and it will all blow up. I can accept the worse-case scenario but I can't involve a wife and children."

Then he added, "Furthermore, to have a family in England is not part of my plans for the future."

Then he added with a smile, "I'd like to help the Soviet Union until it is able to test its atomic bomb. Then I want to go home to East Germany where I have friends. There I can get married and work in peace and quiet. That's my dream." His comments to Eugene certainly suggested that his future plans centered on Germany.

Klaus and Eugene met again soon, at the beginning of April. They ended the meeting by setting up the next one for June 25, and a backup on July 2. Klaus then left for the Mediterranean coast on vacation with his boss Herbert Skinner and wife, Erna, with whom he had become very friendly. While there, he developed bronchial pneumonia—certainly exacerbated by asthma and heavy smoking—and struggled to recover. He spent most of June in bed, nursed by Erna Skinner at her house.

With the three junior researchers fired from Harwell a year earlier for communist ties and spies exposed in Canada, the United States, and Britain, all of which had been covered in the press, Fuchs was wise to lie low. Another reason for increased caution had reached the KGB by way of William Weisband, a naturalized American and double agent who spoke fluent Russian. He worked in the decoding unit for Venona in Arlington, Virginia, and advised on translations. He had passed details of Venona to Moscow Center early on. By late 1948, he could tell them that the decoders were making progress. No specific names yet.

At the same time, KGB records indicate that it worried about the possible arrest of Raymond, Klaus's contact in New York, who knew his real name and background. Raymond had been increasingly exposed since the summer of 1947, when he appeared before a grand jury in connection with the confession of the spy Elizabeth Bentley. The FBI questioned him again a year later. Now the KGB was pressuring Raymond to leave the country illegally. But he wouldn't; he had fallen in love.

Toward the end of July 1949, Fuchs's father and nephew arrived at his new prefab at 17 Hillside Drive, the last house in the row, just as Klaus was moving in. He entertained his family with picnics and dinners with friends, but these occasions made Klaus nervous, especially when Henry Arnold, Harwell's security chief, was a guest. Mary Buneman was there, and she sensed the tension, which was for good reason. Emil was not particularly circumspect, and Klaus was never sure what tales of the Nazi times and Klaus's alignment he might tell.

The conversation within the family was mostly about the future, though. Emil realized that if young Klaus came with him to Leipzig, he might never be able to get him out again. The boy's schooling was an issue, especially after a very spotty education at thirteen different schools during the war. One option was a British boarding school, with Uncle Klaus becoming in loco parentis and covering the costs, something his thrifty lifestyle would make possible.

The three visited some schools, and on the way back to Harwell from one of them, Emil decided that they were too rigid. In Cambridge, Massachusetts, while Emil lectured, young Klaus had lived with Aunt Christel and, along with her children, had attended the progressive Shady Hill School, where he had thrived. They would both go back to Germany, perhaps with young Klaus attending the denazified Odenwaldschule. Sitting in the backseat, the boy saw his uncle's shoulders immediately relax. Something about caring for his young nephew had made Klaus very tense.

Emil had another concern and wanted Klaus's opinion: Would his move to Leipzig be a problem given Klaus's position at Harwell? Klaus said he didn't think so, but he would speak with Henry Arnold. The next evening, Klaus reported that Arnold saw no difficulties with Emil's move to the Russian zone.

Time and events showed this response to be peculiar. Klaus brought the same news to Arnold three months later. On that occasion, Arnold advised that they both think about it and then meet again, at which point Arnold quickly informed MI5.

Did Klaus really ask Arnold in July? This leaves the question of why he asked him again in October. Or did he simply give the answer that his father wanted to hear, knowing that Emil had his mind set and could stir up problems?

IV

RECONNAISSANCE

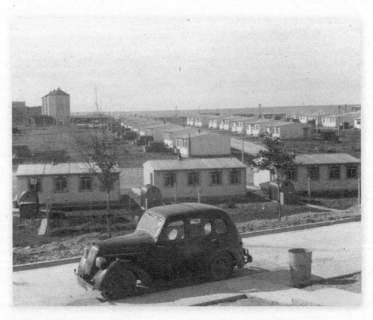

Prefabs at Harwell, 1940s

CHAPTER 15

Suspects, London, September 1949

KLAUS FUCHS'S FIFTEEN YEARS IN BRITAIN HAD TAKEN MANY PATHS, BUT IT TOOK Arthur Martin of MI5, sitting in downtown London in Leconfield House, only a couple of days to scour them in his security file. Now it was time for him to determine if the compilation of rumors and innuendos confirmed that this respected scientist was indeed Rest, the man who had shared the atomic secrets with Soviet Russia.

He composed a note, "Comparison of evidence from source with facts known of Klaus FUCHS," to evaluate how well Fuchs's personal history fit the evidence drawn from Venona, the top secret decoding project run by the U.S. Army Signal Intelligence Service:

1. Male?—yes

2. In US from March 1944 to July 1944?—yes, posted to Oak Ridge in August

3. Had contact with MSN report?—no document yet but probably British

4. Had a sister in US?—Probably

5. Details of the scientific project?—if project is atomic energy, they fit

6. Nationality?—yes, naturalized British

7. Assumption about transferring back to the UK?—fits but not conclusive

8. Movements of sister in October 1944?—fits if sister lives in Cambridge MA

Later that day, September 5, 1949, he melded his appraisal into a cable for the British embassy in Washington. It began by correcting the name of the individual in question—it was Klaus, not Karl. "Your para 1. Presume identical with Emil Julius Klaus Fuchs." He then continued with Fuchs's biographical data, stating that he had found a letter in Fuchs's file from a Mrs. Klaus, signed Kristel, sent from Harvard University. He concluded, "Consider evidence against Fuchs very strong but not conclusive. All above information may be passed to the FBI with request for report on 'Mrs. Klaus.'" He added that since Fuchs's return from the United States, he was a senior researcher at Harwell, the Ministry of Supply's main nuclear research center.

Martin sent this information to his boss, the director of B Branch, Dick White, with augmentation: summaries of what Martin labeled "adverse traces"—the incriminating information on Fuchs's communist past.

1933—Landed UK. German Consulate Bristol inform Police that Fuchs was a member of the German Communist Party.

1940—Interned in UK and later Canada where he was reported to be very friendly with prominent Communist Hans Kahle.

1943—Source Kaspar reported that he belonged to the German Communist Party but, unlike his brother Gerhard, was never a prominent member. Gerhard Fuchs worked in the German Communist Party's secret apparat.

There was good reason for Martin's excluding "adverse traces" from the cable to the embassy: These facts were *not* for the eyes of the FBI. It put Fuchs's security clearances in the spotlight, which might suggest grave lapses on the part of MI5. No need to tell all yet. Conclusions were still preliminary.

Just days into the investigation, a good part of Washington was searching for answers. The security staff at the British embassy, along with the FBI, was prying into every possible file to dig out the spy. All the while more code names tumbled out of the blocks of numbers in the Venona messages, Americans all. For the FBI, Fuchs was but one of many potential suspects in a Russian network.

The almost daily cables from both sides of the ocean threw out new leads, asked for follow-up, and occasionally closed a loop. They read with traditional British aplomb, inadequate to mask the urgency and tension that strained this case.

To narrow the odds on Fuchs, Martin needed a better understanding of the MSN report given to the Russians. For an expert with a high-level security clearance, the natural choice was Michael Perrin, a chemist by training and chief deputy at the Ministry of Supply in the atomic energy section with oversight for Harwell. It was an obvious role after his work coordinating the British bomb project before and during the war. He was fully conversant with Fuchs and the other members of the British mission. Besides that, people trusted his integrity and judgment. His father, an Episcopal bishop, had instilled modesty and an interest in others. He was easy to like, and people naturally turned to him.

Perrin's name was familiar to Martin. He had just read the 1944 exchange in Fuchs's security file between MI5 and Perrin on Fuchs's stay in the United States. Perrin's concern then, vis-à-vis Fuchs's past, was not to "slip up in any way" with the Americans. MI5's concern was to hide Fuchs's possible communist "proclivities." Now, five years after the fact,

Perrin's insights into the murky Venona messages might reveal whether his concern was merited. Martin set up an appointment.

On September 6, an MI5 team of Martin, his counterpart in surveillance, James Robertson, and their boss at B Branch, Dick White, met with Perrin in room 448 at Shell Mex House. The blockish thirteen-story white Art Deco building was home to the Ministry of Supply and only a couple of miles from MI5's location near Hyde Park Corner. Its war wounds from bombing still lingered, but the flow of the Thames, which it fronted, lent a sense of calm and stability.

White opened the meeting by disclosing the source of the information to Perrin, although the chief deputy probably knew through a back channel. White stressed that the top secret nature of the decryptions made it impossible to use them in court. He had two questions for Perrin: Could atomic energy be the project at issue in all these machinations, and could Fuchs be Rest, the man who shared the secrets?

Perrin looked at the fragmentary messages and recognized the paper as "Effect of Fluctuation in the Flow of Nitrogen," part 3 of MSN-12, written by Klaus Fuchs and published on June 6 in New York. He advised that this, together with the term "diffusion method," a process to produce enriched uranium to use in an atomic bomb, indicated almost certainly that the targeted project was atomic energy. The comments about British scientists returning to England to set up their own plant carried weight too. Perrin didn't think the Americans knew of it, but Fuchs, given his specialty in diffusion, could have guessed about the request for his being transferred back to the U.K. Weighing negatively, Perrin explained that the clue in the Venona message on the U.S.-U.K. agreement on atomic energy and the 1941 Atlantic Charter was wrong. The agreement on atomic energy had been signed by Churchill and Roosevelt later, at the Quebec Conference, in 1943.

As for Fuchs's being Rest, Perrin considered it possible. The man's general movements fit those in the messages. Important, though, was that Fuchs had not gone to Oak Ridge to work on diffusion. In this the FBI was wrong. Fuchs had gone to Los Alamos to work on the atomic bomb.

White, Robertson, and Martin left with the understanding that Perrin would follow up on loose threads: the MSN-12 paper; its circulation; Fuchs's movements in the United States; and Fuchs's family, especially his sister. The FBI, White emphasized, must be informed of all outcomes.

Martin's partner, James Robertson, was an expert on surveillance, one of MI5's best. He devised the where, when, and how of tracking a suspect, in this case with the hope of catching Fuchs's handing over top secret documents. With a taboo on using the Venona source in court, and thus exposing the existence of that top secret decoding effort, MI5 needed concrete evidence of spying to prove its case.

Robertson and Martin were the lead team, the ground sleuth and the paper sleuth, men who were as different as their talents. Robertson was very much the British gentleman—the right schools and a master of the hunt, an especially appropriate status given that "Fuchs" was German for fox. He was the outside operational face to Martin's inside interpreter of information.

Success for this very human hunt lay with a comprehensive surveillance web. The one that Robertson and Martin plotted that afternoon revolved around almost every minute of Fuchs's day, every day. An inspection of all mail to and from his home and office; a phone tap in both places; around-the-clock physical surveillance when he left Harwell; a review of all bank records; and bugs in his home and office. Robertson had two choices for that—a microphone, conditional on the layout of Fuchs's house, or something called an SF, a small washer placed in the phone that didn't allow the connection to cut off. If he was spying, he had to pass documents to someone sometime, probably away from Harwell. They would watch twenty-four hours a day, and they would check every contact he made as well as documents he handled. Did he keep them longer than needed, did he take them outside Harwell, could they check for unidentified fingerprints? An effective surveillance net meant no holes.

MI5's director general cautiously approved the plan. His uppermost worry: Fuchs must not sense eyes on him. Safety first, speed second.

Warrants for mail, phone, and bugging were the purview of the Home

Office. Robertson prepared a one-page, single-spaced summary of the basic data on Fuchs's life. He passed it through his boss, Dick White, and the director general. The basics were these:

Emil Julius Klaus Fuchs was born in Rüsselsheim, Germany, on December 29, 1911. He came to the U.K. in September 1933 to study physics at the University of Bristol and received a PhD in 1937. He moved to Edinburgh, Scotland, and received an ScD there in 1939. He was interned in Canada in 1940 after the war broke out and was sent back to the U.K. in January 1941. Later that year he moved to Birmingham to work with Professor Rudolf Peierls, where he began research on the atomic bomb. In 1943, when British scientists went to the United States to aid in research there, Fuchs was part of the team stationed in New York City. In 1944, he was transferred to Los Alamos. Throughout this period, MI5 examined his security record, mindful of the information from the German consulate in 1934, his friendship with Hans Kahle in the internment camp, and the informant Kaspar's 1943 report on his communist leanings. The chief constables in Bristol, Edinburgh, and Birmingham, however, reported no problems. MI5 mail warrants in 1943 and 1947 had produced nothing. During the fortnight of surveillance in 1943, Fuchs didn't receive even a single letter.

To justify the warrants to the Home Office, Robertson explained that a member of the British mission had passed information to the Soviets. Fuchs was under "considerable suspicion" partly because of previous communist views. With his key position at Harwell, he now required scrutiny. The warrants were granted.

The details in the summary were sound, but a discrepancy piqued Valentine Vivian, the deputy chief at MI5's sister agency, MI6. Had Martin, he asked, "queried the Christian name or formed any ideas of your own as to how and why 'Emil Julius Klaus Fuchs' should have turned into 'Karl'"? Martin didn't know and suggested asking the security officers at the embassy in Washington to search their records because they had originally used that particular Christian name.

The instincts of the man from MI6 were astute, but his aim was askew.

The real question was this: How did "Klaus Emil Julius Fuchs" transform into "Emil Julius Klaus Fuchs"?

The answer was that on September 24, 1933, when Fuchs crossed the channel and arrived at the port town of Folkestone, England, he was Klaus Emil Julius, as he had been for his entire twenty-one years. Within a month of his landing, a clerk accidentally transposed the Christian names on his official registration form. From that moment on, no matter the documents that he signed as "Klaus E. J. Fuchs," he was officially Emil Fuchs (his father's name) because his official registration card stated so. It took MI5 seventeen years to make the adjustment. The FBI never did.

Perrin had answers for Martin and Robertson the next day when the three met at Shell Mex House. A search through the records had reminded Perrin of details for the British mission's assignment in the United States. To carry out the U.K.'s agreement on atomic energy made at the Quebec Conference in 1943, British experts on diffusion arrived in New York City at the end of that year. Only four remained there after March 1944. These were Fuchs, Rudi Peierls, Tony Skyrme, and Frank Kearton. All four had received a copy of MSN-12, as had six Americans in the Manhattan office. Staff sent the rest of the copies back to the U.K.

Perrin outlined the movements of these four from March through July 1944. Their movements matched those mentioned in the Venona messages, although Peierls more loosely than the other three. Martin had already learned that Peierls's was the other name intelligence officers in Washington had proposed for "Rest," simultaneously with Fuchs's a few weeks before. A German émigré, Peierls had hired Fuchs to work with him in Birmingham in 1941.

Martin duly recorded Perrin's frank opinions on the two new names. Of Skyrme, he wrote,

A young mathematician probably not more than 32 now. A "queer bird." Wore his hair long and had an odd taste in clothes.

Was always getting into scrapes. Celebrated his arrival in New York by getting arrested for some minor offence and spending his first night in a cell. An old Etonian. Believed to have gone to Cambridge on his return from U.S. and certainly not engaged in government work now.

Of Kearton, he wrote a more sympathetic description,

His duties were purely liaison. He would not have been considered for transfer to the U.K. to work on Diffusion. He was now a senior scientist at COURTLAULDS living in Foleshill Road in Coventry. He is British and, in Mr. Perrin's view, it is practically inconceivable that he could be disloyal.

Martin sent Washington a long cable summarizing Perrin's information. Washington replied with its own revelations. It was almost definite that Kristel Fuchs was Mrs. Robert Bloch Heinemann, who lived in Cambridge, Massachusetts. (MI5 was ignorant of her becoming "Christel.") Meanwhile, information dug up by the FBI on the other three physicists as the FBI searched for any possible sisters streamed in to Martin.

Robertson's surveillance plan included two personnel requests. Both focused on Harwell. One was the MI5 operative William James "Jim" Skardon, who would concentrate on surveillance at Harwell: mail, phone, and visual observation. The other was Wing Commander Henry Arnold, chief of security there. Arnold was a perfect source through his current position and his past experiences. As a wing commander during the war, he had worked on a secret project with scientists to destroy Nazi dams.

Robertson had a long list of needs from Arnold: Fuchs's movement patterns around Harwell and frequency of trips to London; his character, habits, and acquaintances; a full personal description; upcoming trips to

London; handling of top secret documents at Harwell with the possibility to check for fingerprints; the layout of Fuchs's house, including any photography equipment there.

Directly observing Fuchs at Harwell was almost impossible. With the facility carved out of the RAF's airfield, the largely barren fields gave no cover. A chain-link fence topped with three strands of barbed wire protected the scientific community from intrusion; loose rolls of barbed wire surrounded that. Armed security guards, stationed at the four gates, closely controlled the people, cars, and trucks entering and leaving. Adjacent to the compound, just outside the fence, perfectly aligned rows of newly constructed aluminum prefabs created a residential area. Any effort to observe someone's movements would be quickly detected. Robertson needed the help of Henry Arnold at Harwell. It could be done fairly easily. Arnold and Fuchs already knew each other well.

In his early sixties, Arnold was dapper and handsome, friendly and entertaining. An amateur actor, a "superb" mimic, and a cellist, he could easily entertain with a well-told story. Equally evident were his talents as a sympathetic listener, which Arnold coupled with gentle and kindly advice. He encouraged those who sought his counsel, "Spit it all out in Uncle's hand"—him being Uncle of course.

Arnold had a philosophy of security that meshed with his avuncular nature. To the scientists, including Fuchs, he explained that it was

> [his] policy to carry out security in a spirit of trust, friendship and understanding of each individual, and that without such a basis on which to build, physical security controls could never operate successfully.

But beneath Arnold's exterior as a talented raconteur, sympathetic listener, and kindly adviser, there was the dedicated professional who studied Hegel, Engels, and Marx to understand the loyalties of the believers. His warmth also hid certain prejudices:

> By far the most important part of my work was to counter, by
> every means in my power and by personal influence, the forego-
> ing beliefs which might exist in the minds of those employed at
> Harwell and whom I had selected for study.

That is, seeing himself adept at psychological profiling, he watched carefully for those who stood out as different, such as growing up in another
country and being influenced by different "moral and political standards,"
communism being a primary one. A tinge of anti-Semitism was there too, if
not directly with Arnold, then in his office. Someone at Harwell thought
Fuchs was Jewish and printed that word in the margin on a typed Harwell
employment form.

Arnold intentionally suggested unusual security precautions to watch
for reactions out of the norm. He once asked the scientists to leave the key
to their safe with him when they were away. Most scoffed or laughed, but
Fuchs, Arnold noted, willingly agreed.

Fuchs was just the kind of person to grab Arnold's attention, as he said,
one of those "people of alien origin," a prejudicial attitude hardly peculiar
to Arnold in that day.

The relationship between Arnold and Fuchs—one that had a hand in shap-
ing history—began from their first days at Harwell. Within a couple of
months of their both arriving at Harwell, in 1946, Arnold invited Fuchs to
his house for coffee and after-dinner drinks. Before Fuchs arrived, another
couple whom Arnold hardly knew but who lived in the Staff Club, as did
Fuchs then, knocked on the door to bring him a gift of some special cheese.
He invited them in; Fuchs came a little later; and they all chatted. Arnold
assumed that Fuchs had engineered their visit because he didn't want to be
alone with him and his wife.

The episode was awkward, and Arnold didn't wish to repeat it. "In the
early days," he later related, "[Fuchs] was a strangely silent person who

seldom uttered, except when a question was put to him and then, if possible, he answered in a monosyllable." Not a comfortable dinner guest, but someone Arnold wanted to befriend. He tried a different tack.

Arnold lived three doors away from the Bunemans and throughout the next few years dropped in, knowing that Fuchs also came by frequently for a drink. With Arnold's being a bit leery of naturalized citizens, drinks and dinners at the Bunemans' allowed him to keep an eye on two of them, Klaus and Oscar, plus Derek Behrens, who had associated with communists at Cambridge. What Arnold might have missed was that in keeping with the fickle enthusiasms of youth, and the swirling political currents of the times, Derek's interest in communism arose mainly because, at their meetings, the communists had the best sandwiches.

Arnold wasn't the only observer. Even with the conviviality, Mary noted a "distinct" reserve between Oscar and Klaus. It seemed at first that Oscar avoided getting too close socially. Even though neither was comfortable, she eventually realized that it was Klaus who created the distance. He dodged talking to Oscar alone except with regard to the Theoretical Division. To her, it didn't make any sense.

Mary knew that the government's 1940 policy of internment had caught up Oscar and Klaus—along with the thirty thousand other "enemy aliens." She knew that the government had shipped both of them to internment camps in Canada. She knew that to keep away from Nazis in the camps, Oscar had requested to go to a "Kosher camp," even though he wasn't Jewish. She didn't know that they sailed on the same ship to the same camp—or that it was Klaus who had finagled Oscar and other political refugees onto the kosher camp roster.

At Harwell, Klaus reported his former Social Democratic affiliation in Germany on government forms. Oscar Buneman knew the hidden side of Fuchs's life. Mary had no inkling, but it seems that Henry Arnold did.

Around the time that Arnold invited Fuchs to his house in 1946, he contacted MI5. His initial memo didn't indicate any misgivings, but it did set off an unexpected chain of events, all carefully delineated in Fuchs's security file during the winter. Through it, Martin and Robertson learned that even back then Arnold didn't consider Fuchs's security record "above reproach."

When Arnold arrived at Harwell in 1946, the scientists had a lax attitude toward security, and he quickly instituted discipline. One of his first requests to them was to inform him of their travel plans. As instructed, Fuchs wrote to Arnold to say that he would be in London on October 5, 1946, for a lecture of the Physics Club at the Royal Society.

Arnold forwarded Fuchs's note to the MI5 official John Collard in London, asking if Collard wished to receive such information. A confused Collard responded that he wasn't sure why Arnold had written: Did he question Fuchs's integrity, or did he want to use Fuchs as an informant? In either case, Collard explained, he saw no need to act because Arnold had also talked to an MI5 official in field operations.

A few days later Collard had second thoughts, and he entered a note in Fuchs's folder for the B Branch analyst Michael Serpell, one of the many who had reviewed Fuchs's various clearances during the war. Collard suggested that Serpell contact the field operative about his conversation with Arnold. He also mentioned that Fuchs had just arrived back in the U.K. and was engaged in work at Harwell "of extreme importance." This was news to Serpell.

Serpell spoke with the field operative whose information contained an unsettling sentence: "Arnold realizes from some quarter that FUCHS has or had a communist background." This was the fall of 1946. Arnold had known Fuchs for only a couple of months, and he wasn't privy to his security file. No one asked Arnold how he came by this tip.

The incident didn't stop there. From previous security reviews, Serpell knew the Gestapo's allegations against Fuchs. What alarmed him was his new position at Harwell. Serpell wrote a piercing summary of the risks associated with employing Fuchs in a top secret research facility:

> The facts of this case seem to be that FUCHS in his youth acted
> as a communist penetration agent in the NSDAP. That he should

have begun his political career in this undercover style seems to
me to be of considerable significance at the present time. It is also
apparent that as late as 1942 he was engaged in some communist
activities in a refugee group at Birmingham. What does not
seem to be conclusively established is that he was the Claus
Fuchs mentioned as having been a close friend of Hans KAHLE
in a Canadian internment camp. Although the subject of this file
was interned, it was only for a short time (May 1940 to January
1941) and there does not seem to be any direct statement that his
internment was in Canada. However, the identification is probable, and, if it is correct, the association with KAHLE may be
regarded as particularly dangerous, since KAHLE is known to
have acted as an OGPU representative in this country.

To Serpell, the probability that Kahle, a member of the Soviet secret
police, the OGPU, would have recruited Fuchs was high.

He recognized that the British government didn't see "the dangers
inherent in the employment of such people as FUCHS" during the war, but
with the war over he assumed that the danger to security would be a prime
issue. Compelled by this broadside, the head of countersubversion in B
Branch, Roger Hollis, finally requested verification that "Claus Fuchs" in
internment and "Klaus Fuchs" at Harwell were the same person. The answer:
they were.

With that answer, Hollis immediately disputed Serpell's speculation on the Fuchs-Kahle relationship. He argued that the government
had shipped many Nazis to Canada and mistakenly included a few anti-
Nazis. For Fuchs and Kahle to become friends was hardly surprising,
"surrounded as they must have been by Nazis who would have been
uncongenial to them."

Serpell's memo also implicated Rudi Peierls at the University of Birmingham. Peierls consulted at Harwell, was friends with Fuchs, had a Russian wife, and visited Russia in 1937.

Serpell's attack ruffled staff at MI5. Concerned only with security in the postwar era and not science, junior officers pushed to "divorce" Fuchs "from all contact with atomic energy" and no longer use Peierls as a consultant. The chiefs thought there was "nothing of a positive nature" against either of them. Minutes, charged with emotions, flew back and forth into early 1947.

Finally, on January 14, 1947, Hollis ordered warrants on the mail of Fuchs and Peierls. Clerks dutifully hand copied all letters sent to the two physicists for the next two months. A few with sealing wax went unopened. Nothing of importance to MI5 turned up.

Arnold never knew about the buzz in MI5 caused by his initial request to Collard.

With Arnold's suspicions about Fuchs since 1946, Robertson didn't need much context for briefing him on surveillance of Fuchs at Harwell. In their first meeting, he went right to the point: MI5 "had recently received information throwing suspicion upon one of a limited number of British scientists, the particular individual in question having not yet been identified. Fuchs was one of the number." And he warned: Only a handful of people know about this. Tell no one else. Do not make any inquiries. Put little information on paper.

Arnold was able to supply ample background: Fuchs had just moved into a prefab at Harwell; he didn't have a phone but would probably get one; he had an old Morris eight-horsepower motorcar; he traveled to Birmingham, sometimes to Oxford, London rarely, and usually by train; appropriate to his position he had many foreign visitors; and he had a few close friends at Harwell, particularly the Skinners. Herbert Skinner was his boss. Suspected of having TB, Fuchs had lived at the Skinners' and still often slept there. In six months, the Skinners were moving to Liverpool, where Herbert would take up a physics chair at the university. Herbert divided his time between the two places. Fuchs, Arnold reported, "is on more than friendly terms with Mrs. Skinner." He summed up:

[Fuchs] is a very reserved man, and mentally tough. Nevertheless, he is fond of both whiskey and women and can take a large amount of alcohol without being affected. He is a man who is not only brilliant intellectually, but also extremely shrewd from a practical point of view.

Arnold held his cards close, but he certainly signaled to MI5 his own wary attitude toward Fuchs.

CHAPTER 16

Surveillance, Harwell, September 1949

JAMES ROBERTSON READIED AN ELABORATE SYSTEM OF CODE NAMES—FUCHS WAS Ramsey, Peierls was Matthews, and Skinner was Piper (and of course his wife became Mrs. Piper). He had the warrants to tap the phones of Fuchs and Peierls and monitor their mail. He made a request for bank records and three Listeners, young female volunteers from the MI5 transcription team, to work from a side room at the Victorian-era post office in the backwater town of Newbury, near Harwell. All day, all night, they staffed the phone taps and microphones while equipment recorded Fuchs's every word, whether in the office or at home. Just in case, one of them spoke German. When the Listeners were relieved, they had an easy ten-minute walk through the old market square and over the river Kennet to their eighteenth-century coach inn. Their cover story, should anyone ask, was as General Post Office relief staff working on a statistical study of calls passing through the Newbury exchange.

As for mail, the Special Investigative Unit of the GPO, located near St. Paul's in London, opened Fuchs's incoming and outgoing mail, mostly using a steam kettle, and copied it. Checking for invisible ink was also part of the job.

The listening and the mail duplication flowed easily for Robertson, but he wrung his hands over visual surveillance. Because the treeless acres of Harwell offered no cover, a select team of Watchers was on call a few hours away, in a Georgian town house in Regent's Park on the northwest side of London. The chief of the Watchers, Jim Skardon, was described by a colleague as dapper and pipe smoking. His other important qualities were patience and tenacity. He had "a high opinion of his own abilities," said one, but was well liked and an excellent interviewer. Their physical separation from Leconfield House supposedly thwarted foreign agents' observation of comings and goings of this MI5 surveillance team.

The Watchers had a photograph of their target and a basic description—Height: five feet nine, Eyes: brown, Hair: brown. From Arnold they knew that during the week, Fuchs's pattern was office, home, or the Skinners'. Occasionally, he made train trips to London for meetings at Shell Mex House or drives to Birmingham to see the Peierlses. When he traveled by rail, the Watchers waited for him at Didcot Station, the closest one to Harwell. If he drove, Robertson had Watchers pick up his car on a trunk road a few miles into his trip. Lightly trafficked rural roads reasoned against tailing him from Harwell. Information from Arnold or the Listeners kept tabs on his plans. If the Watchers couldn't get to Harwell in time, the backup was to intercept him either at the train station or at his destination.

When he went out on a whim, especially at night, nothing could be done, which was the cause of Robertson's anxiety. With holes, the whole system was worthless. But even if they were on the scene, would they be able to detect a handoff that might take less than a minute and involve a servant, a casual acquaintance, or limitless other possibilities? Besides, they knew they could be spying on someone who was not a spy but merely going on about his business.

The first days of tracking had their tribulations, especially Sundays, a free day with no fixed schedule. The first Sunday, garbled messages sprinkled with the voices of strange men forced Robertson to drive to Newbury to learn details firsthand. It all turned out innocently enough. It seems that car trouble outside Harwell had triggered phone calls from Fuchs, a stay at the Skinners', and—according to a neighbor—unidentified men stopping at the Skinners' in the middle of the night. The muddle involved Fuchs's recent purchase of a car from Herbert Skinner: a used dark gray sedan, which looked like new, its long hood and tall gleaming grille with the prominent MG crest now signaling Fuchs's arrival—when it didn't break down.

Fuchs invited Arnold to drive it sometime. Pleased, Arnold reported to MI5 that he could keep an eye on the mileage, which shouldn't increase much because wartime gas rationing was still in effect. Nevertheless, the next Sunday, MI5 lost Fuchs from 1:00 in the afternoon until 4:00 the next morning; the Listeners heard no sounds from his house. Arnold guessed that he was at the Skinners'.

The first real test of a road trip came on Thursday, September 22, when Fuchs and Skinner drove to the General Electric Company in Wembley, on the western outskirts of London. The prior day's activities, all recorded by the Listeners, involved their secretaries going to and fro about who would drive and in how many cars, given that two others were coming along. Robertson recapped the trip's arrangements as "working satisfactorily enough." The only person disappointed was Erna Skinner, who wasn't allowed to go along.

The investigation slogged along, discovering mostly that Fuchs had a very mundane life and spent most of his time working. The Listeners noted that on weekdays he usually got up around 8:30. Sometimes he whistled. At the other end of the day, it was mostly quiet after 11:30 p.m.—perhaps broken by a sneeze. Weekends were much looser—later rising and later retiring.

Meetings, memos, and list-making clogged the routines of Martin and Robertson. They kept up Fuchs's multiple security files, now exploding with details on every person he spoke with on the phone, corresponded with, or saw face to face. Identifying first names mentioned on the bugs was a tiresome chore. Robertson kept updating his list of code names. The town of Cambridge became "Backwood"—indicating that perhaps the labeler was from Oxford; Maidenhead easily converted to "Virginia"; and Beaconsfield was designated "Primrose," a historical nod to the favorite flower of Benjamin Disraeli, a.k.a. Lord Beaconsfield.

One September morning around 9:40, the Listeners reported two visitors (and maybe a baby) who were not the Skinners. The wife, who had a foreign accent, did most of the talking and was "difficult to follow as her speech was a mixture of shouting and screaming. She addressed RAMSEY by his first name." At 9:46, they probably left the living room, the Listeners noted, to tour the prefab. Not clear who they were (although it was probably the Peierlses).

The prefabs, compact aluminum boxes with two bedrooms, a bath, and a kitchen with built-in fridge, were a marvel to all. They had evolved as a postwar solution to a lack of housing. As though pressed from a cookie cutter, these efficient boxes stretched row upon row across Harwell's gentle hills.

Fuchs's regular visitor was Erna Skinner. The friendship between the Skinners and Fuchs had sprung up in 1947—and particularly between Erna and Klaus. Erna most likely forged the relationship because typically, wherever he lived, the wives of his scientist friends mothered him. His quiet nature with the agreeable but evasive smile appealed to their expressive personalities and challenged the maternal instincts of the likes of Genia Peierls, Mici Teller, and Mary Buneman. The women at Harwell had him over for dinner, hung his drapes, sometimes even came over to cook breakfast for him. Klaus was generally friendly toward people, expressing neither his likes nor his dislikes, and didn't welcome any hint of emotional interest, except from Erna Skinner.

By 1949, he and Erna saw each other almost daily, either for lunch or in the evening, sometimes at his prefab, sometimes at her house. Erna's background and personality made her a natural complement to Klaus's reserve. She was fun-loving, outgoing, very bohemian with many artistic, cosmopolitan friends—the patina of her heritage—and a big drinker. She had been pretty and, although she had gained weight, still "had pretty remains," as Mary Buneman put it. Erna's specialty was acting out hilarious stories of her everyday happenings and poking fun at herself. And sometimes others. She labeled Klaus's discourses "evangelistic sermons on democratic principles."

Being four years his senior might have added to the attraction too. He seemed to prefer older women.

For Erna, an anxious person who required constant companionship, he was a godsend. Caring for him during the summer, while she nursed him back to health from his lung condition, was hardly an imposition. With the impending move, Herbert traveled to Liverpool every few weeks, and she didn't want to be alone.

Henry Arnold described Erna: "Age about 37. Plump. Short (5'4" to 5'5"). Dark. Attractive type of Jewess. Generally well-dressed though inclined to be untidy. Clothes usually darkish." In the Yiddish of her hometown of Czernowitz, she would have been "zaftig"—round and full figured. Listeners' reports indicated that she talked a lot—about trivial incidents that no one seemed to listen to, about her health, and about her kittens. Mary Buneman liked her but thought her a flirt.

Erna Skinner, née Wurmbrand, was nominally Austrian, born in the city of Czernowitz in 1907, a slice of central Europe that was part of the Austro-Hungarian Empire then. Originally a city in Moldova, centuries of submission to Romanian, Ukrainian, Russian, German, and Polish conquerors and the accompanying waves of immigration seasoned it into a multicultural, multiethnic, and prominent intellectual center. It had a slight plurality of Jews, and German was the lingua franca. Erna was a product of this rich culture, and her casual patter, often seemingly frivolous, concealed a lively intelligence and quick mind.

The sterile details from British passport records requested by Robertson listed that Erna divorced a husband named Abrahamson before coming to the U.K. in 1929, visited Boston in 1932 for six months, and traveled extensively on the Continent before the war. She lived in the United States in 1944 while Herbert worked for the Manhattan Project in Berkeley, California. Her parents lived in New York. Not on the passport records—her father was a respected journalist who reported on atrocities in Germany until 1933, when Nazi intimidation forced him out.

The Skinners had married in 1931 and in 1934 had a daughter named Elaine. During this time, Herbert Skinner was on the faculty of the University of Bristol, and Klaus was a student there. Herbert later recalled Klaus as "an uncouth and callow youth." There is no indication that they knew each other well.

Mary Buneman found Herbert Wakefield Banks Skinner a proper English gentleman, reserved, and discreet, as one might expect of a graduate of the elite prep school Rugby and of Trinity College, Cambridge—and now, besides being Klaus's boss, was deputy to the director of Harwell, John Cockcroft. He also had an aptitude for the clerihew, a distinctly British form of poetry, whimsical and often nonsensical, as was his for Fuchs:

> *Fuchs*
> *Looks*
> *An ascetic*
> *Theoretic.*

Herbert and Erna were devoted to each other in their own way. He wanted to keep her happy. But for Erna, one man was not always enough. He knew of her affairs and looked the other way. Klaus, for his part, satisfied her whims and needs and let her take the lead. At the same time, he held an admiration for Herbert and a willingness to please him and do what he asked. Mary Buneman once asked him why he went over to the Skinners' all the time. He answered, "For Herbert." But it seemed more complicated than that.

Arnold considered Erna to be Fuchs's mistress, although Robertson didn't have that impression at first and noted for the record that no evidence existed. He later agreed with Arnold. Herbert evidenced no suspicions about the relationship—except on one particular day, when Fuchs and Skinner had a meeting at Shell Mex House and the relationship between the two men was very cool. The Watchers reported that they arrived at the Didcot Station separately, rode in the first-class car but sat apart, took the same tube car, but didn't speak or sit together. They traveled back to Harwell separately. It was a complete break from their usual routine.

The fracture, whatever its cause, didn't last. The next day Fuchs visited the Skinners for a few minutes, and then they visited him at the prefab along with Herbert's aunt Bess, problem seemingly resolved. The phone bugs offered no explanation.

Other facets of Erna's life Robertson did question. Very shortly he would learn that she had a distinctly peculiar set of friends. By month's end, MI5 had a tap on the Skinners' phone.

Fuchs wasn't the only prime suspect MI5 was following. Rudi Peierls was the other. Robertson already had mail and phone checks on Peierls, but other than maligning his sartorial display ("shabby raincoat with belt, dark grey soft hat with black band—brim turned up all round," and so on), the Watchers didn't report much. Then, on September 19, Martin wrote to Washington with an explosive finding. Peierls had a sister in the United States. This fact came from a 1938 letter supporting U.K. visas for his parents, who were traveling from Berlin to America. Having a sister in the United States was a key factor that came out of Venona. Now Fuchs wasn't the only candidate for "Rest."

The FBI and the British embassy in Washington responded quickly, saying that the time frame in the Venona messages didn't match Peierls's movements. Namely, he took up a position in Los Alamos on July 1, 1944. The government was unlikely to consider transferring him back to the U.K. that same month. MI5's director general, however, didn't want the timetable embedded in the Venona messages, which might not fit exactly with the actual events, to dictate the possibilities. Most, though, still held Fuchs to be the guilty one.

The presence of a sister was an essential factor. The exact details on Peierls were lacking as yet, but evidence on Kristel Fuchs Heinemann and her husband, Bob, crisscrossed between the embassy in Washington and MI5. London uncovered that in June 1937, Bob, then a student at Swarthmore, had visited the U.K. en route to Leningrad. And in 1944, the FBI learned that he had been a member of the Communist Party in Cambridge,

Massachusetts, resigned, and rejoined in 1947 using the alias Robert Hill. Robertson requested any records on Kristel held by the Home Office, and a few days later he applied for a warrant to open mail from her. His minute on September 20 read,

> The address of FUCHS' sister, Mrs. Kristel F. Heineman [sic], has now been obtained from the F.B.I. and is 96 Lake View Avenue, Cambridge, Massachusetts U.S.A.
>
> In view of the information in our records regarding this woman's possible past implication in Russian espionage, and especially the fact that her name was found in a diary of the spy Israel Halperin, I should be grateful if you would approve the operation of a H.O.W. [a warrant] on all correspondence addressed to her from this country.

It wasn't long before Robertson requested that her letters be checked for secret ink.

As the minute indicated, a week or so earlier a cable from Washington had spelled out another troubling fact about Kristel: her name was listed in the diary of Israel Halperin, the mathematician arrested for spying by the Canadians after Igor Gouzenko, a clerk at the Russian embassy in Ottawa who defected in 1945, had implicated him. In 1947, the courts acquitted Halperin, and he resumed his faculty position at Queen's University in Ontario. MI5's director general, Percy Sillitoe, wanted the FBI to investigate his movements between 1942 and 1945. He didn't think Halperin could be the elusive "Goose," the Russians' code name for Rest's courier in New York, but he wanted to make sure.

Similarly, Martin pressured his main contact at the embassy in Washington, Geoffrey Patterson, to find Kristel's whereabouts in 1944. Patterson pushed the FBI agents, and they pushed back. They had already worked for a week and found nothing. It was "extremely difficult," Martin heard, to trace the movements of a U.S. national during 1944. So he abbreviated his request. Could they at least confirm that she was somewhere in the United

States during that time? Was her husband connected with Harvard at the present time, and might Harvard have some information? Urgency pulsed through the request. Until the FBI sorted out the sisters of Fuchs and Peierls, MI5 couldn't eliminate either man as a suspect. They had to cover them both around the clock, and the agency was stretched.

On September 23, 1949, Harry Truman made a public announcement that confirmed the suspicions of Western intelligence and otherwise stunned the world: Russia had exploded an atomic bomb. The next day, eager to watch Fuchs's reaction to the news, Arnold knocked on his door. It was around 11:00 on Saturday morning, and Fuchs was just stirring. Arnold started in right away saying that he had come around because of the news. He feigned confusion. "I don't know what to make of this. Do you?" Fuchs simply replied, "Well we don't—I mean, we want to know the details." After a cigarette and twenty-five minutes of Arnold's mostly one-sided conversation, he departed.

CHAPTER 17

Disposal, London, October 1949

A FEW DAYS AFTER TRUMAN'S ANNOUNCEMENT, FUCHS WENT TO LONDON FOR A TOP secret, two-day government symposium on the bomb. Arnold told Robertson that Fuchs "would almost certainly travel by train." On September 27, from 4:30 a.m. to 10:00 a.m., the Watchers covered Didcot and Paddington stations, but they never saw him. Their first sighting was at 10:30 a.m., when he walked into the Royal Institute with another man whose features they couldn't discern. They stayed in Fuchs's shadow for the next thirty-six hours.

12:45: lunch break, he came out, placed two calls from the post office nearby—one to the Great Western Hotel.

1:00: hailed a taxi to 10 Herbert Crescent, just to the south of Hyde Park. There a woman, known to him, let him in.

2:15: left for the Royal Institute.

2:30: arrived there.

4:55: left the meeting at the Royal Institute accompanied by another man. (One agent followed this man, J. V. Dunworth, to the Regent Palace Hotel where he occupied Room 757. MI5 later discovered that he was director of a division at Harwell and often roomed at the Skinners.)

5:05: fetched his car at the Burlington House courtyard and drove back to 10 Herbert Crescent.

7:45: left the house with the woman who had opened the door and another man and woman.

The four drove to the nearby Blue Cockatoo Restaurant at Chelsea Embankment, a regular meeting place for London's art scene.

9:00: back at 10 Herbert Crescent where he spent the night.

The Watchers ended their preliminary report with this:

1. Wallace Russell HARPER, Ph.D. believed lives at 10 Herbert Crescent.

2. Man from 10 Herbert Crescent who dined with FUCHS traced at 14:30 to Imperial College of Science and Technology, S.W.7. He works here.

3. FUCHS is bad driver.

Fuchs's activities were completely unremarkable.

Fuchs spent the next day at the meeting, and at its end at 6:00 p.m. he visited 52 Lancaster Close, St. Petersburgh Place just off Moscow Road, the city's Russian section. The Watchers noted, "Several aliens live there including one whose name is (approximation) Eliezer Yapou." Perhaps the surveillance had at long last paid off.

Fuchs then returned to Harwell accompanied by a woman whom the Watchers guessed to be Mrs. Skinner. Erna's phone call to a friend the next day confirmed this, along with details on Fuchs's health. Erna told her friend that she was worried about him. He looked "absolutely ghastly" and was easily winded, not able to walk up a few stairs without puffing. She had sent him straight to bed when they returned. She feared another bout of pneumonia. In the morning, she continued, he rested but felt compelled to go to the office after lunch. Herbert was away, and he needed to be there.

The Watchers swiftly garnered facts on Russell Harper were accurate; he was the scientist he appeared to be. He earned a phone tap and a few days of observation because Fuchs and Erna had stayed at his house, but that was the end of it. Eliezer Yapou was different. Robertson quickly discovered that the Registry held a security file on him. According to that dossier, he was the Israeli press attaché in London and had contacts with the Russians, including journalists. He directed "the intelligence activities of the Israeli Legation, and was especially interested in acquiring information concerning Arab affairs." He and his wife, Edith, an Austria-born art historian and friend of Erna's, occupied the Lancaster Close flat in the Russian section. Robertson wrote to MI6 that it was time to intensify the investigation on Yapou.

Erna's friends concerned Robertson. It was she, he noted, who had initiated the few "contacts of any security significance" on the trip. Her somewhat bohemian circle was not well suited to the wife of the deputy director of a top secret research facility, disturbingly so. He requested the Registry to open a file on Erna and her friend Vera Pohle, who had suddenly turned up on another joint trip to London by Fuchs and the Skinners shortly after the one for the conference.

Vera was about forty-five, from Berlin, and recently naturalized. She had trained in liturgical research and antiquarian literature and held several librarian positions in the U.K. For the last six months, MI5 learned, she had been "a domestic help and companion" to Erna. Erna had been diagnosed with anxiety, the main symptom of which was her craving for company and her panic without it. No specific cause was established, but it's not hard to imagine why a Jewish woman living during the Nazi era might have developed "a case of nerves."

Vera Pohle was a new target for MI5, but a friend she shared with Erna had a security file. This was Tatiana Malleson, an actress who was originally from Russia, had lived in Germany, and was possibly a former member of the German Communist Party. Before leaving Germany, her then husband had been in touch "with a small Communist Party group within the *Reichswehr* [the German army], which included Hans Kahle." She lived close to the "pro-Russian" Eliezer Yapou.

Knowing nothing about MI5's information, Arnold kept an eye on the visitors drifting in and out of the Skinners' household. Because of them, he had his own doubts about Erna; moreover, he always kept in mind that "she is of German/Austrian origin."

At times the Skinners' seemed like a boardinghouse. Vera came and went as part of her job as a companion; Tatiana spent the night there when seeing her son in Oxford; Genia Peierls came to visit; John Dunworth, a director at Harwell, lived there much of the time; and of course Fuchs was a frequent visitor. When Skinner's aunt Bess came, Vera was shuffled into the Skinners' dressing room to sleep. The constant flow of people provided Erna with the companionship that she desperately needed, but it was a headache for Arnold.

Robertson kept up with phone taps, mail warrants, and an occasional observation of Erna's friends. They revealed nothing against Fuchs. But the sudden surge of contacts to follow was overwhelming, which required the setting of priorities: (1) Fuchs with twenty-four-hour surveillance; (2) Mrs. Skinner (to be followed anytime she left Harwell because of "obscurity of her past history, her intimate association with FUCHS and the fact that she visited with FUCHS the flat of Dr. Eliezer YAPOU"); (3) Yapou; (4) Peierls.

When Priority 1, Fuchs, made contacts, Robertson established secondary priorities. His rule of whom to follow was this: determine the identity of the contact and report it to Robertson immediately. If he determined the contact significant, this contact became Priority 1 at the next meeting with Fuchs and required all available resources, even "if necessary" to cease observation of Fuchs.

Numerous other people and data cluttered the investigation timeline—significance unclear. There was Simmons, Fuchs's dentist; Frank, his doctor; and Duke, a friend. His cousin Gisela Wagner, who lived in Frankfurt am Main, wrote to him about a visa for Britain. MI6 told Robertson she might have communist connections. He requested a mail warrant, including telegrams, on her—and Emil Fuchs too—with all letters "treated for secret writing." In fact, Robertson ordered all letters to Fuchs from either the United States or any zone in Germany tested and stressed to leave no "trace whatsoever." It was a precautionary measure, he said. He had no indication of secret writing. Furthermore, the delay in delivery was to be no more than "an absolute maximum of 48 hours."

Robertson also received Fuchs's bank records. They listed no large deposits or withdrawals, but he had made out checks to the British Overseas Supply Company, a business based in Oxford that imported and manufactured drugs. It was run by a Polish-born, naturalized Brit. Information to MI5 from "a delicate source" said that it also quietly sent food packages to the Soviet sector of Germany. Was Fuchs sending food to relatives and friends, or was it something more sinister?

For the most part the surveillance was monotonous. But the Watchers did report a curious trip to photography supply shops while Fuchs was in London for a meeting. He was looking for very small Kodak film. They didn't know why.

Like Robertson, Arthur Martin struggled to keep up, integrating information the FBI and the British embassy uncovered as well as feeding them MI5 discoveries. Odds were that Fuchs was Rest, but suspicions lingered about Peierls and even Skyrme. Until the FBI tracked the whereabouts of the sisters in 1944, Martin had no basis to exclude the other two men.

One possible source of information was Frank Kearton, a chemist and one of the four British scientists in New York during the relevant time period. Perrin had described him in the meeting a month earlier as level-headed and potentially useful to the investigation. Another option was to scour the administrative files of the British mission now held at Harwell. Martin went in that direction.

The impassive edifice of Leconfield House masked a deeper problem—the exhaustion of the staff from twenty-four-hour surveillance. Martin crafted an honest and revealing letter to Geoffrey Patterson at the embassy in Washington:

> The elimination of either favorite defeats us. We had thought that with your help in tracing movements of relatives we should be able to clear this up quickly. Now that we realise your difficulties we are going ahead at this end on another tack which may yield the answer. But I must stress that until B.2.c. [Martin] can complete this task a tremendous strain is being thrown on B.2.a. [Robertson] (as I shall explain) so that anything you can do to help or hasten the F.B.I. is of the greatest importance. . . .
>
> I stress all this because it is the biggest and most thorough job we have ever undertaken and it is straining resources to the uttermost. Elimination of one of the candidates would reduce the strain and, more important, allow even greater concentration on the other and his contacts. Moreover, as you can imagine, time is limited.

Martin didn't hesitate to express his fear: that with no elimination of one of the candidates and nothing positive to report, MI5 and the government would pull back resources, and he and the other officers would have to stop the investigation.

By return letter, Patterson wrote of his own troubling situation arising out of the Venona messages: "The FBI had launched 40–50 'grand scale' enquiries and had 'scores' (I might not be too inaccurate if I said hundreds!) of spies to identify."

The investigation of Rest was important to the Americans, but they were focused on unidentified spies who could threaten U.S. security. The FBI had initiated a new policy of giving out no information on current investigations. Patterson read that as an embarrassed reaction to "the new spies in their midst," to which they didn't want to admit. He now had to gather information unofficially from the agents with whom he was on good terms. Consequently, he spent part of most days at the bureau visiting and chatting. His after-hours activities helped to keep them loose and talking:

> I ply the boys with whiskey in the hope of oiling the investigation
> wheels. This system works quite well, but is really hard work and
> one wonders when one will ever get a decent night's sleep.

Patterson promised Martin to press the FBI for information. He also scoured the British mission's files in Washington to pin down Peierls's travels in the United States, and he cabled Martin a timeline. The decision to post Peierls to Los Alamos was made at the end of May; he left New York on June 2 for Albuquerque; he returned to New York on June 20; the report was dated June 6. Therefore, the MSN-12 report wasn't finished before he left; it was handed to the Russians while he was away. His conclusion: "Peierls could not [R] NOT be identical with REST."

MI5 had conducted a six-week inquiry that had produced no evidence to use in a court case. On October 17, Martin sat down to draft another sobering memo, also to Patterson but with the director general's signature. It described MI5's strategy for "disposing" of Fuchs and requested Patterson to determine the FBI's reaction. It was the step prior to MI5's making a recommendation to the prime minister about whether Fuchs should be allowed to remain at Harwell.

Martin's one-and-a-half-page first draft was a terse *a* through *f* framework with disquieting facts, starting with Fuchs as a Soviet agent in 1944.

"FUCHS has been proved beyond all reasonable doubt to be identical with the Soviet Agent REST." The decisive factor for MI5 had been Patterson's timeline that eliminated Peierls.

Martin went on to list the risks to security at Harwell if Fuchs was still spying, as well as the problems of disposing of him. There was still no evidence of suspicious contacts; no means to limit his access to top secret information at Harwell; no grounds for legal prosecution; and no simple administrative way to remove him.

As the list made the rounds for review, MI5 added an assurance: MI5 would not proceed with a recommendation to the prime minister without an FBI response.

Then the next draft suddenly introduced a new tack—"a direct approach" in the form of interrogation. MI5 had reason to believe, or at least hope, that Fuchs might break. The final draft concluded that "an interrogation of FUCHS is in fact the step which is most likely to lead to a satisfactory solution," that is, his removal from Harwell. It gave no rationale, but there was one. During this time, a new issue surfaced, one introduced by Fuchs himself.

On October 17, Arnold met with Robertson for his weekly meeting and reported on a visit from Fuchs. Arnold explained that Fuchs came in to ask for advice concerning his father. Emil Fuchs, who lived in Frankfurt am Main in the western zone, had received an offer of a chair at the University of Leipzig in the eastern zone. Klaus Fuchs asked if he should discourage his father from accepting the offer, given his own position in nuclear research. Arnold said he needed to think about it and that Fuchs might wish to do the same. They agreed to meet in a couple of days. Fuchs departed.

Arnold relayed to Robertson that Fuchs seemed visibly relieved as he left. MI5 told Arnold to advise Fuchs that he should discourage his father because of the Russians' potential for gaining a "hostage" and leverage.

Arnold astutely guessed that Fuchs had pondered this problem for some time. Fuchs, of course, had learned of it when Emil and his nephew Klaus had visited the previous July.

Fuchs had also received another portend of future complications, a letter from an old family friend, a pastor living in Jena in the eastern zone. He had written to thank Fuchs for sending the life-sustaining food packages (hence the entries on the bank record to the Overseas Supply Company) and invited him to visit if he came to see his father in Leipzig. With his father's move, these kinds of Eastern intrusions would multiply.

Because of the mail warrant, Robertson had received and flagged a translation of the letter. He requested a mail check on letters from the pastor because "his letters bear a strong imprint of pro-Soviet propaganda," namely a long paragraph describing the wonderful life in the eastern zone. It seems that Robertson had failed to appreciate the one-sentence reference to Leipzig that signaled Emil's move to the East.

MI5 missed other possibilities too. Early on, while the agency stewed over whether Fuchs had a sister in the United States, friends at Harwell could easily have answered the question. During Emil's visit on his way to Germany from the United States, he dined with them and Arnold as well. None of this was secret.

Arnold and Fuchs met again on October 20 in Arnold's office. Fuchs trusted Arnold and asked that their conversation be kept in "strictest confidence."

Arnold stressed to him that the security services did not want researchers covered by the Official Secrets Act to have ties in Russian-controlled areas. Fuchs should tell his father not to accept. Fuchs replied that his father would not be persuaded by him if he felt he was "doing good" by accepting. Arnold asked if Fuchs thought it strange for his father, who was seventy-five years old, to be offered a chair. Fuchs implied that the question had occurred to him. Would his father take a chair in the western zone? Arnold asked. Fuchs thought not because his father was "disillusioned" by his experiences in Frankfurt. Would his father take a chair in England if one could be found? Maybe, Fuchs replied.

Arnold then asked Fuchs how he would react to pressure from the Russians if his father moved. What if his father's life were in danger? As Arnold described in a memo to Robertson, Fuchs replied "that at present he did not feel he would be induced to cooperate but it was, of course, impossible to say what he might feel under altered circumstances." Fuchs's question in return was, should he resign if his father accepted the position? Arnold said that this was an administrative decision, not his. He suggested that they discuss the matter again, but as he wrote to MI5, he didn't think Fuchs would initiate it.

Martin's boss, Dick White, read Arnold's memo a few days later and saw that someone had highlighted Fuchs's response about reacting to pressure. He addressed a minute in the file to the director general:

> One could speculate a great deal on the meaning of the marked
> paragraph but there is one thing I am tempted to think—that is,
> that FUCHS' answer indicates that there may be something to
> be gained from an interrogation.

The director general and Martin supported White's conviction. Confession could lead to disposal. Although others disagreed, Martin included the idea in the memo for the FBI. It was the director general's call.

CHAPTER 18

Interrogation, London, November 1949

IN A LARGE CORNICED OFFICE ON THE FIFTH FLOOR OF LECONFIELD HOUSE, MI5'S DIREC-
tor general, Percy Sillitoe, faced his deputy, Guy Liddell, over the gnawing question of how to dispose of Klaus Fuchs. Sillitoe subscribed to the
argument for interrogation championed by the chief of B Branch, Dick
White. Liddell expressed concerns about possible repercussions of a confession, most notably, that this accomplished physicist, steeped in British
and American nuclear research, would immediately defect.

Sillitoe and Liddell were very different spirits, with further cause for
tension between them in that Liddell had every reason to believe that he
would be named to head the spy agency when, instead, Sillitoe was given
the position in 1946.

The director general had been a chief constable—famed and knighted
for wiping out gangs and modernizing police forces in large cities. To make
sure the police identified each other in a raid, he fashioned "Sillitoe Tar-
tan," the black-and-white checkerboard bands they wore. He was a policeman's policeman, not reared in intelligence or the lifestyle of London's
old-school clubs.

Those bastions of privilege had been part of Liddell's life for three decades, first with Scotland Yard and since 1931 with MI5, mostly in counter-espionage. In 1933, he had visited Berlin, met many of the top Nazis, and listened to dubious stories about the communists. He knew the territory quite well.

Sillitoe focused on the potential upside of an interrogation; Liddell focused on the downside. The latter argued that they should avoid a confrontation and use Emil's move as an excuse to get Klaus out of Harwell and transferred to a university. It was a logic that harked back to the days of war, when ability topped politics and punishment, if any, was a quiet reassignment or—worst case—a dismissal. But Sillitoe, the policeman, wanted confession and prosecution.

Arnold's assessment—that Fuchs's relating confidences about Emil was "most unusual since he is normally the most reticent and self-sufficient of men"—had captured Sillitoe's imagination, just as Fuchs's reaction to possible Russian pressure had captured White's. They saw themselves stalking a weakened prey.

After the meeting, Sillitoe cabled Patterson in Washington about briefing the FBI on a revised plan using Emil's move "to delve further into FUCHS' mind." That is, Arnold would talk with Fuchs, bring up possible pressure by the Russians, and then go into "the direct question of whether Fuchs had ever come into contact with Russians." They hoped Fuchs would "unburden himself." If not, at least they could observe his thinking. A caveat: the FBI shouldn't construe this move as an alternative to gathering more evidence, particularly from Kristel and Bob Heinemann.

The next day, when Arnold heard about the idea, he was hesitant. Interviewing Fuchs could undermine his personal relationships with staff if his role were known. Weighing whether Fuchs would confess, he saw "a most carefully calculating man" who wouldn't have "an emotional breakdown." Once Fuchs knew the evidence against him, his personal interest would be a heavy factor.

On the other hand, Arnold thought he himself had the best chance of getting a confession. If Fuchs didn't open up voluntarily, he could formally interrogate him relying on their friendship, established trust, and Fuchs's nervous nature. He judged his chances of getting Fuchs to come clean at fifty-fifty.

Fuchs's ultimate fate was not MI5's to decide. The security agency gathered facts and made recommendations and, if possible, gained a confession. The decision on what might follow belonged to the Ministry of Supply, its director Sir Archibald Rowlands, and its controller of production (atomic energy) Sir Charles Portal (Perrin was his deputy)—and overall to the prime minister.

Martin laid out a briefing document for Rowlands and Portal with an analysis of objectives, methods for achieving them, and effectiveness. Options for action were (1) no interrogation with retention at Harwell or transfer to another post; or (2) interrogation with either prosecution, dismissal, or retention. Sillitoe advised that only interrogation resulting in prosecution, not simply dismissal, secured all objectives.

While MI5 waited for a response, the Listeners heard Fuchs mention his passport, an allusion that made a nervous Robertson more so. Arnold assured him that it was innocent. Fuchs had an administrative request for his birth certificate. His passport was the substitute.

In the meantime, Patterson sent Martin the FBI's official agreement for an interrogation provided it safeguarded the Venona source. At least one hurdle was crossed.

On November 15, 1949, MI5 officers gathered to "clear our minds," as Liddell put it in his diary. They were to meet with Rowlands and Portal the next day at the Ministry of Supply at Shell Mex House. To clarify their talking points, Martin wrote up a fourteen-point statement that summarized the other countless memos. It boiled down to one question for Rowlands and Portal: "How important is the need to prevent his defection?" It was an outcome that MI5 couldn't absolutely prevent. For just that reason, Liddell held to his position that edging Fuchs out of Harwell was a better option than a confession.

Martin's minutes of the meeting on the sixteenth filled only one page.

The Ministry of Supply first represented the concerns of Harwell's director, John Cockcroft, that Fuchs's value to Harwell was "extreme." He didn't want to lose him. If not a threat to security, Fuchs could be retained at Harwell; if he went to Russia, that country's gain would be considerable. MI5 turned the argument and convinced Rowlands and Portal that the only way to ensure Fuchs's reliability was interrogation, that "the advantages to be gained from a successful interrogation outweighed the risks involved."

That same day, Sillitoe briefed the prime minister, who agreed with the strategy of interrogation but requested it be postponed for a fortnight until Cockcroft returned from a trip. All agreed.

Robertson determined that other than official trips, which were often with other scientists, Fuchs had left the Harwell area six times since September. The twenty-four-hour net had not produced the slightest odd conversation or unexpected meet up, except when he was with Erna. How much surveillance was needed?

MI5 cut back to not pursuing Fuchs outside London when MI5 was "reasonably sure where he is going and why." A little later, they did the same with telephone checks, suspending the Listeners' services—although not the recording—in Newbury from midnight to 8:30 a.m.

Meanwhile, Robertson delved more deeply into Fuchs's past. He twice noted the name Ronald Gunn in Fuchs's file, the man who had sponsored his naturalization filings in 1939 and 1942 and in whose home he had stayed while studying in Bristol. When Robertson queried the Registry, he found that in 1940 MI5 had opened a security file on Gunn that was filled with informants' rumors but no mention of Fuchs. Reports described Gunn's connection with the Imperial Tobacco Company, as well as the trips he and his wife had made to Russia in July 1932 and June 1936. It wasn't these trips that had drawn the security service to them, though. It was their mail.

An inquisitive postman had informed the Bristol police that Gunn was "in correspondence in suspicious circumstances with aliens," indicating "leanings toward 'either Communism or Nazism.'" His file held the names of "Communists or near-Communists" collected from the addresses on the envelopes. Robertson tracked one of these names to a list of veterans of the International Brigade in Spain available for national service during the war. That list had been compiled by the ubiquitous Hans Kahle.

Robertson requested a mail warrant and telephone tap on Gunn. He asked the Bristol constable to relay any findings, warning that Gunn could be involved in "subversive activity on behalf of Soviet Russia," although, he acknowledged, he had no evidence. Robertson assumed that during the time he had stayed with the Gunns, Fuchs adhered "to the same Communist views."

Also continuing to delve into Fuchs's past was Arthur Martin. On November 21, he and a few others sat down with Frank Kearton, Fuchs's former co-worker in New York. First, they told Kearton that Fuchs was a Soviet spy. An astonished Kearton thought Fuchs the least likely person to suspect. To him Fuchs had been completely absorbed in his work, an extension of Rudi Peierls's "brain," and happy to remain in the background. He had a small furnished apartment and little social life and showed no interest in politics. Not the same Fuchs as now, he added. Kearton had witnessed, as had others, a transformation in Fuchs, whose growing position in the field had not only increased his confidence but widened his interests.

The men from MI5 took Kearton through Fuchs's "movements," specifically the possibility of his knowing about a return to the U.K. in the summer of 1944. Kearton thought that Peierls might have told him about the prospect of a team in the U.K. working on diffusion and that Fuchs could guess that he might be sent back. Kearton didn't know when the decision to transfer Fuchs to Los Alamos occurred, but he knew that Peierls went there at the end of June. Kearton could imagine that once there, Peierls realized how much he needed Fuchs. If Peierls made a request, Fuchs would have heard about it around mid-July.

As for the "friends and relatives" category, Kearton volunteered that

Fuchs had family someplace outside New York City, at least a train ride away, and that he visited them on two weekends. Kearton didn't know of any friends, but he did know that a group of researchers at Columbia was a contractor on the project and used his results. His contact there was someone named Cohen.

On the "clerical staff" side, Kearton listed a couple of secretaries and at least one "machine computer," a person who performed the calculations that Fuchs, Peierls, or Kearton handed her. This woman had a degree in mathematics and was Russian, her parents being recent émigrés. She didn't generally see finished documents, but she could have gained access to and would have understood some of the material. He thought that only he, Fuchs, and Peierls would have had unrestricted access. Even if the typists would have had access, they wouldn't have understood what they were seeing. In fact, they had no knowledge of the mission's purpose. The MSN series of papers, including the one passed along to the Russians, was for the Americans, in particular the group at Columbia.

Kearton offered his own theory about potential spies. If there was one, it was Skyrme, whom he described as "a person likely to have strong convictions, that he almost certainly did develop social contacts in New York, that he got involved in several minor 'scrapes' and that he was generally 'rather odd.'" MI5 listened but, given past experience with scientists' assessment of their own, remained jaded and unconvinced.

Kearton gave them nothing to contradict the information they already had. But the Russian machine computer was a new complication. Martin immediately cabled Washington with the information, including the fact that the Americans had rejected Peierls's recommendation for her employment— probably at Los Alamos—on security grounds. Next, he and John Marriott, an MI5 officer, related the discovery of the Russian machine computer to Liddell, as well as the possibility of her contact with university students. But as Liddell noted, "Neither Martin nor Marriott are in the least shaken in the belief that FUCHS is the man we are after."

The next day Martin received a list of the seventeen MSN papers and an overnight response from Washington about the female Russian mathematician. Neither the embassy nor the FBI knew her identity, and finding it wouldn't be easy. For the embassy, an extensive file search might be a security risk. For the FBI, a trace required either a name or manpower in New York to find it. They wouldn't do more unless MI5 deemed it essential, which it didn't.

Meanwhile, Fuchs kept going about his normal life. In mid-November, he and Peierls went to a three-day conference on elementary particles in Edinburgh organized by his former mentor Max Born. They caught the night train in London—Robertson didn't have them followed—and from Peierls's daily phone calls to his wife the Listeners reported that the two sat together at the conference, hung around together talking physics, and one night went to a terrible movie.

The Watchers did pick up Fuchs on his return to King's Cross at 7:10 a.m. They noted his trip to Paddington Station, a phone call, and breakfast at the station. A man joined him. They ate and paid the bill, and Fuchs took the 9:15 train to Didcot. The Watchers followed his breakfast companion, and they found that his life was about as exciting as Fuchs's. He went to the men's room, took the tube to Trafalgar Square, visited a number of bookstores specializing in scientific texts, ending up at a branch of Butterworth's where he spent the next three and a half hours in the Scientific Research Department. After having a bite to eat and getting his backpack from the coatroom at Paddington, he boarded the 5:35 p.m. train to Didcot. Such was the humdrum of a researcher at Harwell—and those who watched.

A few days later, the esteemed Danish physicist Niels Bohr arrived to give a lecture. Because Cockcroft was busy, Fuchs played host, driving him to Cambridge and then to London to see James Chadwick, the man who had directed the British mission in America during the war.

On November 25, Martin cabled Patterson in Washington that "all necessary clearance has been obtained for the interrogation." Three weeks later,

MI5 officers gathered along with Perrin. They decided that Jim Skardon, their top interrogator, would meet with Fuchs on Wednesday, December 21. If he wanted to confess and needed assurances, they authorized Skardon to tell him that "his position can only be improved by complete frankness." If they were forced to dismiss him from Harwell, they would give Emil Fuchs's move to Leipzig as the reason, ideally blunting any objections from colleagues. With his new chair at the University of Liverpool, Skinner would probably welcome Fuchs there.

Dick White outlined the strategy, saying that Skardon should accuse Fuchs of being a spy and focus on his activities in New York. Skardon, White argued, needed to convince Fuchs that they knew he was a spy and that the inquiry didn't arise simply because the Russians had detonated a bomb. Once again, there were concerns that the solidity of their evidence against Fuchs might compromise the long-standing American decryption program Venona.

Robertson put the Watchers and Listeners on alert for the twenty-first, not only for Fuchs, but for Yapou, Malleson, and Peierls as well. He established that Fuchs should not be detained if he were to leave the country before the interrogation. If the outcome of the interrogation was unfavorable, however, the Metropolitan Police (Special Branch) was "to detain FUCHS on any pretext if he is seen to be intending to leave the country."

On December 21, Skardon took the train from Paddington and arrived in Didcot at 10:27 a.m. Arnold met him and drove to Harwell, where Arnold introduced him to Cockcroft. The latter had been briefed on the interrogation and possible reactions.

Robertson gave Arnold strict instructions not to forewarn Fuchs. So, Arnold came to Fuchs's office around 11:00 and asked the physicist to accompany him. Someone wanted to speak to him about his father. Arnold walked with Fuchs to his office, introduced him to a tall, thin man named Jim Seddon (Skardon's alias), and departed. Skardon opened up by explaining the security risk with his father moving to Leipzig. Fuchs then described his youth in Germany for over an hour. Suddenly, in the midst of this recitation, Skardon broke in and accused him of spying. Fuchs, somewhat stunned, replied, "I don't think so." Skardon continued to prod him until they broke for lunch at 12:45. Skardon wanted Fuchs to eat alone so that he could take time to reflect on what he had said.

Fuchs had other plans. The controlled and contained Fuchs, seemingly unfazed, went to the Skinners', where Erna fixed him a lunch of soft foods. Having broken the plate for his front teeth, he was in significant discomfort. He called a dentist in Oxford to schedule an appointment, then went back to Arnold's office.

In the afternoon, Skardon made it clear that the Ministry of Supply planned to remove him from Harwell because of his father. The Ministry didn't know about the spying, though, and with a favorable report from him on his espionage activities, he might be able to stay at Harwell. The interview ended at 3:45.

Shortly after the interrogation broke up, Skardon called Leconfield House to say that Fuchs had confirmed much of what was known about him but denied being a spy. He then returned to London for a debriefing at 8:00 p.m. Robertson alerted the Listeners, Watchers, and Arnold to pay special attention to Fuchs's reactions and movements.

The Listener on Fuchs's office tap recorded that he seemed preoccupied on his return to his office. When a man came into his office reminding him of the division's Christmas tea party, he departed and returned an hour and a half later. Then he left for home. Part of the evening he spent at the Skinners'. The rest of the evening was a blank. He wasn't home by midnight, when the Listeners signed off. When he came in wasn't recorded.

Deputy Chief Guy Liddell summarized MI5's evening meeting with Skardon in his diary:

> He [Fuchs] went over the whole ground, beginning with his early career, FUCHS admitted everything that we knew and, in fact, volunteered the information with certain additions. He had been associated with the KPD in his activities against the Nazis and after Hitler came into power he went to Paris where he had been in touch with Otto Katz and others. He had not, however, engaged

in any such activities in this country, to which he was extremely grateful for the hospitality that it had extended to him, and for his naturalisation. Finally, Skardon came to the point, when he suggested that FUCHS had been passing information to the Russians. FUCHS smiled and said he did not quite understand. Skardon then put the point quite bluntly, when FUCHS denied flatly that he had ever done anything of the kind; he could not see why he should want to. Skardon then took him very carefully over the ground during the period when he was in America, and told him that our information was positive and that we could not disclose our informants, and said that if it was not FUCHS it "could only be his twin brother." FUCHS said that he could offer no explanation as to how this mistake occurred. He admitted having visited his sister and even possibly to have taken papers with him; he could not conceive, however, that his sister would have betrayed him, even if she had an opportunity to do so.

Liddell further noted that when Skardon asked Fuchs why he went to see Arnold, Fuchs explained that his father was very outspoken, and if he was dissatisfied with the "Soviet zone," he could make a fuss, even be arrested. He wanted Arnold to know of this possibility. He hadn't recognized the potential for pressure on himself. Liddell's conclusion:

> FUCHS demeanor throughout was wholly consistent with guilt or with his innocence and we are, therefore, left with an extremely awkward situation on our hands.

The next morning, the Listeners came back on at 8:00 and heard Fuchs get up at 8:45. Erna's call to him mid-morning at the office centered on herself, telling him that "she didn't know how she was going to get through the day until 3:20 when ELAINE [her daughter] went." Her remedy was lunch with him, suggesting scrambled eggs because of his teeth. She relayed an interesting piece of information. She "told him what a heavy sleeper he was—she had telephoned for about 1½ hours the night before about 2 a.m.!"

After midnight the microphone in his house recorded a knock on the front door that he also didn't answer.

The bugs and phone checks left many unanswered questions. Who knocked on the door? Was he at home when Erna called at 2:00 a.m.? He could have been. Sometimes, in the middle of the night, he didn't answer her calls. Did he go someplace after visiting her? Did he simply drive around and ponder?

MI5 did not address these mysteries the next day, and the Watchers and the Listeners contributed nothing more. MI5's records focused on the outcome of the interview.

Martin boiled it down in a cable to Washington:

1. FUCHS volunteered or admitted all facts except those deduced from [VENONA].

2. He flatly denied espionage and admitted no contacts which might suggest he was unconscious source.

3. We shall re-interrogate.

4. Meeting with Directorate Atomic Energy December 28th will decide disposal.

5. Please inform F.B.I. Stress value of any new information on network they may have.

No one questioned Fuchs's ease of delivery. From Skardon's notes his presentation seemed smooth, organized, and lucid, rehearsed almost—especially his recitation of his background. No unintentional slips of names or details. No entanglement in a web of lies. No crack for MI5 to widen. Skardon's accusation that he had spied did make him pause. But a bit of a surprised response would be expected.

The next day Perrin came over to Leconfield House to talk with Liddell. They decided that the negative outcome required an analysis of the evidence—two columns, with the raw information in one and MI5's explanation of each piece in the other. Perrin wanted to separate accusations of Fuchs's spying from the question of what to do with him, and he wanted to resolve the latter quickly.

At the embassy in Washington, Patterson reacted with disappointment. Complying with Martin's request, he spent several hours at FBI headquarters searching for anything new to help but came away empty-handed. He ventured to Martin that although Fuchs's guilt wasn't definite, all signs still pointed to him.

Most of MI5 felt even more certain than Patterson. The 10:30 meeting on the twenty-eighth at Shell Mex House included a full roster: Portal, Cockcroft, Perrin, Liddell, White, Skardon, and Martin. Skardon reviewed the information from the interrogation, and others dissected the evidence.

Martin's minutes noted a difficult moment when Portal suggested that he and Cockcroft interview Fuchs to get him to confess. He wanted to pledge to Fuchs that if he confessed, "no legal or repressive action would be taken against him for his activities in New York." Dick White quickly pointed out a number of problems with the suggestion and gently reestablished the responsibility for the interrogation within MI5. The question of what was to become of Fuchs was deferred once again until after Skardon's next round with Fuchs.

That afternoon the MI5 group reviewed the morning's discussion. Their first concern was to maintain Fuchs's impression that MI5 would not inform the Ministry of Supply about the espionage allegations. Their second was to disabuse Portal firmly about interrogating Fuchs. They spun a rationale to offer Portal: he had to disassociate himself so he couldn't be questioned by Parliament or the press about the source material. He needed to maintain deniability.

Another problem, quietly brewing, brought the meeting to an end with a tense discussion. The decoders in Arlington had just identified a Venona message that referred to a trip Goose, Rest's handler, made to Rest's sister in Cambridge, Massachusetts, on September 20, 1944. Because of a corrupt number group, it wasn't clear if a certain sentence referred to Rest's departure on that date or his sister's. If it was Rest's, Fuchs's movements did not fit the timeline in the messages. He was already in Los Alamos then. Liddell reflected in his diary, "It is evident we are on somewhat shifting sand, and that it is never possible to be certain that we have got the correct solution unless we have all the groups in the sentence. This is rather disturbing."

In the midst of his uncertainty, Skardon's second interrogation of Fuchs took place on December 30.

Emil and Else Fuchs in front of the old parsonage in Rüsselsheim, Germany, around 1914. (COURTESY OF THE FUCHS FAMILY)

Else with baby Klaus in 1912. (COURTESY OF THE FUCHS FAMILY)

Emil Fuchs, Lutheran
minister, Quaker,
and theologian.

(COURTESY OF THE FUCHS FAMILY)

Children playing with toy soldiers in trenches, ca. 1915 (*left to
right*): Christel, friend, Klaus, Gerhard. (COURTESY OF THE FUCHS FAMILY)

A day riding in Eisenach (*left to right*): Gerhard, Elisabeth, Christel, Klaus.

Klaus doing calisthenics with his cousins in 1926 (*left to right*): Christel, cousin, Klaus.

A happy twelve-year-old Klaus.

Klaus in a school play in Eisenach.

Klaus playing the violin, self-taught.

A somber family meal on the porch in Eisenach in the mid-1920s (*left to right*): Christel, Gerhard, Else, Elisabeth, Klaus.

Elisabeth and Klaus sawing wood in Kiel, 1932.

The Fuchs children in the early 1930s; first row (*left to right*): Karin (Gerhard's future wife), Elisabeth, Christel; second row (*left to right*): friend, Gerhard, Klaus.

Gerhard during his underground days in Berlin leading the Red Student Group, 1933.

Klaus's registration photo when he arrived in the UK in September 1933.

The physics department at the University of Bristol, 1935–36; first row: Herbert Skinner (*second from left*) and Nevill Mott (*fifth from left*); second row: Klaus (*third from left*).

Gustav and Max Born in their backyard in Edinburgh in the late 1940s.

Rudi and Genia Peierls in New York, 1943.

Elisabeth Fuchs-Kittowski and young son Klaus, 1937.

The Quaker Meeting House in Bad Pyrmont, Germany; a smiling Elisabeth far to the right in the left-hand window on the day before she died in 1939. (COURTESY OF THE FUCHS FAMILY)

Internment Camp N in Sherbrooke, Canada; internee wearing uniform with red circle on his back, early 1940s.

Ernest Hemingway with Hans Kahle during the 1937 Madrid Front in the Spanish Civil War (*left to right*): Hemingway, Kahle, German author Ludwig Renn, filmmaker Joris Ivens.

Klaus Fuchs's ID photo for Los Alamos, 1944.

The tech area at Los Alamos, early 1940s. (*THE MANHATTAN PROJECT: AN INTERACTIVE HISTORY, U.S. DEPARTMENT OF ENERGY—OFFICE OF HISTORY AND HERITAGE RESOURCES*)

Oscar and Mary Buneman with sons Peter and Michael in 1946.

A picnic near Harwell during the July 1949 visit of Emil and young Klaus (*left to right*): a woman in a bathing suit, Klaus Fuchs-Kittowski, Klaus Fuchs, Erna Skinner, a friend, Elaine Skinner, Emil Fuchs (white hair showing), and another physicist.

Guy Liddell, deputy director of MI5 and disciplined diarist.

Harry Gold in an FBI mug shot after his arrest in 1950.

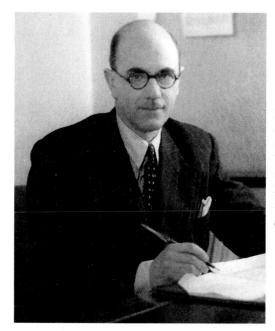

Michael Perrin, the coordinator for the British atomic bomb project during WWII and deputy for atomic energy at the Ministry of Supply while Fuchs was at Harwell.

(COURTESY OF THE PERRIN FAMILY)

Jim Skardon, MI5 Officer, and Henry Arnold, chief of security, Harwell, on March 1, 1950, the day of the Fuchs trial.

(COURTESY OF TOPFOTO)

Grete Keilson and
Klaus Fuchs-Kittowski
as they wait for Klaus's
plane to land on June
23, 1959, in East
Germany.

The three Fuchs men in the garden of Klaus's weekend house near
Dresden ca. 1960 (*left to right*): Klaus, Emil, and nephew Klaus.

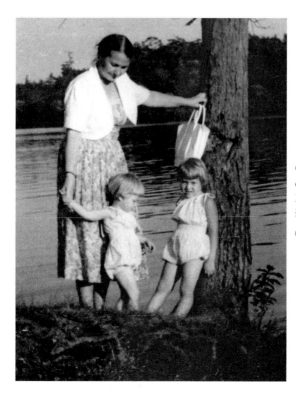

Christel with her daughters Heidi and Marianna visiting Klaus in Germany, 1960.

(COURTESY OF THE FUCHS FAMILY)

Klaus and Grete in the mid-1960s.   (COURTESY OF THE FUCHS FAMILY)

V

RESULTS

Wormwood Scrubs Prison, London

CHAPTER 19

Disposal Again, London, January 1950

AS THE SECOND HALF OF THE TWENTIETH CENTURY BEGAN, THE QUESTION LOOMING over MI5 was what to do about Klaus Fuchs. They had no hard evidence to support prosecution, but the circumstantial evidence was overwhelming. A new episode in the five-month saga of Fuchs's investigation—the interrogations—had unfolded in just the last two weeks.

On January 2, Liddell reviewed the case for Prime Minister Attlee. He reminded the PM that after careful analysis MI5 had determined that interrogating Fuchs promised the best resolution and that Fuchs's report of his father's move to the Soviet zone opened up this option. They had undertaken two interrogations, so far with no results. The interrogator had conveyed three important "facts to him"—that his father's move jeopardized his remaining at Harwell; that MI5 knew he had spied; and that MI5 had not relayed his spying activities to his employer, the Ministry of Supply (which wasn't true). Fuchs's demeanor throughout was ambiguous, consistent with either guilt or innocence, and the government had yet to make a final decision of how to dispose of him. But they had decided that retaining Fuchs at Harwell was an unacceptable risk. How to dispose of him and when were the questions that vexed them.

January 4, 1950, became the day of decision. The Ministry of Supply's directors along with Guy Liddell met at 4:00 p.m. at Shell Mex House to finalize Fuchs's disposal. They outlined three steps:

1. Harwell's director, John Cockcroft, will inform Herbert Skinner, Fuchs's direct boss, that Fuchs must leave Harwell because of his father's move. Cockcroft will ask Skinner if he can find a position for him at the University of Liverpool, where Skinner will take a chair at the end of March. If all agreed, the government would publicly indicate Fuchs's departure to take another job. Nothing more said.
2. Cockcroft will tell Fuchs that he must resign because of his father's move, that MI5 is "adamant" about that.
3. Fuchs will prepare to hand over the department to his successor and can leave when Skinner does so in March, the risk to his staying not high, because he can pass any information he has to the Russians "as long as he is alive."

They mulled over whether they should interrogate him one more time, perhaps softening him up by confronting his obvious concerns about implicating his sister. They could guarantee him that "anything he told us would not be passed to the Americans." Of course, the gathering cynically noted, the Americans already knew, and MI5 could do nothing to stop the U.S. government from prosecuting Christel if it had evidence. Protecting Christel wasn't MI5's problem; getting Fuchs to confess was.

In fact, MI5 had no real interest in absolving her. As Sir Percy Sillitoe, MI5's director general, declared, "We ourselves think the Heinemans [*sic*] were in it up to the neck."

The steps unfolded on January 10. Some time after lunch, Fuchs met with Cockcroft and heard that he had to resign from Harwell because of his father's move.

Michael Perrin talked to Cockcroft about the discussion, and as he

reported to MI5 officer John Marriott, the time limit Cockcroft gave Fuchs
for his departure was vague. Arthur Martin and Marriott journeyed to
Harwell to hear Cockcroft's account of the meeting.

Cockcroft's account disturbed them. He had offered to help Fuchs find
a university position, perhaps with Skinner in his new post in Liverpool or,
as he added at his own discretion, maybe one at the University of Adelaide
in Australia, where there was also a post. Fuchs, in turn, admitted that he
had thought of taking such a position for some time. He had delayed the
decision while waiting for results from the "fast" reactor, a pet interest that
would lead to exploiting atomic energy for large-scale commercial nuclear
power. These reactors generate more fissile material than they use and so
are also known as "breeder" reactors. Reprocessing the excess creates more
plutonium to fuel another reactor and leaves less nuclear waste to deal
with, a boon to civilization.

Cockcroft suggested a six-month leave of absence starting at Easter
and told him that only he, Perrin, Perrin's boss, Lord Portal, and Arnold
knew that he was to resign, something MI5 was adamant about unless
Fuchs gave them further information about his life and background. Otherwise, they could help reverse the Ministry's decision.

The suggestion of Fuchs's teaching in Australia, the lack of specificity
for the basis of his departure—whether a university offer or his father's
move—and especially the delay until Easter seriously aggravated Marriott. He told Cockcroft that he would speak with the DG, Sillitoe, to determine if MI5 would maintain surveillance until Easter.

Folded into this mix of aggravations were tentative travel plans for
Fuchs. Just prior to Klaus's conversation with Cockcroft on January 10, he had
spoken with Erna, and she had expressed concern that he might be getting
sick. He thought not. Why then, she wanted to know, was he now "all wonky"
again? He had been much better. What was the mystery? A long meeting, he
explained. Maybe he would take off the whole of next week. Erna suggested
leaving on Monday night.

Erna's chitchats the next day exposed another travel option—a potential trip to Switzerland with some Harwell neighbors. Erna doubted whether

he would go, she told her friends. "He's in such a state of indecision about everything, I just don't know. I've been trying to push him hard."

A few hours later, MI5 picked up hints from another phone conversation between Erna and Klaus that he might have told her about "his forced resignation." Herbert wanted him to come over for a chat that evening. In all probability, Cockcroft had, in accordance with the MI5 disposal plan, briefed Herbert on Klaus's resignation, making it equally likely that he leaked the information to Erna.

The proposed travel interrupted James Robertson's plans to reduce surveillance further, something the overtaxed MI5 team desperately needed. With Fuchs informed about his resignation, Robertson had decided to eliminate the Listeners at Newbury. He saw no need for fast feedback to MI5 or the SF reception equipment (the small washer on the phone that kept the connection open). The regular taps on Fuchs's home and office phones, and on the Skinners', would continue to chronicle life in Harwell, picking up the usual dinners, lunches, teas, and an upcoming party at Klaus's prefab for a departing colleague. As for travel outside the U.K., MI5 advised that Fuchs not be restrained. They couldn't justify it; they had no hard evidence.

Robertson postponed the additional decrease in surveillance until after Fuchs and Erna Skinner returned from their three-day vacation that would start on January 16.

The Skinners' daughter, Elaine, always maintained that a chaperone—one of her mother's regular companions—accompanied Klaus and her mother on these outings, of which there had been a few others. MI5's surveillance didn't confirm that version. Klaus and Erna timed their travels to coincide with Herbert's now regular trips to the University of Liverpool.

Skardon met with Fuchs for the third time on January 13. As with the previous interrogations, Skardon checked on a few details such as Fuchs's address in New York and his friendships there, both important to Arthur Martin's efforts to match up information and liaise with Washington and the FBI.

As sure as MI5 was of Fuchs's espionage, they weren't sure enough.

The intelligence from the Venona decodes received six months earlier had to reconcile with those from the administrative files of the British Diffusion Mission in New York. Martin had waded through layers of bureaucracy to track down the files and then dig through them. The Venona messages gave him Fuchs's dates of travel to Los Alamos, mode of transportation, specifics on a call to Kristel in November 1944 while in Chicago on a business trip, visits by his handler to Kristel, worries of the handler when "Rest" disappeared from New York.

Everything pertaining to Rest needed to agree with Fuchs's actual record. This circumstantial evidence was the bulk of their proof. The only hard evidence of secrets passed on was the MSN-12 document on fluctuations in the flow of nitrogen.

Given Martin's burden, Fuchs's corroboration helped him, but Skardon's goal for the meeting was to determine Fuchs's understanding of his conversation with Cockcroft, which Skardon summarized in his report: "He had been told that he must go, but that there was nothing very urgent about it and he had not so far made any positive enquiry to find any job."

In this third interview, Skardon found Fuchs "completely composed." None of the "wonkiness" that Erna had observed a few days before showed through.

MI5 was less composed when hearing of Fuchs's understanding about his departure. Dick White called Perrin stating that the director general "would be extremely averse" to Fuchs's going to Australia and that if he stayed at Harwell indefinitely, MI5 would take no responsibility. The next day, a letter from the director general to the director of the Ministry of Supply diplomatically stated that Fuchs needed to leave Harwell "as soon as it is decently possible."

On January 19, the day that Klaus and Erna returned to Harwell from their brief retreat, he spent a few hours at the Skinners' in the evening. One result was that the next morning Skinner called Henry Arnold requesting to see him about Klaus. Skinner also said that he wanted to speak with John

Cockcroft, who apparently had said something out of turn to him, such as
"he wished Fuchs had been more co-operative." Arnold, who well understood the personalities in his charge, guessed that during his trip with
Erna, Klaus had revealed his sessions with Skardon. He put off Skinner
until 5:00 that evening. He needed guidance from Robertson on how to
handle the situation.

The advice was straightforward: for Arnold to acknowledge basically
what Skinner already knew and no more—that is, a security officer had
talked with Fuchs about his father's move to the Russian zone and that the
authorities insisted that Fuchs resign because of it. As for Cockcroft, Arnold
was to tell him to admit to those points, again nothing more.

In the convoluted world of espionage, it wasn't that straightforward.
MI5 had to coordinate three players, Arnold, Skinner, and Cockcroft, each
of whom had a different level of knowledge and different concerns. MI5
didn't trust the one in charge, Director Cockcroft, to appreciate the seri-
ousness of the situation. A kindly academic, he seemed to lack the necessary guile. Skinner, on the other hand, had additional information from
Fuchs. How inclusive it was, MI5 didn't know. So, Arnold (whose knowledge was limited) was to tell Cockcroft that Skinner might believe that
other factors had led to Fuchs's resignation. If there were other factors (ones
that Arnold himself didn't know), Cockcroft should not reveal them to
Skinner. MI5 also alerted Perrin, who knew all.

Most important, Fuchs understood from Skardon that only MI5 knew
he had spied, not Cockcroft or the Ministry of Supply—who both, of course,
did know in a general way. If Klaus perceived their deceit, the scheme to
get him to open up could crumble.

Over the next few evenings, Klaus visited the Skinners to talk about the
situation. The discussions ended with Herbert's expounding on the obliga-
tions of friendship. What Klaus might have told Erna—and then she told
Herbert—while on their trip was never made explicit, but whatever it was,
it was sufficient to set off Herbert on one's responsibilities to friends, how

one's actions reflect on others. Klaus later ascribed this discussion to his next decisions that determined his fate.

On January 21, he called Henry Arnold, who wasn't home. When Klaus reached him the next morning, he said he wanted to have a "long, quiet talk." They made plans for lunch the following day and then discussed the Bunemans.

Harwell, its insular environment inhabited by exceptionally talented and intelligent people, wasn't immune to the ordinary, or maybe extraordinary, problems of everyday life, including affairs of the heart and all the attendant complications. In addition to the complexities of the Skinner relationship, the marriage of Mary and Oscar Buneman was in trouble. Mary was having an affair with one of Klaus's staff members, and thus a close colleague of Oscar's. The wives gossiped in their kindly, concerned way, and the Skinners and Klaus spent late nights discussing the personal as well as the professional. No one took sides. Arnold and Klaus were doing as much as they could to help, including Klaus's promise to Oscar to help him find a new job. Everyone supported both Mary and Oscar, all the while Erna, Herbert, and Henry Arnold circled around Klaus's situation.

Seemingly, Arnold made his call to MI5 for guidance about the meeting with Fuchs. Robertson instructed Arnold to try to get Fuchs to open up. If Fuchs wanted a guarantee of immunity, Robertson advised, Arnold must say that he doesn't know the details and doesn't have the authority. If Fuchs adds information that Arnold isn't supposed to know or information completely new to Arnold, he should listen and then make it clear to Fuchs that he has to report this information to the authorities. "Arnold should however," forewarned Robertson, "postpone any statement to this effect until the latest possible stage of the conversation." MI5's idea of a caution was to wrench as much information as possible from the confessor before warning about the legal consequences.

Arnold and Fuchs had lunch on January 23 at the Railway House Hotel, a few miles outside Harwell, close to Abingdon. Their relationship a friendly one, they chatted a while, and then Fuchs came to the point: he asked to speak to the MI5 security officer the next day. Notes from Arnold's later call to Leconfield House suggest that Fuchs revealed more, but Arnold didn't provide the details on the phone. The notes said that Arnold, trying not to be too optimistic, "had the impression that FUCHS wanted very much to talk and to talk a lot. Arnold thought that he might well now be ready to make a confession." MI5 couldn't hope for more than that.

By 4:30 that afternoon, both men were at the Skinners'. Erna needed their help with Mary Buneman. She had fallen apart and was at the Skinners' on her way to the hospital. Oscar was there as well. In the midst of the to-do, Henry Arnold slipped in a phone call to his deputy at Harwell to ask him to "ring Jimmy or James on 126 and leave a very cryptic message—11 a.m. as arranged prefab."

Arnold also talked with Erna that afternoon. She was concerned about Klaus's level of anxiety, which seemed out of proportion to his father's move to Leipzig, she remarked, perhaps fishing for more. He had told her that there were other factors but they weren't very serious. She assured Arnold of Klaus's integrity. The rumors about Fuchs's resignation and his father's move to Leipzig had already started at Harwell. But the Skinners knew more. How much more was MI5's question.

The next morning, Skardon left London and took the train to Didcot, where Arnold picked him up, then dropped him off in the compound to walk alone on this cold and wet day to Fuchs's prefab for the 11:00 meeting.

It was just the two of them. Robertson had dismantled the monitoring system at Newbury, and Fuchs was probably unaware that he was more alone than he had been in months.

Fuchs and Skardon hadn't seen each other for ten days. The Fuchs who opened the door was a changed person to Skardon—agitated and extremely pale. Skardon said to him, "You asked to see me, and here I am." Fuchs replied, "Yes. It's rather up to me now."

A pause followed. Skardon waited, thinking that some uncertainty had unsettled Fuchs. Then Fuchs began to unburden himself. For the next two hours, he told the story of his life, from his days in the underground to his present work, of its importance to him and to Harwell, and of his friends at that institution. He stressed the belief that Russia had made the only sincere effort to defeat the Nazis. Internment had "to some extent" reinforced his view of the British government's making shameful compromises with the Nazis (as he had explained to Walter Kellermann years earlier).

This was their fourth interview, and previous ones had revealed much the same details to Skardon. He listened and waited as Fuchs held his head in his hands, looking haggard. Even though there was little new information, telling it seemed to drain Fuchs. There was a different emotional quality this time.

Finally, Skardon said, "You have told me a long story providing the motives for actions, but nothing about the actions themselves." Seeing Fuchs's emotional stress, Skardon counseled that he relieve his conscience. Fuchs replied in a steady voice, "I will never be persuaded by you to talk."

Skardon suggested a lunch from a daily food truck, but Fuchs chose for them to go to Abingdon. Once behind the wheel of his MG, he drove fast and recklessly—passing vehicles within inches. At the town's main hotel, the two men ate a quick lunch mixed with a somewhat strained, gossipy conversation about Harwell. Fuchs was distracted. After coffee in the lounge, he quickly got up, saying, "Let's go back."

CHAPTER 20

Confession, Harwell, January 1950

WHEN DID IT START?" SKARDON ASKED WHEN THEY ARRIVED BACK AT THE PREFAB.
"About the middle of 1942," Fuchs answered, "and it continued until about a year ago."

Skardon was startled. MI5's only evidence came from the Venona messages and exposed activities in New York. But if Fuchs started in 1942, it didn't require a mathematician to add in the years for Birmingham, Los Alamos, and Harwell nor his intimate involvement in the development of the bomb for Britain and the United States.

This second half of the narrative went on for an hour and a half, the facts tumbling out so quickly that Skardon said he didn't take notes. Fuchs began at the beginning: his first meeting in London, which he initiated; the meetings that took place every few months; and the type of general information he passed on, first his own work and later everything he could, including the details for making the atomic bomb, "the worst thing," he said. He told of questions from his contacts that didn't arise from material he handed them but gave few details on his contacts whose names he didn't know. Skardon later wrote that Fuchs understood the risk, that "he was carrying his life in his hands, but that he had done this from the time of his under-ground days in Germany." He was compelled by "a duty to the world" to pass information to the Russians.

He ended at what was the end for him—a belief in communism but disillusionment with its practice in the Soviet Union. In February 1949, he had cut the tie by missing a rendezvous. He wanted to settle in England. His sister, he stressed, knew nothing of his activities.

At 3:55, Skardon called Arnold to say he was about to leave and had set up another interview with Fuchs for two days hence. He then proceeded to Arnold's office, where he called MI5 at 4:30 and reported that Fuchs had made a full confession. Because the line wasn't secure, the conversation was short. His instructions were to inform Cockcroft and return home. He would brief MI5 the next morning at 10:00 in the director general's office. Arnold drove him to the train station.

The lights stayed on at Leconfield House late that night as four mem-bers of the MI5 team huddled to mull over new surveillance procedures. Their first priority was to reestablish monitoring with Listeners and SF reception equipment in Newbury on a twenty-four-hour basis. The deci-sion on observations they delayed until the next day. They informed the director general and Perrin of all developments.

With the confession, MI5 could now issue a warrant should Fuchs try to leave the country, a worrisome but unlikely possibility. Immediate arrest wasn't a priority. MI5 had already revealed its suspicions about his spying in the three previous interviews, and he had not fled. Skardon's report was crucial for the next decisions.

Arnold called Robertson at 8:00 that same evening to report suspicious activity. He had earlier noticed Fuchs in his office neatly stacking documents on his desk. "Was Fuchs planning a 'get-away'?" Arnold wondered. Robert-son proposed another interpretation: that he was preparing for his succes-sor. They agreed that Arnold should check out Fuchs's office if he wouldn't be detected. The Listeners, quickly put in place, then reported that for the last half an hour Fuchs appeared very occupied with his home fire. On a 10:00 p.m. call, Robertson and Arnold discussed his entering Fuchs's house

CONFESSION, HARWELL, JANUARY 1950

the next day, again depending on the risk, to check for burned documents. The next morning Arnold reported a quiet night.

Robertson called Arnold later to tell him to do no investigating, just maintain the "status quo." No disturbances.

Skardon's 10:00 a.m. debrief in the director general's office lasted one hour. The main decision was to extract as much information as possible and "to maintain FUCHS in his present state of mind, and for this state of mind to be in no way disturbed."

Guy Liddell's full description of the meeting in his diary revealed no shock or hand-wringing. Besides logging in a broad sweep of the details, he pondered about what had finally made Fuchs break, ideas tossed around perhaps with his colleagues. His initial thoughts were prosaic: Cockcroft's comment to him about his lack of frankness with the MI5 interviewer; open knowledge of his relationship with Erna; discussions with Herbert. Maybe it was all of these, he surmised, combined with Skardon's undermining of his defenses.

His list overlooked one key factor, perhaps because, even though MI5 had heavily depended on it all along, they had just as much undervalued it: Henry Arnold. Without Fuchs's trust in Arnold, MI5's highly prized confession might never have come about. In Michael Perrin's view, it was Arnold who, "by slowly working on him and becoming almost his personal friend, got all the information out of him which really led to his arrest."

But it was the deeper psychology that intrigued Liddell. In thinking through why Fuchs had confessed, he noted, "In the light of what he said, it is clear that vanity plays a great part. . . . In his conversation he made it perfectly plain that in his view he was indispensable at Harwell . . . and should be retained. He evidently thinks that he can, without too much difficulty, persuade the authorities to retain his services. This is, I think, where his vanity and megalomania come in."

No doubt, a vain streak ran through Fuchs, and in that vulnerable moment of baring all, he relied on it to shield himself and to present his case for remaining at Harwell. He had little else to wield. That Liddell labeled it "megalomania" might have spoken more to his own understated personality than to Fuchs's having an imperious one.

In addition, Skardon's official report made no mention of his promise to Fuchs to stay at Harwell if he confessed nor Cockcroft's repetition of it, and Liddell was unaware. This factor arose that afternoon when Skardon and Robertson briefed Perrin. Perrin's perceptive questions brought the key legal issue to the fore: inducement. It appears that Skardon had not disabused Fuchs of this quid pro quo during the confession. In keeping the tone of a comfortable, friendly chat, Skardon had not cautioned Fuchs about his legal rights either. As Robertson pointed out to Perrin when the latter asked about prosecution, "The statement so far from FUCHS had been obtained without a caution, and *in circumstances in which it might possibly be argued* [italics added] that there had been inducement." That is, inducement could make legal proceedings against Fuchs invalid.

MI5 had effectively manipulated Fuchs's weak spot—his desire to stay at Harwell. It wasn't the reason for his confession—that was friendships— but his vanity was just potent enough to let him believe what Skardon and Cockcroft told him: if he confessed, he could stay. Cockcroft was surely sincere; he considered Fuchs essential to Harwell. He simply repeated to Fuchs what he had been told. Skardon was anything but sincere.

Did Fuchs confess? Yes. Did the government gain the confession legally? No, there was inducement. Could it prosecute him? Not under these circumstances.

Skardon proposed a solution to Robertson and Perrin: to obtain a formal, written statement from Fuchs to use as evidence. With such a statement in hand, they could seriously consider prosecution.

Perrin brought up concerns about Fuchs's reaction. Would he try to escape or commit suicide? Skardon thought neither option likely. Fuchs had "complete confidence in the likelihood of his remaining at Harwell." He regarded himself as the "lynch-pin" there. Skardon assured Perrin, "In his present state of mind it is almost inconceivable to FUCHS that he might be removed."

There had been no Listeners, no tape recording on that rainy afternoon of the twenty-fourth when Fuchs confessed. Just Skardon. MI5 later
released a one-and-a-half-page report of the several-hour interview. Skardon wrote a longer version that it did not release. The surety of Skardon's
remark to Perrin—"complete confidence in the likelihood of his remaining
at Harwell"—certainly creates questions of what further assurances Skardon had offered Fuchs.

Nor were any further tapings to occur at the prefab. MI5 reestablished
SF (the washer inserted into the phone) there but decided not to reinstall
the Listeners in Newbury because the advantage was unclear. The mic
didn't always provide a clear transcript. Besides, Skardon indicated that
a tape recording might embarrass him. He didn't explain why—maybe
offering more inducements? The DG agreed that its use was at Skardon's
discretion.

Fuchs's actions backed up Skardon's confidence in his state of mind.
After his confession, he had gone to the office for half an hour, busied himself at home between 7:00 and 8:00 p.m., and then was out until 10:00. The
bugs gave no hint of where he was for those two hours.

Robertson had reduced surveillance after Klaus and Erna returned
from their short holiday. No one expected Fuchs to flee or to spy. It was a
calculated risk, but they also didn't want the possibility of surveillance to
unnerve him.

Around 11:00 the next day, Fuchs stopped in Arnold's office to apologize "for having been secretive hitherto." Skardon had always maintained
that only MI5 knew about the allegations and had never suggested that
Arnold was involved. For his part, Arnold indicated no awareness. But
Fuchs sensed otherwise and said that he thought Arnold knew more than
he admitted. As he had throughout, Arnold stayed mum.

Then Fuchs lunched with a potential new staff member at his office and
showed the recruit around Harwell and houses in Didcot. Erna went along
for the ride. An ordinary day, and no hint of concern on the part of MI5.

Fuchs arrived at his office around 10:00 on the morning of January 26
and checked in with Arnold to ensure that MI5 understood his position at

Harwell in light of an upcoming conference. Arnold told him that Skardon did understand and appreciated it. Using the opportunity, Arnold asked Fuchs if he had handed information to the Russians. Fuchs said yes—on the plutonium bomb, the hydrogen bomb, and diffusion. Arnold told him that "it was a dreadful blow" and hurt him deeply. To Arnold, Fuchs seemed "much affected."

Then Fuchs met Skardon at his prefab at 11:00. They discussed Fuchs's main concern, resolving his position at Harwell as quickly as possible and ensuring that the authorities understood his importance to the research program.

Skardon's memo for the meeting shows that immediately after Fuchs shared his worry, Skardon "asked him whether he would like to make a written statement incorporating any details that he thought to be borne in mind." Between the lines, one can almost hear Skardon, polite and friendly, say, "Sure, just write down what happened and then we can figure it out." Fuchs wanted to believe, and Skardon let him.

For the rest of the interview, Fuchs generally described his rendezvous over the years. He disagreed with Skardon that "espionage is properly considered to be an offense." He countered that he had supplied information to the British obtained from the United States, which the McMahon Act had made illegal to reveal. Skardon had no response. At this moment, the legality of spying wasn't the issue. The issue was whom you chose to spy for.

Skardon left just after 1:00, and Fuchs quickly called Erna. She asked how he was. Sounding confident, and obviously pleased with the outcome of the interview with Skardon, he answered, "I think it's under control."

He told her he was going to see Mary Buneman in the hospital in Oxford.

Erna demanded, "Why do you do things without consulting me? I mean, you promised you wouldn't."

Klaus had a simple but confident answer: "Yes, I'm sorry. Just now I'm in the habit of taking things into my own hands."

When she couldn't persuade him not to go, she asked, "Well, can you

drive? Because if you're going to drive as you've driven me lately—!"
Apparently, the death-defying ride Skardon had experienced with Fuchs
at the wheel was not an isolated event.

The next morning, Friday the twenty-seventh, Fuchs took the 9:28
train from Didcot to London. He had told Erna that he was meeting up
with Perrin.

While he traveled, White and Robertson called Perrin to brief him
about Fuchs's interview with Skardon later that morning. Robertson stated
in his minutes, "We regard this as of over-riding importance at the moment
in view of its bearing on the possibility of a successful prosecution which—
although it would be unreasonable to be too optimistic—now seems by no
means out of the question."

They also reminded Perrin that Fuchs was coming to London supposedly to see him. It was a ruse; he wasn't to be available. The real reason was
that room 055 in the War Office in Whitehall had recording equipment.

Fuchs met Skardon at Paddington Station, and from there they traveled to the War Office, just minutes south of Trafalgar Square. This time,
Skardon cautioned him of his legal rights beforehand, and Fuchs said he
understood. He dictated his statement to Skardon, read it over, made some
edits, and signed it. His last sentence was "I have read this statement and to
the best of my knowledge it is true."

Fuchs's statement gave a largely accurate, although cursory and carefully crafted, description of his personal history, especially his becoming a
communist. Protecting Gerhard, he omitted any mention of his leadership
and tutelage during the early 1930s. The only name included other than his
father's was Rudi Peierls's, and this in the context of claiming that, initially,
he had not known the nature of Peierls's work in Birmingham. (He might
have forgotten that he and Born had discussed Peierls's work on the bomb,
or not.) He declared that Britain's strategy was to have Germany and Russia fight each other to the death, but differing from his oral confession, he
omitted that internment reinforced this perception. Instead, he stated that
he understood the necessity of internment. Only one sentence related any

specifics about spying, but it was all that MI5 needed. In that one sentence, he stated what he considered the worst, "namely to give information about the principle of the design of the plutonium bomb." It was a confession that befuddled analysis because it revealed so little other than that he had spied. Interpretation offered the opportunity for misguided perceptions.

Not everyone was satisfied. Liddell's diary entry for January 27 once again brought up inducement. He had read the troublesome sentence in Fuchs's statement: "I was given the chance of admitting it and staying at Harwell or of clearing out." A prosecution would be difficult, Liddell thought, if Fuchs made his confession because of promises to stay at Harwell.

Fortunately for MI5, the statement was top secret, so the government could bury those words or, if made public, twist them. A few years later, MI5 hired a journalist to write up the Fuchs case to improve its image. In explanation, he wrote, "He had confessed, and that was that. It was all over and done with. And the price Skardon had to pay for the confession was that he had to ensure that Fuchs remained on at Harwell." Fuchs had an "absurd illusion."

That Friday night Fuchs returned home about 7:00 and went to the Skinners' until the wee hours of the morning. After that, the weekend was quiet. Klaus puttered about, spending some time in the office.

Herbert Skinner, though, made noises. He had three roles: Klaus's boss, Harwell's deputy director, and Klaus's friend. Cockcroft and he had discussed Fuchs, with Cockcroft naively revealing, once again, more to him than authorized. Skinner planned to take steps "to ensure that FUCHS remain at Harwell," even perhaps to gain access to a meeting of Lord Portal's to discuss the case. MI5 assigned Perrin to warn off Skinner sharply. The message: the Fuchs case was very serious, and he must stay out of it and not reveal anything he has learned.

The FBI, as yet, had received no report on the interrogation and demanded a full one. The British embassy in Washington told Martin that the FBI suspected MI5 of being "cagey." MI5 knew it had to send the reports that day or the next to appease J. Edgar Hoover.

On Monday morning, January 30, Fuchs took the train to London once more for a prearranged visit with Perrin, this time without any pretense. They met with Skardon in room 055 at the War Office, where, for more than four hours, Fuchs explained the technical information he had given to the Russians.

In a soft but firm voice, Perrin questioned him, going over the details from each era, one by one.

First there was Birmingham, and as Fuchs explained, he confined the information passed along to his own research on gaseous diffusion, usually handing the agent carbon copies of his reports. He also gave the general scope of the atomic project in the U.K.

In the second period in New York, as part of the British mission, he expanded beyond his own work and gave any important documents that came to hand, though still mostly on gaseous diffusion, such as one on the type of membranes used in the filtration process. Most were the product of his team, and half of those were his own. Given that the copies and the names of those to whom they were distributed were meticulously indexed, he handed over his handwritten manuscript. Besides that, he indicated the construction of an industrial superstructure for producing U-235, such as a large production plant somewhere (it was Oak Ridge, Tennessee). He told Perrin that he didn't have the impression that the Russians were intensively pursuing a bomb at that time.

Once he arrived in Los Alamos in August 1944, he realized for the first time the extensive scope of the American program. When in Cambridge visiting his sister in February 1945, he met his agent "Raymond," as he knew him, for the first time since seeing him in New York. Until this, Fuchs had provided no data on a plutonium bomb. While there, he wrote a six-page report on the problems of constructing an atomic bomb—the differences in triggers for plutonium and U-235 bombs and in critical mass. Many details remained to be worked out.

By the time he and Raymond met in Santa Fe in June 1945, he had the mother lode, the design of the plutonium bomb, the Gadget, that the Americans would soon test at Alamogordo. The documents he handed Raymond included a sketch and a full description of the components, such as the tamper, aluminum shell, and lens system, as well as the dimensions, all of which he had checked out at Los Alamos to ensure precise figures.

In the fall, the two met in Santa Fe again, and Fuchs gave him a bit more precise information on the metallurgy of plutonium, but none on how to produce it.

Back at Harwell, in the fourth period, he didn't make contact with an agent until 1947, six months after he returned. He had begun to question Stalin's Russia, and he didn't answer all the questions put to him or pass on all he knew. Still, the Russians received data on the British Windscale Piles (reactors) on the northwest coast of Britain, along with more mathematical details on the plutonium bomb. He told what he knew about the hydrogen bomb from his time in Los Alamos.

Throughout the years, his various Russian agents had occasionally asked him about research not derived from material he had provided, so it was clear the Russians had other sources. When he was at Harwell, those questions increased. In the past, he often didn't know the answer, because he was unfamiliar with the research. Now he pleaded ignorance or gave them only a piece, extracts of information from Los Alamos but much less from the U.K. research. As he rattled off as many as he remembered, Perrin hastily wrote up a list.

Perrin felt Fuchs was sincere in recalling all that he could.

They went on to assess the bomb tested by the Russians in August 1949, which largely duplicated the Gadget. A plutonium bomb was Fuchs's initial expectation, and measurements of airborne fissile material confirmed this, even though lack of evidence of plutonium in the clouds made it inconclusive. What had surprised Fuchs was the Russians' ability to create the industrial superstructure to manufacture the components so quickly, especially considering the devastation they suffered during the war. Fuchs estimated that the research he furnished to the Russians saved them one or two years, an estimate that other physicists generally agreed with.

In 1942, as the Russians fought the Germans to the death, Stalin had assigned one of his top physicists to launch an atomic bomb project. The Russians knew from intelligence sources that the British, Germans, and Americans already recognized the potential of this new class of weapons.

They had a year's worth of Fuchs's research on diffusion—his actual espionage beginning in August 1941, not 1942 as he confessed, perhaps conflating the year with signing the Official Secrets Act in 1942 or, perhaps, protecting Peierls. Fuchs shouldn't have known any secrets until signing the act. Impossible to conduct their research with that restriction, Peierls had largely ignored it.

In any case, it was a date with little scientific significance. With the Germans' invading its cities and a meager supply of uranium ore, Russia's prospect for an intensive U.S.-style program was nil. Diffusion was not a research path that could bring a bomb to fruition quickly.

Fuchs's details of the plutonium bomb in 1945 did have consequences, but only after Stalin saw the extraordinary results of Hiroshima and Nagasaki. Afterward, fearful rather than cowed (as the American military had hoped), he ordered a crash atomic bomb program so that Russia wouldn't be next.

No scientist doubted the Russians' ability to create a bomb on their own. As Edward Teller later said, "From what I have seen of the competence of Soviet scientists, I have reason to believe that they could have produced the weapons independently, once they knew that an atomic bomb could be produced."

But an implosion bomb, one using plutonium, required more than knowledge of the relevant science and engineering. With the explosive lenses all needing to detonate within one-millionth of a second, it required precise timing and symmetry. The state of Russian electronics technology lacked this degree of exactness. By replicating the design of the Trinity bomb that Fuchs passed to "Raymond" in Santa Fe, they circumvented the electronics problem and gained a design proven to work.

But even with secretly obtained information, the Russians faced additional hurdles. The political director for the Soviet bomb project was the ruthless and paranoid Lavrentiy Beria. He demanded that the scientists ensure that the intelligence wasn't "disinformation." The science director Igor Kurchatov kept the American design under wraps in his desk drawer. He masked its origins by creating a fiction of other Russian scientists' working on the bomb and forced his scientists to check out all the specifications.

The technical information Perrin took down at the War Office on Monday, the thirtieth, was damning. At Leconfield House, Liddell still struggled with the role of inducement in Fuchs's confession. When a visitor (unnamed) scanned the confession in Liddell's office the next day, he allayed fears, confidently claiming, "We ought to get away with it." The idea was to stress the moral side, as Fuchs had done, that he confessed because of his friends—which was, in fact, his reason.

After he stated in his written confession that he had a choice of quietly leaving or of confessing and staying at Harwell, he related his struggles over the possible effect on his friends of not confessing:

> I would deal a grave blow to Harwell, to all the work which I had loved and furthermore that I would leave suspicions against people whom I loved who were my friends and who believed that I was their friend. I had to face the fact that it had been possible for me in one half of my mind to be friends with people, be close friends and at the same time to deceive them and to endanger them. I had to realise that the control mechanism had warned me of danger to myself but that it had also prevented me from realising what I was doing to people who were close to me.

Fuchs self-diagnosed this inner conflict as "controlled schizophrenia"; that is, he compartmentalized his mind, one part for making friends and being a good person and one part for spying. His conceptualization—certainly not psychosis—spoke to the whole person who rigidly divides his life's actions: a nice person who leads a secret life, whether it is betraying information, stealing from the business, or having an affair. Fuchs had his belief system to reinforce his actions, so similar to many people where the belief in the cause transcends the rights of the individual and excuses the harm done to others. "Controlled schizophrenia" rationalized an irresolvable conflict, a trap he had unwittingly created for himself—loyalty to friends whom he had come to love or to communism, which he believed in with religious zeal. Stripping away the certitude of the cause as promulgated by Stalin exposed the conscience of a human being overwhelmed by turmoil completely new to him.

Fuchs took the train back to Harwell after his interview with Perrin and was in the prefab by 9:00 p.m., the late arrival caused by a visit to his doctor in London for a prescription, probably sleeping pills. Once home, he rang Erna. Seemingly recovered, she insisted that they see each other. He had no car but said he would ride his bike over. He was back by 10:45. January 30 had been a long day for everyone. Perrin later reflected that the experience had caused him to feel "years older."

February 1 was a Wednesday, eight days since Fuchs had first confessed to Skardon. He was in the office by 10:00 a.m., having gotten a second call from Erna at the early morning hour of 1:00 to visit, then not returning home until 5:20. He had also just received a letter from his father touting his inaugural lecture at the University of Leipzig. That was the good news. Otherwise, Emil asked for funds to care for his grandson Klaus for two months, and he expressed worries about Christel, still hospitalized. He wanted her to come to Germany, but her German passport had long ago expired. "To think of her is a constant torment," he wrote to Klaus.

Fuchs called Henry Arnold too, requesting to see him. Arnold in turn called MI5 once again and was told to "plead ignorance." Fuchs "does not suspect any punitive action against him," Robertson said. And he had no reason to. His life rolled on exactly as promised. Arnold reminded Robertson that Fuchs and Skardon had arranged a meeting for the next afternoon at 3:30 at Harwell. Arnold needed to know if he should make any arrangements. Robertson confided that Skardon might not come.

When Arnold and Fuchs met in mid-afternoon, Fuchs asked if he had seen Skardon's report, and Arnold pleaded ignorance as ordered, even, as he put it to Robertson afterward, "feigning lack of understanding of FUCHS' question."

At Harwell, the tension was filled with secrets.

CHAPTER 21

Arrest, London, February 1950

FEBRUARY 1 WAS A SCRAMBLE AT MI5. THEY PLANNED FOR AN IMMINENT ARREST BUT were nagged by second thoughts. The most vexing question had moved from "Can we get a confession?" to "Will inducement scuttle a prosecution?" The legal issue was whether Fuchs's confession was truly voluntary.

MI5's legal adviser, B. A. Hill, declared there was a prima facie case for prosecution. In a meeting that day with the director of public prosecutions, Sir Theobald Mathew, Commander Leonard Burt from Scotland Yard, and Skardon, Hill outlined the evidence and the inducement problem, specifically Skardon's quid pro quo on December 21 and Cockcroft's on January 10, the only ones documented. Although requiring the attorney general's approval, Sir Theobald stated assuredly that these inducements "would not prevent the voluntary statement being admitted in evidence."

That afternoon, Hill and the others met with the prosecuting attorney Christmas Humphreys, an esteemed barrister and the founder of the Buddhist Society of England, whose tall, lanky profile was a valued asset in the courtroom. Humphreys would present the formal charges for the Crown after Fuchs's arrest.

In the meantime, Fuchs, unsuspicious, kept his schedule at Harwell.

Or so they hoped. The worry persisted: Would he flee? With Skardon's assurances that Fuchs had no such intentions, Scotland Yard left well enough alone. It was legally in charge of the actual arrest, not MI5.

The setup began early on February 2. Perrin called Fuchs in the morning to ask him to come to London for a 3:00 meeting at Shell Mex House. Fuchs told him that he had a full day planned but said if it was urgent, he would do so. Perrin assured him that it was.

MI5 used that morning to settle the charges against their confessed spy. Hill consulted with the director of public prosecutions at 11:45, and they laid out two counts: one of espionage in the United States in 1945, and one of espionage in Britain in 1947, both contrary to the Official Secrets Act. The one related to the United States, they decided, required approval from the Foreign Office or the prime minister. Hill immediately called Dick White and Guy Liddell, who rushed from Leconfield House to the Foreign Office to meet with Michael Perrin and Roger Makins, a top official there. Time was getting on.

Neither MI5 nor the Foreign Office wanted the U.S. charge included: MI5 because of possible embarrassment to the FBI, the Foreign Office because of the appearance of political maneuvering. Perrin carried a contrary point from his boss, Lord Portal, that if not included,

> it was certain that the arrest of FUCHS in the U.K. would cause an outcry against British security, and that even though subsequent disclosures would make it plain that the major leakage took place from Los Alamos, a good deal of the original mud was likely to stick.

Portal's point overrode the objections. At 2:35, White and Liddell called Hill at Leconfield House. When they arrived back about fifteen minutes later, they heard that Sir Theobald was still leery of the American charge. Hill enlisted Liddell to convince him.

Fuchs arrived at Shell Mex just after 3:00 p.m. to see Perrin. He strolled through the long marble lobby and climbed into the rickety lift that took him to the fourth floor. Being in a restricted area, he passed through the Bostwick folding security gate, the so-called cage. In Perrin's anteroom, he sat and waited.

Perrin was at Shell Mex by 2:30 and expected Commander Burt with a warrant. When he didn't arrive, Perrin anxiously made a few calls, unaware of the wrangling over the charges.

At 3:45, Burt finally showed up in Perrin's office. Perrin called Fuchs in, introduced him to Burt, and slipped quietly out the side door. He had insisted beforehand that he did not want to witness the arrest.

As Fuchs stood there, Burt matter-of-factly read the charges, cautioned him, and arrested him. It was over in a couple of minutes. Fuchs, making no reply, slumped into Perrin's chair, astounded. As he had said earlier to Erna, he thought he had it under control.

He told Burt that he wanted to speak to Perrin—"the smooth Perrin [who] got me unsuspecting," as he put it later—who opened the door for him to face the police and disappeared without a word.

When Perrin stepped back in, Fuchs said the first thing that came to him: "You realise what this means?"

"I realise it means that we shall be deprived of your services at Harwell," Perrin answered.

"It means more than that," said Fuchs. "Harwell will not be able to go on."

He later said of the remark, "Silly, isn't it?" It was silly, but his ego was a useful protection at that moment.

On that rainy afternoon, Burt marched Fuchs, ashen and dazed, off to the Bow Street prison, where he was formally charged and processed. Police took away his eyeglasses and personal ID papers. The magistrate asked him if he needed help with legal representation, and in a low voice Fuchs replied that he didn't know anyone. He spent the night in a cell, talking to an "old hand" whose petty offenses had occasioned multiple arrests. Recalled

Fuchs, "In spite of his long experience, . . . he seemed much more shaken by the Court than I was."

Burt traveled on to Harwell, where he searched through the prefab, the office, and the safe for an hour and a half removing possible evidence. Robertson collected his own cache of papers there the next day.

A master of understatement, Liddell wrapped up the day with a line in his diary: "According to what we heard from Burt afterwards, FUCHS was not in any sense in a communicative mood: he seemed stunned by events."

The next morning, February 3, Fuchs was remanded into custody before the Bow Street magistrate under his full and proper name, Klaus Emil Julius Fuchs. The judge asked Humphreys, the prosecutor, whether the defendant could afford representation and was assured that he could. The magistrate asked that Fuchs bear this in mind because come next Friday, when the case would be heard, neither the magistrate nor Humphreys wanted to hear that he didn't have an attorney. Fuchs's only response was to request his glasses and his money. And then it was on to Brixton Prison until his hearing in a week.

Fuchs had spent most of the last ten years inside a fence—from imprisonment in internment, to the confines of top secret research at Los Alamos and Harwell—but this new one was the least forgiving.

The morning's short court appearance made Fuchs's arrest public, the information limited to the charges of two counts of espionage, but no details. MI5 expected calls from the press. MI5's legal adviser, B. A. Hill, worried about John Cockcroft's making a statement and asked Perrin to tell him to say only that the "case was now *sub judice,*" meaning under judicial review and therefore off-limits for discussion elsewhere. Hill similarly advised all other personnel.

When parsing the charges against Fuchs, Lord Portal at the Ministry of Supply had warily evoked the noxious element "blame." The same dread of facing up to who was responsible for this egregious breach had consumed Guy Liddell, Dick White, and their friend Roger Makins from the Foreign Office the day after Fuchs's confession. That evening, they pondered how they had overlooked Fuchs, and they fixed on the vetting in

1946 when he arrived at Harwell. They recalled "the considerable amount of argument" from the junior officers, but that the information against Fuchs didn't "add up to anything positive." In fact, the officers had urged "divorcing" Fuchs from contact with atomic energy, while those at the top had concluded that "the security risk is very slight."

But the "blame game" was about to take on an international dimension. Within a day, the Fuchs case was front-page news in every city and town in America, feeding off brief reports from London and the FBI's seemingly innocuous two-line news item: "A case involving Dr. Fuchs was developed by the British on information originally furnished to them by the F.B.I. The F.B.I. has been co-operating very closely with the British on this case." *The New York Times* carried a lead story that juxtaposed the FBI's rapid exposure of Fuchs's long-held communist sympathies against ostensible British ineptitude. A senator "declared himself unable to throw light on the fact that the British apparently had not learned of this background, while Dr. Fuchs worked for years in atomic matters." Another said, "It is re-assuring to note that our own F.B.I. has uncovered this information of the alleged disclosures." The hoopla built the case for placing the blame exactly where the British had feared that it would land. The verdict: the Brits had been lax with security.

An American lawyer, writing to a British colleague after reading the article, feared "irreparable damage to Anglo-American relations," with "misguided people" using it to cut off international collaboration, even with trusted allies.

When the news broke, the Skinners' maid Grace could do little more than answer the waves of phone calls and fend off news reporters. She coped alone. The Skinners had left for Liverpool the morning before to set up for their move. On hearing the news, Herbert phoned to tell her to say nothing to anyone "about anything that everybody doesn't know." They would be home sometime the next day.

By the time the Skinners arrived in Harwell the next afternoon, Rudi

Peierls had already made his way to London and entered the high redbrick walls of Brixton Prison on the south side of the Thames. He found Klaus, No. 994, lodged in the hospital, not because of illness, but because, according to the warden, it offered better accommodations than a dismal cell. The more probable reason was a suicide watch.

The night before, Rudi had called Scotland Yard, talked with Commander Burt, Fuchs's arresting officer, and asked to visit Fuchs. Burt, with MI5's consent, agreed, requesting Peierls to speak with him first. For an hour, Burt interviewed Peierls, the latter professing shock and disbelief, a Harwell-wide reaction. He ran through his background with Fuchs, including a sense—not sure from where—that Fuchs undertook anti-Nazi activities in Birmingham. Peierls considered Fuchs's politics "no different from that of the general run of his colleagues." To Burt's question whether he would help them, Peierls deferred. He recognized that the authorities must have good evidence to take this course, he told Burt. He wanted to make his own determination of Fuchs's guilt first. If he agreed, he would help.

Burt relayed to MI5 that Peierls's sincerity and candor impressed him. He also said Peierls's description of Fuchs offered nothing they didn't already know.

After the interview, Peierls saw Fuchs in the room of the deputy governor for the allotted fifteen minutes. An MI5 officer, a Scotland Yard policeman, and the deputy chief warden stayed with them. Smith, the policeman, took notes on tidbits he gathered from the softly spoken conversation. There was the functional: need for underwear and books; a woman wanting to visit (Erna); Herbert's offer of financial help. And there were the difficult questions. Peierls asked Fuchs why he had spied. He answered, "Knowledge of atomic research should not be the private property of any one country but should be shared with the rest of the world for the benefit of mankind."

Peierls pressed him to tell the authorities all he could, and Fuchs said he had told them a good deal.

Smith noted that the conversation sounded "a trifle embarrassed" and twice used "indifferent" to describe Fuchs's response to offers of help. He mentioned no other emotional responses. In Smith's eavesdropping account, the characteristically quiet Fuchs now seemed numb.

Within a day or so, Scotland Yard installed a microphone in the visiting room.

Peierls's phone call that night with the Skinners described a Fuchs who was depressed at the beginning of the visit and upset at the end. The three of them reviewed whether Klaus wanted to see Erna and whether the Skinners should go. That was one of Rudi's questions that Klaus had met with indifference. The Skinners thought they might go after the weekend, and Rudi assured them, "I don't think you can do any harm to him whatever you do."

The Skinners had yet to comprehend the maelstrom that would soon overwhelm them: constant phone calls and knocks on the door from reporters, rumors about themselves, queries from people who wanted to make movies—and jarring realizations of betrayal.

It seems that Klaus had told Erna details of his passing information on diffusion. The day after they returned home, Herbert claimed to a friend, "I know everything about it; we have been through hell for the last two weeks." They thought they knew the full story. They felt the hurt and betrayal as more secrets tumbled out.

The following day, Peierls wrote Commander Burt a letter that began, "I want to say first of all that I can now undertake to help you in any way you wish without reservations." He wondered, though, if Klaus had "cracked up" and imagined what he confessed. Klaus's work pressure for the last two years had been extreme, and he had been seriously ill. Should one believe everything in his statement?

Peierls admitted confusion too. When he had asked Klaus whether, during their time in America, he really believed in the superiority of the Russian system, Klaus said that he did. He added, he would have stood up and said what was wrong with communism once it had taken over. Peierls thought this remark too foolish and naive to fit the Klaus he knew.

The letters Peierls wrote to Hans Bethe and Niels Bohr restated much of what he had written in his letter to Burt. Did Klaus have "hallucinations"?

To Bethe, Peierls also worried about the political atmosphere in the United States with the "anti-British outburst in the American Press. . . . Tough times ahead for everyone." To Bohr, he wondered if it was possible to maintain secrecy without "creating the atmosphere of a totalitarian country in which everyone is ready to suspect his best friend of being an informer." At what point does the price of security exceed the value of having it? he asked.

Peierls's prediction of "tough times ahead" was hardly overstated, given the atmosphere. Anyone who had worked with Fuchs during the 1940s came under scrutiny and was considered unreliable, including Oscar Buneman and Derek Behrens (Mary's cousin). Oscar was the subject of an active MI5 investigation, as was Derek. Henry Arnold wrote to Oscar that "his position in Harwell also could no longer be guaranteed." Oscar soon left, and Derek was transferred to an administrative position. MI5 put mail and/or phone warrants on Peierls for years without a hint of suspicion ever arising. Frank Kearton, one of the four at the British mission in New York, called 1950 "the worst time in my life."

Peierls tried to reconcile the Fuchs he had known with the communist dogmatist he now heard. He settled on a "psyche of overwhelming importance concealed under that cloak of self-effacing modesty." Peierls didn't reckon with the self-assurance of the true believers, those select few who know "the Truth." He needed to look no further than all the religious wars throughout the centuries that had championed a "truth" that made devastation, widespread suffering, and bloodshed acceptable to those who inflicted it. For Klaus the Truth was equality and social justice. It had blinded many besides him to the millions murdered by way of Stalin's show trials, gulag, and cruel policies that led to mass starvation.

To Genia Peierls, it seemed that Klaus had taken the fate of the world on himself.

And so the time slowly rolled on to the hearing on February 10. Brixton meted out Fuchs's perquisite of one visitor a day within specified hours. A list formed: the Skinners; his former hosts in Bristol, the Gunns (though separately, because they had divorced); a cousin who was a refugee; Corder Catchpool, a Quaker who sent Emil Fuchs updates; and Erna's friends Vera Pohle and Tatiana Malleson. They all received their twenty or so minutes with the prisoner, which left far too many hours vacant for him to fill. No other close friends from Harwell came, and he heard that they said they didn't want to intrude. He interpreted that as people were waiting until after the trial to decide about him.

After a bit of high drama with Erna's making a midnight call to Arnold, asleep and exhausted, the Skinners went to Brixton on February 8, the warden allowing them to visit in tandem for twenty-five minutes. The bug didn't capture much except for Erna's tears mixed with a desultory conversation about finances, lawyers, doctors, and her mother's cable from New York City that her father was in the hospital, very ill. Erna was unable to go there because of the Klaus "cloud." She did ask him "what had happened at the finish" but didn't get an answer.

She asked the warden for a glass of water. At the end of the visit, when the warden asked her if she wanted more water, she said she needed a stiff drink.

Genia didn't visit. She wrote a direct, honest, uncompromising letter after Rudi returned from his visit on the fourth. It came from the depths of her own life: growing up in Russia during the revolution, when she learned to trust no one. She berated him for putting his friends in England and America in such a difficult position that people wouldn't trust them, because if he could spy, why couldn't they? She thanked him for not taking his life and leaving a terrible mess for others to sort out.

"This is your job, Klaus. . . . You are now going through the hardest time a man can go through, you have burned your god."

Klaus responded in kind:

> I have told myself almost every word you say, but it is good that
> you should say it again. . . . They gave me a much easier way out;
> I could have left Harwell to go to a university a free man, free

from everything, free from friends, with no faith left to start a
new life. I could even have stayed at Harwell if I had admitted
just one little thing and kept quiet about everything else. I bungled the "take your life" stage; yes, I went through that too, before
the arrest. The elaborate precautions taken after my arrest, I am
glad to say, were quite unnecessary. . . .

Klaus

Then, in a postscript, he added, "And don't worry if you don't see the
tears. I have learned to cry again. And to love again."

Liddell, who had access to all of Fuchs's mail, rated Genia's letter "first
class." He made no comment on Klaus's.

Most colleagues questioned the news. Those who didn't question it were
simply shocked. Robert Oppenheimer read *The New York Times* headlines
while having breakfast at Grand Central Terminal. Said his breakfast partner, "Robert was in shock. He just stared at the story shaking his head. He
could not believe the man had done this." Fuchs's former next-door neighbor at Los Alamos, Richard Feynman, understood. He had led a double life
in 1945, carefully hiding his wife's fatal illness and his torment over it, only
letting out his carefree, bongo-drumming side. At a press conference on
February 4, Hans Bethe remarked off the record that he understood Fuchs's
attitude because "a scientist is of the world and works for the world." In an
interview with the FBI, he added another emotion: that he had considered
Fuchs trustworthy; now he didn't know whom to trust.

Dick White, who became director general of both MI5 and MI6, considered Fuchs's motives "relatively speaking pure. Different from other spies,
money was not the goal. He was a scientist who got cross at the Anglo-
American ploy in withholding vital information from an ally fighting a
common enemy." White, too, understood him.

Of course, Max Born, Nevill Mott in Bristol, and Skinner from his days there knew that Klaus was a communist, but none of them knew that he was a spy. Once while Born lectured at Oxford in 1948, he dined with Fuchs, who expressed a certain boredom working at Harwell. Born stated the obvious—that he could find a professorship—and Fuchs responded that he had "a greater task at Harwell." When Born mentioned the remark in March 1950, everyone interpreted it as related to spying. It is just as likely that his investment in and feeling of importance at Harwell prompted the remark.

The obliviousness of MI5 was equally shocking to some. At a party at Harwell, Francis Simon, Fuchs's erstwhile collaborator on gaseous diffusion during the Birmingham days, remarked on the reaction of Gustav Born, who was living with them. "Young BORN . . . who after learning of the arrest of FUCHS from the newspapers, came downstairs with a very white face. . . . How was it we [the government] did not know that he had Communist sympathies, when this was widely known in Edinburgh University?"

Those from the internment camps had the same question as Gustav. One wrote to an MI5 officer that he had been impressed with Fuchs's lectures at Camp L and "repelled by his apparent doctrinary communist fanaticism." This was his second letter to them, he explained. When he returned from internment, he wrote a similar note to the government and never heard back.

Skardon had visited Fuchs the same day as the Skinners at Fuchs's request, a necessary precursor for Skardon to have a thirty-minute interview. Fuchs wanted to confide meeting places and descriptions of Russian contacts in the United States and the U.K. But as Skardon discovered, vagueness still clouded them. His U.S. contact was "about 40, fairly tall, 5'10", fairly broad with a round face," probably a first-generation American, origins unknown, some sort of technician. More useful was his description of "Alexander," his first contact in London. With it, MI5 was able to match "Alexander" with Simon Kremer, secretary to the Soviet military attaché. Including the intermediary who introduced him to Alexander and another who found a courier for him in 1947, that was one person out of six identified.

Fuchs asked Skardon if the government had other evidence besides his confession. Skardon answered that no other evidence would be presented at trial because his confession was a "complete case." He left Fuchs's curiosity unsatisfied. Then again, turnabout was fair play.

Martin cabled Washington with the description of the U.S. contact, along with a warning: "If F.B.I. show a tendency to regard this as a success for pressure tactics by them, you should emphasise this development wholly unexpected and springs solely from F. himself."

Fuchs was a controlled and contained risk-taker, his demeanor calm, quiet, and polite in most situations. He never gave hints of tension or anxiety. After his arrest, Genia Peierls reflected on the years he had lived with them in Birmingham. She realized that maybe there was something. Although generally healthy, he would sporadically develop a nasty cough, stay in bed—although he had no fever—and look depressed and miserable. (Of course, he was a chain smoker and did have asthma.) She now diagnosed this regression as a psychological reaction correlated, in her mind, to his guilt for betraying his friends whenever he met his Russian contact.

If Edinburgh is the control, a period before spying, her intuition was accurate. Over Klaus's three years there, neither Max Born in his extensive correspondence, Hedi Born in her diary, nor Walter Kellermann in his memoir noted Fuchs ever being sick. If Fuchs's illness had hampered Born's research, he would have mentioned it to friends.

His illnesses in 1949 certainly strengthen Genia's premise. On February 12, Klaus met "Eugene," and on February 21, 1949, Klaus wrote to his father that he was sick. Although to MI5 he always pegged the twelfth as his last rendezvous, on April 2, they met again, and a few weeks later, while in the Mediterranean with the Skinners, the illness developed into bronchial pneumonia, ultimately sending him to convalesce at the Skinners' through the end of June. Recuperating under Erna's doting care, he had a protected space for pondering his fate and making decisions.

Had he simply picked up a persistent bug? Or was this serious illness a reaction to stress, as Genia would have surmised?

Fuchs always maintained ignorance of MI5's eye on him in the fall of 1949. In May 1950, he sent his father a different message. Sitting in a prison cell, he wrote him to apologize for his deception during the visit of the previous July. "I am sorry if I had to deceive even you. I don't know whether you felt it, but I expect you know now that I could not take [nephew] Klaus here, however much I would have liked to do so." The release of tension witnessed by young Klaus from the backseat of the car as they returned to Harwell from the school visits was very real.

But what did he learn, how did he learn it, from whom, and when exactly? His awareness of a threat almost had to stem from the steady, although still vague, advances on cracking the Venona messages. This information didn't crystallize until August 13, 1949, when MI5 received a telegram with the first hint of "Rest." If Fuchs's identity had come from a confession—Raymond knew it as did his Russian controllers—MI5 and the FBI wouldn't have needed Venona or the surveillance. And KGB notes might have reflected it. Years later, that security agency was still anxious to know what had happened.

We may never know the truth. Fuchs never met Eugene after April, later claiming to MI5 disillusionment with Stalin's regime and appreciation of the British character. After a frank examination of conscience, these may well have been true, if incomplete—and the reason, built on hope of deliverance from suspicion, he didn't flee.

His calm recitations to Skardon do suggest foreknowledge. Although momentarily flustered in his first interview when Skardon accused him of spying—the intended effect of the boldness—he recovered quickly and error-free, as though he had seen the hand they held. He had had time to firm up his defense.

As for suspecting MI5's interest in him, in London with Erna at the end of September 1949, his "bad" driving reported by MI5 surveillance would have served to spot a tail. And, coincidentally, the next day, she noted to friends his ghastly appearance and difficulty breathing. A week later, while in London for another meeting, he ran in and out of photography supply shops looking for film, a basic technique for identifying a Watcher. Fuchs was well-practiced in the tools of spycraft.

Moscow Center had another very important asset: a mole deep inside the British embassy in Washington. It was Kim Philby, a member of the infamous Cambridge Five spies, a double agent since the war who would not be exposed until 1963, and an officer in MI6. During the 1940s, he had eagerly served up to Moscow the names and activities of MI6 agents and anticommunist partisans in Eastern Europe who fought to create democracies in their countries and be free from Russia. Collectively, hundreds died at Philby's hand—a hand that pushed Soviet expansion and weighed heavily on the balance of power.

Philby didn't learn that Fuchs's name had emerged from Venona until the fall of 1949. He gave the information to Guy Burgess, another Cambridge Five spy, who supposedly bungled alerting the Russians. Confusion has always existed around these events. In effect, it doesn't matter. By the time they knew, Fuchs already had a plan.

CHAPTER 22

Trial, London, March 1950

IT TOOK ONLY A DAY AFTER FUCHS'S ARREST FOR THE WIRES BETWEEN THE U.S. AND the U.K. security services to become, as Liddell described them, "red hot." The charges against Fuchs in his court appearance on February 3, 1950, had roused the ire of the FBI director, J. Edgar Hoover, whose career had been built on tracking down subversives, beginning with German agents during World War I, then moving on to communists. In a closed hearing of a Senate Appropriations subcommittee, he testified that Fuchs had given the Russians information on the "super-secret" hydrogen bomb. A subcommittee member leaked this testimony to a reporter from *The Washington Post*. Before another committee, Hoover said (and later denied) that "the British made a muck of the FUCHS case." They had a noncooperative security service and a cumbersome legal system. MI5 told the FBI's newly arrived representative Lish Whitson that Hoover's words could jeopardize the whole case if the British press published them.

In British law, a fair hearing in court overruled the freedom of the press to report on a case. If a newspaper article was deemed prejudicial to the defense, the case could be thrown out. One British reporter had tumbled on Fuchs's cleaning lady and heard assurances that he was a wonderful person, but generally the stories stuck to the revelations directly from the courtroom and so far there wasn't much.

The problem for Hoover was the charge of spying in the United States, raising the obvious question: Why had his agency not detected it? The problem for the U.K. was that MI5 was Hoover's excuse. The British intelligence agency had cleared Fuchs and assured U.S. officials of a thorough vetting. Even so, MI5 would have none of the FBI's demands for details on the clearance. "Wrong in principle," scribbled Liddell.

It was one of many demands from the FBI that MI5 ignored: The meeting places in the United States? Fuchs's confession? No details. A copy of Skardon's interviews for the FBI agent Whitson? No, sub judice. (Whitson was allowed to read them but not to have a copy of the documents.) Information on what Fuchs passed on to the Russians? Maybe after conferring with other government agencies.

Sillitoe wrote to Hoover, trying to tiptoe around by emphasizing that MI5 earnestly wanted to cooperate, but British legal procedures restricted its ability to give the FBI the access it desired. At the same time, the FBI's Whitson took whatever MI5 gave him, always relieved to have something to pass on to Hoover, "of whom everybody in the F.B.I. is terrified!" quipped Liddell.

Hoover wasn't the only anticommunist firebrand in the United States in 1950. Long before Fuchs, there was HUAC, the House Un-American Activities Committee, which embodied all the hysteria of "the Red Scare." Soon after the Russian Revolution in 1917, the fear of Bolshevism had gripped the minds of politicians, and for more than three decades the committee, under one name or another, had hammered away to uncover threats of communist subversion and to enhance its own power, stirring panic whenever possible. Its prominence escalated to dizzying heights with an investigation into communists in the motion picture industries in 1947 (the Hollywood Ten, blacklists), quickly followed in 1948 by sensationalized probes of Whittaker Chambers, a journalist, and Alger Hiss, a former high-level official in the State Department. It propelled the rush to judgment that executed the Rosenbergs for turning over largely inconsequential information.

In the early days of February, the FBI warned the Foreign Office that HUAC wanted to send a representative to Britain to investigate the case, warning that without prior notification the committee had recently done so in Canada.

The Fuchs case emboldened the anticommunist fervor in the United States. Within days of Fuchs's arrest, Joseph McCarthy, the demagogic Republican senator from Wisconsin, proclaimed in a speech in West Virginia that he had a long list of communists who worked in the State Department. McCarthy quickly became the standard-bearer, carrying his banner to a Senate permanent subcommittee on investigations to hunt out communists, amassing massive political influence along the way. Congress saw that those he supported won; those he didn't lost. Those who criticized him he tarred as communists or sympathizers. His Republican Senate colleagues stayed mum for the most part—cowards all—until public opinion shifted and McCarthyism collapsed.

With emotions running high, J. Edgar Hoover continued to be the zealous avenger of the perfidious communists, refining the art of exploiting fear and manipulating public perceptions.

The British political air was less contaminated. Morale at Harwell did fall, and while a few, such as Buneman, felt pressure, Peierls could write to Bethe at the end of March that except in the tabloid press things had settled down without demands for increased security. Gossip continued, and the Theoretical Division struggled as personnel were investigated and transferred, such as Buneman and Behrens, but it functioned.

Nonetheless, MI5 had instituted a covert "purge system" of Communist Party members employed by SIGINT, signal intelligence. The thought that anyone who believed in communism could be turned to betray the government was pervasive. If such a brilliant mind as Fuchs could be misled, what was to stop anyone? Others recommended that the Communist Party be outlawed. Liddell agreed with the necessity of the purge, so long as it was restrained by an intensive investigation of cases. Declaring the party illegal, he considered ill-advised, fearing that any party with sympathies for Russian foreign policy could be penalized.

The first weeks of February 1950 had been mild to very mild as London winters go. Friday, the tenth, was no exception. That morning, police drove Fuchs from Brixton Prison to Covent Garden in London's West End. He entered the Bow Street Magistrate's Court for the start of the 10:30 hearing in the mahogany-paneled courtroom No. 3, then walked to the dock—a raised, oblong platform with a heavy iron railing—and sat on the bench inside. When Commander Burt, who had arrested him the week before, asked if he felt all right, he answered, "Yes, thank you." Those were the only words he spoke throughout the hearing. Otherwise, he sat somewhat motionless in a rumpled brown suit, occasionally writing on a pad of paper or gripping his knee with his left hand.

Government officials, two U.S. representatives, and about sixty reporters who had stood in line for two hours crammed into the tiny courtroom that usually held twenty-five. Members of the public were barred.

Christmas Humphreys presented the evidence for the Crown. His ten-page opening statement began with the two charges of violating the Official Secrets Act. The first half of it listed generalities about Fuchs's background: from internment to the high value of the scientific information to Russia and his "controlled schizophrenia." Humphreys minced no words, referring to what Fuchs had done as the "planned and deliberate treachery" of a "political fanatic" driven by "unswerving devotion to communism." Then he read the last two pages of the confession, noting beforehand that Fuchs had made it "without threat or promise." "He corrected it himself, he paragraphed it himself, and finally signed it, and I understand that he actually wrote in his words the final phrase, to the effect that 'I have read this statement and to the best of my knowledge it is true.'" Humphreys's words strongly implied that he would read a verbatim statement.

These last pages dealt with Fuchs's confidence in the rightness of Russian policy and his growing doubts and ended with his concerns of how his actions could affect his friends. Humphreys omitted a few sentences—one because Perrin wanted to omit reference to Fuchs's giving the Russians the plans to the plutonium bomb and their having an atomic bomb. Fearing the public's "alarm and despondency," he would agree only to their having "caused an atomic explosion."

The most important deletion was "I [Fuchs] was given the chance of admitting it and staying at Harwell or of clearing out." Humphreys thus avoided the specter of inducement.

Reporters sent a note to Humphreys to request a copy of the confession. The director of public prosecutions denied it and asked the magistrate to declare it secret, which he did.

Humphreys called four witnesses: Commander Burt, Henry Arnold, Michael Perrin, and Jim Skardon, the first three, one by one, substantiating the charges by summarizing Fuchs's admissions to them. Humphreys himself contrived Skardon's longer statement to emphasize Fuchs's worry about "the effect of his behaviour" upon friendships at Harwell. MI5 wanted to emphasize the conclusion that Fuchs confessed because of friendships, not because of inducement, which in fact was true.

Skardon also gave Fuchs's interpretation of his oath of allegiance; that is, Fuchs took it seriously but qualified it: "He claimed the freedom to act in accordance with his conscience should circumstances arise in this country comparable to those which existed in Germany in 1932 and 1933."

Fuchs later remarked to Erna, "What Skardon said was not all true. I think he knows it was a wrong statement." Fuchs didn't clarify, although Skardon's statement closely adhered to Fuchs's written statement except for omitting the offer to stay at Harwell.

At the end of the hearing, the magistrate asked Fuchs two questions: Did he wish to respond to the charges? His solicitor answered, "Not at this stage." Did he wish to call witnesses? His solicitor answered, "Not here." Fuchs stood, the magistrate charged him, and his solicitor stated that he pleaded "not Guilty." He was committed for trial at the Old Bailey at the session beginning on February 28.

As Fuchs left, his solicitor allowed Skardon to speak with him at the back of the courtroom. Skardon showed him selected photographs of possible contacts in the United States and U.K. Fuchs pointed to an image of Simon Kremer, thus confirming "Alexander" as his contact in London. He didn't admit to recognizing others. A few days later, Skardon made a visit to Brixton with more photographs of Russian embassy staff. All embassy personnel had photographs on file with MI5, Fuchs's contact Eugene included. If that photograph was among the stack, Fuchs didn't pick him out. Having seen him only a year before, he certainly would have recognized him.

At the same time, the governor of Brixton Prison alerted his staff: "It would be advantageous to Russia if anything were to happen to the prisoner before his trial and before he divulged the names of his contacts and other vital information." They needed to watch for lethal poisons, and ensure this prisoner's safety. The Russians were ruthless.

They knew that Fuchs had arrived basically healthy. A full physical revealed the chronic lung problem for which his doctor in London had earlier prescribed him rest, iron, and arsenic. Fuchs confided to the doctor that he had contemplated suicide as a way out but those thoughts were now gone.

On the afternoon of Fuchs's arrest, Dick White had sent Washington an "emergency" cable so that the FBI could interview Christel and Bob Heinemann before the news broke. MI5 had already reported that Fuchs had not implicated them.

Two FBI agents found Christel at Westborough Hospital, a psychiatric facility where her husband, Bob, had committed her a year before. She had been seriously depressed, a condition that ran in her mother's family. The doctors, perhaps mistakenly, had diagnosed her with schizophrenia. Unusual for a schizophrenic, she never had another episode or took medication. In the hospital, the doctors administered electric shock, a treatment favored at the time for depression.

On that Thursday—and several more—she was perfectly rational and cooperative, although her doctor always stayed near in case questions

stressed her. He, in fact, suggested administering a truth serum. The FBI
agents said they would not be responsible. Incomplete FBI records leave it
unclear what was decided.

Over the weeks, Christel told them the story of the man who came to
their house on Lakeview Avenue in Cambridge, Massachusetts. She looked
out the window to see a stranger on the sidewalk in front of the house, then
heard a knock on the door. Her version differed slightly from others by date
and number of visits, but not in its essence. She didn't know much.

Christel's and Bob's descriptions of the visitor (whom Bob met only once)
generally coincided with Klaus's, that of a stocky man with a round face,
which was accurate. They were all off on height. The five-foot-six Raymond
must have stood tall. The Heinemanns measured him around five feet eight;
Klaus put him at five feet ten, perhaps a deliberate error to throw off the
investigators. Same with his age. He was thirty-five, and they estimated him
to be in his late thirties or forty. Klaus placed his city of origin as Philadelphia (here he was correct), Bob as Buffalo because they talked about the
weather there, and Christel guessing Chicago because he seemed very tired
from his trip. The picture didn't tally well with those on the FBI's suspect
list, which comprised every physicist with leftist proclivities that Fuchs
encountered on the Manhattan Project, including Robert Oppenheimer,
and anyone tangential to a communist ring in the United States or Canada.

As the FBI and MI5 knew, a person of interest linked to the 1945 defection of the cipher clerk at the Russian embassy in Ottawa was a professor
of mathematics named Israel Halperin. When the police arrested him, they
seized piles of documents from his home. One was an address book that
contained the names and addresses of Klaus and Christel. At the time,
Klaus's addresses were internment Camps L and N.

In March 1950, FBI agents interviewed Halperin and found no other
connection to Fuchs. MI5 questioned Fuchs, who said he had received
journals from Halperin while in internment but had never met him.

How did Halperin come to send Fuchs magazines and—according to
Christel—cigarettes? The most probable connection was the Harvard physicist and Halperin's brother-in-law, Wendell Furry, also a member of Bob

Heinemann's Communist Party group in Cambridge. More roundabout was Halperin's association with John von Neumann, Fuchs's later colleague on the Manhattan Project. Max Born had written to von Neumann, among many others, to send Fuchs reading material. Halperin had been von Neumann's sole PhD student at Princeton and sufficiently close for Halperin to complete two of his manuscripts after von Neumann's early death. Von Neumann might have written to him.

The interest in Halperin's diary wasn't its relevance to espionage; it earned a closer look because of its murky provenance. The Canadians assured MI5 that early on they had passed the diary to them and to the FBI. MI5 insisted they had no record of it. In a speech, the lord chancellor had denied they ever received it. Unfortunately, they had, in a way. An MI6 agent, in Canada at the time, was allowed to poke through the piles of documents to extract anything of interest but missed the diary. MI5's copy ultimately came from the FBI in the fall of 1949. Originating from internment, it wasn't relevant to the case. It did, however, become a tool for the press to accuse MI5 of poor security clearance.

Meanwhile, Hoover whipped up a storm. He had heard a ridiculous story supposedly spread by Michael Perrin and his boss, Lord Portal. Although it was absurd in substance, he believed they had spread it—that MI5 had learned about Fuchs in February 1949 and told Walter Winchell, the American gossip columnist who then told the FBI. Hoover ordered Lish Whitson to tell Sir Percy Sillitoe that Perrin and Portal must stop—or as one FBI memo stated five times, "to put up or shut up." Otherwise, repercussions would follow. Whitson was to be aggressive and not cowed by "big titles" and to ask Sir Percy if he had any doubt "as to whether the Bureau had broken the Fuchs case." Hoover remarked, "The sly British are gradually getting around to having unearthed Fuchs themselves!"

The fact is, the American and British code breakers had wrestled together with the thorny Venona decryption project since 1944. Slogging away in Arlington, Virginia, the British analyst Philip Howse unearthed, either alone or with others, the existence of a possible British spy on August 13, 1949, and the British embassy hurriedly telegraphed the news to MI5 and MI6. A month later, the Americans dug up the name "Karl Fuchs" as the author of a document noted in the messages. The British were about a day from finding it, and they fit the puzzle pieces together to prove the rest. Walter Winchell had nothing to do with it.

When Whitson saw Sillitoe on a Sunday afternoon, as Whitson wrote in his report, Sillitoe agreed emphatically that the FBI had supplied the information in the Fuchs case. He planned to speak with Perrin and Portal the next day. Whitson described an almost fawning Sillitoe, saying that "he would do whatever the Director [Hoover] desired, even coming to the US after the trial if it would help." Or, perhaps, Whitson was merely soothing Hoover's ego and rage.

Liddell spent the next evening dining with Whitson and John Cimperman, the American embassy's FBI liaison to MI5. Whitson wondered who was to be the scapegoat in the Fuchs drama. Liddell thought neither of them. The Russians, he said, had scored two victories already—gaining the information and eliminating one of the U.K. 's leading scientists. They should not let them get another by "throwing a spanner into the works of Anglo-American co-operation." The congenitally diplomatic souls of the British worked hard to keep the peace.

Brixton was a real prison for Fuchs. He walked around the oval path in the yard counting his steps, correlating fewer steps with a better mood. He read. He wrote letters, especially to the Skinners, trying to explain to himself and to them what he had done and why. He had had a few lines from his father. "He won't ever believe that his children can do wrong," he told the Skinners. "So, he will be all right. I sent him a message through the Society of Friends to get out of the Russian Zone. That is all I can do."

The Skinners came down toward the end of February for a twenty-minute visit, their second. The recording suggested another conversation filled with awkward pauses and stabbing comments, such as Erna telling him that he "looked rotten." As they left, the tape caught his last remark. Putting it in the third person, the transcription read, "It was strange how he kept his spirits high when he really could not look to the future." He knew that people went to the gallows for his crime.

The Peierlses visited on the twenty-eighth, the day before the trial. Then Skardon arrived for one more photo-ID session. Fuchs had examined the dozens and dozens of pictures that flowed in regularly, none of which looked familiar, although one day he picked out a remote possibility if it was a very bad likeness. In his report, Skardon identified that photograph as "the notorious Whittaker Chambers."

Throughout the month, Skardon had gently worked on Fuchs for descriptions of meeting places and pulled out a few dribs and drabs of information. A map of New York helped with the first meeting place at Henry and Market streets on the Lower East Side. Another of Kew Gardens, southwest of London near Richmond, let Fuchs identify places involved in re-establishing contact or indicating danger, including tossing a magazine over a fence. Checking out the geography the next day, Skardon found it as Fuchs described.

Fuchs described the young woman who replaced "Alexander" and with whom he met in the countryside near Banbury; the American he saw about half a dozen times in New York City, once in Philadelphia, and twice in Santa Fe; and the Russian he met in pubs later in London.

On this visit he gave Skardon a couple of names too: the intermediaries who introduced him to his contacts in Britain. The first was Jürgen Kuczynski, erstwhile promoter of the Left Book Club, co-founder of the Free German League of Culture, very short-term internee, professor at the London School of Economics, possible recruiter for the OGPU (the Soviet secret police) in England, and introducer to Alexander. The other was Johanna Klopstech, German-born, longtime member of the Communist Party, associate of Kuczynski's, refugee to Britain from Czechoslovakia, and, like Kuczynski, probable good friend of the Fuchs brothers from the Berlin underground days. Both had already returned to Berlin, Kuczynski for a time employed by the U.S. military with a rank of lieutenant colonel working for the Strategic Bombing Survey.

Before the trial, Fuchs's attorney Derek Curtis-Bennett, a well-known criminal defense lawyer, visited him to discuss the case. Curtis-Bennett persuaded him not to mention inducement, even though, as Fuchs later wrote, it "should have been of great value in a plea for mitigation." The prosecution for the Crown had told his lawyer that revealing it could be "prejudicial to the country." Fuchs consented with this decision. Fuchs's confession certainly proved his willingness to acknowledge his guilt and not to blame others.

His lawyer also said that he should expect the maximum sentence. To qualify this statement, he asked Fuchs if he knew what that was, and Fuchs simply said, "Yes, I know. It's death." "No," said Curtis-Bennett. "It's fourteen years." Charges under the Official Secrets Act did not carry a death sentence. Russia had been an ally during the war, and its present designation was "friendly nation." He wasn't to be tried for treason.

Fuchs later said, "Strangely enough at that instant I felt nothing. I was convinced I would get capital punishment and was ready for it. That was my mistake: a real secret agent should fight for his life until the end. Then I felt what someone who is on death row must feel when he's told, 'You will not be executed; you're going to live.'"

Wednesday, March 1, 1950, was the date for Fuchs's trial in the Central Criminal Court at the Old Bailey, the 275-year-old institution in the heart of London near St. Paul's Cathedral. Many famous trials had been held there, including the fictional proceedings against Charles Darnay, tried for treason in Dickens's *Tale of Two Cities*. Fuchs, in the midst of reading it, wrote to Henry Arnold that its opening sentence, "It was the best of times, it was the worst of times, it was the age of wisdom, it was the age of foolishness," had completely "knocked" him out.

The bewigged attorney general, Sir Hartley Shawcross, with Christmas

Humphreys in attendance represented the case for the Crown. Derek Curtis-Bennett represented Fuchs. The lord chief justice, enrobed in scarlet, was Lord Rayner Goddard, who cast himself as "an avenging enemy of criminals and a vigilant lord protector of society."

On this morning, Fuchs entered directly into the dock, climbing the stairs from cells below the chamber. In the audience were reporters from eighty-one international news agencies, including the Russian news agency TASS, and special guests, such as the Duchess of Kent, in the distinguished visitors' seats.

Since the hearing, the charges against Fuchs had doubled, with transgressions added from Birmingham in 1943 and others in New York City from December 1943 to August 1944. To all of these accusations, Fuchs said in a low voice, almost a whisper, "Guilty." After this plea, the purpose of the trial shifted to determining the sentence.

Absent Humphreys's inflammatory rhetoric, Shawcross opened with Fuchs's motives, interspersing long excerpts from Fuchs's original statement. This time Shawcross read the inducement sentence: "I was given the chance of admitting it and staying at Harwell or of clearing out."

Lord Goddard jumped on this: "Does he mean this was in his own mind?" Clearly anticipating him, Shawcross dissembled with ease: "My Lord, that is what he seems to have understood. It is not a correct account of what happened but that is what he appears to have understood. What he was being confronted with were the incidents in America. His whole course of conduct had not at that time been discovered."

Next Shawcross stressed Fuchs's desire not to leave a shadow over his friends. And with that, having called no witnesses, Shawcross closed his case.

Shawcross's portrayal of Fuchs hinted at his being a victim of unfortunate circumstances, a depiction that Curtis-Bennett embraced for his defense. His first act was to call Skardon to the stand as a witness, who reinforced that Fuchs had made his confession as "a free man, quite patently acting on his free initiative." Curtis-Bennett didn't challenge him on the now open secret of inducement. Instead, he calmly stressed that Fuchs was a known communist.

Startled, Lord Goddard questioned him closely on this point. Curtis-Bennett said that Home Office records indicated he was a member of the German Communist Party and "never pretended he was anything else." Shawcross interjected that at the enemy alien tribunals in 1939, Fuchs was a refugee from Nazi oppression because he was a communist.

Curtis-Bennett produced no document from the Home Office or from MI5 files. Max Born's official reference letter for Fuchs at the tribunal stated that he had been a Social Democrat. Notes from the tribunal had long since been destroyed. There was no evidence of the word "communist" mentioned. It was, however, catnip for the press.

Curtis-Bennett stated his intent "to build before your Lordship his state of mind at the time of the various periods of the indictment." Lord Goddard interrupted and sputtered that he had read "this statement several times and I cannot understand this metaphysical philosophy or whatever you like to call it. I am not concerned with it. I am concerned that this man gave away secrets of vital importance to this country. He stands before me as a sane man and not one relying on the disease of schizophrenia or anything else."

Hoping to soften Fuchs's sentence, Curtis-Bennett continued on with a defense centered on Fuchs's state of mind and the wartime fate of the Russian allies who had suffered something on the order of twenty-five million deaths, along with the devastation of their eastern territories, as they turned the tide that led to Hitler's defeat.

At the end, Lord Goddard asked Fuchs if he had anything to say. Fuchs stood, holding a piece of paper. His voice barely audible, he read five sentences that acknowledged his guilt and thanked the government for a fair trial and the staff at Brixton Prison for their courtesy. He noted his own failings by deceiving his friends.

Lord Goddard then peered at him and spoke with a hard voice:

> Your statement which has been read shows to me the depth of self-deception into which people like you can fall. Your crime to me is only thinly differentiated from high treason. In this country

we observe rigidly the rule of law, and as technically it is not high treason, so you are not tried for that offense.

I have now to assess the penalty which it is right I should impose. It is not so much for punishment that I impose it, for punishment can mean nothing to a man of your mentality.

The maximum sentence which Parliament has ordained for this crime is fourteen years imprisonment, and that is the sentence I pass on you.

The trial was over. It had lasted all of one hour and twenty-eight minutes.

At first, Fuchs didn't move. A warden patted him on the back to nudge him out of the dock. He later admitted that at that moment the prospect of years ahead filled with nothingness terrified him. A journalist noted spots of color highlighted on Fuchs's pale cheeks as he left the courtroom.

Back in his office at FBI headquarters in Washington, J. Edgar Hoover must have been pleased. With journalists' passions aroused by the allegation that the Home Office knew of Fuchs's communist ties, *Time*, quoting the Manchester *Guardian*, wrote, "Luckily, the Americans were not sleeping too. . . . The slowness of the British government's detectives is something which the free world will not forget or forgive in a hurry."

TASS, on the other hand, published the Soviet government's official statement a few days later: that the case against Fuchs was a "gross fabrication since Fuchs is unknown to the Soviet Government and no 'agents' of the Soviet Union had any connection with Fuchs."

CHAPTER 23

The FBI, London, May 1950

WITH THE TRIAL OVER, HOOVER AND HIS FBI EXPECTED ACCESS TO MI5'S DOCU-
ments, and to Fuchs as well. MI5 said no to both. Fuchs's attorney had
three weeks to decide whether to appeal, and an appeal itself could take
another two to three weeks. During this period, sub judice prevailed,
therefore no interrogation.

"How can there be an appeal when he pled guilty?" stormed Hoover.
Lish Whitson offered an insight: "A strong inference exists that Fuchs
believed his cooperation would substantially reduce his sentence."

A few weeks later, MI5 provided the FBI with Fuchs's scientific statement, a background memo on Fuchs's family members, and the all-important
confession. Whitson's sop that MI5 had fully cooperated met with "Hog-
wash!" from Hoover. He wanted his men to interview Fuchs. MI5 had snared
its spy, but the FBI had yet to find his American contact.

Director General Sillitoe had his own problems. He gathered his officers
for a postmortem on the Fuchs case and hailed them with congratulations
on their success. Then he surprised them with an unexpected reprimand.

Parliament had buzzed for a month on MI5's failure to uncover Fuchs, and especially the clearance they gave him to work at Harwell. The press reveled in the gossip. Sir Percy wanted to end all this and to support his officers, so a couple of days after the trial he had met with Prime Minister Attlee and handed him a brief on the case—Fuchs's background, work history, investigation, and confession. Relying on Sillitoe's brief, the prime minister addressed the House of Commons on March 6 to defend the security service, declaring, "There was no means by which we could have found out about this man."

Before the prime minister spoke, Sillitoe had not read Fuchs's security file. He did so afterward and was stunned. Liddell paraphrased Sir Percy's reaction in his diary: "Had an enquiry been ordered, he felt that he would probably have lost his job and the department would have been split from top to bottom."

Enlightening his officers, Sillitoe rattled off what he considered three remarkable blunders in the file. In 1944, MI5 had advised Perrin not to mention the reports of Fuchs's communist history to the Americans. In 1946, shortly after Fuchs's arrival at Harwell, Henry Arnold reported that he was a spy. A few months later, Michael Serpell conducted a security clearance for Fuchs's Harwell appointment and, alarmed, recommended his removal. How, Sillitoe asked, given these minutes, could they do nothing but a mail check for his clearance at the end of 1946? Especially because they knew full well that spies don't communicate by mail!

Many spoke up in their defense. Skardon clarified that the black marks in Fuchs's security file were so tepid that they had provided nothing of material value when it came time to interrogate him. Another officer rationalized that with hundreds of émigrés fitting Fuchs's profile, resources didn't exist to investigate them all. Yet another, referring to the Kahle association in internment, shifted the blame to incompetent camp intelligence officers and leaned on the myth of Fuchs's being surrounded by Nazis.

After the meeting, Liddell spoke to Sillitoe alone, giving a bleak assessment of their situation. "We had to realise that we were permanently sitting on a hornet's nest. A huge increase of staff would not produce the answer. It would only turn us into a mass-production organisation like the F.B.I. It would not be tolerated by the public, and it would produce no better results." He didn't yet know that the most insidious spies weren't immigrants but homegrown, many from Liddell's upper-class stratum. One of these, Guy Burgess, later made infamous as a member of the Cambridge Five of Soviet moles, was a close friend.

Two days after Attlee's speech, Asik Radomysler, a professor at the London School of Economics, wrote a letter that ultimately reached the prime minister. Radomysler had known Fuchs in Camps L and N in Canada and objected to Attlee's claim of ignorance. All the internees knew Fuchs was a communist.

The result was an interview for Radomysler with MI5's Michael Serpell in room 055 in the War Office. It was Serpell who, outraged in 1946, had urged Fuchs's removal from Harwell in large part because of the link with Hans Kahle in the camps. The bug in the interview room provided fifteen single-spaced pages of transcript.

Radomysler began with his background in the camps. Like Fuchs, whom he knew, he had been a hut father and a member of the Refugee Committee. In this latter capacity, he had helped Fuchs divvy up internees between the "Aryan" camp and the kosher Camp N.

Serpell wanted to know why he identified Fuchs as a communist. Radomysler explained that terminology was the "distinguishing characteristic" for him and his camp friends: language created to step around the complications of the Russian-German pact signed in 1939. The party had imposed it, he said, within a week of the war's breaking out. Serpell questioned his ability to recognize this "line of conversation." "Because of course, as you know," he noted, a tad condescendingly, "some people find difficulty in deciding whether a man is extreme Left Wing or Communist or whatever he may be." It was a point he belabored throughout the interview.

Radomysler had an answer. "When others were sort of whole-heartedly, say, for the war or against the Germans, they [communists] would try and join the sentiment without subscribing to any particular form of words which would contradict the official Russian policy. . . . It was that which made it so startling." He assured Serpell that his friends, whom he had recently met with, agreed on who were communists. "FUCHS was certainly one of those who we knew was."

Serpell asked him about the proportion of Nazis in the camps, a key point given MI5's excuse for Fuchs's being friends with Kahle. Radomysler said Camp L was largely Jewish—"Out of a given 700, I should say 600 were Jewish"—and the kosher Camp N even more so. And many of the non-Jewish were anti-Nazi too. Serpell was taken aback. "Predominantly anti-Nazi, was it? There's no doubt of it. I see, yes." Not an answer that aided MI5's exculpation.

Did you report this information to the intelligence officer? asked Serpell. No, said Radomysler, but there were plenty of informants in the camp. And the camp records had to be someplace. Even without them, he insisted that "there were so very many people with whom he had been close enough for sufficient time to give a reliable account of this one single fact."

Radomysler and his friends were disappointed never to be asked. As they saw it, MI5's ignorance about Fuchs was simply unacceptable.

Serpell tried to salvage an excuse by advancing the difficulty for the uninformed person—of course, not Radomysler, he added—to know whether a person was a communist. "I hope you understand that . . . it wasn't a very straightforward issue, from the point of view of the Intelligence Officer."

Radomysler gave some ground: "I can see that it looked different from the outside, much more difficult."

Even without hard evidence, Serpell considered Radomysler's judgment of Fuchs as a communist convincing. In his report, Serpell justified MI5's error by exploiting the excuse of camp personnel not reading Fuchs's communist activities. The report allowed the prime minister's secretary to state dismissively "that further enquiry has hardly confirmed the criticism of the Security Service implied in [Radomysler's] letter." If Serpell had dug further, he would have found camp intelligence reports naming Fuchs a communist. An even simpler course would have been merely to speak with Oscar Buneman at Harwell who had witnessed it all.

None of this addressed why MI5 hadn't contacted internees, an omission contrary to its meticulous fact-checking. Nor did it correct its story. In mid-June 1950, the MI5 officer Roger Hollis, who worked in counterespionage in B Branch, and Michael Perrin traveled to Washington, D.C., to discuss security changes with the FBI. Once again, Hollis rather shamelessly offered up the "surrounded by Nazis" defense for Fuchs's association with Kahle in the camps. A few years later, bewildered by many lapses, Arthur Martin and other MI5 officers investigated the possibility of a high-level mole in MI5. Their hunting served up a target, Roger Hollis, who, in 1946, had clearly rebuffed Serpell's security objections. He was interviewed in the mid-1960s and never confessed. He was MI5's director from 1956 to 1965.

Before Fuchs's arrest, the FBI had snuck around peeking into dimly lit corners to unearth his American contact. Afterward, agents scoured the country unchecked for the unknown chemist whom they called the "unchem." A "top-grade man-hunt for Goose," as Patterson described it to Martin.

Location circumscribed MI5's participation, but it did have the source—and a photo identification was worth gold. So Skardon carried slews of photographs to Wormwood Scrubs, Fuchs's new home—another dismal, Victorian-era, redbrick prison five miles to the west of downtown London. According to his jailers, Fuchs was settling into prison discipline, in "good fettle," and, to Skardon's and everyone else's relief, not resentful toward him or the government. An FBI special agent told Patterson, "That guy Skardon of yours is sure doing a swell con-job to keep Fuchs talking after the Judge threw the book at him."

It was essential to keep Fuchs talking until they had exposed all his contacts. It wasn't easy. One spoiler was prison rumors, and the case spawned many. Recently, British tabloids had reported a "national search" for an unknown woman friend.

On this particular day, when Skardon spread out photographs on the table in the visitors' room, one stood out to Fuchs—that of a man named Joseph Arnold Robbins. After a long look, he said to Skardon, "I cannot swear, but I am pretty sure that this is the man I met in the U.S.A."

Martin dispatched the name to Washington, and Patterson replied the next day with positive anticipation—his own and the FBI's. It was short-lived. Neither of the Heinemanns recognized Robbins, even with Bob's traveling to Philadelphia and viewing him in a lineup. Sillitoe thought both were dissembling. In fact, Robbins's schedule definitively eliminated him.

The FBI, assuming they would find Goose, desired more than a photo ID; they wanted Fuchs in America to testify in Goose's trial. Would MI5 transport him? they asked. After a week of silence, the director general responded emphatically, "You may take it that this is entirely out of the question." Fuchs could give evidence, if needed, from England.

Days later, Cimperman hand carried a letter to Sillitoe from Hoover. The delay in receiving the confession, barriers to interviewing Fuchs, and lack of forewarning of Fuchs's arrest had outraged the director. Rather than argue those charges, Sillitoe sought to pacify, offering to intervene with the Home Office—the department blocking the interview—about granting the FBI access to Fuchs.

The Home Office feared the precedent of a foreign government's interviewing a British prisoner. When the prime minister belatedly learned about the to-do from Sillitoe, he was "slightly peeved," not caring a whit about precedent in the current "unprecedented world." Sillitoe cabled Patterson to give the FBI permission.

A week later, the press splashed the secret agreement onto the front page, and the British Foreign Office sent the U.S. State Department a telegram of protest. It was the fourth leak in quick succession. As Liddell lamented, "It appears to be impossible to do anything in the U.S. without consulting the Congressional Committee or the semi-public (?) Commission where representatives of the Press take copious notes."

Two weeks afterward, on Friday, May 19, 1950, Special Agent Bob Lamphere, a counterespionage expert, and the assistant FBI director Hugh Clegg, a sycophantic admirer of Hoover's, arrived in London after the thirteen-hour flight from New York. As they rode in from the airport, Lamphere was surprised by the debris still piled up on London's streets from wartime bombing.

The next day, trying to thwart reporters and photographers, Lamphere and Clegg drove with Skardon to Wormwood Scrubs in an unmarked van. Hoover was aggravated that Skardon was on hand, but sensing a trap, Liddell had insisted. He saw the interrogation as a PR stunt. "It seems to us that it was their intention to represent this visit as a scoop for the FBI where the British had failed." Two weeks later he returned to that thought.

Sitting at a circular table in a drab, unheated interview room across from the warden's office, Lamphere met a colorless, sallow-complexioned, slightly stooped Fuchs, a dramatic transformation from his arrival in Harwell four years before. The agents had to handle this sad-looking prisoner very carefully. Although they had MI5's agreement for the interview, they needed Fuchs's agreement, and Fuchs saw no reason to give it because he didn't trust the FBI and he had no intention of answering questions. The United States had refused a visa to someone who knew Fuchs. He had already put Skardon on notice that he wouldn't name names if it led to pursuit by a "foreign intelligence organisation."

At first, Lamphere made no progress. He then tried the only leverage he had—Christel. He assumed that protecting Christel had hardened Fuchs's reluctance. By mentioning her cooperation and acknowledging her innocence (a statement that in reality offered no protection), he persuaded Fuchs to answer questions.

Lamphere and Clegg had brought several photographs of a man named

Harry Gold. Fuchs had rejected one of him six weeks earlier. On this particular Saturday, however, Fuchs told Lamphere, who conducted the interviews while Clegg took notes, that he couldn't exclude this person as his contact.

Sunday, they all rested, and on Monday, the twenty-second, Lamphere started in on Fuchs again, discussing details of his meetings with the contact, trying to wring out an ID. After forty-five minutes, the wardens blacked out the interview room, and Fuchs watched a film clip of a man walking down a street. "I cannot be absolutely positive," Fuchs said, "but I think it is very likely him. There are certain mannerisms I seem to recognize, such as the too obvious way he has of looking around and looking back."

But something didn't fit. Fuchs saw the film again and spotted the problem. His contact was always happy when they met; the person in the film was very serious. He watched it a third time with the projector moved back to enlarge the picture. This time Fuchs said, "Very likely."

Two days later, on the afternoon of the twenty-fourth, Fuchs viewed another film of the man taken the day before and declared, "Yes, that is my American contact."

Lamphere was relieved but surely not surprised. Two days earlier, the FBI had taken Gold into custody and obtained a confession. The news had broken immediately in the press. Rumors in the prison could have tipped off Fuchs before he fingered Gold, but Fuchs had a different reason for his ID. In the first clip, he saw a very nervous Gold, perhaps concerned that he was being followed. In the second one, filmed in jail, he saw a man, as he later said, "who had just gotten a big load off his chest." It was only then that he identified him.

His interviewers, MI5 and the FBI, had already noted a pattern. Fuchs withheld names of his contacts until he knew that he couldn't cause them harm. He never implicated anyone through an unguarded moment. His record was perfect.

Harry Gold—"Goose" to the Russians, the FBI, and MI5; "Raymond" to Fuchs—was about the same age as Klaus. He was also a scientist of sorts with a passion for chemistry. He'd studied at the University of Pennsylvania until his father lost his job, both victims of the Great Depression. With the economic crash blighting all opportunity and devastating the hard-up immigrant family, they tottered on the edge of eviction and homelessness. The industrious Gold worked a night job to support them while he took a two-year course in chemistry, earning a diploma and eventually a college degree. But he was a gentle and sensitive person, and the hardships and humiliations, especially for his family, had deeply affected him.

A friend began to proselytize to him about communism. He resisted at first but eventually surrendered—not to the politics of meetings and lectures and ranting, but to the Soviet Union's social and economic needs. Gold engaged in small-scale industrial espionage for a while, but he still longed to make a difference for a principle he had come to believe in: the fair and just society promised by communism.

Gradually, Gold went deeper into the underground, and there he met "Paul Smith." Gold had no specifics other than the name, obviously a cover. He didn't know that Smith was an agent for the KGB or that he was based in the Soviet consulate in New York. When Smith assigned him to be Fuchs's handler, Gold saw his chance to make a difference.

It was not any connection to Fuchs that initially called the FBI's attention to Gold. It was his original small-scale industrial espionage. In 1945, the American Elizabeth Bentley, who had spied for the Russians, confessed, and a domino effect implicated Gold with a suspicious chemical company. In 1947, he was called before a federal grand jury and lied himself out of an indictment. The principal fallout was an FBI file with his name on it. In 1950, this file produced the poor photograph Fuchs had rejected at the end of February, choosing Joseph Robbins instead.

A sharp FBI agent with a good memory, noting a resemblance between Robbins and Gold, dug deeper. Clues from Fuchs and the Heinemanns matched details in Gold's file. Knowing that photographs from different angles boosted the odds of identification, agents started following him and snapping pictures.

On May 15, 1950, two agents interviewed Gold in Philadelphia about specifics of the earlier grand jury case. On May 20, the same day that Lamphere and Clegg first met Fuchs, they interviewed Gold again, this time for seven hours straight. They showed him photographs of the Heinemanns, whom he denied knowing, and discussed his travels. He had never been west of the Mississippi, he said. The next day, Gold held to his story during another long interview and agreed to their searching his residence.

On the morning of the twenty-second, the agents showed up at 8:00, climbed the stairs, and entered his cluttered bedroom. Methodically, they searched, extracting incriminating items one after the other, including a map of Santa Fe, where supposedly he had never been. With inconsistencies in his story mounting, his defenses crumbled until he simply stated to the agents, "Yes, I am the man to whom Klaus Fuchs gave the information on atomic energy."

A voluble Harry Gold emptied his conscience to the FBI. Besides the specifics in the Fuchs case, agents heard about David Greenglass, a machinist at Los Alamos working on lenses for the plutonium bomb—a name that led to his brother-in-law Julius Rosenberg, an engineer living in New York, and his wife, Ethel, later executed for crimes of espionage. Julius passed on secrets gained from his brother-in-law on lenses and gave over whatever tidbits he could find on electronics for other advances, such as radar. Neither Rosenberg nor Greenglass had the scientific understanding of Fuchs. The Russians couldn't have created a bomb from their information.

Fuchs had no knowledge of them, or they of him.

Washington headquarters cabled details from the confessions to Lamphere in London. No suspicious differences emerged between the statements made by Fuchs and by Gold—more matters of date and time. Lamphere did spot one inconsistency and confronted Fuchs.

When Fuchs visited Christel in February 1945, he wrote up several pages of notes from memory. He insisted that he handed this material to Gold two days later on the banks of the Charles River, not at his sister's house, where, according to Fuchs, they only set up the next meeting. Gold had no such recollection of visiting Boston proper. He said that Fuchs gave him the material at Christel's. Lamphere saw Fuchs's story as protecting Christel and judged it "the only time during our long interviews, I think, when he did not come entirely clean."

KGB records based on Gold's report showed that he and Fuchs had gone into Boston to buy gifts for friends at Los Alamos. Gold had misremembered, although the transfer of documents seems to have occurred upstairs in Klaus's room at Christel's.

Fuchs was adamant that he never involved Christel. Other than relating that he gave her a phone number for Klaus to call, and then checking in with her, Gold supplied no evidence to the contrary. Although he visited a few times on his own, he and Klaus had only one meeting there. Christel, outspoken and somewhat ingenuous like her father, would have been a poor choice for a spy. She might have guessed what her brother was doing, but it is highly unlikely that he told her that he was handing information to the Russians. She professed no involvement—then and over the years to her children.

Fuchs had given Perrin an account of what he passed on. Gold filled out the story of where the transfers had occurred, their meetings in Santa Fe being the most significant. The KGB's methods tantalized the FBI and MI5.

That Fuchs never, as he claimed, saw Gold again seems clear from Gold's own testimony. Did he meet someone else? When, in January 1950, Fuchs detailed for Perrin the information passed to Gold, Perrin wrote down, "He had several further meetings with him [Gold] in Santa Fe in the autumn of 1945 and spring of 1946 but could not remember precise dates." Fuchs never repeated this statement. Perrin might have misunderstood. Or Fuchs might have come to realize that MI5 had little actual knowledge of his activities, and he could simply erase events.

Arguing against their meeting—or Fuchs using a new agent—were the two espionage cases in 1945–46—Gouzenko in Canada and Bentley in the United States—that had put the KGB on high alert and forced them to suspend meetings.

When Gold's arrest hit the press on the twenty-third, MI5 reeled with surprise, completely blindsided. Hoover had directed Lamphere and Clegg to reveal nothing about the U.S. investigation into Gold. Lamphere thought it "ludicrous" but had followed orders. Hoover demanded that all FBI agents swear a personal allegiance to him.

A perturbed Liddell penned an exceptionally convoluted sentence in his diary that spoke to the PR stunt he had feared when Lamphere and Clegg had first arrived:

> The arrest of Harry GOLD has broken. *As we rather expected, the reflection in the Press here is that the Americans told us about FUCHS, leading to the latter's arrest, but we refused to allow them to interrogate FUCHS, but that now we have done so they have solved their case in forty-eight* [sic] *hours, where we failed.* The question arose as to whether I should have said anything to Clegg before the break. I took the view that it was difficult to accuse the F.B.I. of trying to make a scoop before they had done so, and that in any case we had to reckon with the fact that we were dealing with a cross between a political gangster and a prima donna, who had no intimate knowledge of the case and who, even if he had, would be quite prepared to sacrifice anything and anybody if his own position was at stake.

An equally perturbed Patterson sent a telegram to Dick White: "He confessed before (R) BEFORE F.B.I. knew F had positively identified photographs." Gaining Fuchs's belated identification let Liddell's political gangster/prima donna, J. Edgar Hoover, do exactly what Liddell had predicted—make MI5 look like a failure. Liddell considered the tactics "childish"; Patterson, seeing a bit more maturity, used the term "adolescent."

Two days later, Fuchs signed two statements prepared by Clegg, one with sensitive technical information and one without, the latter for possible grand jury use. Lamphere interviewed Fuchs for another week, during which time Lamphere learned that each answer required a very precise question. Fuchs responded as narrowly as possible with each detail requiring a further probe. Teasing out every tidbit of Fuchs's meetings with Gold this way took time and patience. In the end, Lamphere mined little more than Skardon had already dug out.

Soon after they left, Klaus wrote to Erna that it was his choice whether to be interviewed and reassured her that he didn't answer questions about "purely personal relations." MI5 toyed with censoring this comment but let it pass through.

Sillitoe returned from a trip to the United States and Canada on May 30, 1950, "profoundly dissatisfied." He had experienced the news coverage in America firsthand. He asked Lamphere and Clegg to meet with him before departing.

Holding the meeting in a drab conference room, rather than his paneled office, Sir Percy had brought in his senior officers and introduced them to the two agents. He calmly addressed both Hoover's criticisms from earlier letters and the press reports on the Fuchs case. The implications that MI5 had failed where the FBI had succeeded affronted him.

The impact of the meeting rippled for weeks. According to Clegg's report to Hoover, Sillitoe accused Hoover of leaking information detrimental to MI5, something Hoover denied. Clegg urged Sillitoe to apologize and, when he did not, recommended that the FBI retaliate. Hoover did just that, ordering his agents to share no intelligence on Gold that wasn't specific to the U.K. MI5's relationship with the FBI spiraled down to a "mere formality." Furious though MI5 was, it affirmed that it would continue providing the FBI with access to its intelligence and personnel.

On June 25, 1950, four weeks after Clegg and Lamphere left London, North Korea launched a full-scale invasion along the 38th parallel that had separated it from South Korea since the end of World War II. The threat of nuclear attack hung over the peninsula for the first year of the conflict, at which point the bombs and bombers sitting on a tarmac at the Okinawa air force base went back home. President Truman did not authorize the use of nuclear bombs.

CHAPTER 24

Prison, Wormwood Scrubs, 1950 and On

A FEW DAYS AFTER THE FBI LEFT, SKARDON WROTE A LETTER TO THE HEAD OF THE Prison Commission commending the governor and staff at Wormwood Scrubs for the excellent arrangement during the ten-day interrogation. He ended it by quoting Fuchs, who said that "he had been agreeably surprised to find the Americans so courteous and forbearing." The FBI's questioning seemed to leave little mark.

A couple of days later, Klaus wrote to Christel, the first time since his arrest, and began with "a short lecture":

> It seems to be a general family weakness that we feel so strongly
> about our convictions that we take a good deal on ourselves. We
> have to pay for that and I think that again may be characteristic
> for us that we do not complain [about] the price. With our strong
> convictions we are apt to forget the rights of other people and if
> we do that, the price is so much heavier.

Klaus understood his betrayal, which was not handing secrets to the Russians. In that he did what his conscience dictated and was proud. Prison was someone else's sense of justice, and he accepted that as well. Where he had to carry the burden of guilt was in his disloyalty to his friends.

Christel knew that her family had paid a price too, but for that she never chastised her brother. Her husband, who had committed her to a psychiatric hospital and cut her off from her children, left her there during the search for Klaus's handler. Meanwhile, FBI agents silently followed their eleven-year-old son on his two-mile walk to school every day. His father told him it was the FBI; he didn't know what that was, and it scared him.

Despite the four months Klaus had spent behind bars, the rest of his letter had a lighter tone. He said that he felt young, "almost ready to throw away the whole past and start again on something quite different." His new direction was "going to school," reading everything he had never found time for, such as Gibbon's *Decline and Fall of the Roman Empire*. Otherwise, every day was the same: sewing mattresses—advancing, with his usual efficiency and focus, from the typical household sewing machine with a pedal to a motorized model.

It was as though he had his life, however changed, back under his control.

More change was a few weeks away. At the end of June, officials moved him to HM Prison Stafford in the West Midlands, not far from Manchester. From prison to prison was a four-hour drive, but Skardon arranged a detour. With the MI5 driver Reeve and two prison officers, Skardon and Fuchs first went south to Kew Gardens Station so that Fuchs could confirm the locations of the chalk-mark signals as well as the house where he would throw the men's magazine over the fence to change a meeting date. As when Skardon had checked on his own, he reported that it was all exactly as Fuchs had described.

On arrival at Stafford, Fuchs was held in maximum security "at all times." He read philosophy and worked in the Mail Bag Shop, sewing again. Letters were fewer, as were visits. The Skinners, for one, complained to him that he didn't write anymore. Their letters to him reported that they were both unwell, especially Erna, who suffered everything from mumps to a nervous breakdown, lived on sedatives, and was out of bed for only half the day.

Living in Liverpool, they were about two hours away from Stafford and close enough to visit. There's no record that they did. Letters seemed to cease as well. Herbert continued with his work and died suddenly in January 1960, apparently of a heart attack. He was only fifty-nine. Erna died a decade or so later, having never recovered health-wise from the traumas of January 1950.

In keeping with his words to Christel about throwing out the past, which might have included people, Klaus decided to forgo physics and study economics.

Gaps in Fuchs's contacts still pestered MI5. Who was the young woman in Banbury who walked along the country road with him in 1943? Who was the man who began meeting him in London pubs in 1947? Perhaps in the Christmas spirit, Fuchs gave up one at the end of 1950: Ursula Kuczynski, a.k.a. Ruth Werner, a.k.a. Hamburger, a.k.a. Sonya. Skardon was pleased.

Ursula claimed never to have seen Klaus after their "trysts" in Banbury. The Russians, for a reason she either didn't know or didn't tell, deactivated her in January 1946. The next year, two MI5 officers, having no idea of her ties to Fuchs, knocked on her door to question her about her previous activities in Switzerland.

In the fall of 1949, tired of her inactivity, she began to organize her departure from Britain. At that time, she lived in Great Rollright, thirty-five miles north of Harwell and on the edge of the Cotswolds. Having already made preparations, she was exfiltrated soon after Klaus's arrest, leaving for Berlin on February 28, 1950.

The proximity of Harwell to Great Rollright certainly leads to speculation. Did she, as Klaus had, learn of trouble early in 1949? Did they meet again to strategize about MI5? Did Klaus slip off to see her after his first interview with Skardon? Given the visit from MI5, it would have been very risky but not impossible.

Wanting more from Fuchs, MI5 realized that their approach had to be gentle. When the Home Office pushed to take away his citizenship quickly, Liddell fended them off, not wanting to give him "a body blow until we had got all the information we wanted." The Home Office waited to send Fuchs notice of the denaturalization process until June 1950. He responded with a long letter arguing and then pleading for them not to strip it away. It was against the law, he said, to reverse naturalization as a punishment. It was to be based on consideration of his present and future loyalty, which his cooperation with MI5 and the FBI demonstrated. His consent to exclude charging inducement at the trial attested to his loyalty. He asked that the Home Office confirm this with MI5 and the prosecutor's office.

Skardon met with Fuchs just after the Home Office letter arrived. In tears, Fuchs asked for his advice. As Skardon stated in a letter to the Home Office, "There is no doubt whatever about his feelings at the prospect of being deprived of British citizenship. . . . Having read FUCHS' letter with care, I am satisfied that it is wholly true." He had come to know Fuchs well and did not consider him a security risk now or in the future. He emphasized that without Fuchs's voluntary confession, they could not have arrested him, that he had been free from espionage for a year before that, and that he had newfound friendships and loyalties. Skardon did not think that denaturalization "should necessarily follow automatically" from conviction.

The Deprivation of Citizenship Committee met to hear his case in December 1950. Fuchs chose not to attend or be represented because he didn't want to incur publicity or cause stress to friends or the authorities. To no consequence. A version of his letter showed up in the *Evening Standard*, and every London newspaper carried the story.

Attorney General Shawcross presented the history of the case and read parts of Fuchs's letter. The committee then adjourned to consider its recommendation to the home secretary. On February 12, 1951, the Home

Office canceled his citizenship because, according to the committee, it was not conducive to the public good. Politics clearly played a part.

Fuchs was devastated, but other than the letter he wrote, he made no remarks or complaints. It seems, though, that he began to isolate himself from Britain.

Although overwhelmed by Klaus's conviction, Emil Fuchs wrote to his son regularly. His traditional Christmas letter to friends in 1950 thanked them for their love during the difficult year and passed on some good news, that Christel, although still hospitalized, was improving and that Gerhard had finally returned from Switzerland. Emil, seventy-six and president of the peace committee at the University of Leipzig, ended on a note of courage as written in 2 Corinthians 12:9, "My grace is sufficient for thee: for my strength is made perfect in weakness."

It was strength he would soon need to draw on. With Klaus's arrest, the Swiss police had questioned Gerhard about his communist ties and political activities. It resulted in their revoking his entry pass and forcing him to return to Germany in June 1951. He found a job at an economic research institute in Berlin.

Even with twelve years in the sanatorium, Gerhard had never regained his health and had become obese. Now the stress of the move and the change from the pure air of the mountains to the pollution of the big city caused his asthma to come rushing back almost immediately. Then he contacted his former wife, Karin, who wrote that she had to finish her PhD dissertation. Their son, Jürgen, born while the Nazis held Karin in the women's prison in Berlin, had drowned a few years before. Gerhard never saw him.

At Christmas, Emil visited Gerhard in a clinic in the Harz Mountains where he was trying to recover from asthma. He didn't, and he died on February 10, 1951. Emil wrote to Klaus a week later about the bitter reality: "Every moment I feel as if the pain should kill me and I live on." This was just days after Klaus had the final word on losing his citizenship.

It took Klaus three months to respond. He explained that he "found it difficult to write, since it is not easy to get one's feelings in perspective if one has so little chance to take one's sorrows away from the eyes of the curious." He wrote the day before his father's birthday and ended the letter with good wishes: "So for your 77th birthday, I send you the faith of optimism and youth, that youth which you have always retained through all trials and which perhaps we should trace back to our French ancestors. But tempered a little by Socrates wisdom, which perhaps shows that I am beginning to grow old." Klaus, at thirty-nine, and imprisoned for one year, had begun to realize the limits of his knowledge.

In spite of the strained relations between the United States and the U.K. over Fuchs's arrest and the McMahon Act of 1946, one common concern had kept them talking—uranium ore, particularly the lode in a mine in the Belgian Congo. If the United States wanted to build more bombs, it needed that ore. The two countries had signed an agreement with a very favorable distribution for the United States, and in 1949 it was about to expire. Without another, the split reverted to fifty-fifty. The U.S. government thought the chances of gaining congressional approval for a renewal, no matter the need for the ore, were slim. Congress feared that the U.K. would use it to blackmail them, wringing out concessions on atomic energy and weakening the McMahon Act, which it guarded zealously.

Even so, by the summer of 1950, the two governments had established talks on a uranium agreement and on security standards. A year later, at the Americans' urging, the British introduced a new security system as a move to encourage Congress to amend the McMahon Act and to cooperate more closely on atomic energy. It had had many setbacks. As Secretary of State Dean Acheson said, every time they were to do it, another spy scandal erupted. First, there was Fuchs; then the British physicist Bruno Pontecorvo fled to Moscow in September 1950. In May 1951, the British diplomat Donald Maclean, who had worked at the British embassy in

Washington, followed, taking along another British diplomat, Guy Burgess. A sobering account.

Acutely aware of its tattered image, MI5 took an opportunity to shape the story. The respected war correspondent turned public relations officer at the Ministry of Defence, Alan Moorehead, proposed writing "a serious study of Fuchs" to examine "the schizophrenia of the high, scientific mind." The Ministry of Supply was "enthusiastic" about the project, and MI5 was "keen," especially Sillitoe and White. They saw that it could be "anti-Communist propaganda" and offered to provide Moorehead with "factual information . . . not of a secret character."

To interview Fuchs, Moorehead needed the permission of the Prison Commission, which objected. It didn't want to set a precedent should someone ask to interview a notorious murderer for a book. Moorehead proceeded without meeting Fuchs and shifted his focus. Writing to Max Born, he described the project as a book on Soviet atomic espionage for the purpose of putting forth the British case, especially to the Americans. Moorehead explained to Born that "Fuchs can be understood only in the light of these early days before the war, at first in Germany and then when he came first to Bristol and then to you." True enough, but unfortunately for Moorehead, Born answered that he didn't have any information.

Other friends and acquaintances did have something to say. Erna Skinner even handed over all her correspondence with Klaus. From a collection of letters, memories, and MI5 input, Moorehead re-created every motive and behavior that he assumed Fuchs felt. Some were accurate; others completely bowed to whatever MI5 needed to repair its status.

Skardon was Moorehead's minder. He handed him "factual information" that Moorehead sometimes quoted verbatim and massaged to excuse MI5's security failures and the inducement, turning Fuchs's thinking that he could stay at Harwell if he confessed into an "absurd illusion." Moorehead's opinions served as the official Fuchs character template for years.

Published in 1952, *The Traitors* featured Fuchs and two other atomic spies, Alan Nunn May and Bruno Pontecorvo. The book was very popular in Britain, where thirty thousand copies were quickly snatched up. In the United States, *The Saturday Evening Post* published an excerpt. The British film producer and director Alexander Korda planned to turn the book into a movie but never did. Fuchs wouldn't give him permission. The book, however, did little to alter the opinion of the U.S. Congress about MI5's lax security procedures.

The well-known literary critic Raymond Mortimer wrote in his review, "Mr. Moorehead acquits our security officers of all blame; and maintains that the Americans, if they had investigated him [Fuchs] independently, could have discovered nothing."

Mortimer recommended the book but faulted Moorehead's condemnation of Fuchs for following "his own conscience and society afterwards." Mirroring the overblown tone of the entire text, Moorehead had written, "How that conscience was formed, who gave it authority—this he [Fuchs] did not discuss. The conscience was divine, unquestioned, and inexplicable; it simply gave forth its inevitable light, and one obeyed." Mortimer, finding Moorehead's statement "shocking," reminded him of the martyrs who died for their faith and quoted E. M. Forster: "If I had to choose between betraying my country and betraying my friends, I hope I should have the guts to betray my country."

Emil Fuchs had his own unique response to issues of conscience. A pastor published a newspaper article about Emil titled "Conscience Without Reason!" It blamed him for the problems that had befallen his children. Emil explained to his friends with a smile, "The man is right. Had we been as reasonable as the mass of our bourgeoisie, we would have said 'Heil Hitler' and spared ourselves everything. Then maybe my children, like so many, would have died for Hitler instead of their own convictions."

Even after two years of his silence, stories of Fuchs sold newspapers. Besides Moorehead's book, Rebecca West, noted British author and critic, featured him in articles on treason, "friends" from prison sold false information, and the American government held hearings and published white papers about him. When Emil Fuchs and his grandson Klaus Kittowski applied for a visa to attend a Quaker world conference in 1952, the British government refused. The cabinet feared that the American press would sensationalize the story.

One news story that went around in America in 1951 was that from his prison cell Fuchs continued to do research, particularly on the hydrogen bomb. Embassy staff in Washington cabled London for a denial.

The rumor seemed to precede the facts. In May 1952, Dr. William Penney requested an interview with Fuchs to review information he gave to the Russians. Within the atomic weapons section of the Ministry of Supply, Penney was charged with designing Britain's first atomic bomb. While Fuchs was at Harwell, he was one of Penney's main theoretical consultants. They knew each other well from working together at Los Alamos and having an ongoing debate on the blast waves of the Hiroshima bomb.

MI5's Guy Liddell was doubtful that Penney would find anything substantive but agreed that he, with the appropriate permission from the prison and accompanied by Skardon, could see Fuchs. Months later, on February 23, 1953, with all permissions in hand including Fuchs's, Penney, Skardon, and an MI6 officer traveled from Paddington Station to Stafford. Penney checked that the train schedule allowed for a three- to four-hour interview. This was no ordinary visit with a twenty-minute limit.

What the three men talked about on the twenty-third wasn't set down. In various letters, the subject was intentionally not named, referred to instead as "the matter about which we spoke," "real grounds for you to have another dig," or "technical issues." Regardless of what Penney told Liddell, it was likely not about information given to the Russians but about what Fuchs knew—the importance of which was narrowing quickly. By the time Penney saw Fuchs, Britain had tested its first atomic bomb, so it didn't need him for that, although when Penney first made the request, that wasn't true. More relevant in 1953, the Americans had detonated their first hydrogen bomb. Could the Russians be far behind? The question for Fuchs might have been, what could he tell Penney about the hydrogen bomb?

Fuchs had as much to say as any other physicist in Britain, perhaps even more. He had heard lectures at Los Alamos in 1945 on Teller's classical Super, as it was called, which didn't work. Before leaving there in 1946, he had searched the library for any additional information—for the British and the Russians. On his declassification trip to the United States in 1947, he had gathered hints on recent research on the hydrogen bomb at the behest of the British. Earlier at Los Alamos, he and von Neumann had designed a trigger device for which they applied for a secret patent. Fuchs hadn't told Perrin about it, because he didn't ask. KGB files indicate that he did tell the Russians. Did he tell Penney?

The Russians, led by Andrei Sakharov, exploded a hydrogen bomb in 1955. The British with Penney detonated theirs in 1957. They both used radiation compression as the trigger, an original idea from the Americans Edward Teller and Stan Ulam. With this device, high levels of electromagnetic radiation compress the core of the bomb to set off the chain reaction. Sakharov always equivocated about how he came to this concept. His friends decided that he wasn't trying to obfuscate the use of foreign intelligence. He wasn't quite sure of the origin himself.

Implicit in the Fuchs–von Neumann design, which as a whole didn't work, was the idea of radiation compression—so implicit that if one did not already know it, it wasn't obvious.

Ideas are amorphous creatures. An impression one absorbs subconsciously can provoke images and designs without awareness. A fully developed idea often has many parents. Whether the hidden insights of the Fuchs–von Neumann design, which Fuchs later stated was mostly his work, seeped in can never be known, nor whether he shared it with Penney.

By April 1953, the prison system had moved Fuchs a hundred miles north of Stafford to Wakefield prison, his permanent home for the remainder of his sentence. The first reports indicated that he settled in nicely and did surprisingly well with the other prisoners. His physical health and mental health were good. The wardens noted that he had no time for any "spiritual reasoning" and was cheerful and no longer interested in communism, considering it a "vile and vicious organisation."

As he moved farther away, the distance from Harwell increased in more than miles. Henry Arnold, who agreed to pay his bills, also disposed of his belongings, from pots and pans to bed linens to his violin, skis, and two cars. Science books to the Harwell library; various items to friends; correspondence—seemingly every personal letter sent to him since 1933—stored in boxes, along with his German school reports and two dozen letters received during internment, all scoured by MI5. From under his bed, Arnold pulled out a uniform. On the back of the jacket was a red circle a foot in diameter, the target, as the internees in Camps L and N had thought of it. Arnold wrote to Fuchs that he wanted to burn it. And Fuchs indifferently agreed.

Such was the disposal of a life.

In the summer of 1956, Fuchs's twenty-one-year-old nephew, Klaus Kittowski, successfully applied for a British visa. Having a last name other than Fuchs made it easier. Before visiting his uncle, he worked at a Young Friends Work Camp in the south of England, building a brick house in the community. When finished, he hitched rides for two weeks over two hundred miles to Wakefield, sleeping in barns and living with a gang in Birmingham. When he finally reached Wakefield, they allowed him one whole hour with Klaus. It had been seven years. A report to the prime minister said that they spoke in English and talked about the family.

Nephew Klaus brought two presents: a radio that he had bought with the money earned from translating at the Quaker camp, and greetings from "Margot." "Margot" was the French diminutive for Margarete used that summer so long ago by Grete Keilson, Klaus's comrade in Paris in 1933. She now worked for the Foreign Ministry in the East German government, and it was from her that the young man had received his visa. Klaus sent greetings in return.

The next year, 1957, Emil Fuchs made one more attempt to see his son. There was another European Friends conference, and this time the government decided that it was unlikely the press would be interested. Finally, father and son reunited. They talked about where Klaus would go and what he would do when he was released. Following standard policy, Fuchs's good behavior would reduce his sentence by a third, releasing him in June 1959. Klaus saw his prospects as "dismal," discredited in England and probably unwanted in socialist countries. Emil assured him that East Germany would welcome him and use his talents.

Fuchs became a full member of the prison community at Wakefield and more than a model prisoner. He was, as a warden wrote, "held in high esteem by other men on the Wing." He shared his cigarettes; he listened to and tried to solve their problems; he joined clubs (French, German, Modern Science, and the Atomic Physics Radio Listening Club); he enjoyed chess matches with members of the Irish Republican Army; he regularly donated blood; he was a Stroke (a trusted prison leader); he advanced from the laundry to the library and in the last two years to education, organizing and teaching courses in math and physics. He later wrote that creating the courses was a difficult task that "demands the whole man." He always kept the notebooks he used for the classes, a positive memory to hold on to from the long nine years of lost life.

In 1958, the British government began to contemplate Fuchs's release. Its primary goal with any activity surrounding this prisoner was not to upset the Americans and the endless negotiations on atomic energy. When the governor of Wakefield requested that Fuchs be transferred to an open prison—one with no walls or fences that prepared inmates for the outside world—the Foreign Office rejected it. Talks to amend the McMahon Act were taking place in the U.S. Congress. Part of the reason for the request was Fuchs's deteriorating health. The Foreign Office hoped it didn't worsen in the next six months.

The Americans wanted him to remain in Britain and not disappear behind the Iron Curtain. The British pressured him to stay, but he had made up his mind. The home secretary did gain assurances from the U.S. government that it would not lodge a formal protest if Fuchs went to East Germany.

The British government had hemmed itself in. It had no control over Fuchs. Because it had revoked his British citizenship, he was stateless. It couldn't deport him if no country would take him in; it couldn't prevent him from staying in Britain if he wished to nor from leaving if a country gave him entry.

First, officials needed to know what he wished. The governor of Wakefield, who liked Fuchs very much and tried to persuade him to become a Christian, had already learned that he wanted to go to his father in Leipzig, but only if the "Stalinists are not in power." They, of course, would mete out very rough treatment. Fuchs ruled out West Germany, Britain, and America because of the stigma of being a traitor. If East Germany wasn't an option, he would consider India or Brazil.

Turning eighty-five and not well, Emil could still draw on his lifelong tenacity to ensure that Klaus arrived in East Germany as desired. He had arranged entry permits early and even sent a friend to London in March 1959 to smooth out details with prison officials. In fact, the whole East German government wanted to ensure that he made it there, unimpeded by the Brits or the Americans. As the KGB wrote, "We attach exceptionally serious significance to [Fuchs's] presence in [East Germany]." From the German side, the senior official in the Foreign Office in charge of Klaus's immigration process was Grete Keilson, Margot from 1933 Paris.

Arrangements for him to leave the country weren't simple. The British didn't recognize East Germany. Going by a British boat or plane meant traveling to another country first. They debated which travel mode, what date, from what prison, consulting Fuchs throughout. The final plan, kept secret, was for Fuchs to leave on June 23 on a Polish airliner from London Airport, traveling to Schönefeld Airport in East Berlin.

Members of Parliament had a slew of questions. During the deliberative ritual of Question Time, Home Secretary Rab Butler stressed that any scientific information Fuchs had possessed was out of date. One member asked if "his brain will be of no future use to the Russians" because at his trial the attorney general had described him as "this brilliant scientist." The home secretary answered, "I cannot extend my influence as far as that."

Newspapers were abuzz with rumors about his release. No one could miss that he was about to leave. Rudi Peierls sent him a short note:

> Dear Klaus,
>
> I saw from the papers that you are soon going to be released.
>
> If you need any help in getting started in life, financial or otherwise, or if you need advice, please let me know. I shall do what I can.
>
> Yours Sincerely,
> Rudi

The two had had little contact over the years. The letter must have been hard for Rudi to send and for Klaus to receive, so hard for the latter that he did not respond, although he did save it. According to Genia, Rudi never forgave that slight. As for Klaus, a normally courteous person, he felt his friends had abandoned him, even though Erna Skinner had complained about his not writing to her. It was one of those misperceptions that would never be resolved.

The one person Fuchs did trust was Henry Arnold, the last familiar face he saw. Arnold, although retired since 1957, had stayed in touch with Fuchs about his finances and helped with plans for his release. He defined his feelings about Fuchs with two remarks—one about relief and one about regret. The first one he made in 1956, referring to an anticipated last visit to Fuchs to discuss finances: "I'll be glad enough, you may be sure, when that's over and done with." The other was years later: "I can't call him a friend exactly, but I had affection for him. . . . Well, was it affection? More than friendship, I felt sorry for him, because I knew for a long time how it had to end." That Arnold did whatever he could for Fuchs throughout his stay in prison suggests that it was probably more than that, that genuine caring took hold of him. It did, in fact, take hold of Fuchs.

At 7:00 on Tuesday morning, June 23, 1959, reporters who had staked out Wakefield prison saw a thin, older Klaus Fuchs walk out wearing an over-sized, double-breasted brown suit—three pens in the top pocket—and a brown trilby. He and three policemen quickly climbed into a black Morris police car that was followed by another police car to keep reporters from getting too close. The night before at midnight, security had carried out a decoy removal to confuse reporters, unsuccessfully.

Zipping through the city of Wakefield at fifty miles per hour, they drove south on Great North Road, through old villages and towns, past miles of fields, and stopped for lunch at the Bedford police station. It had been six years since Fuchs had seen the outside world, and on this Tuesday a clear vista greeted him, the temperature comfortably in the midseventies. He probably didn't see much change, though, because Great North Road hadn't changed in decades, maybe centuries. But it was coming. Out of sight, just to the west, the government was about to open the country's first modern motorway, the M1, to replace it. They were driving to London Airport, southwest of the city. If his journey took him close to London, the change would have left him awed.

At London Airport, he sat in a private room with his security men until the flight was ready for departure. The aim to minimize publicity had failed, but security kept reporters and photographers at a distance. That his reservations were under the name Herr Strauss didn't help a bit.

Mixed feelings accompanied his departure. One headline read, "Good Riddance!" and another, "Fuchs: No Resentment." A former inmate was quoted as saying, "The Doc—one of the best." Fuchs didn't have too much to say. In conversation with a reporter, he expressed some regret at leaving

Britain but pleasure in being reunited with his father "on the other side of the Iron Curtain."

The Polish Airlines flight was a regular commercial one, and Fleet Street reporters had all bought seats with dreams of an exclusive story. The police cleared a path through the photographers. Fuchs climbed the stairs to board the plane and disappeared.

VI

RETURN

The Loschwitz neighborhood in Dresden where the Fuchses had a weekend house

CHAPTER 25

East Germany, Berlin 1959

AROUND 7:00 P.M. ON JUNE 23, 1959, THE POLISH AIRLINER CARRYING KLAUS FUCHS approached Schönefeld Airport in Berlin's eastern sector. This flight was the final leg in a twenty-six-year journey, almost to the day.

From the West Berlin side of the border, a dozen or so reporters sat in cars watching. Those who had obtained entry permits from East Germany crowded into the airport's restaurant, waiting. Once the plane landed, the ground crew waved the pilot to a space beyond the terminal where a state limousine could pull up. The gangway wasn't in position when the door opened, and with the crush of reporters on the plane trying to get in front of him, Fuchs almost fell out.

Once the stairs were in place, Fuchs descended to the tarmac with a gray overcoat over his arm and a small bag clutched in his hand. A tall young man and a middle-aged woman walked up to him, their faces beaming. His nephew Klaus gave him a hug; the government official and old friend Grete Keilson handed him a bouquet of red carnations. In just over a minute, the three were in the back of the black ZIS heading south, customs and immigrations formalities not required. After all, Klaus had no passport; he was a stateless person.

All the same, Walter Ulbricht, first secretary of the Socialist Unity Party of Germany (the SED) and effectively the country's president, had personally supervised to ensure Klaus's safe arrival. The KGB had warned, "It is possible that the English and Americans are making efforts to keep [Fuchs] from leaving England for the GDR, and it is even possible that they are arranging to have him abducted."

The only threat evident at the moment was from reporters, who jumped into their cars and sped along behind. The driver of the limousine took a dirt road through the woods until the cars trailing began to fall away. When a railroad crossing barrier forced the driver to stop, the occupant of the only car to have hung on got out and knocked on the window of the limousine to ask for an interview. Klaus told Reuters' East German bureau chief and sole reporter Peter Johnson that he could visit him in the next day or two.

The limo then headed to the modest summerhouse in the resort town of Wandlitz, just north of Berlin, where eighty-five-year-old Emil was waiting, just as he had waited for years.

Reuters' Peter Johnson had heard that Emil had a house in Wandlitz on Karl-Marx-Strasse, and on the morning of the twenty-third he drove by. He went again that night around 10:00 to make sure Klaus was there and returned the next morning at 8:00. A woman came out when he rang the bell. She told him that Klaus was still sleeping. Shortly, Klaus came out wearing the same brown suit he had worn on the plane, and they spoke through the fence. He apologized to Peter for not opening it, but he didn't have the key.

Klaus, maintaining his usual polite and friendly demeanor, told Johnson that he planned to become an East German citizen, which he did a few days later. When Johnson pushed him, he admitted that he was a Marxist. At the end of their chat, Johnson asked, "Why did you pass the atomic secrets to Russia?" With a slight smile, Klaus answered that he didn't wish to say.

Johnson called at Wandlitz again the next day at lunchtime for another scoop. This time the gate was open, and Klaus invited him to join them for a dessert of strained apple puree. Johnson gave Klaus a copy of *The Times* from the previous day, Wednesday, June 24, 1959, with articles describing his departure from London, and snapped an iconic picture of Klaus reading it, sitting on a chair next to a white trellis, legs crossed and his face wearing a somewhat curious expression.

Klaus had arrived in a city and country filled with cold war tensions and unmet needs, including housing, certain food staples, and fuel. Nonetheless, leaders were proud of the progress since the war, given the nearly complete destruction of Berlin. On the ride to Wandlitz the driver had detoured through East Berlin on streets near Alexanderplatz for Klaus to see the new socialist construction.

Its counterpart, West Berlin, was a sliver of land in the eastern side of Germany divided up and controlled by the Americans, British, and French in their individual sectors, but Nikita Khrushchev, premier of the Soviet Union, wanted Berlin to be whole and wholly his. The western sectors had no direct land link to the Federal Republic of Germany, and earlier Stalin had tried starving the West Berliners out. In 1948 and 1949, with the Berlin airlift, the United States shipped in tons of food and coal to defeat that strategy, but failure did not decrease Russia's fixation. West Berlin's rising prosperity, which lured East Berlin citizens to cross the boundary in droves, made the obsession more intense. In 1958, Khrushchev searched for another solution to stop the bleeding. A year of talks between the Americans and the Russians produced no results.

It was an unusual backdrop against which to establish a "normal" life, the first such opportunity for Klaus since 1930, when he took the train from Eisenach to Leipzig to study mathematics and, as it turned out, to become a resister to fascism. Much later, his four years at Harwell seemed normal, but his conflicts and contradictions roiled inside.

As with most transitions in Klaus's life, this one rolled out quietly and quickly. He simply settled in and got on with what was expected of him. No complaints, no drama, no joy or suffering shared.

His mailbox filled with greetings from his old Free Socialist Student

Group in Kiel; his math teacher in Eisenach, Dr. Erich Koch; repatriated
friends he had seen in London at the Free German League of Culture
events; even a couple of former inmates from Wakefield prison reporting
on their lives and thanking him for his good counsel and the education he
gave them there. At least initially, there were no messages from former
friends in Britain.

In the coming years, a few notes of good wishes arrived irregularly
from Max and Hedi Born and from Nevill Mott. In 1979, the East German
Academy of Science invited Mott to lecture in Leipzig and Halle. Fuchs
was invited but chose not to attend. Mott was relieved, writing in his memoir, "I could not have embraced my long-lost pupil with 'all is forgiven,'
neither could I have shown any hostility to a man who had done what he
thought right and suffered for it."

Other requests were equally tied to the past: a letter from Jim Skardon's son asking for information for a biography of his father, one from a
lawyer for the sons of Julius and Ethel Rosenberg asking for an interview,
and one from the brilliant mathematician John Nash asking for help in
getting an East German visa and passport. There is no indication whether
Fuchs responded to the last three or not. He did send a package to Wakefield prison and received a thank-you note from its "Tutor Organization"
for his gift of books to the German Club, of which he had been a member.
Requests for interviews from reporters, authors, and movie producers kept
him in contact with the West.

He relived memories with old friends too—as reported by Nitschke,
the limousine driver who had met him at the airport and continued to
drive him around. An employee of the Stasi (the East German secret
police), he was a precaution against abduction or assault and one of its
informants on him. One day, Nitschke drove Klaus to visit a woman who
fought with him against the Nazis in Kiel. She had lived through a two-
year imprisonment and severe beatings and carried the scars from injuries
that forced her to walk with two canes. Another day, Nitschke brought the
Fuchs family's old friend Arthur Rackwitz to Wandlitz from West Berlin.

After hiding Klaus, Gerhard, and others in Berlin's underground, Rackwitz had been arrested in 1944 and survived, barely, in the Dachau concentration camp.

But a new world immediately sprang up as well. After spending eight days with his father in Wandlitz, Klaus and Nitschke traveled to Dresden-Rossendorf and the ZfK, the Central Institute for Nuclear Physics, an institution with more than eight hundred employees, mostly scientists and engineers. His stay included tours, discussions with scientists, and a hotel reception—the subtext being a kind of job interview.

Nitschke, impressed with Klaus's humble and simple nature in spite of his "bourgeois origins," became a confidant during this period. Klaus was open about his concerns at the ZfK—that the scientists and students there "have no purposeful work in mind and are experimenting haphazardly without it." As someone being considered as a potential deputy director, Klaus didn't know if he could accomplish the changes needed. To decide, he wanted a discussion with First Secretary Walter Ulbricht.

Having been Jürgen Kuczynski's contact in Moscow during the 1940s, Ulbricht was well acquainted with Klaus's story, and a meeting between the two took place in Berlin. Here in the East, the cloud over Fuchs's reputation wasn't spying but his confession and possible identification of agents. He admitted frankly to Ulbricht that he had made mistakes, an acknowledgment that Ulbricht accepted. He gave Klaus his support, and as a first step the SED leadership appointed Klaus deputy director of the ZfK, presumably with assurances that he would have the resources for his work. As a second option, he also extended an invitation from the KGB to live and work in Russia, which Klaus declined.

In 1959, the director of the three-year-old ZfK was Heinz Barwich, whose personal interest was nuclear reactors, as was Fuchs's. In a meeting with the chair of the scientific council in August, Barwich asserted his rights as director and refused to have Fuchs as his deputy director, or to decrease his own role in developing reactors, or to have Fuchs in an independent role at the institute. Barwich wanted Fuchs to create a theoretical department squarely under his control.

Displeased with this response, the chairman of the scientific council strongly suggested that Barwich take a few days to think it over, and after the few days Barwich complied with the council's wishes. Fuchs's positions as deputy director of the institute and head of a theoretical division (that was independent) were announced on September 1, 1959. He also soon became a professor at the Technische Hochschule in Dresden.

Émigrés to East Germany were regarded cautiously by those who had escaped to the East rather than the West, the latter often considered tainted by liberal democratic ideals. Some of these *Westemigranten*, though, had successfully navigated treacherous political chasms and become trusted and powerful members in the SED. Their shared history in Britain—refugee status, internment, KPD activities—together with a similar worldview had created a bond that they honored. Enough of them gave support to Klaus—not only an émigré, but one who had confessed—to make a difference.

Klaus had another important backer as well, Grete Keilson. From his arrival, he and Grete, a widow for six years, saw a lot of each other. Nitschke would frequently drop him off at Grete's in the evening and fetch him the next day to travel back to Wandlitz. Klaus had been enamored of Grete in Paris and, according to Christel, never quite left the feelings behind. At the beginning of Klaus's stay in Bristol, he had sent her amusing letters. She had not passed up the opportunity to send him the "Hello from Margot" via young Klaus when he visited his uncle in prison in 1956.

Now in a high position in the SED as well as an assistant director in the Foreign Office, Grete had a deep history with the German Communist Party, having signed on as a teenager. Before the Nazi power grab, she was secretary to Georgi Dimitrov, the leader of the Comintern in Germany later arrested for complicity in the Reichstag fire. She escaped to Prague and then Paris to organize, with Klaus's help, the peace conferences in

1933. She stayed there to evaluate the situation in Germany and report to Moscow. In 1939, she went to Moscow and worked with Dimitrov and Ulbricht in the Comintern.

This was Stalin's Russia, and after the war he wanted to liquidate anyone who had operated outside Russia. One day, Grete sat at a meeting and watched as comrades were ushered out, never seen again. With blood pulsing, she waited to see if she would be next. The terror of the moment lasted for the rest of her life.

Klaus and Grete were opposites—she "arrived," whereas he blended in—that complemented each other well. Her outgoing personality allowed his reserved one to sit back and observe. In fact, she had many traits similar to Erna Skinner. Like Erna, she was a few years older than Klaus, smart and chatty, and she liked to take charge, especially in organizing their social life. Unlike Erna, she dressed elegantly and took care with her appearance. Klaus was, at best, a gray-suit-and-white-shirt man and, when anxious, a bit disheveled.

Whether for physical, mental, or ideological reasons or all of them, Klaus took a short break from his new life and underwent a checkup at a health spa at the government's request. His comments to Nitschke indicated irritation at the stay. Once back, he and Grete sat down with Emil and told him of their plans to marry. Then at Klaus's request, the government provided him with three weeks at another health spa, this one in the Thuringian Forest near Eisenach. Reports from Nitschke indicated all sounded well.

Their wedding on September 9—the groom was forty-seven, the bride fifty-three—was a simple, nonreligious ceremony followed by a small dinner at the Hotel Johannishof in central Berlin and a party at the summerhouse in Wandlitz. It was just family, Emil and young Klaus, and a few friends, two of whom were members of the Central Committee of the SED. By the end of September, the new Fuchs family had moved to Dresden, Klaus began work at the ZfK, and a routine developed that included guests from the institute and lecturers who came from Russia. They seemed happy from the start.

In three months, Klaus transformed thirty years of delayed opportunity into life in full bloom: a wife, a high-level job, an apartment in the city, a large weekend house, a car, and an application to become an SED party member that was quickly accepted. A professorship at a university would follow, all arranged by the East German government. A letter to the local party secretary in Dresden from Kurt Hager, the East German secretary responsible for science and a fellow British émigré and internee with Klaus, directed:

> Fuchs is an outstanding scientist, and we attach great importance to his getting the best living and working conditions. On behalf of Walter Ulbricht, I ask you to ensure that Fuchs gets an appropriate house . . . and that trustworthy housekeeping personnel will be hired.

On his first visit to the ZfK, Klaus had identified the lack of theoretical input to the experimental research. He struggled with this institutional problem and one of his own, catching up with recent scientific advances. After a while the British prison system had allowed physics books, but he couldn't keep current. His solution to both was to select talented young scientists, who were primarily "misused" for calculations by the experimentalists, and establish an "independent school" for basic modern theory. Presumably a primer for them as well as for him. His nephew often saw them having discussions in his uncle's garden.

But there were intrigues from the start, especially on the part of the scientists now assigned to him who at first resented his insertion. With foreign press reports highly restricted, he was largely unknown to them and introduced with little of his scientific background shared. Or his personal background—a history not discussed by the older scientists who knew. There were too many invisible listeners for those knowledgeable to gossip.

No celebrations and accolades welcomed him. The Russians wanted no reference to his passing them information. According to them, they had discovered the atomic secrets themselves. Russia's denial of any connection to him made his past taboo. Even his nephew Klaus had felt the long arm of the KGB. When he applied for admission to Leipzig University in 1956, he included that his uncle had spied for Russia. University officials accused him of lying: Russia didn't have spies. They forced him to delete the information.

Staff problems gradually straightened out, but over the next few years rumors swirled about confrontations with the Russians and the East Germans, breakdowns, and recoveries in spas. Some of these stories ended up in Western newspapers; others remained tightly held in intelligence files.

One reporter manipulatively arranged a telephone interview with him for an article in the *Sunday Express* in London. Afterward, the reporter admitted that the article was a "garbled version" but thought Klaus came out well in it—"a person determined to refuse to yield to pressure," referring to accounts that he had had a nervous breakdown because of Russian pressures to do weapons work. Klaus acknowledged to the reporter that he was sick but not seriously and said it was untrue he was going to Russia: "My work has nothing to do with arms—it is pure research." Declaring the article a "distortion," he told officials that he would decline future phone interviews.

The East Germans kept an eye on him by way of reports from Nitschke and from the maids who cleaned the apartment (with similar cleaning arrangements for Emil in Leipzig). Everyone was a potential informant, even family members. The Stasi made an effort to recruit his nephew Klaus, who reported the overture to Klaus and Grete. Grete said no, not in the family; Klaus agreed with her. No informing on anyone, family or otherwise.

By April 1960, after nine months in his new country, Klaus was ready for another cure at a spa, this time in Czechoslovakia and with Grete and with benefits and accommodations at the "Party level," that is, as a VIP. He had a hard entry into the ZfK to recover from and a first-time trip to Russia to prepare for.

CHAPTER 26

Expectations, Dresden 1960

AT THE END OF MAY, KLAUS WAS PART OF A DELEGATION TO THE JOINT INSTITUTE FOR Nuclear Research in Dubna, Russia, an international research facility with 50 percent of its budget from Russia, 20 percent from China, and the remainder from smaller satellite countries. The Russians' one-sentence consent for the trip painted a backdrop for the bureaucracy that Klaus faced daily in his administrative role at the institute:

> The Central Committee of the CPSU gave consent to invite Klaus
> Fuchs, Dep. Director of the GDR's Central Institute for Nuclear
> Research, through the Chief Administration on the Peaceful Use
> of Atomic Energy under the SM USSR as a member of the GDR's
> delegation to a conference, in May of this year, of the Academic
> Council of the Joint Institute on Nuclear Research.

The system in Russia differed little from that in East Germany, and intrigues and manipulations easily festered.

From the government's point of view, the main purpose of the trip was

ATOMIC SPY

for the KGB to "find out tactfully from K. F. the circumstances of, and possible reasons for, his arrest." The "circumstances" included why he confessed, how much he told counterintelligence about the information he passed, the reasons for his "failure"—that word signifying an uncovered agent, not necessarily a personal failure of the agent.

Klaus had his own agenda, which was to make progress toward harvesting and harnessing nuclear power with breeder (fast) reactors to secure the future energy needs of the East Germans. He resisted any pressure to do atomic weapons research, instead pushing his dream for the peaceful use of atomic energy. He hoped scientists in Russia would support his efforts and tilt the politics in East Germany in his favor.

This breeder reactor—which generated more fissile material than it used and reprocessed the excess to create more plutonium to fuel another reactor—was similar in concept to the one he had worked on at Harwell in 1949. Then he had told John Cockcroft that he wanted to stay in his position until there were test results from it. Presumably, in his heart-to-heart talk with Ulbricht about coming to the ZfK, he had discussed this interest and had received support.

Klaus saw breeder reactors as the solution that would meet the world's energy needs for millennia. One of the major drawbacks, though, was that the plutonium created could be removed and used for weapons. Klaus's answer for this problem was an international disarmament agreement to dismantle nuclear weapons.

Carrying out plans for the peaceful use of atomic energy at Rossendorf, even with Ulbricht's support, was a difficult task. The organization wasn't efficient, and the staff wasn't trained for the work needed. Klaus could warn that meeting the country's electrical needs in 1970 depended on building reactors immediately. He knew that without the support of the party nothing would happen.

Four days after arriving in Moscow on May 24, Klaus dined for over two hours with two KGB agents in an almost empty Chinese restaurant. KGB memos reported a friendly luncheon where the agents expressed "gratitude" for "the great help he rendered to the Soviet Union." Sensing that he was "very unsure of himself and guarded," they treated him carefully.

Klaus related his conversation with Ulbricht to them, admitting that he had made mistakes. As for his "failure," which is to say his getting caught, he explained that the British had relied on suspicions from the Americans but not direct evidence. He confessed of his own free will because the influence of "bourgeois propaganda" had led to his losing faith in Soviet policies. He concluded that "the Soviet Union had violated the principles of democracy." To their question of whom he had identified, he said only Gold, and then only after Gold confessed.

As to what he told the British of his intelligence activities, he detailed it for them but denied telling the British about passing information on the hydrogen bomb, even though he had done just that.

It wasn't a rough interrogation, but Fuchs canceled his activities for the rest of the day. He was sick with a bad cold, and he stayed in Russia for only a week, turning down a twenty-day tour of the country for him and Grete—a KGB arrangement in order to "study him."

Informants seemed to be well represented at the conference. One KGB agent spoke with "Hans," who was the head of the East German delegation and himself an agent of the KGB in East Germany. Hans described Klaus as "closed off and taciturn" and someone who hadn't recovered from the "moral" trauma of his arrest and years in prison. Klaus, he explained a bit peeved, didn't even discuss his impression of Moscow, let alone his past. Obviously, Hans's expectations revealed that he didn't know Klaus well.

A Stasi informant reported back that Klaus's personal scientific agenda hadn't gone well. When he visited the research center at Dubna, he came as too much of a supplicant, asking that experts on reactors be posted to East Germany for an extended period. In charge of training personnel, Klaus had "fallen behind" with the science, the informant said. Klaus said he would take any "bread crumbs" that fell from the Russian researchers' table at Dubna.

The scientists briefed him on their experiments—"published ones of course"—and were deferential with regard to his past, treating him warmly. His "appearance," they offered, however, "made him look like he was at the end of his power and scientific capabilities and would, therefore, not know how to lead the theoretical work in Dresden [ZfK, Rossendorf] further." The conclusion in Dubna was that it was senseless to give aid without an embryo to nurture, and the scientists didn't see one.

This description undermines a later rumor that Klaus had helped the Chinese develop their first atomic explosion in 1964. Although a Chinese delegation did visit the ZfK, it strains credulity to think that they would seek information from him when China was a significant partner in the Russians' scientific institute in Dubna and had access to all its scientists. Why would they need Klaus's ten-year-old knowledge?

And there the situation remained. Klaus debated with various SED committees to redirect research efforts at Rossendorf toward the peaceful use of energy, and he wrote articles and went to conferences about it. He complained to the SED Central Committee that he felt constricted by his colleagues, sometimes "cut off dead." He had few friends in the scientific world, fostering a sense of partial isolation. Whether the construction of the Berlin Wall in 1961 reinforced this feeling isn't known. He didn't record any thoughts.

Klaus simply didn't have the government behind him. In 1959, two months after he had returned to Germany, and just as he prepared to start at the ZfK, one top party official had explained to another that he didn't see why they should expend tight resources on nuclear energy when the country had a cheap and plentiful supply of brown coal. That mind-set held.

Finally, in January 1964, a man named Werner, the first secretary of a committee on science, called Klaus to a meeting and told him, "No breeder reactor." Klaus was deeply, deeply disappointed.

It wasn't just the East Germans' lack of interest or their strained economic resources; the Russians wanted to lead the effort. And there was a side issue: his leadership. Werner asked if the months-long debates on nuclear energy derived from "subjective" opinions of some top scientist or from him as the leader.

Klaus informed Werner that Comrade Ulbricht had expressed no reservations about him during their discussion. On his application for party membership, he had disclosed mistakes, and he was accepted into the party. He saw no reason for there to be protests against him.

Werner wanted to know if the description in a recent book was true: Had he confessed of his own accord? Klaus acknowledged that he had "turned himself in but not on his own initiative." Other than that, Klaus said he could speak only to Ulbricht about this question. Werner suggested that the Planning Commission and the Economic Council take up the reactor issue and if that produced no better results, Klaus should speak with Ulbricht again. Such was the dismissal of Klaus's dreams.

Klaus did add an interesting aside that Werner included in his report: "For understandable reasons, the SU [Soviet Union] has not confirmed to this day that something had been received from him and had no interest in the fact that there are constant reports in the Western press about him." A two-part TV movie made the next year by a West German film company, titled *Klaus Fuchs: History of Atomic Treachery*, must not have sat well with the Russians.

A year later, a quick political evaluation recorded Fuchs as being connected to the party, but critical and impulsive: "He exaggerates his criticism that then leads to being disrespectful toward state functions, and he generalizes his critiques too quickly. But he is open and honest." For the last report in 1973, his minder wrote that his position at Rossendorf between 1964 and 1970 had steadied, and he had become a member of the Central Committee of the SED for the Eighth Party Congress and, in 1972, a member of the Academy of Science of East Germany. Conclusion: his political and scientific stability required no further interviews.

However upset he was about the cancellation of the breeder reactor, he had held it in check and, as he was wont to do, gone on with his life, taking an interest in science policy and garnering positions on various esteemed scientific committees. But he didn't forget.

In an interview a year before his death, Klaus explained that at Harwell his research had been, in part, on the "peaceful use of nuclear power." And then he added, "It was a research area that at that time—to be sure, I did not know it—was forbidden in Germany. In general, there was little information about processes in the Soviet-occupied area." As well as confirming his disappointment twenty-three years after his conversation with Werner, was there a tinge of remorse about his return?

Emil Fuchs died in 1971, a few months shy of ninety-seven, a man whom Klaus loved but couldn't entirely forgive for past sins, as he had obliquely remarked to his nephew Klaus. Steadfast, ideologically driven, determined, and righteous by his own definition, Emil was the template from which Klaus was drawn. Both father and son fought for the working class, and they worked for a world without weapons. One cited the influence of Marx, the other faith in God.

Emil held to his pacifism and came to communism once the revolution was over; Klaus held to his communism and came to pacifism once the Nazis were defeated. The intellectual journey wasn't difficult for either. Like many Social Democrats, Emil subscribed to the social goals of communism without the revolution. As a child, Klaus became a vegetarian in part not to kill animals, a pacifist at heart.

In Britain, Klaus seemed to repudiate communism and professed an admiration of the British people and their lifestyle. His friends believed he had changed his heart, Rudi Peierls even remarking on the sadness of Klaus's sitting in jail for something he no longer believed in. Once back in East Germany, they heard that Klaus had reverted to his earlier, firm beliefs. But in his confession and during his time in prison, it may be that he repudiated Stalinism—the implementation, not the ideology. As Klaus said of his father, "He was never a man of the church but of faith." The same could be said of the son.

Since his arrival in the East, Klaus was a sought-after speaker at conferences and on radio shows as well as a regular interviewee in newspapers. A strong priority was lectures to young people, and he was relentless in espousing themes he deeply believed in. What started as criticism of U.S. nuclear tests in the 1960s and early 1970s became a call for both sides to disarm and use nuclear energy peacefully to power the globe. Politics entered too, sometimes directly by his celebrating the twenty-fifth anniversary of East Germany and the U.S.S.R.'s fiftieth, and more indirectly when he expounded on the joys of a scientist working in a socialist system. Given his own bitter experience in 1964 with the fast reactor, he could not have believed what he was saying. With the exception of his open and perilous resistance to the Nazis, he maintained the same nonconfrontational demeanor affected throughout his life.

Klaus and Grete experienced life at the VIP party level, enjoying vacations in Russia, Hungary, even faraway Cuba. And then there were their houses and the car and the nice clothing. Grete enjoyed dining in nice restaurants and had no compunction about accepting priority over others in line to secure a table. They mostly socialized with her friends. Klaus's closest was another ZfK physicist, Max Steenbeck, whom Grete didn't quite approve of. His four children had all gone to the West.

But the advantages of their party membership couldn't compensate for smog from the brown coal or lack of hard liquor or missing labels on packages of food when the factories ran out of ink. They still had to squeeze the bags to know if the contents were sugar or flour.

Unlike Grete, Klaus never used his position for favorable treatment. When Christel needed entry visas to bring her two young daughters, Marianna and Heidi, for a visit, he wouldn't intercede on their behalf. The task fell to his nephew Klaus.

Released from Westborough Hospital in the mid-1950s, Christel's life had come back together. She met and then worked for Albert Holzer, a bookbinder, resuming her connection to an art she had first learned at the

Odenwaldschule. They married and moved to Vermont, where she built a life around the peace movement, Quakerism, and environmental sustainability. At age sixty-eight, she walked from Washington to Moscow—both towns in Vermont—as part of the nuclear freeze movement.

Christel made four family visits to see Klaus, frequent enough for her younger daughter Heidi to decide to study at the University of Leipzig in 1981. Klaus took her in hand and set up her program. Having retired in 1979, he had time, although he probably would have made time even if he were working.

On weekends, Heidi often visited Dresden, where they walked in the park and chatted or went to a museum, often the Zwinger for its old masters and porcelain collections. One day they saw an art exhibit on Russian social realism, the official art of Russia that portrayed the idealized proletarian worker. Heidi giggled, and Klaus didn't react much, but she could tell he thought it was silly. Klaus was neither deaf nor blind to ideological shortcomings. He was silent, though.

In 1983, Markus Wolf, head of East Germany's foreign intelligence service (akin to the CIA and MI6), requested that Klaus sit for an interview in which the scientist dutifully described his childhood, his education, his exile, and the atomic bomb, something he had never done before, except with the Soviets.

By mid-1987, it was clear that Klaus was dying from lung cancer. He lay in the hospital for a number of weeks, and when his nephew Klaus visited him on January 28, 1988, they chatted as always, but his nephew had a particular question. The film director Joachim Hellwig was pushing to make a movie of his life. Is that something he wanted? Klaus said absolutely not. A few hours later he died.

The next day, obituaries in Western newspapers highlighted his conviction for espionage, one noting that he had died thirty-eight years and a day after his confession in London. Those in Eastern newspapers spoke of his lifelong dedication to the party as a scientist, professor, and communist while successfully developing nuclear energy for East Germany. The condolence from the Academy of Science listed honors he received including the Karl Marx Medal, the country's highest civilian honor.

His funeral, a solemn state affair, took place on Thursday, February 11, 1988, at Friedrichsfelde Cemetery in Berlin, the resting place of honored socialist and communist leaders, starting with Rosa Luxemburg and Karl Liebknecht, murdered during the Weimar troubles that first roused Klaus to activism. It was carefully arranged to last fifty minutes.

Just before 3:00 p.m., Grete and the family entered the Festival Hall door, which was flanked by an honor guard, and walked to the first row. In front of them were the East German flag, the urn, and Klaus's fifteen medals resting on pillows. In the background were numerous wreaths from scientific groups and the East German government that added softness and warmth. One was from the Russian delegation, the first time that the Soviet Union had ever openly acknowledged him.

The organist played Chopin and a string quartet played Vivaldi, after which Herbert Weiz, the minister of science and technology, gave the eulogy, a respectful and thankful description of Klaus's scientific contributions and sense of responsibility for humanity. He also cited Klaus's hope for a future dependent on nuclear power that enabled the economic growth of "the Lands of Red October." He described Klaus's life path through Los Alamos and the end of World War II, then compressed time to have Klaus suddenly appear in Dresden—no mention of Harwell and prison.

In the audience among the 115 invited guests were state officials, members of the scientific committees, the SED Central Committee, colleagues from the ZfK, and Johanna Zorn, a member of the Free Socialist Student Group in Kiel in 1932, the woman who used canes to walk because of beatings by the Nazis and whom Klaus had visited in Berlin when he first arrived. Another guest was thirty-five-year-old Vladimir Putin, a KGB agent stationed in Dresden. No high-level Russian officials attended.

Except for the eulogy, music accompanied every movement. The Polish socialist protest song, "Whirlwinds of Danger," and a Chopin funeral march accompanied mourners and the soldiers carrying the urn, the wreaths, and the medals from the hall to the Pergolenweg section and Klaus's marble tombstone. He was laid to rest amid drumrolls, a trumpet solo, and finally the "Internationale." A film crew captured the moment for the documentary about Klaus, his rejection of the project notwithstanding.

The actual production of the documentary began a few months later. Its proposal requested that knowledge of the project be limited to a few and that interviews be held with his KPD contacts from the London days: Jürgen Kuczynski and his sister Ursula (a.k.a. Sonya) and the friends and relatives of Hans Kahle. Even forty years after his death, Kahle haunted Klaus's life. Included in the proposal was the caveat to the producer "where necessary, give a signal to the intended interviewees, 'You are allowed to talk about Klaus Fuchs, the circumstances, and the times!'" Also included were many interviews with family—Grete, Christel, and his nephew Klaus—and surviving physicists from Los Alamos (for example, Hans Bethe) and German physicists who worked on a bomb for the Nazis.

Väter der tausend Sonnen (*Fathers of a Thousand Suns*), a production of the East German government's film studio, premiered in (the former East) Berlin at the Academy of Arts on January 4, 1990, two years after Klaus's death. For the first time it revealed his espionage activities, the fall of the Berlin Wall two months before having brushed aside any hesitation related to this taboo.

The disintegration would probably have disappointed him, watching the ideals of communism crumble to the ground—ideals he held so close and had risked so much for. His faith was such, however, that he might well have seen it as another stage in the development of socialism.

Remembrances, Berlin, March 1989

A WHITE-HAIRED MAN DRESSED SOMBERLY IN A GRAY SUIT AND DARK OVERCOAT walked on the hard dirt path of Pergolenweg, in his right hand a small bouquet of Shasta daisies tied with a pink ribbon. He squinted into the sun on a chilly March day at Friedrichsfelde Cemetery. He was searching for something, and upon seeing it, he approached, leaned the daisies against the stone, and knelt down. He was in front of the grave of Klaus Fuchs. He bowed, straightened up, and paused—perhaps saying something to himself—bowed again, straightened up and paused, and bowed once more.

The man, Alexander Feklisov, bowed the first time to acknowledge his gratitude for having met Klaus; the second was on behalf of the Russian people; the third was to reflect the gratitude of all the people of the world. As he wrote in his memoir, "He [Klaus] wished we could live in a safer world and we probably owe him our lives."

Feklisov was in East Germany so that the director Joachim Hellwig could interview him for the documentary. The next day he drove to Dresden to see Grete Keilson. When he had first communicated with her and said that he knew Klaus in London in the late 1940s, she knew who he was: Klaus's last handler, the one never identified by MI5. "But why have you come so late?" she asked. Klaus and Feklisov never saw each other after their meeting in April 1949, even though Feklisov was in Russia much of the time that Klaus was in Dresden.

Feklisov didn't have an answer. In normal KGB procedure, he would have met Klaus in Berlin in 1959 to interview him about his "failure." When he didn't receive the order to do so, he assumed that another intelligence officer had been dispatched. In his occupation, one didn't ask about those things. He didn't learn of the KGB's 1960 interrogation of his former agent until after Klaus's death. At that time, he asked why he had not been allowed to do the interrogation and never received a satisfactory answer.

Feklisov explained that he didn't make that decision, and she told him, "Klaus waited to see you for some thirty years. Lately, he was saying that no Soviet comrade who had known him was probably still alive." Feklisov stuttered a few remarks, not knowing how to respond.

Quoting Rabelais, Feklisov recorded in his memoir his final thought on Klaus: "Science without conscience is only ruin for the soul." For Klaus, his conscience was a solid core at the root of a very complex man.

Someone once asked me if Klaus Fuchs was evil. Over the years, many have weighed in on this question. Some—especially back in the 1950s—thought he was a traitor, clear and simple. Others, mostly his scientific friends, thought him misguided but an honorable person, true to his beliefs—the person with noble ideals who otherwise would not have betrayed country and friends. And others commended him for saving the world—Official Secrets Act be damned.

He had his own answer, which he gave during his 1983 taped interview. As in any of his interviews, he wasn't emotionally effusive, no baring of the soul to reveal what sustained him. Instead, he offered a simple moral reckoning, his own reflective evaluation:

There have been things in my life that I must admit I would do differently. Looking back at those 72 years I have lived, I can see all the mistakes I made and those I could have avoided. But I am deeply convinced that, in spite of all their mistakes and their negligent behavior, if the line of your life still took you towards the goal you had set once and for all; if you were able to reach that goal, or at least get closer to it, if going in that direction you did not lose yourself, nor squander your strength, committed anything contemptible, humiliated yourself, climbed over dead bodies, nor harmed others to get there; if you were able to maintain the moral course within your soul which in every language is called conscience, you can consider that your life is a success.

Whatever others thought, Klaus Fuchs deemed his life a success, undoubtedly feeling "the moral course" within his own soul. It sprang from his father's teachings, zealously pursued, on the innate worth of the workingman uniquely blended with the political fire in Leipzig that reshaped the arc of his life. From there on, he never wavered even when his chosen goal compelled him to risk his life.

What does one make of a man whom many considered a hero for fighting the Nazis and whom others considered a traitor for betraying his country?

Fuchs's actions left most people confused, but what they didn't see was that his life, circumscribed from within, was consistent and constant to his unwavering set of ideals. He sought the betterment of mankind that transcended national boundaries. His goal became to balance world power and to prevent nuclear blackmail. As he saw it, science was his weapon in a war to protect humanity.

And what of the consequences of his deed?

Most of the scientists at Los Alamos shared his strong feeling that the United States should not have a monopoly on nuclear weapons, that the Russians should take part in the secrets and be partners. They would have their own bomb soon enough anyway, probably by 1951. The information

Fuchs provided advanced their timeline by a year or two at most. Their nuclear stockpile of a couple of weapons in 1950 might have kept the United States from dropping an atomic bomb on North Korea. If so, was that a bad outcome? Was the person who made that happen evil or good, guilty or innocent, a traitor or a hero?

Acknowledgments

I owe a tremendous amount to many people.

Most of all, I thank the extended Fuchs family, the patriarch of which is "young" Klaus, who is now all grown up and who sat for many, many interviews with me, and his wife, Sabine, who was a gracious hostess for my multiple visits. His son Gerhard was instrumental in my acquiring court records from the 1930s and documents at the Bundesarchiv as well as passing on family lore. Heidi and Marianna Holzer answered all my questions about their mother, Christel Fuchs, as did Steve Heinemann. Fuchs's cousins Silke and Dietmar Göbel shared family genealogy and photographs.

Without their collected memories and mementos Klaus's story would have lacked the understanding that Alan Moorehead tried to find from Max Born almost seventy years ago.

Another family intimately involved is that of Max Born, whose children and niece and nephew knew Klaus Fuchs. Many of them we have lost: his son, Gustav, and wife, Faith, daughter Irene Newton-John, niece Renata Koenigsberger, and nephew Ralph "Rolli" Elliott. His grandchildren who had heard the stories have been extremely supportive, with granddaughter Carey and husband Darren reading chapters and offering advice and grandson Bash giving guidance. Both Walter Kellermann and Walter Ledermann worked with Born and played in the physics/math quartet in Edinburgh with Klaus. Walter Kellermann's recollections of internment and his memoir were priceless. And then there are the Born cousins: Anita Pollard, Katie Fischel, and Sophia Kingshill who regularly entertained me, offered advice, and read some chapters too.

The same is true of friends, many of whom I made along this long path. The Buneman family (Peter, Michael, and Naomi) and their late mother, Lady Mary Buneman Flowers, who was a very lovely and lively lady—and her memoir—gave me a strong sense of Harwell and Klaus. Others who agreed to interviews, tours, meetings, teas, and lunches and in every way were supportive are Brian Pollard (Bristol), Kathy Behrens Cowell (Derek Behrens), Charles Perrin and Nicola Perrin (Sir Michael Perrin), Thomas Giesa, Wolfgang Gleiser, and Peter Schütz (Martin Luther Gymnasium, Eisenach), Patricia Shaffer (Los Alamos), Lili Hornig (Los Alamos), Stewart Purvis (the Free German League of Culture), Jo Peierls Hookway (the Peierlses), Nigel West (MI5), Mike Rossiter (Klaus Fuchs), Alexander Vassiliev (the KGB), Victor Ross (internment), Günther Flach (the ZfK, Dresden), Henry Richardson (ethics), Derek Leebaert (the cold war).

And then there were those who read most or some of the manuscript: Bill Leahy, always checking in with me and keeping me moving, reading and critiquing everything I gave him, and his wife and my college friend, Chris, too; Robby Brewer, who also read everything and weighed in with a good critical eye; Margaret Ayres and Steve Case, who gamely suffered through some bad chapters early; Kathryn Johnson, who advised on creating a stronger narrative style; Richard Squires, whose insightful critique of several chapters reformed my narrative; Joe Martin, and Cameron Reed, who bolstered the physics; Cristina Fischer, who critically reviewed the chapters on student unrest in Germany; Cindy Kelley, who, at the last minute, obliged my needs for review of the chapters on the Manhattan Project; Allen Hornblum, who reviewed background material on Harry Gold; John Earl Haynes, who introduced me to Venona; and Peter Collisson, Ed Mayberry, and John Korbel, who read the MI5 chapters early and gave me helpful feedback.

Without German friends to help with some of the translation, I'd still be struggling through the videos and some German archival material: Robert Metzke, Matthias Rolke, and Jan Ehrhardt. My skating coach Alexei Kiliakov tackled some Russian for me, and Caroline Danforth set her mind to a very difficult letter in Sütterlin.

A special thanks to everyone who offered a suggestion, or a reference, or entry to something or someone: Andrew Farrar, Dieter Hoffman, Alex Wellerstein, John Wilhelm, Michael Goodman, Tom Steiner, Andrew Robinson, Sabine Lee, Geoff Andrews, Steve Feller, and an extra special thanks to Kathryn Imboden, who rushed to the Swiss Alps to rescue copies of the Geheeb archives for me and who offered unending support along with Anne Wesp, both friends for more than fifty years.

The archivists at the thirty or so libraries and archives that I visited deserve a big thanks. They were always gracious and informative, often identifying files I wouldn't have thought to look at, especially those for the University of Kiel at the archives in Schleswig.

Then there is the "team," which began with Merloyd Lawrence introducing me to Carolyn Savarese, my agent at Kneerim & Williams—thank you, Merloyd—who made the connection to Wendy Wolf at Viking. They are both tough taskmasters when needed who cushioned the required rigor with support, kindness, and humor. The immeasurable and deft skills of Bill Patrick added the polish—and then some—at the end.

Terezia Cicel, Wendy's assistant at Viking, answered technical questions quickly and knowledgeably and kept everything on schedule, and my friend Laura Cohen worked willingly and tirelessly on the endnotes. And the copy editor, Ingrid Sterner, saved me from so many mistakes.

Last, but certainly not least, are my three children—Elizabeth, Jake, and Sarah—who listened patiently to my problem of the day with love and caring. The smiles and hugs from my two granddaughters kept the joys of life in mind for me.

Abbreviations

PEOPLE

EF: Emil Fuchs

HA: Henry Arnold

KF: Klaus Fuchs

PG: Paul Geheeb

RP: Rudolf "Rudi" Peierls

ARCHIVES

AFSC: American Friends Service Center Archives, Philadelphia

BA: Bundesarchiv, Berlin

BFC: Library of the Society of Friends, Friends House, London

BODLEIAN-P: Rudolf Peierls Papers, Bodleian Library, Special Collections, Oxford University

BODLEIAN-S: Papers of the Society for the Protection of Science and Learning, Bodleian Library, Special Collections, Oxford University, Klaus Fuchs file

BRISTOL: University of Bristol Archives, Special Collections

BRITLIBE: British Library (Sound and Vision), London

CAMB: Cambridge University Archives, Department of Manuscripts and University Archives, Sir Nevill Mott Collection

CHURCH: Churchill Archives Centre, Born Collection, Cambridge University

EISENACH-C: Eisenach City Archives

FAM: Fuchs family papers formerly held by Klaus Fuchs-Kittowski, transferred to the Berlin-Brandenburg Academy of Sciences and Humanities (Fall 2018)

FBI: U.S. Federal Bureau of Investigation, online Vault, vault.fbi.gov/rosenberg-case/klaus-fuchs

GEHEEB: Papers of Paul and Edith Geheeb, formerly held at the École d'Humanité, Hasliberg Goldern, Switzerland, transferred to the Hessische Staatsarchiv, Darmstadt (Fall 2017)

HARVARD-B: Harvard University Archives, Percy Bridgman Collection

HAV: Quaker and Special Collection, Haverford College, Haverford, Pa.

IWM: Imperial War Museum, London

LAC: Library and Archives of Canada, Ottawa

LANL: Los Alamos National Laboratories

LASH: State Archives of Schleswig-Holstein, Schleswig, Germany

LEIPZIG: Leipzig University Archives

LOC-N: Library of Congress, John von Neumann collection

MEPO: Metropolitan Police, London

NA: Public Records Office, National Archives, London

NBLA: Niels Bohr Library and Archives, American Institute of Physics, College Park, Md.

NUFFIELD: Nuffield College, Oxford University, Lord Cherwell Papers

ROYSOC: Royal Society, London

RÜSSEL: Stadt und Industrie Museum, Rüsselsheim am Main

STABI: Staatsbibliotek zu Berlin, Preussischer Kulturbesitz, Max Born Papers

STASI: Archives of the Ministry of State Security of the former German Democratic Republic, Berlin

TH: Technische Hochschule, Berlin

USHMM: U.S. Holocaust Memorial Museum, Washington, D.C., Library and Archives, AFSC Refugee Case Files: Fuchs

VENONA: Wilson Center, Cold War International History Project, Washington, D.C., online, www.wilsoncenter.org/article/venona-project-and-vassiliev-notebooks -index-and-concordance

WIENER: Wiener Holocaust Library, London

Notes

PROLOGUE: REVELATION, LONDON, AUGUST 1949

1 **Perrin, deputy director:** Moss, *Klaus Fuchs*, 130–31.

1 **One week later, Perrin:** NA, KV 4/471, 9.24.1949, 178–79.

2 **"The [Joint Intelligence Committee]":** NA, KV 4/471, Liddell diary, 9.24.1949.

3 **"We have discovered Material":** NA, KV 6/134, Maurice Oldfield to Arthur Martin, 8.17.1949.

4 **"From Stettin in the Baltic":** Churchill, speech at Westminster College, Fulton, Mo., March 5, 1946.

4 **"blot this country out":** NA, KV 4/472, Liddell diary, 1.1.1950.

5 **they cabled Martin:** NA, KV 6/134, 8.17.1949, 8.24.1949, 8.25.1949.

5 **"To VIKTOR":** NA, HW 15/23, 6.15.1944, Venona.

6 **Martin was different:** Nigel West, interview with author, March 2016; Wright, *Spy Catcher*, 207, 224, 237.

6 **The director of B Branch:** Nigel West, interview with author, March 2016.

6 **Scrutinizing the text:** NA, KV 6/134, 8.30.1949.

7 **The messages indicated:** NA, KV 6/134, 8.30.1949.

7 **Venona was run by:** This decryption project had several name changes. It is now known as Venona.

7 **On September 1:** NA, KV 6/134, 8.30.1949.

8 **The FBI offered up:** NA, KV 6/134, 9.1.1949.

8 **"this file when in transit":** NA, KV 2/1245, cover.

9 **"there is, as far as we":** NA, KV 2/1245, HA to J. S. McFadden, 9.18.1947.

9 **The file began with a letter:** NA, KV 2/1245, 9.7.1934 and 9.9.1934.

10 **"a short-term certificate":** NA, KV 2/1245, 10.6.1934 and 10.23.1934.

10 **Martin requested the Home:** NA, AB 46/232, extract from file, residence permits.

10 **"The Student Klaus Fuchs":** NA, KV 2/1245, 10.6.1934.

11 **"The above-named German":** NA, KV 2/1245, 11.5.1934.

11 **"identical with a certain":** NA, KV 2/1245, 6.19.1942.

12 **Was "Claus Fuchs" the same:** NA, KV 2/1245, 12.3.1946.

12 **"He bears a good":** NA, KV 2/1245, 2.3.1943.

13 **"I said I thought":** NA, KV 2/1245, 10.10.1941.

13 **whether a man of this nature":** NA, KV 2/1245, 7.15.1943.

13 **Perrin said no:** NA, KV 2/1245, 10.6.1943.

13 **"This is a very":** NA, KV 2/1245, 10.6.1943.

13 **"[Fuchs is] rather safer":** NA, KV 2/1245, 1.16.1944.

14 **"It would not appear":** NA, KV 2/1245, 1.17.1944.

CHAPTER 1: BEGINNINGS, LEIPZIG 1930

19 **On March 3, 1918:** RÜSSEL, Emil Fuchs, "Der zweite Friede," *Evangelisches Gemeindeblatt*, 3.3.1918, 1.

20 **The church had assigned:** Fuchs, *Mein Leben*, 2:11.

20 **little Klaus made a gizmo:** Fuchs, *Mein Leben*, 2:12.

20 **Klaus and his sister Kristel:** Heidi Noroozy, "My Uncle, Klaus Fuchs—Beyond the Cold War," noveladventurers.blogspot.com/2012/01/my-uncle -klaus-fuchs-beyond-cold-war.html.

20 **His concern for animals:** GEHEEB, EF to PG, Jan. 1924.

20 **Emil transferred his older son:** GEHEEB, EF to PG, 8.23.1923.

21 **"But little by little":** Fuchs, *Mein Leben*, 2:12.

21 **Emil wandered dead:** Fuchs, *Mein Leben*, 2:10.

21 **"But what is so much":** GEHEEB, EF to PG, 8.23.1923.

22 **"the bourgeois world":** Fuchs, *Mein Leben*, 2:133.

22 **"the existing theology":** EISENACH-C, Hochheim, "Emil Fuchs: Eine Biographie."

22 **Emil's notoriety fell:** Fuchs, *Mein Leben*, 2:128.

22 **"Pastor, hurry up":** Fuchs, *Mein Leben*, 2:127.

23 **Emil wanted Klaus:** STASI, video interview of Klaus Fuchs, 1983.

23 **"known and famous":** NA, KV 2/1259, translated letter from Dr. A. Burghardt, Munich, 12.24.1952.

23 **Even so, Klaus:** NA, KV 2/1252, KF to the Skinners, 2.27.1950.

23 **"You can be proud":** Fuchs, *Mein Leben*, 2:128.

23 **Goaded, Klaus pinned:** Fuchs, *Mein Leben*, 2:127.

23 **"None of these masters":** Fuchs, *Mein Leben*, 2:128–29.

24 **"quiet and pale" young man:** Wolfgang Gleiser, "Gratwanderer Klaus Fuchs vulgo 'Atomspion,'" Lutherschule Friends, Eisenach, 2009, 50.

24 **"It was the power":** Fuchs, *Mein Leben*, 2:130.

24 **"big, lively house":** EISENACH-C, Letter from Heinrich Gaertner, n.d.; GEHEEB, EF to PG, 10.30.1930.

24 **"hints and reminders":** Fuchs, *Mein Leben*, 2:126.

24 **"a martinet":** NA, KV 2/1552, H. Skinner to HA, 2.12.1950; Marianna Holzer, interview with

author, May 4, 2013; Heidi Holzer, interview with author, Sept. 12, 2013.

24 **"I'm jealous of you":** Klaus Fuchs-Kittowski, interview with author, Nov. 2017.

24 **mathematics and physics:** LEIPZIG, doc. 577522.

24 **His brother, Gerhard:** LEIPZIG, docs. 577522 and 577513.

26 **"It was totally futile":** Krause, *Alma Mater Lipsiensis*, 251–52.

26 **Candidates from the Social:** Krause, *Alma Mater Lipsiensis*, 252.

26 **"But we know":** LEIPZIG, Plakat 0562.

26 **Gerhard organized lectures:** FAM, photos; GEHEEB, PG to Gerhard Fuchs, 3.13.1930, 7.4.1928, and EF to PG, 7.10.1929.

27 **"To achieve something":** GEHEEB, Gerhard Fuchs to PG, 3.13.1930.

27 **The petition accused:** LEIPZIG, Socialist Student Union to Rector Falke, 5.10.1930.

27 **Klaus would later say:** Klaus Fuchs-Kittowski, interview with author, March 2019.

27 **The duplicity of the leaders:** NA, KV 2/1263, 1.27.1950, 1.

27 **As roommates, Klaus:** STASI, video interview of Klaus Fuchs.

27 **But to Klaus's dismay:** Klaus Fuchs-Kittowski, interview with author, March 2017.

27 **At semester break in August:** GEHEEB, Edith Geheeb to Gerhard Fuchs, 9.27.1930.

28 **The next day a meeting:** Eisenach Online timeline.

28 **a "hair-raising" experience:** Fuchs, *Mein Leben*, 2:128; GEHEEB, EF to PG, 5.30.1930.

28 **For two hours, Hitler:** Yale University Avalon Project, chap. 7, no. 1; *New York Times*, Sept. 26, 1931, 1 (in Bill Downs, blogspot, May 16, 2017).

29 **On November 18:** LEIPZIG, Socialist Student Union (KF) to Rector, 11.25.1930.

29 **"a decisive position":** LEIPZIG, Socialist Student Union to Rector, 11.25.1930 and 12.3.1930.

29 **"The best should 'prevail'":** LEIPZIG, Plakat 0529.

30 **"The great unrest":** LEIPZIG, Socialist Student Union (KF) to Rector, 11.25.1930.

30 **"a very passionate resistance":** GEHEEB, EF to PG, 10.30.1930.

30 **"Of the three of us":** Fuchs, *Mein Leben*, 2:190.

CHAPTER 2: LOSS, KIEL 1931

31 **Kristel, he told him:** GEHEEB, EF to PG, 10.29.1930.

32 **In the early 1920s:** Richard F. Hamilton, "The

Rise of Nazism: A Case Study and Review of Interpretations—Kiel, 1928–1933," *German Studies Review* 24, no. 1 (Feb. 2003): 44.

33 **The culprit ran out:** LASH, Abt. 47, no. 1931, Rector's Report, 7.2.1931.

33 **Sunkel and his friend:** Irene Dittrich, "Die 'Revolutionäre Studentengruppe' an der Christian-Albrechts Universität zu Kiel (1930–1933)," *Beirat für Geschichte in der Gesellschaft für Politik und Bildung Schleswig-Holstein* e.V, 2012, n2; LASH, Abt. 47, no. 1103.

34 **Klaus arrived in August:** NA, KV 2/1245, 10.6.1934.

34 **Klaus was the political leader:** Behn, *Ein Spaziergang war es nicht*, 19.

35 **"What comes now":** Fuchs, *Mein Leben*, 2:205.

35 **"Mother is on the floor!":** Fuchs, *Mein Leben*, 2:205; Family genealogy documents, Silke and Dietmar Göbel.

35 **"powerful and shattering":** Fuchs, *Mein Leben*, 2:205.

35 **Emil had immediately:** GEHEEB, correspondence between EF and Odenwaldschule, 10.10–12.1931.

35 **"We ask you to refrain":** GEHEEB, EF to PG, 10.12.1931.

36 **Gerhard held his lecture:** LASH, Abt. 47, no. 1284.

36 **In a letter printed:** "Die Erhoehung der Gebühren," *Der Volkskampf*, Nov. 14, 1931; LASH, Abt. 47, no. 1092, NS leaflet, 11.13.1931.

36 **In their newsletter:** Dittrich, "Die 'Revolutionäre Studentengruppe,'" 176.

CHAPTER 3: REVOLT, KIEL 1932

39 **They issued warnings:** LASH, Abt. 47, no. 1092, University Senate, 5.4.1932.

39 **"the decision that determined":** FAM, Klaus Fuchs statement, n.d., after 1959.

40 **the "bourgeois parties":** NA, KV 2/1263, KF confession, 1.27.1950.

40 **The Fuchs brothers:** NA, KV 2/1245, Gestapo note, 10.11.1934.

41 **"They are all":** GEHEEB, EF to PG, 3.1.1932.

41 **In communist neighborhoods:** Hempel, *Die Kieler Hitlerjugend*, 5–6.

41 **But Klaus transferred to the local:** BA, R58/3622, police president, Kiel, 10.12.1931; Dittrich, "Die 'Revolutionäre Studentengruppe,'" n15.

41 **The troupe crisscrossed:** Behn, *Ein Spaziergang war es nicht*, 21–22; interview with Lisa Behn, Berlin 2004, erinnerungsort.de/interviews.

42 **"the sea-embraced Nordmark":** Mühlberger, *Hitler's Voice*, 1:220.

42 **According to her:** Behn, *Ein Spaziergang war es nicht*, 18–19; Hempel, *Die Kieler Hitlerjugend*, 1–3.

42 **Klaus and his colleagues:** Behn, *Ein Spaziergang war es nicht*, 19.

42 **One day, city authorities:** Behn, *Ein Spaziergang war es nicht*, 8, 21.

42 **"the Beast and the Devil":** NA, KV 2/1253, KF to the Skinners, 2.27.1950; interview with Lisa Behn, Berlin 2004, erinnerungsort.de/interviews.

43 **"Heil Hitler":** Frank Omland, "Siegeszug in der Nordmark," in Dohnke et al., Schleswig-Holstein und der Nationalsozialismus, 43; Hamilton, "Rise of Nazism," 53.

43 **The Nazis had rolled up:** AFSC, Mary Goodhue Carey, MS, Jan. 15, 1932, chap. 1, p. 2.

43 **"'fascization' of worker rights":** LASH, Abt. 47, no. 1353, 5.2.1932 and 5.28.1932.

44 **Meanwhile, the Nazis:** LASH, Abt. 47, no. 1932, Anlage D, in "Vorgeschichte," and Abt. 47, no. 1932, Antwort an den VDA, in "Vorgeschichte."

44 **"The Nazi leadership":** LASH, Abt. 47, no. 1932, Anlage C, in "Vorgeschichte."

45 **Lichtenfeld, seeing no overt conflict:** LASH, Abt. 47, no. 1932, Anlage F and H, in "Vorgeschichte."

45 **"unspeakable ways":** LASH, Abt. 47, no. 1932, Freie Kieler Studentenschaft to Rector, 6.23.1932, in "Vorgeschichte."

45 **The Nazis swiftly:** LASH, Abt. 47, no. 1932, NS Notice, 6.24.1932, in "Vorgeschichte."

45 **At the University Senate:** LASH, Abt. 47, no. 1932, Senate Meeting, 6.25.1932, in "Vorgeschichte," and LASH, Abt. 47, no. 1931, Rector Action notice, 6.27.1932.

46 **"masters in the methods":** LASH, Abt. 47, no. 1932, flyer enclosure, Essmann to Hoepner, 7.5.1932.

46 **"immediate dispersal of the Red Student":** LASH, Abt. 47, no. 1932, Freie Kieler Studentenschaft to the Rector, 8.8.1932, copy of article in the *Kieler Neueste Nachrichten*, Aug. 1932, and note by Universitäts-Sekretariat, 7.18.1932.

46 **On July 20:** LV Schlüsseltexte zum NS: Hitler-Wahlreden, July 1932, 1n7.

46 **"With subhumanity":** LV Schlüsseltexte zum NS: Hitler-Wahlreden, July 1932, 1n7.

47 **When Klaus heard:** NA, KA 2/1263, KF confession, 1.27.1950.

47 **The broken spirit:** LASH, Abt. 47, no. 1932, "Ultimatum to the Rektor from the Hochschuler Gruppe der KPD," n.d.

47 **From then on:** NA, KV 2/1263, KF confession, 1.27.1950.

47 **When the winter semester:** LASH, Abt. 47, no. 1932, Rector to Gerhard Fuchs, 11.7.1932; Essmann statement to Schepp, 7.13.1932; Gerhard Fuchs statement to Hoepner, 7.27.1932.

48 **The communist leadership:** NA, KV 2/1248, Robertson memo, 11.23.1949; Helmut Gruber, "Willi Münzenberg's German Communist Propaganda

Empire, 1921–1933," *Journal of Modern History* 38, no. 3 (Sept. 1966): 287.

CHAPTER 4: LEADER, KIEL 1933

49 **With the Nazi students:** LASH, Abt. 47, no. 1932; Rector's, University secretary to KF, 11.8.1932.
49 **"Fighting the Suppression":** FAM, KF, "Lebenslauf für VdN," 3.12.1960.
49 **"the dragged-out battle":** LASH, Abt. 47, no. 1932, Rector's "Remarks," 11.15.1932.
49 **The new orders:** LASH, Abt. 47, no. 1294, Kossel to Rector, 12.18.1929.
50 **"he would tell this":** LASH, Abt. 47, no. 1932, Rector's "Remarks," 11.15.1932.
50 **"On the basis":** LASH, Abt. 47, no. 1932, KF to Rector's, 11.18.1932.
50 **On November 22, Klaus:** LASH, Abt. 47, no. 1932, KF to Hoepner, 12.17.1932.
51 **"Against the University":** LASH, Abt. 47, no. 1932, FRSG flyer, 12.8.1932.
51 **"I therefore thought":** LASH, Abt. 47, no. 1932, KF to Hoepner, 12.17.1932.
51 **Essmann, feeling besmirched:** LASH, Abt. 47, no. 1932, Essmann to Hoepner, 12.13.1932.
52 **"I came to accept":** NA, KV 2/1263, KF confession, 1.27.1950, 4. It is not entirely clear to which fee protest Fuchs's feelings of guilt corresponds. His confession omits Gerhard's role in the student group, so the chronology is confusing.
52 **A few days later:** LASH, Abt. 47, no. 1932, Skalweit note, 12.20.1932.
52 **"a certain agitation":** LASH, Abt. 47, no. 1932, Skalweit report, 2.22.1933.
52 **In the meantime:** LASH, Abt. 47, no. 1353, meeting notices, Jan. 1933.
52 **On a cold, wintry night:** Pieper-Wöhlk and Wöhlk, *Kiel*, 46.
53 **Kiel's chief of police:** Pusch, "Die Goldberg-Affäre."
53 **It took the Nazi students:** FAM, KF, "Lebenslauf für VdN," 3.12.1960.
54 **On Friday afternoon:** LASH, Abt. 47, no. 1932, Skalweit report, 2.22.1933, 1; Dittrich, "Die 'Revolutionäre Studentengruppe,'" 175; FAM, KF, "Lebenslauf für VdN," 3.12.1960; Fuchs, *Mein Leben*, 2:220; Behn, *Ein Spaziergang war es nicht*, 22.
54 **Miraculously, he survived:** NA, KV 2/1252, Herbert Skinner note, 2.12.1960. In Emil's version,

relayed to him by Elisabeth, Klaus escaped from the mob and ran to a friend's house. His children shielded him from the truth. Fuchs, *Mein Leben*, 2:220.
54 **The Nazis' calls for a strike:** LASH, Abt. 47, no. 1932, Skalweit report, 2.22.1933.
54 **"We knew, however":** FAM: KF, "Lebenslauf für VdN," 3.12.1960.
54 **During the riot:** LASH, Abt. 47, no. 1231, Skalweit to KF, 2.22.1933.
54 **Gerhard, in Kiel:** Fuchs, *Mein Leben*, 2:221; USHMM, AFSC Refugee case file no. 18809.
55 **"In ten years":** *Kieler Zeitung*, Feb. 9, 1933.
55 **The morning of February 28:** Fuchs, *Mein Leben*, 2:220.
55 **"Even anti-communist journals":** WIENER, "More Arrests in Germany," Reuters, March 2, 1933.
55 **"as a defensive measure":** German History in Documents and Images, germanhistorydocs.ghi-dc.org.
55 **The number one student:** Behn, *Ein Spaziergang war es nicht*, 22.
55 **At four o'clock:** NA, KV 2/1263, KF confession, 1.27.1950, 3.
56 **"Why are you searching":** Behn, *Ein Spaziergang war es nicht*, 23.
56 **The authorities searched:** Fuchs, *Mein Leben*, 2:220–21; Behn, *Ein Spaziergang war es nicht*, 23.
56 **"It concerns your son":** Fuchs, *Mein Leben*, 2:237.
56 **Emil stayed in Kiel:** Fuchs, *Mein Leben*, 2:219–20.
57 **"Please wear dark":** LASH, Abt. 47, no. 1584, announcement, 3.4.1933.
57 **On orders from the Prussian:** LASH, Abt. 47, no. 1932, Wolf to Haupt, 12.14.1933.
57 **With the new regime:** LASH, Abt. 47, no. 1232, Frei Kieler Studenten to Rector Scheel, 4.2.1933.
58 **"All my children":** GEHEEB, EF to PG, 12.16.1932.

48 **"Gerhard has the doggedness":** GEHEEB, EF to PG, 2.11.1933.

CHAPTER 5: UNDERGROUND, BERLIN 1933

60 **Despite this menace:** STASI, video interview, Klaus Fuchs; Brothers, *Berlin Ghetto*, 55.
60 **Liddell, who spoke fluent German:** NA, KV 4/111, Liddell, 4; Hamilton, "Rise of Nazism," 55.
61 **"Those in authority":** NA, KV 4/111, Liddell, 17.

61 **Liddell himself was not convinced:** NA, KV 4/111, Liddell, 2–3.
61 **Liddell's specific interest:** NA, KV 4/111, Liddell, 13.
61 **"The Liquidation of Communism":** NA, KV 4/111, Liddell, 17.

61 **Klaus had no footprint:** FAM, KF, "Lebenslauf für VdN," 3.12.1960.

61 **Klaus had an aunt:** FAM, KF, "Lebenslauf für VdN," 3.12.1960.

62 **Rackwitz's combined rectory:** Brothers, *Berlin Ghetto*, 65.

62 **Hitler's simple and fiery message:** WIENER, "Germany's Choice," *Manchester Guardian*, March 4, 1933; "Fruits of Efficient Propaganda," *Manchester Guardian*, March 7, 1933.

63 **The press reported:** WIENER, "Large Nazi Gains," *Manchester Guardian*, March 6, 1933; "Large Guns," Press Assoc. Foreign Special, March 6, 1933; "Disorder."

63 **"It is these hitherto":** WIENER, "Fruits of Efficient Propaganda."

63 **"Yes," one German:** AFSC, Hertha Krause to Clarence Pickett, 3.27.1933; HAV, Yarnall, n.d., summer/fall 1933.

63 **Beggars vanished:** HAV, Yarnall, end of 1933.

64 **"For in the last analysis":** HAV, Yarnall, n.d., summer/fall 1933.

64 **"Few passers-by":** WIENER, "Imperial and Foreign, Violence in Germany," *Manchester Guardian*, March 14, 1933.

64 **The auxiliary police:** WIENER, "The NS Terror Goes On," March 16, 1933.

64 **The communist leadership:** WIENER, "Efforts to Escape," *Manchester Guardian*, February 4, 1933.

64 **The mid-level staff:** Beatrix Herlemann, "Communist Resistance," in Benz and Pehle, *Encyclopedia of German Resistance to the Nazi Movement*, 14–24.

65 **"without bourgeois Germany":** Fuchs, *Mein Leben*, 2:223.

65 **Emil had little to fall back on:** Fuchs, *Mein Leben*, 225–26.

65 **The election and tensions:** BA, ZC 14566 Kirchgatter u.a., Court records, Berlin, 12.4.1936, 2. Today these mountains are between Poland and the Czech Republic.

65 **But Karin, just twenty:** BA, ZC 14566 Kirchgatter u.a., Court records, Berlin, 12.4.1936, 2.

65 **The Gestapo estimated:** BA, ZC 14566 Kirchgatter u.a., Court records, Berlin, 2.4.1936, 2.

66 **Klaus's girlfriend Lisa:** Behn, *Ein Spaziergang war es nicht*, 23–24; BA, Gustav Kittowski, Court records, Berlin, 4.27.1937.

66 **Gerhard's job was:** FAM, KF, "Lebenslauf für VdN," 3.12.1960.

66 **Gerhard relied on his brother:** I thank Cristina Fischer for her valuable information on the TH.

66 **It had had no official:** Hans Ebert, "The Expulsion of the Jews from the Berlin-Charlottenburg Technische Hochschule," *Leo Baeck Institute Year Book* 19, no. 1 (Jan. 1974): 161.

66 **"German Students!":** TH, Die Technische Hochschule, *Nachrichtenblatt der Studentenschaft* no. 1 (May 1933): 1.

67 **"cautiously living illegally":** FAM, KF, "Lebenslauf für VdN," 3.12.1960.

67 **For those on the streets:** Herlemann, "Communist Resistance," 18.

67 **everyone had a code name:** Taleikis, *Aktion Funkausstellung*, 7; BA, ZC 14566 Kirchgatter u.a., Court records, Berlin, 12.4.1936, 2; BA, p. 2.

67 **Whatever Klaus learned:** BA, ZC 14566 Kirchgatter u.a., Court records, Berlin, 12.4.1936, 2; BA, p. 19.

67 **Since newsletters:** Taleikis, pp. 41–45, Ehrlich, pp. 12–15 (general descriptions), Brothers, 66.

68 **"Certainly, these people":** Fuchs, *Mein Leben*, 2:227.

68 **They parted amicably:** HAV, Howard Yarnall, "Trial of Pastor Emil Fuchs," handwritten, Sept. 1933; Fuchs, *Mein Leben*, 2:227; HAV, Gilbert MacMaster, 4th installment, "Visiting Political Prisoners," 1933, 11.

68 **Wary of the police:** Fuchs, *Mein Leben*, 2:227; HAV, MacMaster, 4th installment, "Visiting Political Prisoners," 1933, 11.

68 **A week later:** HAV, MacMaster wrote "a son," but Gerhard was still in Riesengebirge.

68 **Emil had been arrested:** HAV, MacMaster, 4th installment, "Visiting Political Prisoners," 1933, 11.

69 **"The whole horror":** Fuchs, *Mein Leben*, 2:228.

69 **"Why did so very many":** Fuchs, *Christ in Catastrophe*, 9.

69 **The young couple hid:** Pusch, "Die Goldberg-Affäre," 157–58.

69 **The court sent Guschi:** USHMM, ITS Archive, doc. 30466334#1; Wiki, "KZ Gründung 1933."

69 **Elisabeth languished in the women's jail:** Fuchs, *Mein Leben*, 2:237.

69 **Emil's Quaker friend:** HAV, Gilbert MacMaster, 1933 diary, 160.

70 **Gerhard reassembled the shack:** Mary Flowers, interview with author, Oct. 22, 2011; Fuchs, *Mein Leben*, 2:238–39.

70 **He said goodbye:** FAM, KF Fragebogen, 1961; Fuchs, *Mein Leben*, 2:239.

CHAPTER 6: INTERLUDE, PARIS 1933

71 **As arranged with his father:** Fuchs, *Mein Leben*, 2:239.

71 **When he had to fill out:** NA, KV 2/1245, registration card.

71 **About eighty other:** Taleikis, *Aktion Funkausstellung*, 23.

72 **A longtime party member:** "Grete Keilson," German Wikipedia.

72 **As Grete organized:** "Keilson, Max," Biographische Datenbanken, Bundesstiffung zur Aufarbeitung der SER-Diktauer.

72 **Klaus spent his Parisian summer:** NA, KV 4/4/471, information from first interview with Skardon, Liddell diary, 12.21.1949.

72 **Emil's trial took place:** "Trial of a German Friend at Weimar, *Times* (London), Sept. 29, 1933, 833–34; Fuchs, *Mein Leben*, 2:235.

CHAPTER 7: SAFETY, BRISTOL 1933

77 **When the immigration officer:** NA, KV 2/1245, "Conditional Landing," 9.25.1933.

77 **"white-faced, half-starved":** Moorehead, *Traitors*, 75, in a letter from Jessie Gunn.

77 **Klaus was deemed:** NA, KV 2/1245, "Conditional Landing," 9.25.1933.

77 **The photograph on Klaus's registration:** NA, KV 2/1245.

77–78 **He could also continue:** FAM, KF, "Lebenslauf für VdN," 3.12.1960, 2.

78 **Ronald was at least:** NA, KV 2/3223, 3.9.1944.

78 **Klaus attended a few:** BRISTOL, Fuchs course card, 1933–36; Kellermann, *Physicist's Labour in War and Peace*, 61.

79 **It was with another article:** Dieter Hoffmann, "Fritz Lange, Klaus Fuchs, and the Remigration of Scientists to East Germany," *Physics in Perspective* 11 (2009): 415. Fuchs wrote the article "The Conductivity of Thin Metallic Film According to the Electron Theory of Metals" in 1936, but it wasn't published until 1938 in the *Proceedings of the Cambridge Philosophical Society.*

79 **"Be careful what you write":** USHMM, Kraus to William Eves, 4.21.1936.

79 **In the spring of 1934:** NA, AB 46/232, 9.13.1949.

79 **Gerhard, whose underground work:** BA, Gustav Kittowski, Court records, Berlin, 4.27.1937.

79 **Gerhard looked for:** BA, Gustav Kittowski, Court records, Berlin, 4.27.1937, 4.

79 **Early on, the family:** FAM, "PS zu einem Lebenslauf," Studio 80 am Vormittag, 10.20 Radio DDR II, n.d.

80 **The government had granted her:** GEHEEB, EF to PG, 5.16.1934.

80 **In October 1934, Klaus's stateless condition:** BODLEIAN-S, [Klaus Fuchs files], 10.23–11.28.1934.

80 **Registering with the police:** BODLEIAN-S, [Klaus Fuchs files], 11.30–12.28.1934.

80 **Unknown to Klaus:** NA, KV 2/1245, 8.7–11.5.1934.

73 **By the time the World Congress:** Moorehead, Traitors, 75, in a letter from Jessie Gunn.

73–74 **His father contacted:** FAM, KF, "Lebenslauf für VdN," 3.12.1960.

74 **"the shock brigade":** Pikarski, *Jugend im Berliner Widerstand*, 44; MEPO, 38-16 pt. 1, 7, Henri Barbusse, "You Are the Pioneers."

74 **"the living incarnation":** MEPO: 38-16 pt. 1, 3–4, Barbusse, "You Are the Pioneers."

74 **"We will win":** *L'Humanité* (Paris), Sept. 25, 1933, 1.

81 **Students and faculty often:** FBI, Hans Bethe statement, 2.14.1950.

81 **Klaus didn't participate:** NA, KV 2/1254, Edward Corson, 3.17.1950.

81 **He also belonged:** NA, KV 2/1255, Rev. L. G. Folkard, 4.13.1950.

81 **Studying Marx and Lenin:** NA, KV 2/1256, "The Case of Emil Julius Klaus Fuchs," 11.24.1950, 1.

81 **Gunn was chairman:** Society for Cooperation in Russian and Soviet Studies, London, 11th Annual Report, 1934–35, 8.

82 **The 1934–35 annual report:** Society for Cooperation in Russian and Soviet Studies, London, 11th Annual Report, 1934–35, 1–2.

82 **MI5 considered the SCR:** archive.org /stream/KlausFuchs/fuchs79_djvu.txt, 99.

83 **But Mott also knew:** Mott, *Life in Science*, 52.

83 **"Half a million":** CAMB, Nevill Mott to his mother, 9.29.1934.

83 **millions were exiled:** Sebag Montefiore, *Stalin*, 84.

83 **Mott also saw the physicist:** CAMB, Nevill Mott to his mother, 9.10–21.1934.

84 **It began with Karin:** GEHEEB, EF to PG, 5.16.1934; BA, ZC 14566 Kirchgatter u.a., Court records, Berlin, 12.4.1936.

84 **In 1935, the Gestapo:** BFC, 7 letters, 9.30.1935–2.10.1937, FCRA/19/2 c-F, correspondence with Mrs. Mary Ormond.

84 **According to the Gestapo report:** BA, ZC 14566 Kirchgatter u.a., Court records, Berlin, 12.4.1936; BA, Gustav Kittowski, Court records, Berlin, 4.27.1937.

84 **With Gestapo agents:** BFC, 7 letters, 9.30.1935–2.10.1937, FCRA/19/2 c-F, correspondence with Mrs. Mary Ormond; GEHEEB, Basel Liechtenhan to group of subscribers, 12.26.1935; EF to PG, 5.16.1934.

84 **Guschi, now Elisabeth's husband:** USHMM, Kurt Cassirer to Hertha Kraus, 2.6.1936.

84 **The Gestapo had figured out:** BA, Gustav

Kittowski, Court records, Berlin, 4.27.1937, 4–5; GEHEEB, EF to PG, 12.28.1934.

84 **Working as a liaison:** BA, Gustav Kittowski, Court records, Berlin, 4.27.1937, 4.

85 **Guschi was in prison:** USHMM, Kurt Cassirer to Hertha Kraus, 2.6.1936.

CHAPTER 8: WAR, EDINBURGH 1937

88 **"weak in appearance":** Born, *My Life*, 285.

88 **Born's daughter Irene:** Irene Born Newton-John, interview with author, Jan. 1997.

88 **Refugee aid organizations:** Kellermann, *Physicist's Labour in War and Peace*, 69–70.

88 **Throughout the day:** Kellermann, *Physicist's Labour in War and Peace*, 50.

88–89 **When Hedi became a Quaker:** National Records of Scotland, Edinburgh monthly meeting minutes, 1927–38, ref: CH10/1/13. I thank Andrew Farrar for this information.

89 **Klaus also played:** Walter Ledermann, interview with author, March 2007; Ralph Elliott, interview with author, Jan. 1997.

89 **Fuchs had amassed:** FAM, KF, "Lebenslauf für VdN," 3.12.1960.

89 **the Carnegie Trust:** Carnegie Trust, 1938–39, Appendix B, 30.

89 **Born frequently described:** BODLEIAN-S, Born to Simpson, 7.5.1940.

89 **Klaus continued to send:** BODLEIAN-S, Born to Esther Simpson, 11.5.1937; GEHEEB, Clara Ragaz to friends, 5.2.1939.

90 **"Dear Frau Geheeb":** GEHEEB, KF to Edith Geheeb, 1.11.1938.

90 **Emil heard a whistle:** Fuchs, *Mein Leben*, 256–57.

91 **He acted as a conduit:** Brinson and Dove, *Politics by Other Means*, 6.

91 **The Borns knew Klaus:** Renate Koenigsberger and Ralph Elliott, interviews with author.

92 **Klaus lived in a miserable:** Walter Kellermann, interview with author, March 2007.

92 **Afternoons often found:** Kellermann, *Physicist's Labour in War and Peace*, 69–70.

92 **Many Britons, especially those:** Walter Ledermann, interview with author, March 2007.

92 **Gerhard was still in Prague:** GEHEEB, Clara Ragaz to friends, 5.2.1939.

85 **While Klaus waited:** BRISTOL, *Bristol Evening Post*, Jan. 23, 1937.

85 **As in Kiel with the agitprop:** www.phy.bris.ac.uk/history/11.%20Mott%27s%20Memories.pdf.

86 **He told Born:** Kellermann, *Physicist's Labour in War and Peace*, 51.

92 **In July, he flew:** NA, KV 2/1248, Robertson, 11.23.1949.

93 **Elisabeth calmed herself:** Fuchs, *Mein Leben*, 256–61; family photos, Marianna Holzer.

93 **On the morning of August 7:** USHMM, AFSC Refugee case file no. 18809.

93 **A few months later:** FAM, EF to friends, 10.24.1939.

93 **Within a week:** NA, CSC 11/103, 11.4.1948.

94 **Two days later:** Dorothee Rausch von Traubenberg Fuchs, interview with author, 1997.

94 **Klaus argued that:** Walter Kellermann, interview with author; Kellermann, *Physicist's Labour in War and Peace*, 67–68.

95 **The government watched:** NA, HO/45/25521, 9.28.1939.

95 **On November 2, 1939:** NA, CAB 67/6/15, 4.29.1940.

96 **Those in attendance:** NA, KV 2/1259, 5.7.1951.

96 **Fuchs had a new grant:** Carnegie Trust, 1939–40, Appendix B, 32.

96 **A tribunal classified Jürgen:** NA, KV 2/1871; Brinson and Dove, *Politics by Other Means*, 4.

97 **"Obviously, no decision":** NA, CAB 67/6/15, 4.29.1940.

97 **On May 11, he had to issue:** NA, CAB 66/13/43, 11.25.1940.

97 **"All male Germans":** CHURCH, Hedi Born diary, 5.11.1940.

97 **"Fanaticism versus fanaticism":** CHURCH, Born to Hedi Born, 5.25.1938.

98 **Churchill and others:** NA, CAB 67/6/31, 5.17.1940.

98 **The situation in Britain:** NA, CAB 65/7/23, 5.18.1940.

98 **The War Cabinet met:** NA, CAB 67/8/109, 11.20.1940.

98 **"a considerable number":** NA, CAB 65/8/18, 7.17.1940.

99 **According to Born:** Born, *My Life*, 286.

CHAPTER 9: INTERNMENT, ENGLAND 1940

101 **Guard towers that loomed:** Seidler, *Internment*, May 29 and 31, 1940, 40–41.

102 **Each man filled a sack:** IWM, Hermann Wallach diary, 6.

102 **Klaus and Walter shared a room:** Kellermann, *Physicist's Labour in War and Peace*, 77–78;

Brinson and Dove, *Politics by Other Means*, 7; Walter Kellermann, interview with author.

102 **In the chaos, an internee:** NA, KV 2/1561, 4.23.1940.

102 **Local police had picked him up:** Lynton, *Accidental Journey*, 20.

102 **"He never raised his voice":** Lynton, *Accidental Journey*, 22.

103 **Internees later described:** KV, 2/1252, 2.16.1950.

103 **In the first weeks:** Seidler, *Internment*, May 26, 1940, 42.

103 **Finally, the camp commander:** Seidler, *Internment*, May 25, 1940, 42.

103 **In the mess tent:** IWM, Hermann Wallach diary, 4.

103 **"Today again we got":** Seidler, *Internment*, May 30, 1940, 43.

104 **The government later admitted:** NA, CAB 66/13/43.

104 **He told Kellermann:** Kellermann, *Physicist's Labour in War and Peace*, 80.

104 **As the government came:** NA, KV 4/390, 6.22.1940.

104 **In the early morning dew:** Seidler, *Internment*, June 14, 1940, 49–50.

105 **Workers had grappled:** "Spectators' Searchlight," *Isle of Man Examiner*, May 17, 1940, 4.

105 **A newspaper reported:** "Internment of Aliens," Governor's statement, *Isle of Man Examiner*, May 31, 1940, 1, 7.

105 **A local newspaper:** Seidler, *Internment*, June 20, 1940, 53.

105 **The refugees referred:** Kellermann, *Physicist's Labour in War and Peace*, 79.

106 **With a nod to democracy:** Kellermann, *Physicist's Labour in War and Peace*, 81.

106 **With limited resources:** NA, CAB 67/6/48, 6.13.1940.

107 **John Anderson stressed:** Koch, *Deemed Suspect*, 74–75.

107 **The pragmatists insisted:** Igersheimer, *Blatant Injustice*, xii; NA, CAB 67/7/20, 7.2.1940.

107 **No one told the Canadian government:** NA, CAB 67/7/20, 7.2.1940.

107 **"Dear Professor Born":** CHURCH, STABI, KF to Born, n.d. (approximately July 2, 1940).

108 **At nine o'clock that night:** NA, HO/215/267.

108 **He was also classified:** NA, HO/215/265.

108 **Once in Liverpool:** "Launched 1938: MV Ettrick," *Shipping Times*, www.clydesite.co.uk /clydebuilt/viewship/asp?id=4095; IWM, Hermann Wallach diary, 14.

108 **The thirteen hundred refugees:** IWM, Hermann Wallach diary, 14–16.

109 **"There is no way out":** Igersheimer, *Blatant Injustice*, 34.

109 **Down the middle of each deck:** Lynton, *Accidental Journey*, 33.

109 **Kellermann claimed a place:** BA, NY/4301, KF to Horst Brasch, 9.1.1986.

110 **The second night:** IWM, Ernst Pollak interview, 30.

110 **Finally, the colonel was persuaded:** Coleman, Cornish, and Drake, *Arndt's Story*, 35.

110 **"The whip of hunger":** Igersheimer, *Blatant Injustice*, 37.

110 **The Nazis goaded:** Kellermann, *Physicist's Labour in War and Peace*, 85.

110 **At night they sang:** Igersheimer, *Blatant Injustice*, 39; IWM, Ernst Pollak interview, 25.

110 **"A sight worse than anything":** Igersheimer, *Blatant Injustice*, 38–40.

111 **The refugee doctors:** Seidler, *Internment*, July 10, 1940, 60; Igersheimer, *Blatant Injustice*, 40.

111 **A detachment of volunteers:** Coleman, Cornish, and Drake, *Arndt's Story*, 35; Lynton, *Accidental Journey*, 32, 34.

111 **Accenting the blur:** Lynton, *Accidental Journey*, 35.

111 **Klaus insisted that Lingen's crew:** Victor Ross, interview with author, March 2016; BA, NY/4301, KF to Horst Brasch, 9.1.1986; NA, HO/215/210, "Summary Report of the Internment of German and Austrian Refugees in Canada," 2.

111 **On the third day out:** NA, CAB 66/13/43.

112 **On the seventh day:** Seidler, *Internment*, July 10, 1940, 60; Igersheimer, *Blatant Injustice*, 41.

112 **"It was the longest 10 days":** IWM, Peter Wayne interview.

CHAPTER 10: INTERNMENT, CANADA 1940

113 **One internee estimated:** Igersheimer, *Blatant Injustice*, 43.

113 **By 4:00 p.m., the men:** NA, HO/215/210, diary section, 1.

114 **It was 7:30 before the refugees:** Igersheimer, *Blatant Injustice*, 44.

114 **As motorcycle police:** Seidler, *Internment*, July 13, 1940, 61–62.

114 **The buses reached the heights:** Seidler, *Internment*, July 18, 1940, 65.

114 **Newly outfitted as a prison compound:** NA, HO 215/210, diary section, 6.

115 **The inspectors found:** NA, KV 2/1253.

115 **At one o'clock that morning:** Igersheimer, *Blatant Injustice*, 50–51.

115 **In each hut that first night:** Igersheimer, *Blatant Injustice*, 78.

115 **The next day a couple:** Seidler, *Internment*, July 14, 1940, 62–63.

115 **Pondering whether the Canadians:** Seidler, *Internment*, July 14, 1940, 63.

115 **Early in the morning:** Igersheimer, *Blatant Injustice*, 51–52.

115 **The men did hear:** Victor Ross, interview with author, London, March 11, 2016.

115 **He was taken:** Seidler, *Internment*, July 17, 1940, 64.

115 **A report attributed the death:** LAC, Camp L report no. 25, Red Cross, 8.29.1940.

115 **The fact is:** Koch, *Deemed Suspect*, 80.

116 **The leaders of the Ettrick's:** IWM, Walter Wallich interview; Michaelis, *Scientific Temper*, 23.

116 **Kahle and Klaus fumed:** NA, KV 2/1249, KF, interview with Skardon, 12.21.41.

116 **The majority of refugees:** IWM, K. Hirsch diary and Walter Wallich interview; Koch, *Deemed Suspect*, 84–87.

116 **Fearing negative publicity:** NA, FO 371/24424/5873, CAB, 66/15/48.

116 **The few times he was allowed:** IWM, Walter Wallich interview.

116 **The polar opposite:** NA, KV 2/1561, 11.28.1939 and 10.18.1930.

117 **Internees uniformly found Klaus:** IWM, Walter Wallich, Alfred Lane, and Alfred Doerfel interviews; Koch, *Deemed Suspect*, 84.

117 **Others found his "fanatical" expression:** NA, KV 2/1252, 2.15.1950.

117 **The camp's intelligence officer:** IWM, Walter Wallich interview.

117 **At the first council meeting:** IWM, Walter Wallich interview.

117 **The Canadian government's official answer:** NA, HO 213/2391, from the Undersecretary of State, U.K., to a Canadian official, n.d.

117 **Within the camp:** Coleman, Cornish, and Drake, *Arndt's Story*, 37–38.

118 **"In contrast to the camp":** FAM, KF, "Lebenslauf für VdN," 3.12.1960.

118 **While everyone resented:** BA, NY/4301, KF to Horst Brasch, 9.1.1986.

118 **One young Jewish refugee:** Seidler, *Internment*, July 27, 1940, 67.

118 **Canadian authorities prominently:** Igersheimer, *Blatant Injustice*, 62.

118 **The censors in Ottawa:** Seidler, *Internment*, July 17, 1940, 64.

118 **Some refugees gave in:** BA, NY/4301, KF to Horst Brasch, 9.1.1986; Igersheimer, *Blatant Injustice*, 62; Seidler, *Internment*, Aug. 7, 1940, 70.

119 **"Friendly Aliens, Grave Injustice":** *Times* (London), Aug. 16, 1940.

119 **A few outraged members:** NA, HO/215/254, July and Aug. 1940; HO/215/150, Oct. 1940.

119 **"I am not here to deny":** Koch, *Deemed Suspect*, 175.

119 **He had already pushed:** ROYSOC, Born to Francis Simon, 7.25.1940.

119 **In a letter to von Neumann:** LOC-N, Born to von Neumann, 8.20.1940; HARVARD-B, Born to Percy Bridgman, 8.30.1940.

120 **His friends did comply:** Kellermann, interview with author.

120 **Then Born pressured:** NA, KV 4/372, 10.24.1940, 3; STABI, Ralph Fowler to Born, 9.9.1940, and A. V. Hill to Born, 9.12.1940.

120 **The bountiful Canadian fields:** Igersheimer, *Blatant Injustice*, 56–57.

120 **The internees' only assigned task:** Igersheimer, *Blatant Injustice*, 56–57; K. Hirsch diary, 65–67.

120 **Initially, guards removed:** LAC, report by Colonel H. de N. Watson, 7.22.1940; Seidler, *Internment*, July 22 and 26, 1940, 66–67.

120 **"Some of the brainiest people":** IWM, Hermann Wallach diary, Aug. 22, 1940, 34.

120 **From within the barbed wire:** Michaelis, *Scientific Temper*, 23–24.

120 **Fuchs, whose pupil Perutz:** Seidler, *Internment*, Sept. 2, 1940, 78; Max Perutz, "Spying Made Easy," *London Review of Books*, June 25, 1987, 6–7.

120 **The sympathetic major Wiggs:** Seidler, *Internment*, July 21, 1940, 65–66.

121 **Through the layers of barbed wire:** Igersheimer, *Blatant Injustice*, 67; Seidler, *Internment*, Aug. 11, 1940, 73.

121 **News of the white paper:** Seidler, *Internment*, Aug. 23, 1940, 75.

121 **As icy winds and rain:** Seidler, *Internment*, Aug. 31–Sept. 3, 1940, 77.

121 **Within two weeks, the director:** Kellermann, interview with author.

121 **The hut fathers called:** NA, HO/215/166/8, 10.12.1940, 1.

121 **That same day the guards:** Seidler, *Internment*, Sept. 23, 1940, 82, and Oct. 2, 1940 84.

121 **On September 27, the internees:** Coleman, Cornish, and Drake, *Arndt's Story*, 37; IWM, Walter Wallich interview.

122 **"[We] should like to protest":** NA, HO/215/166/8, Appendix 1, 10.12.1940.

122 **Canadian officials knew:** NA, HO/215/166/8, 10.12.1940, 4.

122 **Major Wiggs wanted:** K. Hirsch diary, 95, and NA, HO/215/166/8, 10.12.1940, Nos. 39 and 56, pp. 4, 6.

122 **Jews who considered:** Koch, *Deemed Suspect*, 123, quoting the diary for Peter Heller on September 17.

123 **"I was especially responsible":** BA, NY/4301, KF to Horst Brasch, 9.1.1986.

123 **Major Wiggs sent off:** HO/215/166/8, 10.12.1940, no. 60, p. 6.

123 **On the morning of October 15:** Igersheimer, *Blatant Injustice*, 100; Seidler, *Internment*, Oct. 15, 1940, 89.

123 **The men looked out the windows:** IWM, Heinz Bing interview.

123 **When they objected:** Igersheimer, *Blatant Injustice*, 123.

124 **An internee equated them:** IWM, Hermann Wallach diary, 14.

124 **The word "release" was in the air:** NA, CAB 67/8/109, 11.20.1940.

124 **"The rough and ready measures":** NA, CAB 65/10/13.

124 **Paterson arrived at Camp N:** Igersheimer, *Blatant Injustice*, 128.

CHAPTER 11: TUBE ALLOYS, BIRMINGHAM 1941

129 **Born wanted Kellermann:** ROYSOC, Born to Francis Simon, 10.23.1940.

129 **An obvious employer:** BODLEIAN-S, KF to Esther Simpson, 1.23.1941.

130 **While Klaus was in Canada:** NA, AB 1/572, RP to Born, 11.5.1940.

130 **Ultimately, the uncertainty:** NA, AB 1/572, RP to Born, 11.27.1940.

130 **Born approached Peierls:** NA, AB 1/572, correspondence between RP and Born, 3.12–22.1941.

130 **needed a good physicist:** NA, AB 1/574, correspondence between RP and KF, 5.10–22.1941.

130 **He included a detailed letter:** NA, AB 1/572, RP to Born, 5.12.1941.

130 **Fuchs's friends from the camps:** NA, KV 2/1249, KF, interview with Skardon, 12.21.1949.

130 **Kuczynski, an outsider:** NA, KV 2/1879, 3.11.1941.

131 **Bringing German art, literature:** Brinson and Dove, *Politics by Other Means*, introduction.

131 **Klaus could easily see friends:** NA, KV 2/1259, police note, 4.15.1941; FAM, Wilhelm Koenen to Fuchs, 1959; Brinson and Dove, *Politics by Other Means*, 6, 27–29, 34–35. There are various accounts of where Fuchs and Kremer met. One is a party in April at the Kuczynski's house. Fuchs himself reported a house on the south side of Hyde Park. He probably wouldn't have named the house of a friend. During his trip in April, he did go to the league. So it is somewhat confusing.

131 **an agent for the GRU:** NA, KV 2/1561, 10.1939; AB 46/232, 9.6.1940; KV 2/1248, Robertson, 11.23.1949.

132 **Klaus found himself:** NA, KV 2/1259, Metropolitan Police memo, 4.15.1941.

134 **"Vast Power Source":** NUFFIELD, *New York Times*, May 5, 1940, in D.30.

134 **the article drew special attention:** NUFFIELD, Simon to Frederick Lindemann, May 7, 1940, in D.230.

134 **The outcome was a blithe memo:** NUFFIELD, Lindemann to Churchill, n.d., D.230/3,4.

134 **Government regulations excluded:** NA, KV

125 **Unlike during the trip over:** IWM, Walter Wallich, Hermann Wallach diary, and Heinz Bing interviews; Kellermann, *Physicist's Labour in War and Peace*, 95.

125 **Air raid sirens screamed:** www.culture24.org.uk/history-and-heritage/military-history/world-war-two/tra28260.

125 **After the all clear:** BODLEIAN-S, KF to Esther Simpson, 1.13.1941; Kellermann, *Physicist's Labour in War and Peace*, 96.

2/1658, G. P. Thompson to Air Marshal R. H. M. S. Saundby, 5.3.1940.

134 **they became full members:** Farmelo, *Churchill's Bomb*, 180.

135 **"When Fuchs went to Birmingham":** CHURCH, Born to Gustav Born, 9.2.1945.

135 **"And so all illusion":** Klaus Fuchs, "Wenn die Neugier nicht wär'!," *Meine Jugendstunden*, Teilnehmerheft 77/78, 26.

136 **the deadliest raids were over:** ROYSOC, Born to Franz Simon, 8.2.1942.

136 **Klaus became their lodger:** Peierls, *Bird of Passage*, 163.

136 **Peierls was enthusiastic about Fuchs:** NA, AB 1/575, RP to Frisch, 5.31.1941.

136 **Fuchs had recalculated:** NA, AB 1/576, RP to Maurice Pryce, 6.8.1941.

136 **Even though Fuchs:** CHURCH, Born to Gustav Born, 6.25.1941; ROYSOC, Born to Simon, 8.8.1941; Peierls, *Bird of Passage*, 164.

136 **he was the perfect fit:** BODLEIAN-P, Rudolf Peierls, taped interview.

136 **By August, Klaus was well:** FBI, "VI. Fuchs' Espionage Contacts Outside United States," 109; NA, KV 2/1256, Nov. 1950.

138 **They could build an atomic bomb:** U.S. Department of Energy, Manhattan Project, MAUD Report, 1941.

138 **create a partnership on the bomb:** Farmelo, *Churchill's Bomb*, 196–99, 203–5.

138 **required filtering uranium gas:** NA, AB 1/576, 12.23.1941; AB 1/572, 2.24.1942, 3.29.1942, 3.31.1942.

139 **They plowed through the research:** NA, AB 1/572, 8.15.1944.

139 **examined German science journals:** NA, AB 1/576, RP to Simon, 9.15.1941; Simon to RP, 2.1.1943; AB 1/578, W. A. Akers to Gorell Barnes, 6.22.1942; AB 1/574, RP to H. Halban, 8.22.1942.

139 **Sonya and Klaus first met:** NA, KV 2/1963, Fuchs note, 2.24.1950; Werner, *Sonya's Report*, 250–52; VENONA, Vassiliev yellow notebook no. 1, 86.

140 **Fuchs didn't limit himself:** Brinson and Dove, *Politics by Other Means*, introduction.

140 **the involvement of both in the KPD:** IWM, Alfred Doerfel interview.

140 **Fuchs now had authority:** NA, AB 1/574, 6.18.1942.

140 **Fuchs became a naturalized British citizen:** NA, CRIM 1/2052, 6.18.1942; KV 2/1263, 7.31.1942.

140 **MI5 officers questioned employing him:** NA, KV 2/1245, 10.10.1941.

141 **"We must . . . face the fact":** Farmelo, *Churchill's Bomb*, 215, as quoted from Margaret Gowing, *Britain and Atomic Energy, 1939–1945* (London: Macmillan, 1964), 437–38.

141 **The British and Americans reached consensus:** NA, AB 1/578, 10.29.1943.

142 **the agreement didn't specify mutual trust:** IWM, Rudolf Peierls, taped interview.

CHAPTER 12: MANHATTAN PROJECT, NEW YORK 1943

143 **The East Coast headquarters:** NA, KV 2/1255, Fuchs's notebook (addresses) from Arnold on 5.31.1950; FBI Vault, "V. Fuchs' Scientific Knowledge and Disclosures to Russians," 100. The building occupies a corner. Some references cite the address as 37 Wall Street.

144 **Meetings between the British team:** NBLA, Williams Collection [DOE Archives], box 2, folder 11, War Department, 12.8.1943; FBI: "V. Fuchs' Scientific Knowledge and Disclosures to Russians," 88.

144 **They needed special permission:** NBLA, Williams Collection [DOE Archives], box 2, folder 11, War Department, 3.18.1944.

144 **Permission was granted automatically:** FBI, File no. 5, 2.13.1950, 79–80.

144 **the plant's thousands of components:** IWM, Rudolf Peierls, taped interview.

145 **her life had changed dramatically:** USHMM, correspondence between Christel Fuchs, Hertha Kraus, and members of Quaker and refugee organizations, March–June 1938.

145 **An intensive refugee crisis:** USHMM, "Immigration to the United States, 1933–41," Holocaust Encyclopedia.

145 **From Cambridge, she worked tirelessly:** USHMM, correspondence between Christel Fuchs, Hertha Kraus, and members of Quaker and refugee organizations, June–Jan. 1939.

146 **This, their first encounter:** VENONA, Vassiliev yellow notebook no. 1, 2.5.1944.

146 **Klaus explained his assignment:** VENONA, Vassiliev yellow notebook no. 1, B, 2.5.1944, 31.

146 **Before going their separate ways:** Williams, Gold FBI statement, 197.

146 **Klaus had brought no materials:** LANL, Fuchs FBI interviews, LA-UR-14-27960, 3, 7, 10.

147 **He began his report:** VENONA, Vassiliev yellow notebook no. 1, B, 2.5.1944, 31.

147 **The KGB knew a lot about Klaus:** VENONA, Vassiliev yellow notebook no. 1, 1.29.1944, 119, 121.

147 **But there were also reservations:** VENONA, Vassiliev yellow notebook no. 1, C-NY 2.15.1944, 148.

147 **they had fleeting encounters:** VENONA, Vassiliev yellow notebook no. 1, 2.25.1944, 150.

148 **Raymond had his own drill:** LANL, Fuchs FBI interviews, LA-UR-14-27960, 14.

148 **Klaus asked about the reaction:** VENONA, Vassiliev yellow notebook no. 1, B, 48, NY-C 3.22.1944.

148 **Why had he, "Goose":** VENONA, Vassiliev yellow notebook no. 1, C—to May, 7.28.1944, 416.

148 **fabricated a detailed cover story:** VENONA, Vassiliev yellow notebook no. 1, B, 48.

148 **The work of the British team:** VENONA, Vassiliev yellow notebook no. 1, B, 49; C/t NY-C, 6.15.1944, A, 171.

149 **The scientists and engineers at Los Alamos:** NA, AB 1/5, RP to KF, 6.14.1944, 74.

150 **Fuchs's deployment remained a subject:** NA, AB 1/639, James Chadwick to RP, 7.14.1944.

150 **bringing Fuchs back to England:** NA, AB 1/639, James Chadwick to RP, 7.14.1944.

151 **"He was a student of Born":** LANL, Teller to Mayer, 2.8.1944.

151 **Fuchs sent Peierls his latest report:** NA, AB 1/575, KF to RP, 6.17.1944.

151 **he complained to Peierls:** NA, AB 1/575, Fuchs report, 7.22.1944.

151 **Fuchs succinctly summarized their work:** LANL, Klaus Fuchs, personnel form, 6.27.1945, 5.

151 **The British mission's seventeen reports:** NA, AB 1/575, KF to RP, 7.17.1944; AB 1/575, 7.22.1944.

152 **Klaus made two more trips:** LANL, Fuchs FBI interviews, LA-UR-14-27960, 16.

152 **It returned a qualified:** NA, KV 2/1245, 1.17.1944.

152 **Klaus and Raymond were to meet:** VENONA, Vassiliev yellow notebook no. 1, cipher cable NY to C, 8.29.1944, D, 154.

152 **Fuchs was on his way to Camp Y:** NA, KV 2/1249, Patterson, 1.10.1950.

153 **he learned that Klaus had left:** VENONA, Vassiliev yellow notebook no. 1, cipher cable NY to C, 8.29.1944, D, 154.

CHAPTER 13: TRINITY, LOS ALAMOS 1944

155 **transported Klaus to a new world:** McKibbin, "Under a Pinon Tree," 13, 15, 17.

156 **Dorothy McKibbin, the indispensable gatekeeper:** McKibbin interview, 1965, *Voices of the Manhattan Project*, Atomic Heritage Foundation.

156 **The research site:** Densho Encyclopedia, encyclopedia.densho.org. Today it is the Japanese Internment Remembrance Site on La Loma Vista Road in Santa Fe.

156 **they reached the Pajarito Plateau:** Jette, Inside Box 1663, 31–32; Lilli Hornig, interview with author, Aug. 2011; Patricia Shaffer, interview with author, Oct. 2016.

157 **Fuchs's next-door neighbor:** Gleick, *Genius*, 190, 187.

157 **Evenings when they were free:** FBI, Feynman interview, 78.

157 **Fuchs worked in the Theoretical Division:** FBI, "V. Fuchs' Scientific Knowledge and Disclosures to Russians," 103s; LANL, Theoretical Divisions—Personnel, Building E, 9.1.1944, "Inter-office Memorandum, 11.8.1944, Bethe to Oppenheimer.

157 **Implosion was a completely different:** Bruce Cameron Reed, in "Electronics and Detonators," Atomic Heritage Foundation.

158 **Teller was a brilliant physicist:** Lilli Hornig, interview with author, Aug. 11, 2011.

158 **When he refused to head:** BRITLIBE, Rotblat interview C464/17/01-17; Joel N. Shurkin, "Edward Teller, 'Father of the Hydrogen Bomb,' Is Dead at 95," *Stanford Report*, Sept. 23, 2003.

159 **The best minds in physics:** NA, AB 1/576, RP to George Placzek, 9.10.1944.

159 **Los Alamos a "scientific paradise":** BRITLIBE, Nicholas Metropolis, taped interview, in Moss, "We Built the Bomb." BBC Radio 4, July 16, 1985, T8056R C1.

159 **a perfect research environment:** NBLA, Williams Collection [DOE Archives], box 2, folder 11, War Department, 4.24.1944, 3.7.1945, 3.17.1945.

160 **Fuchs's first invitation to a colloquium:** NBLA, Williams Collection [DOE Archives], box 2, folder 11, War Department, 4.24.1944, 3.7.1945, 3.17.1945.

160 **Bethe considered him vital:** Bethe, interview with author, 1997; FBI, Bethe interview, 2.14.1950; Lilli Hornig, interview with author, Aug. 2011.

161 **Weisskopf was yet another:** Teller, interview with author, Dec. 1999.

161 **The scientists were sworn to silence:** John Wickerham interview, *Voices of the Manhattan Project*, Atomic Heritage Foundation.

162 **The British team was particularly close knit:** BODLEIAN-P, Genia Peierls, taped interview.

162 **He dated a couple:** NA, KV 2/1253, KF to the Skinners, 2.27.1959; FBI, Skyrme interview, 78.

162 **filling the few down hours:** Conant, *109 East Palace*, 260.

162 **He also had a reputation:** BODLEIAN-P, Special Collections D.54, R. Peierls to Schneir, Dec. 1962, and to Hans Bethe, 2.15.1950.

163 **Everyone on the Hill was entitled:** McKibbin, "Under a Pinon Tree," 77; Szasz, *British Scientists and the Manhattan Project*, 27.

163 **Raymond and Rest were reunited:** VENONA, Vassiliev yellow notebook no. 1, 70–73. Klaus, Christel, and Gold all gave separate descriptions of this encounter from memory. This account is from Gold's contemporaneous notes to the KGB.

164 **principles of the A-bomb construction:** FBI, "Fuchs' Scientific Knowledge and Disclosure to the Russians," 107H-I.

164 **He did have a request:** VENONA, Vassiliev yellow notebook no. 1, 73.

164 **Fuchs remained an enigma:** Jette, *Inside Box 1663*, 118; Laura Fermi, in Conant, *109 East Palace*, 245.

164 **"He was willing to help":** Teller, *Memoirs*, 185.

164 **Fuchs was everyone's favorite:** BODLEIAN-P, Genia Peierls, taped interview.

165 **the creation of an atomic bomb should end:** BRITLIBE, Moss, "We Built the Bomb."

165 **Churchill and Roosevelt had secretly agreed:** The Roosevelt-Churchill "Tube Alloys' Deal," 10.19.1944, Atomicarchives.com.

165 **But also in April:** Fuchs, "Wenn die Neugier nicht wär'!," 26.

165 **Fuchs, in a lecture to students:** Fuchs, "Wenn die Neugier nicht wär'!," 26.

166 **On June 2, 1945, Fuchs:** Daniel Lang, "Letter from Harwell," *New Yorker*, Oct. 6, 1956, 153.

166 **the bomb would not be ready:** Williams, Appendix C, FBI Gold statement, 213–14.

167 **the nuclear detonation would ignite:** McKibbin, "Under a Pinon Tree," 102–5; Jette, *Inside Box 1663*, 94, 198–200; Lilli Hornig, interview with author, Aug. 11, 2011.

167 **Russian radio interference:** BRITLIBE, Norris Bradbury, interview, in Moss, "We Built the Bomb."

167 **"an unholy light":** McKibbin, "Under a Pinon Tree," 106.

168 **"bedraggled and depressed":** BRITLIBE, Mrs. Deutsch and Martin Deutsch, interviews, in Moss, "We Built the Bomb."

168 **One exception to the funereal mood:** Bird and Sherwin, *American Prometheus*, 313.

168 **The next day a petition circulated:** Szilard petition, Atomic Heritage Foundation.

168 **Whatever warning the Japanese:** Alex

Wellerstein, "A Day Too Late," *Restricted Data: Nuclear Secrecy Blog*, April 26, 2013.

168 **The military argued that:** BRITLIBE, Rotblat interview, tape side A, 5, 7.25.1999. Some historians believe that Rotblat's memory was faulty, that it was out of character for Groves to have said this at a dinner party. Rotblat repeated this claim many times in interviews. Although memories are often faulty, it's usually not the content but the context: who said it, when, and where. That Rotblat heard this from some important person is likely, if not Groves.

169 **After learning of the massive:** FBI, interview of associates of Fuchs, Martin Deutsch, 80.

169 **Scientists gravely cautioned their government:** NA, AB 16/705, "Memorandum from British Scientists at the Los Alamos Laboratory, New Mexico," n.d.

170 **"We, a group of the scientists":** LANL, "An Open Letter to the President," Bethe, draft memo, n.d.

171 **they rendezvoused on the outskirts:** Williams, *Klaus Fuchs, Atom Spy*, 214–15.

171 **His first remark was:** VENONA, Vassiliev yellow notebook no. 1, 76.

CHAPTER 14: DIRECTOR, HARWELL 1946

176 **Britain's stature was declining:** Hyde, *Atom Bomb Spies*, 124; Leebaert, *Fifty-Year Wound*, 42, 43, 203.

176 **He accepted the offer:** NA, AB 1/444, 3.6.1946, 3.11.1946, 3.14.1946.

177 **advised Fuchs on staff possibilities:** NA, AB 1/574, RP to KF, 3.29.1946.

177 **"The location of the place":** NA, AB 1/574, RP to KF, 5.6.1946.

177 **The similarities with Los Alamos:** NA, AB 27/8; Alan Dick, "Didcot Days: Atom Scientist Lifts the Veil."

178 **Fuchs advised the British:** NA, AB 6/30, KF and Chadwick correspondence, 4.1–6.3.46.

178 **he visited Christel in Cambridge:** NA, AB 1/574, KF to RP, 8.7.1950; memoir of Christel Fuchs Heinemann, family material of Dietmar and Silke Goebel.

178 **Harwell was impatient:** NA, AB 1/444, McMillan to KF, 6.25.1946.

178 **One of his first "duty calls":** Flowers, "Friends and Fences," in *Atomic Spice*.

179 **required a more extensive background check:** NA, KV 4/202, 9.27–12.4.1946.

179 **the counterspies opened an investigation:** NA, KV 2/1658, 12.20.1946.

179 **ordered mail inspections on both men:** NA, KV 2/1658, 1.23.1947.

180 **Fuchs was to meet his new handler:** VENONA, Vassiliev yellow notebook no. 1, 80–81; Feklisov, *Man Behind the Rosenbergs*, 189–93.

171 **Fuchs later related:** LANL, LA-UR-14-27960, issued 10.10.2014, 24.

171 **Alamogordo is approximately:** Hornblum, *Invisible Harry Gold*, 149.

172 **What had been theory:** FBI, "V. Fuchs' Scientific Knowledge and Disclosure to the Russians," 107J.

172 **Before parting, they set:** VENONA, Vassiliev yellow notebook no. 1, 76.

172 **Fuchs's only time away:** NA, KV 2/1249, 12.2.1949.

172 **The foursome had a relaxed trip:** Teller, *Memoirs*, 223; Peierls, *Bird of Passage*, 205–6.

172 **When Raymond met with his contact:** VENONA, Vassiliev black notebook, 11.12.1945, 125.

173 **caution was very much in order:** VENONA, Vassiliev black notebook, 126.

173 **one more visit to Cambridge:** VENONA, Vassiliev yellow notebook no. 1, 12.27.1946, 80.

173 **During Fuchs's twenty-two-month stay:** LANL, Alan Brady Carr, "Lists of Material Held at the Los Alamos National Laboratory Research Library," *Project Y Inventory*, 11/5/2009.

173 **"I developed the theory":** LANL, Klaus Fuchs, personnel form, 6.27.1945, 5.

181 **nuclear energy for domestic use:** NA, AB 27/8, Cockcroft to Basil Schonland, 2.22.1950.

181–82 **use in an atomic bomb:** Farmelo, *Churchill's Bomb*, 371–72.

182 **preserve its monopoly on atomic energy:** NBLA, Williams Collection, T. O. Jones and Ralph Carlisle Smith report, 9.18.1945.

182 **"As a result of the passage":** NA, AB 1/444, McMillan to KF, 8.21.1946.

183 **the British moved forward:** NA, AB 27/8, Cockcroft to Basil Schonland, 2.22.1950.

183 **Fuchs's Theoretical Division:** NA, AB 27/8, Cockcroft to Basil Schonland, 2.22.1950.

183 **he took a personal hand:** Hyde, *Atom Bomb Spies*, 94, as quoted from Gowing, *Independence and Deterrence*, 144.

183 **He kept his ties to American scientists:** NA, AB 6/30, Awbery to KF, 7.16.1946.

183 **He brought back invaluable intelligence:** VENONA, Vassiliev yellow notebook no. 1, 82.

183 **Fuchs's approach to running the division:** BRITLIBE, Flowers, interview.

184 **a director who energetically intervened:** BODLEIAN-P, RP to Hans Bethe, 2.15.1950.

184 **She saw none of the "opinionated conceit":** Flowers, "Friends and Fences," in *Atomic Spice*.

184 **all of the disparate assessments:** BODLEIAN-P, RP to Hans Bethe, 2.15.1950.

184 **In 1948, Rudi Peierls:** ROYSOC, LC/1951/08.

184 **Klaus missed his first meeting:** VENONA,

Vassiliev yellow notebook no. 1, 82–83; Feklisov, *Man Behind the Rosenbergs*, 195–96, 205.

185 **"kind, generous, quiet"**: Michael Buneman, interview with author.

185 **Mary remembered a hesitant Klaus**: Flowers, "Harwell and Hamburg," in *Atomic Spice.*

185 **The two men became good friends**: Kathy Behrens Cowell, interview with author, Oct. 27, 2016.

186 **asked them to search**: NA, ES 1/493, KF to Akers, 2.8.1946.

186 **to exit Germany was almost impossible**: USHMM, memo on conference, 6.5.1947.

186 **What it was and what he had done**: USHMM, AFSC memo to Jones and Gallagher, 6.10.1950.

186 **assumed name of Strauss**: Feklisov, *Man Behind the Rosenbergs*, 225.

186 **He reported back that his father**: Flowers, "Harwell and Hamburg," in *Atomic Spice*; NA, KV 2/1254, Skardon memo on questions, 4.5.1950; Klaus Fuchs-Kittowski, interview with author, March 15, 2017.

186 **Surviving the war**: All information on these war years from author interviews with Klaus Fuchs-Kittowski.

187 **It was a harsh life**: GEHEEB, EF to PG, 10.18.1945; Klaus Fuchs-Kittowski, interview with author, March 2014.

187 **Emil suffered from exhaustion**: USHMM, AFSC correspondence, 6.5.1947.

187 **he found a niche lecturing**: NA, KV 2/1247,

10.6.1949; AFSC correspondence, 8.19.1946; GEHEEB, EF to PG, 11.3.1947.

188 **Emil's ultimate objective**: GEHEEB, EF to PG, 9.11.1947.

188 **provided a visa for Emil only**: AFSC correspondence, 4.22.1948.

188 **Eventually, they both received**: USHMM, AFSC correspondence, 8.22.1947, 3.8.1948, 5.14,1948.

188 **trying to immigrate to the United States**: USHMM, Kraus to Pendle Hill, 12.13.1948.

188 **the university wanted him**: USHMM, EF to "Friends," 6.16.1949.

188 **Christel sat despondent**: USHMM, AFSC note for file, 4.4.1949.

188 **Klaus and Eugene met**: Feklisov, *Man Behind the Rosenbergs*, 198.

189 **They ended the meeting**: VENONA, Vassiliev yellow notebook no. 1, 83.

189 **he developed bronchial pneumonia**: NA, AB27/8, KF to John Cockcroft, 6.8.1949; Moorehead, *Traitors*, 126.

189 **Another reason for increased caution**: John Simkin, "Venona Project," Spartacus, Yuri Bruslov, memorandum on William Weisband, Feb. 1948.

190 **Mary Buneman was there**: Mary Flowers, interview with author, March 2012.

190 **if young Klaus came with him**: USHMM, AFSC note, 1.1.1949.

190 **the progressive Shady Hill School**: Klaus Fuchs-Kittowski, interview with author.

191 **Emil had another concern**: Klaus Fuchs-Kittowski, interview with author.

CHAPTER 15: SUSPECTS, LONDON, SEPTEMBER 1949

195 **"Comparison of evidence"**: NA, KV 6/134, no. 11, 9.5.1949.

196 **"Consider evidence against Fuchs"**: NA, KV 6/134, no. 10, 9.5.1949.

196 **Martin labeled "adverse traces"**: NA, KV 6/134, no. 12, 9.5.1949.

197 **It was an obvious role**: Charles Perrin, interview with author.

199 **Perrin would follow up**: NA, KV 6/134, 9.7.1949.

199 **Robertson was very much**: Nigel West, interview with author.

199 **a comprehensive surveillance web**: NA, AB 46/232, 9.7.1949; Nigel West, interview with author.

199 **they would check every contact**: NA, AB 46/232, 9.12.1949.

199 **Fuchs must not sense**: NA, AB 46/232, minutes 116 and 135.

200 **Emil Julius Klaus Fuchs was born**: NA, AB 4/232, no. 120, 9.8.1949, and KV 2/1245, no. 32, 8.30.1943.

200 **he now required scrutiny**: NA, AB 46/232, minutes 120 and 123.

200 **a discrepancy piqued Valentine**: NA, KV 6/134, 9.13.1949.

201 **a clerk accidentally transposed**: NA, KV 2/1245, registration.

201 **duly recorded Perrin's frank opinions**: NA, KV 6/134, 9.8.1949.

202 **summarizing Perrin's information**: NA, AB 46/232, 9.9.1949, and KV 6/134, 9.7.1949.

202 **surveillance plan included**: NA, AB 46/232, minute 115, 9.7.1949.

202 **Arnold was a perfect source**: Lang, "Letter from Harwell," 148.

202 **his talents as a sympathetic listener**: Flowers, *Atomic Spice.*

202 **Arnold had a philosophy**: KV 2/1257, 1–7.

202 **His warmth also hid**: KV 2/1257, article.

204 **he watched carefully for those**: NA, KV 2/1245.

204 **Fuchs was just the kind of person**: KV 2/1257, "Notes on Dr. K E J Fuchs," 1.

204 **Arnold invited Fuchs to his house:**
KV 2/1257, "Notes on Dr. K E J Fuchs," 4.

204 **"In the early days":** KV 2/1257, "Notes on Dr.
K E J Fuchs," 2.

205 **What Arnold might have missed:** Kathy Behrens Cowell, interview with author, Oct. 27, 2016.

205 **He dodged talking to Oscar:** Mary Flowers, interview with author, March 2012.

205 **he contacted MI5:** NA, AB 46/232, Robertson's minutes of meeting, 9.7.1949.

206 **a lax attitude toward security:** NA,
KV 2/1245, minutes 45 and 46.

206 **Serpell spoke with the field operative:** NA,
KV 2/1245, minute 47.

206 **information contained an unsettling sentence:** NA, KV 2/1245, minute 48.

206 **Serpell wrote a piercing summary:** KV
2/1245, no. 49, 11.13.1946.

207 **danger to security would be a prime issue:**
KV 2/1245, no. 55, 12.4.1946.

207 **Serpell's memo also:** KV 2/1245, nos. 51 and
49, 11.26.1946.

207 **Serpell's attack ruffled staff:** KV 2/1245,
no. 57, 12.20.1946.

208 **Hollis ordered warrants:** KV 2/1245, Nos. 50,
53, 57, 58, 59.

208 **Arnold's suspicions about Fuchs:** AB 46/232,
9.9.1949.

208 **supply ample background:** AB 46/232,
9.9.1949.

CHAPTER 16: SURVEILLANCE, HARWELL, SEPTEMBER 1949

211 **recorded Fuchs's every word:** NA, AB
46/232, Progress Report, 9.16.1946; Wright, *Spy Catcher*, 55.

211 **Fuchs's incoming and outgoing mail:** Wright,
Spy Catcher, 57.

212 **a select team of Watchers:** NA, AB 46/232,
Progress Report, 9.16.1946.

212 **The chief of the Watchers:** Wright, *Spy Catcher*, 63; Hyde, *Atom Bomb Spies*, 100.

212 **a basic description:** NA, AB 46/232, 9.12.1949.

212 **Fuchs's pattern was office:** NA, AB 46/232,
Skardon to Storrier, note, 9.12.1949.

212 **kept tabs on his plans:** NA, AB 46/232, 9.16.1949.

212 **With holes, the whole system:** NA, AB
46/232, Progress Report, 9.16.1946; NA, AB 46/232,
night duty officer, 9.17.1946.

212 **tracking had their tribulations:** NA, AB
46/232, 9.19–20.1949.

213 **Fuchs invited Arnold:** NA, AB 46/232,
9.22.1949 and 9.26.1949.

213 **Arnold reported to MI5:** NA, AB 46/232,
Robertson note, 9.19.1946; AB 46/232, call with
Arnold, 9.19.1949; AB 46/232, visit to Harwell,
9.20.1949.

213 **The first real test:** NA, KV 46/232, 9.21.1949.

213 **recapped the trip's arrangements:** NA, AB
46/232, 9.26.1949.

213 **The only person disappointed:** NA, KV
2/1266, 9.21.1949.

213 **The investigation slogged along:** NA, AB
46/232, 9.21.1949.

214 **Listeners reported two visitors:** NA, KV
2/1266, 9.20.1949.

214 **The friendship between the Skinners:** Flowers, *Atomic Spice.*

214 **he and Erna saw each other:** Flowers, *Atomic Spice.*

215 **prefer older women:** Fuchs's girlfriend in
Kiel, Erna Skinner, and his later wife were all older.

215 **Arnold described Erna:** NA, KV 2/1246,
9.29.1949.

215 **she talked a lot:** Mary Flowers, interview with author.

215 **details from British passport records:**
NA, KV 2/1248, 11.11.1949, and KV 2/2080,
3.9.1950.

215 **her father was a respected journalist:**
JTA, "Daily New Bulletin," March 19, 1952, 6.

215 **The Skinners had married:** NA, KV 2/2080,
draft book review, 1952.

216 **Skinner a proper English gentleman:**
Moorehead, *Traitors,* 62.

216 **He knew of her affairs:** Mary Flowers, interview with author, March 2012.

216 **Erna to be Fuchs's mistress:** NA, KV 2/1248,
minute note, no. 335, 11.21.1949.

217 **Fuchs visited the Skinners:** NA, KV 2/1248,
11.7.1949.

217 **MI5 had a tap on:** NA, AB 46/232, note and
passport request, 9.19.1949; KV 2/1247, passport
check, 9.28.1949; KV 2/1246, 9.29.1949.

217 **MI5 was following:** NA, KV 2/1658, 10.6.1949
and 10.7.1949.

217 **an explosive finding:** NA, KV 2/134, 9.19.1949
and 9.21.1949.

217 **unlikely to consider transferring:** NA, KV
6/134, 9.21.1949.

217 **didn't want the timetable embedded:** NA,
KV 6/134, 9.30.1949.

217 **The presence of a sister:** NA, KV 6/134,
9.15.1949 (2) and 9.16.1949.

218 **requested any records on Kristel:** NA, AB
46/232, 9.16.1949 and 9.21.1949.

218 **His minute on September 20:** NA, AB
46/232, 9.20.1949.

218 **another troubling fact about Kristel:** NA,
KV 6/134, 9.14.1949, and Liddell diary, approx.
9.9.1949, date redacted.

218 **Martin pressured his main contact:** NA, KV 6/134, 9.21.1949.

218 **Could they at least confirm:** NA, KV 6/134, 9.23.1949.

CHAPTER 17: DISPOSAL, LONDON, OCTOBER 1949

221 **Fuchs went to London:** NA, AB 46/232, Arnold meeting, 9.26.1949.

221 **Their first sighting:** NA, KV 2/1246.

221 **They stayed in Fuchs's shadow:** NA, AB 46/232, 9.27.1949 and 9.28.1949.

222 **ended their preliminary report:** NA, AB 46/232, 9.27.1949 and 9.28.1949.

222 **Fuchs spent the next day:** NA, AB 46/232, 9.29.1949.

222 **details on Fuchs's health:** NA, AB 46/232 and KV 2/1266, both 9.29.1949.

223 **Watchers swiftly garnered facts:** NA, KV 2/1247, 10.6–19.1949.

223 **According to that dossier:** NA, AB 46/232, note, 9.29.1949; KV 2/2080, 3.9.1950, and 2/1247, 10.5.1949.

223 **it was time to intensify the investigation:** NA, KV 2/1247, 10.4.1949.

223 **Erna's friends concerned Robertson:** NA, KV 2/1248, 11.23.1949, 12.

223 **to open a file on Erna:** NA, KV 2/1248, 11.4.1949 and 11.24.1949, and KV 2/1247, 10.13.1949.

223 **Erna had been diagnosed with anxiety:** NA, KV 2/1248, 11.2.1949, 11.4.1949, 11.23.1949, 14.

224 **This was Tatiana Malleson:** NA, KV 2/1248, 11.23.1949, 13.

224 **her then husband had been in touch:** NA, KV 2/1248, 11.8.1949.

224 **Arnold kept an eye on the visitors:** NA, KV 2/2080, 10.16.1951.

224 **the Skinners' seemed like a boardinghouse:** NA, KV 2/1248, 11.3.1949.

224 **required the setting of priorities:** NA, KV 2/1247, 10.4.1949.

225 **data cluttered the investigation timeline:** NA, KV 2/1247, 10.17.1949.

219 **MI5 couldn't eliminate:** NA, AB 46/232, Sillitoe letter, 9.30.1949.

219 **suspicions of Western intelligence:** NA, KV 2/1266, 9.24.1949.

225 **Robertson ordered all letters:** NA, KV 2/1247, 10.7.1949.

225 **Fuchs's bank records:** NA, AB 46/232, 9.22.1949; KV 2/1247, 10.5.1949.

225 **a curious trip to photography supply shops:** NA, KV 2/1247, report, 10.7.1949; KV 2/1248, general October surveillance, 11.2.1949.

226 **scour the administrative files:** NA, KV 6/134, 10.7.1949.

226 **MI5 and the government would pull back resources:** NA, KV 6/134, 10.7.1949.

227 **Patterson promised Martin:** NA, KV 6/134, 10.14.1949.

227 **scoured the British mission's files:** NA, KV 6/134, 10.13.1949.

227 **framework with disquieting facts:** NA, KV 6/134, 10.19.1949.

228 **There was still no evidence:** NA, KV 6/134, 10.19.1949.

228 **Fuchs might break:** NA, KV 6/134, 10.19–22.1949.

228 **advice concerning his father:** NA, KV 2/1247, 10.17.1949.

229 **a letter from an old family friend:** NA, KV 2/1247, Hertzsch letter, 10.5.1949.

229 **He requested a mail check:** NA, KV 2/1247, 11.7.1949.

229 **Arnold and Fuchs met again:** NA, KV 2/1247, 10.17.1949, and KV 4/471, Liddell, 195–96, 10.31.1949.

229 **Arnold described in a memo:** NA, Arnold to Robertson, note, KV 2/1247.

230 **Fuchs's response about reacting to pressure:** NA, KV 2/1247, MS, 10.26.1949.

CHAPTER 18: INTERROGATION, LONDON, NOVEMBER 1949

231 **Sillitoe subscribed to the argument:** NA, KV 4/471, Liddell diary, 10.31.1949.

231 **Sillitoe and Liddell were very different:** NA, KV 6/134, 11.1.1949; KV 4/471, 10.31.1949, 176.

232 **Sillitoe cabled Patterson in Washington:** NA, KV 6/134, 11.1.1949.

232 **Weighing whether Fuchs would confess:** NA, KV 6/134, 11.2.1949.

233 **Fuchs's ultimate fate:** NA, KV 6/134, 11.2.1949 and 11.4.1949.

233 **Listeners heard Fuchs mention his passport:** NA, KV 2/1248, 11.10.1949.

233 **agreement for an interrogation:** NA, KV 6/134, 11.10.1949.

233 **edging Fuchs out of Harwell:** NA, KV 4/471, 11.15.1949 and KV 6/134, 11.16.1949.

234 **Fuchs's value to Harwell:** NA, KV 6/134, 11.17.1949.

234 **agreed with the strategy of interrogation:** NA, PREM 18/1279, 11.17.1949.

234 **not pursuing Fuchs outside London:** NA, KV 2/1248, Marriott, minute 293, 11.3.1949.

234 **suspending the Listeners' services:** NA, KV 2/1249, 12.1.1949.

234 **Robertson delved more deeply:** NA, KV 2/1248, 11.3.1949 and 11.7.1949.

234 **An inquisitive postman had informed:** NA, KV 2/1248, 11.7.1949.

235 **Gunn could be involved in:** NA, KV 2/1248, 11.23.1949 and 11.22.1949.

236 **theory about potential spies:** NA, KV 2/1248, 11.21.1949.

236 **Americans had rejected Peierls's recommendation:** NA, KV 2/1248, 11.21.1949.

236 **the discovery of the Russian machine:** NA, KV 4/471, 11.21.1949.

236 **Martin received a list:** NA, KV 6/134, 11.22.1949.

237 **Fuchs kept going about:** NA, KV 2/1248, 11.12.1949.

237 **The Watchers followed:** NA, KV 2/1248, 11.14–17.1949.

237 **Fuchs played host:** NA, KV 2/1248, 11.19.1949 and 11.21.1949.

237 **"all necessary clearance":** NA, KV 6/134, 11.25.1949.

238 **Jim Skardon, their top interrogator:** NA, KV 6/134, 12.15.1949.

238 **Watchers and Listeners on alert:** NA, KV 2/1249, 12.21.1949.

238 **"to detain FUCHS on any pretext":** NA, KV 2/1249, 12.21.1949.

238 **not to forewarn Fuchs:** NA, KV 2/1249, 12.21.1949.

238 **Skardon opened up:** NA, KV 2/1249, 12.21.1949.

239 **denied being a spy:** NA, KV 2/1249, 12.21.1949.

239 **Fuchs's office tap recorded:** NA, KV 2/1249, 12.21.1949.

239 **Liddell summarized MI5's evening meeting:** NA, KV 4/471, 12.21.1949.

240 **Liddell's conclusion:** NA, KV 4/471, 12.21.1949.

240 **Listeners came back on:** NA, KV 2/1249, 12.21.1949.

240 **Erna's call to him:** NA, KV 2/1269, 12.22.1949.

241 **recorded a knock on the front door:** NA, KV 2/1249, 12.21.1949. The surveillance sheet is very confusing on the time of the knock on the door. The typed notation directly follows "midnight" on December 21, 1949. It reads, "21.15 (22.12.49) There was a knock on the front door—unanswered." The time signature would translate to 9:15 p.m. on the next day. Following this note is "08.45 R. [Ramsey] got up." I have assumed that the time recorded is a typo, and the time is either 1:15 a.m. or 2:15 a.m. This surveillance sheet covers through 9:35 a.m. of December 22, 1949, only.

241 **many unanswered questions:** NA, KV 2/1269, 1.21.1950. Erna called Klaus on that night, and he also didn't answer. Perhaps he was out both nights, but no departure and return were picked up on the bug.

241 **MI5's records focused on:** NA, KV 6/134, 12.22.1949.

241 **"FUCHS volunteered or admitted":** Venona changed names a few times. Early on it was STOCK, and in this message "STOCK" was used.

241–42 **analysis of the evidence:** NA, KV 4/471, 12.22.1949.

242 **all signs still pointed to him:** NA, KV 6/134, 12.23.1949.

242 **what was to become of Fuchs:** NA, KV 6/134, 12.28.1949.

242 **MI5 group reviewed:** NA, KV 6/134, 12.29.1949.

242 **The decoders in Arlington:** NA, KV 4/471.

CHAPTER 19: DISPOSAL AGAIN, LONDON, JANUARY 1950

247 **Liddell reviewed the case:** NA, KV 4/472, Liddell diary, 1.2.1950.

248 **finalize Fuchs's disposal:** NA, KV 4/472, Liddell diary, 1.4.1950.

248 **no real interest in absolving her:** NA, KV 6/134, 1.4.1950.

248 **he had to resign from Harwell:** NA, KV 2/1269, several surveillance records, 1.10.1950.

249 **Cockcroft's account disturbed them:** NA, KV 2/1250, Marriott memo, 1.13.1950; KV 2/1249, Robertson memo, 1.11.1950; KV 2/1263, 2.1.1950, summary report.

249 **exposed another travel option:** NA, KV 2/1249, 1.11.1950, and KV 2/1269, 1.11.1950.

250 **MI5 picked up hints:** NA, KV 2/1249, 1.11.1950. Little in the conversation of January 10, 1950, that MI5 released to the public suggests that Fuchs told Erna much. There are later suggestions that he told her about giving the Russians informa-

tion on diffusion. Erna's conversations with friends the next day also don't hint at anything. It is possible that MI5 didn't release a document that contained that discussion.

250 **plans to reduce surveillance:** NA, KV 2/1249, Marriott note, 1.5.1950, restated in KV 2/1250, Robertson note, 1.24.1950.

250 **The regular taps on Fuchs's home:** NA, KV 2/1249, 1.11.1950.

251 **"He had been told that":** NA, KV 2/1263, Skardon report, 1.18.1950.

251 **Fuchs's understanding about his departure:** NA, KV 2/1250, White note, 1.18.1950.

251 **Fuchs needed to leave Harwell:** NA, KV 2/1250, 1.19.1950.

252 **In the convoluted world of espionage:** NA, KV 2/1250, Robertson note, 1.20.1950.

252 **the Skinners to talk:** STASI, Klaus Fuchs, filmed interview.

253 **he called Henry Arnold:** NA, KV 2/1269, phone bug, 1.21.1950; KV 2/1250, Robertson note, 1.23.1950.
253 **then discussed the Bunemans:** NA, KV 2/1269, phone bug, 1.22.1950.
253 **Seemingly, Arnold made his call to MI5:** NA, KV 2/1250, Robertson note, 1.23.1950.
253 **he asked to speak to the MI5 security officer:** NA, KV 2/1250, Robertson note, 1.23.1950.
254 **both men were at the Skinners':** NA, KV 2/1269, phone bug, 1.23.1950.
254 **She was concerned about Klaus's level:** NA,

KV 2/2081, Arnold to Robertson, 10.7.1952; KV 2/1250, Robertson memo, 1.23.1950.
254 **It was just the two:** NA, KV 2/1250, 1.20.1950.
254 **The Fuchs who opened:** Moorehead, *Traitors,* 139; NA, KV 4/472, Liddell diary, 1.25.1950.
255 **seemed to drain Fuchs:** Moorehead, *Traitors,* 139.
255 **Seeing Fuchs's emotional stress:** NA, KV 2/1263, 4th–7th interviews, 1.31.1950; Moorehead, *Traitors,* 138.
255 **Fuchs was distracted:** Moorehead, *Traitors,* 140.

CHAPTER 20: CONFESSION, HARWELL, JANUARY 1950

257 **"About the middle of 1942":** Moorehead, *Traitors,* 140. Fuchs pegged his spying as beginning in 1942. In fact, it began in August 1941, six weeks after Hitler invaded Russia. Whether the invasion played a role or he misremembered isn't clear.
257 **This second half of the narrative:** NA, KV 2/1250, Robertson note, 1.24.1950; Moorehead, *Traitors,* 141. Even though Moorehead wrote that Skardon didn't take notes, this may not be true. MI5 still retains documents on this interview. Moorehead used Skardon as his main source along with documents shown to him. MI5 saying it had no documents excused them from providing any. Moorehead wouldn't necessarily have known the truth. That there was no SF does seem true. That decision was made as of January 5. NA, KV 2/1249, 1.5.1950.
257 **Fuchs understood the risk:** NA, KV 2/1263, 4th interview, 1.24.1950.
258 **"a duty to the world":** NA, KV 4/472, Liddell diary, 1.25.1950.
258 **he had cut the tie:** NA, KV 2/1263, 4th interview, 1.24.1950; KV 4/472, Liddell diary, 1.25.1950.
258 **Fuchs had made a full confession:** NA, KV 2/1269 (2), KV 2/1250, Robertson note, 1.24.1950; Moorehead, *Traitors,* 141.
258 **reestablish monitoring with Listeners:** NA, KV 2/1250, Robertson note, 1.11.1950.
258 **report suspicious activity:** NA, KV 2/1250, Robertson memo, 1.24.1950.
259 **do no investigating:** NA, KV 2/1250, Robertson note, 1.25.1950; Moorehead, *Traitors,* 147–48.
259 **extract as much information:** NA, KV 2/1250, Robertson diary of events, 1.25.1950.
259 **what had finally made Fuchs break:** NA, KV 4/472, Liddell diary, 1.25.1950.
259 **Without Fuchs's trust in Arnold:** Hyde, *Atom Bomb Spies,* 123.
259 **it was the deeper psychology:** NA, KV 4/472, Liddell diary, 1.25.1950.
260 **Skardon had not cautioned Fuchs:** NA, KV 2/1250, Robertson minutes of Perrin meeting, 1.25.1950.

260 **Did the government gain:** NA, KV 2/1250, Robertson minutes of Perrin meeting, 1.25.1950.
260 **"In his present state of mind":** NA, KV 2/1250, Robertson minutes of Perrin meeting, 1.25.1950.
261 **a tape recording might embarrass him:** NA, KV 2/1250, Dick White to Marriott, 1.25.1950; KV 2/1250, Robertson minutes on Perrin call, 1.27.1950.
261 **No one expected Fuchs:** NA, KV 2/1250, MI5 meeting with Perrin, 1.25.1950.
261 **Arnold knew more than he admitted:** NA, KV 2/1250, Robertson diary of events, 1.25.1950.
261 **An ordinary day:** NA, KV 2/1269, phone records, 1.25.1950.
262 **Arnold asked Fuchs if he had handed:** NA, KV 2/1263, Appendix B to MI5 report on Fuchs, n.d.
262 **They discussed Fuchs's main concern:** NA, KV 2/1263, interviews, 12.24–30.1949, 2.
262 **Fuchs generally described his rendezvous:** NA, KV 2/1250, Robertson minutes on Perrin call, 1.27.1950.
262 **he was going to see Mary Buneman:** NA, KV 2/1269, Skinners' phone check, 1.26.1950.
263 **It was a ruse:** NA, KV 2/1250, note on White's call with Perrin, 1.27.1950.
263 **Fuchs's statement gave a largely accurate:** NA, KV 6/134, Fuchs's written confession, 1.27.1950.
264 **"namely to give information":** NA, KV 2/1263, KF confession, 2.24.1950, 8.
264 **if Fuchs made his confession:** NA, KV 4/472, Liddell diary, 1.27.1950.
264 **government could bury those words:** Moorehead, *Traitors,* 143.
264 **Klaus puttered about:** NA, KV 2/1269, phone checks, 1.28–29.1950.
264 **Skinner planned to take steps:** NA, KV 2/1250, Robertson minutes on Perrin call, 1.27.1950; KV 2/1250, note on White call with Perrin, 1.27.1950.
264 **The FBI, as yet, had received no report:**

NA, KV 2/134, Martin cable from Washington,
1.26.1950; KV 2/1250, White to Perrin, 1.27.1950.
266 **Russians had other sources:** NA, KV 2/1250,
Robertson note, 2.1.1950.
266 **What had surprised Fuchs:** FBI, "V. Fuchs'
Scientific Knowledge and Disclosures to Russians,"
107F; NA, AB 1/695, Perrin report, 1.30.1950.
267 **Fuchs's details of the plutonium bomb:**
David Holloway, interview with Cindy Kelly, May
14, 2018, Atomic Heritage Foundation.
267 **"From what I have seen":** Teller, *Memoirs*, 276.
267 **The state of Russian electronics:** Hans
Bethe, interview with Richard Rhodes, 1993,
Atomic Heritage Foundation.
268 **the Russians faced additional hurdles:** David
Holloway, interview with Cindy Kelly, May 14,
2018, Atomic Heritage Foundation.

CHAPTER 21: ARREST, LONDON, FEBRUARY 1950

271 **Hill outlined the evidence:** NA, KV 2/1263,
Hill memo, 2.1.1950.
271 **Humphreys would present:** NA, KV 2/1263,
note on the case against Fuchs for the Director
General and the Prime Minister, 1.31.1950; KV
2/1263, Hill note on 2.1.1950 conference, 2.2.1950.
271 **Fuchs, unsuspicious, kept his schedule:** NA,
KV 2/1250, Robertson note on 1.31.1950 meeting,
2.1.1950.
272 **Perrin called Fuchs:** NA, KV 2/1270, phone
check, 2.2.1950.
272 **they laid out two counts:** NA, KV 2/1263,
Hill, meeting in public prosecutor's office, 2.2.1950.
272 **possible embarrassment to the FBI:** NA, KV
4/472, Liddell diary, 2.2.1950.
272 **Portal's point overrode the objections:**
NA, KV 4/472, Liddell diary, 2.2.1950; NA, KV
2/1263, Hill, meeting in public prosecutor's office,
2.2.1950.
273 **Bostwick folding security gate:** Interview
with Charles Perrin and observations of author
273 **Perrin was at Shell Mex:** Some sources report
that Burt arrived at 3:15. Burt distorted most of the
information on Fuchs in his autobiography. Given
the times that Hill wrote in his memo, it would have
been impossible for Burt to be there then. Liddell
writes in his diary on February 2 that it was at 3:45.
273 **he wanted to speak to Perrin:** NA, KV
2/1252, KF to the Skinners, 2.3.1950.
273 **Fuchs said the first thing:** NA, KV 4/472,
Liddell diary, 2.2.1950; NA, KV 2/1252, KF to the
Skinners, 2.3.1950.
273 **He later said of the remark:** NA, KV 2/1252,
KF to the Skinners, 2.3.1950.
273 **formally charged and processed:** NA, KV
2/1263, Inspector Smith, Metropolitan Police note,
3.6.1950, and AB 126/383, 2.3.1950.

268 **he confessed because of his friends:** NA, KV
4/472, Liddell diary, 1.31.1950.
268 **"I would deal a grave blow":** NA, KV 6/134,
Fuchs's written confession, 1.27.1950.
269 **Fuchs took the train back to Harwell:** NA,
KV 2/1269, phone check, 1.30.1950.
269 **Perrin later reflected:** "Profile: Michael
Perrin, the Man to Whom Fuchs Confessed," *New
Scientist*, Jan. 24, 1957, 28.
269 **He wanted her to come to Germany:** NA,
KV 2/1250, EF to KF, 1.19.1950, rec'd 1.30.1950.
269 **Fuchs called Henry Arnold:** NA, KV 2/1269,
phone check, 1.31.1950.
270 **Arnold pleaded ignorance:** NA, KV 2/1250,
Robertson note, 2.1.1950.

273 **He spent the night in a cell:** NA, KV 2/1252,
KF to the Skinners, 2.3.1950.
274 **Burt traveled on to Harwell:** NA, KV 2/1270,
phone checks, 2.2.1950.
274 **Robertson collected his own cache:** NA, KV
2/1250, Robertson notes, 2.2.1950 and 2.3.1950.
274 **"According to what we heard":** NA, KV 4/472,
Liddell diary, 2.2.1950; Moorehead, *Traitors*, 150.
274 **Fuchs was remanded into custody:** NA, AB
126/383, 2.3.1950.
274 **MI5 expected calls from the press:** NA,
KV 2/1263, Hill memos, 2.3.1950.
274 **they pondered how they had overlooked:**
NA, KV 4/472, Liddell diary, 1.25.1950.
275 **Fuchs case was front-page news:** NA, CSC
11/103, "Scientist Accused of Atomic Leak," *Daily
Telegraph*, Feb. 4, 1950.
275 **juxtaposed the FBI's rapid exposure:** NA,
KV 2/1263, Arthur J. Cohen to Elwyn Jones, MP,
2.7.1950.
275 **"It is re-assuring to note":** NA, AB 126.383,
British Embassy Washington to Cabinet, 2.8.1950.
275 **the Brits had been lax:** NA, KV 2/1263,
Arthur J. Cohen to Elwyn Jones, MP, 2.7.1950.
275 **The Skinners had left:** NA, KV 2/1270, Skinners' phone check, 2.1.1950 and 2.3.1950.
276 **Burt interviewed Peierls:** NA, KV 2/1263,
Marriott note, 2.6.1950.
276 **Peierls asked Fuchs why he had spied:** NA,
KV 2/1661, Metropolitan Police note, 2.6.1950.
277 **Scotland Yard installed a microphone:** NA,
KV 4/472, Liddell diary, 2.4.1950.
277 **Fuchs who was depressed:** NA, KV 2/1270,
Skinner phone check, 2.4.1950; KV 4/472, Liddell
diary, 2.4.1950.
277 **Klaus had told Erna details:** NA, KV 2/1970,
Skinner's phone call to Cherwell, 2.5.1950.

277 **They felt the hurt and betrayal:** NA, KV 2/1254, Skinners to KF, 3.17.1950; KV 2/1259, minute 968, Robertson, and Skardon note, 9.24.1950.

277 **Klaus's work pressure:** NA, KV 2/1661, RP to Commander Burt, rec'd 2.6.1950.

278 **At what point does the price:** BODLEIAN-P, Special Collections, RP to Bohr and Bethe, 2.14–15.1950.

278 **Anyone who had worked with Fuchs:** FBI, B. interviews of associates of Fuchs, 84Fn2.

278 **Henry Arnold wrote to Oscar:** Flowers, *Atomic Spice*, 10.

278 **MI5 put mail and/or phone warrants:** Sir Norman Wooding, CBE, "Christopher Frank Kearton, Baron Kearton of Whitchurch, Bucks, Kt, O.B.E., 17 February 1911–2 July 1992," *Biographical Memoirs of Fellows of the Royal Society*, 224; Cathy Cowell, interview with author, Oct. 2016.

278 **Peierls tried to reconcile:** Peierls, *Bird of Passage*, 9.

278 **Klaus had taken the fate:** BODLEIAN-P, Genia Peierls, taped interview.

278 **Brixton meted out Fuchs's perquisite:** NA, KV 2/1270, Gunn's visit, 2.16.1950.

279 **The bug didn't capture much:** NA, KV 2/1270, Skinner phone check, 2.6.1950; prison bug, 2.8.1950.

279 **She wrote a direct, honest:** NA, KV 2/1661, Genia Peierls to KF, 2.4.1950.

279 **Klaus responded in kind:** BODLEIAN, KF to Genia Peierls.

280 **Liddell, who had access:** NA, KV 4/472, Liddell diary, 2.7.1950.

280 **colleagues questioned the news:** Conant, *109 East Palace*, 244.

CHAPTER 22: TRIAL, LONDON, MARCH 1950

285 **wires between the U.S. and the U.K. security:** NA, KV 4/472, Liddell diary, 2.7.1950.

285 **he testified that Fuchs:** Marshall Andrews and Alfred Friendly, "Hydrogen Bomb Secret Feared Given Russians," *Washington Post*, 4.2.50, 1.

285 **They had a noncooperative security service:** NA, KV 4/472, Liddell diary, 2.7.1950.

286 **"Wrong in principle":** NA, KV 4/472, Liddell diary, 2.7.1950.

286 **British legal procedures restricted:** NA, KV 2/1263, DG to Hoover, cable, 2.6.1950.

287 **the FBI warned the Foreign Office:** NA, FO 371/82902, 2.6.1950.

287 **The British political air:** BODLEIAN-P, RP to Bethe, 3.30.1950.

287 **Liddell agreed with the necessity:** NA, KV 4/472, 6.2.1950, and Liddell diary, 6.9.1950.

288 **That morning, police drove Fuchs:** Williams, *Klaus Fuchs, Atom Spy*, 126; NA, KV 2/1263,

280 **Fuchs's former next-door neighbor:** Gleick, *Genius*, 191.

280 **In an interview with the FBI:** FBI, File no. 5, 2.5.1950, 25; interview with Hans Bethe, 2.14.1950.

280 **considered Fuchs's motives:** MI5 website, 1950 box, comment by Dick White.

281 **none of them knew that he was a spy:** NA, AB 27/8, Philip Lee to Cockcroft, 3.15.1950.

281 **The obliviousness of MI5:** NA, KV 2/1252, Robertson note, 2.15.1950.

281 **Those from the internment camps:** NA, KV 2/1252, Martin J. Muller to Mr. Sykes, 2.13.1950.

282 **Fuchs asked Skardon:** NA, KV 6/134, Skardon notes, 2.8.1950.

282 **Martin cabled Washington:** NA, KV 6/134, Martin cable to Washington, 2.8.1950; KV 4/472, Liddell diary, 2.3.1950 and 2.8.1950.

282 **Genia Peierls reflected on the years:** BODLEIAN-P, Genia Peierls, taped interview.

282 **Klaus wrote to his father:** FAM, KF to EF, 2.21.1949.

282 **his last rendezvous:** Feklisov, *Man Behind the Rosenbergs*, 199n61. Feklisov explains that information in the KGB archives says the meeting was on April 1. Since he would never meet on such a day—they usually met on a Saturday—he wrote that they met on April 2.

283 **Sitting in a prison cell:** NA, KV 2/1255, KF to EF, 5.10.1950.

283 **When MI5 received a telegram:** NA KV 6/134, Patterson memo about PH.60, 8.16.1949.

283 **As for suspecting:** NA AB 46/232, 9.27.1949 and 9.27.1949; AB 46/232 and KV 2/1266, both 9.29.1949; KV 2/1247, report, 10.7.1949.

"Confession Alleged in Atom Case," *Daily Telegraph*, Feb. 11, 1950.

288 **Fuchs's confidence in the rightness:** NA, KV 2/1263, Humphreys's opening statement, 2.10.1950.

289 **Humphreys omitted a few sentences:** NA, KV 2/1265, Hill note, 2.8.1950.

289 **Humphreys called four witnesses:** NA, KV 2/1263, Humphreys's conference meeting, 2.3.1950; CRIM 1/2052, Skardon testimony, 2.10.1950.

289 **"What Skardon said":** NA, KV 2/1270, Skinners' prison visit, 2.25.1950.

289 **At the end of the hearing:** NA, KV 2/1263, Humphreys statement; CRIM 1/2052, court documents; KV 2/1263, Hill note, all on 2.10.1950.

290 **Skardon made a visit to Brixton:** NA, KV 6/134, Skardon memo, 2.15.1950.

290 **the governor of Brixton Prison alerted:** NA, PCOM 9/2377/2, minute from governor, 2.15.1950.

290 **Fuchs had arrived basically healthy:** NA, PCOM 9/2377/3, note from physical exam, 2.14.1950.

290 **On the afternoon of Fuchs's arrest:** NA, KV 6/134, cable to Washington, 2.2.1950.

290 **Two FBI agents found Christel:** Heidi Holzer and Marianna Holzer, interviews with author.

290 **she was perfectly rational:** FBI, Fuchs File no. 8, 3.3.1950, 93–94. Technically, it was deleted. It was not released by the FBI.

291 **She didn't know much:** NA, KC 6/134, Washington to Martin, 2.13.1950.

291 **FBI agents interviewed:** FBI, 3.24.1950.

291 **MI5 questioned Fuchs:** NA, KV 2/1251, Martin to Washington, 2.7.1950.

292 **The interest in Halperin's diary:** NA, KV 4/472, Liddell diary, 3.31.1950.

292 **Hoover whipped up a storm:** FBI, no. 3, 2.20.1950, 29–33.

292 **American and British code breakers:** NA, KV 6/134, Patterson to Martin (Sillitoe), 8.16.1949; KV 6/134, Oldfield to Martin, 8.17.1949; Hamrick, *Deceiving the Deceivers*, 36–38.

293 **Sillitoe agreed emphatically:** FBI, no. 3, 2.20.1950, 29–33, and no. 6, 2.28.1950, 65.

293 **American embassy's FBI liaison:** NA, KV 4/472, Liddell diary, 2.16.1950.

293 **Brixton was a real prison:** NA, KV 2/1252, KF to the Skinners, 2.21.1950.

293 **The Skinners came down:** NA, KV 2/1270, Skinners' visit, 2.25.1950.

CHAPTER 23: THE FBI, LONDON, MAY 1950

299 **Fuchs's attorney had three weeks:** FBI, no. 8, Ladd to Hoover, 3.6.1950.

299 **MI5 provided the FBI:** NA, KV 6/135, Sillitoe to Patterson, 3.9.1950.

299 **Whitson's sop that MI5:** FBI, 3.17.1950.

299 **Director General Sillitoe had his own problems:** NA, KV 4/472, Liddell diary, 3.17.1950.

300 **Parliament had buzzed:** NA, KV 2/1253, "The Case of Klaus Fuchs."

300 **Relying on Sillitoe's brief:** NA, PREM 18/1279, extract from the PM's address, 3.6.1950; KV 2/1263, Hill note, 2.20.1950; Liddell to Mathew, 2.23.1950.

301 **the most insidious spies:** NA, KV 2/1263, Edward Bridges to Sillitoe, 3.8.1950.

302 **"I hope you understand":** NA, KV 2/1270, Serpell interview, 3.23.1950.

302 **Serpell considered Radomysler's judgment:** NA, KV 2/1254, Serpell memo, 3.23.1950.

302 **The report allowed:** NA, PREM 18/1279, memos to Sir Edward Bridges and the PM, 3.30.1950.

294 **The Peierlses visited:** NA, KV 6/134, Skardon memo, 2.15.1950.

294 **Fuchs identify places involved:** NA, KV 6/134, Skardon memo, 2.11.1950.

294 **Fuchs described the young woman:** NA, KV 6/134, Fuchs note, 2.17.1950.

294 **he gave Skardon a couple of names:** NA, KV 2/1879, Skardon note, 3.9.1950. MI5 seemed to use the Soviet secret police organizations GRU and OGPU interchangeably.

294 **Johanna Klopstech, German-born:** NA, KV 6/135, DG to Patterson, 3.17.1950.

295 **He wasn't to be tried for treason:** Moorehead, *Traitors*, 152.

295 **"Strangely enough at that instant":** Feklisov, *Man Behind the Rosenbergs*, 216, as translated from 1983 Stasi interview of Fuchs.

295 **the date for Fuchs's trial:** NA, KV 2/1255, KF to HA, 4.14.1950.

296 **the charges against Fuchs:** NA, CRIM 1/2052.

296 **Shawcross opened with Fuchs's motives:** NA, KV 2/1264, trial transcript, 10.

296 **Shawcross's portrayal of Fuchs:** NA, KV 2/1257, McBarnet minute and White to Perrin, 4.6.1951 and 5.18.1951.

297 **Hoping to soften Fuchs's sentence:** NA, KV 2/1264, trial transcript.

298 **"Luckily, the Americans were not":** "Thank You, My Lord," *Time*, March 13, 1950.

298 **"gross fabrication since Fuchs":** TASS, March 7, 1950, archive.org/stream/KlausFuchs /fuchs98_djvu.txt.

303 **MI5 hadn't contacted internees:** NA, CAB 126/338, 6.16.1950; NBLA, Williams files, "Talks on Security Standards at Washington, July 19–21, 1950."

303 **unearth his American contact:** NA, KV 6/135, D.C. to Martin, cable, 3.8.1950.

303 **Fuchs was settling into prison:** NA, KV 2/1253, Skardon memos, 3.9–10.1950; KV 2/1255, Skardon memo, 5.11.1950.

303 **"That guy Skardon of yours":** NA, KV 26/135, Washington to Martin, 3.9.1950.

304 **they wanted Fuchs in America:** NA, KV 6/135, Martin to D.C., 3.8.1950; Washington to Martin, 3.9.1950.

304 **Would MI5 transport him?:** NA, KV 6/135, Sillitoe to Patterson, 3.14.1950.

304 **granting the FBI access:** NA, KV 4/472, Liddell diary, 3.24.1950.

304 **The Home Office feared the precedent:** NA, KV 4/472, Liddell diary, 4.28.1950.

304 **Sillitoe cabled Patterson:** NA, KV 4/472, Liddell diary, 4.28.1950.

304 **It was the fourth leak:** NA, KV 4/472, Liddell diary, 5.6.1950.

305 **He saw the interrogation:** NA, KV 4/472, Liddell diary, 5.19.1950.

305 **they needed Fuchs's agreement:** NA, KV 2/1253, Skardon memos, 3.9–10.1950; KV 2/1255, Skardon memo, 5.11.1950.

305 **He assumed that protecting Christel:** Lamphere interview, in "Secret Victories of the KGB," Red Files, PBS.

305 **Lamphere and Clegg had brought:** NA, KV 2/3797, Marriott to D.C., 5.20.1950; KV 4/472, Liddell diary, 5.20.1950.

306 **Fuchs saw the film again:** FBI, FBI confession, edited by Roger Allen and Linda S. Meade, July 26, 1950.

306 **"Yes, that is my American contact":** Hornblum, *Invisible Harry Gold*, 208. Marshall Perlin, an American attorney, visited with Fuchs in prison years later. According to him, Fuchs said that he never identified Gold as his courier. Hyde, *Atom Bomb Spies*, 120. However, according to KGB files, Fuchs told them he did after Gold had confessed.

306 **the FBI had taken Gold:** VENONA, Vassiliev yellow notebook no. 1, 64.

307 **Gold engaged in small-scale industrial espionage:** Hornblum, *Invisible Harry Gold*, 32–58.

307 **called the FBI's attention to Gold:** FBI, File no. 4, Teletype between FBI offices, 2.24.1950, 76.

308 **his defenses crumbled:** FBI, "VII. Identifica-tion of Harry Gold as 'Goose' and Subsequent Developments," 125–30; Hornblum, *Invisible Harry Gold*, 207.

308 **When Fuchs visited Christel:** Lamphere and Shachtman, *FBI-KGB War*, 156.

309 **he never involved Christel:** Heidi Holzer and Marianna Holzer, interviews with author.

309 **"He had several further meetings":** NA, AB 1/695, Perrin notes on Fuchs interview, 1.3.1950.

310 **When Gold's arrest:** Lamphere and Shachtman, *FBI-KGB War*, 147.

310 **Hoover demanded that all FBI:** Henry T. Gallagher, "Behind Hoover's FBI and Ole Miss, Clegg Was a Force," *Clarion Ledger*, June 13, 2015.

310 **"The arrest of Harry GOLD":** NA, KV 4/472, Liddell diary, 5.22.1950.

310 **Patterson sent a telegram:** NA, KV 2/3797, D.C. to MI5, 5.25.1950.

310 **Liddell considered the tactics:** NA, KV 4/472, Liddell diary, 6.9.1950; KV 6/135, Patterson cable, 5.25.1950.

310 **Fuchs signed two statements:** Lamphere and Shachtman, *FBI-KGB War*, 152.

311 **Klaus wrote to Erna:** NA, KV 2/1255, KF to Christel, 6.5.1950; and KF to Erna, 6.6.1950.

311 **He asked Lamphere and Clegg to meet:** NA, KV 4/472, Liddell diary, 6.1.1950; Lamphere and Shachtman, *FBI-KGB War*, 158–59.

311 **According to Clegg's report:** NA, KV 4/472, Liddell diary, 6.9.1950, 6.13.1950, 6.26.1950.

CHAPTER 24: PRISON, WORMWOOD SCRUBS, 1950 AND ON

313 **Skardon wrote a letter:** NA, KV 6/135, Skardon to Paice, 6.8.1950.

313 **Klaus wrote to Christel:** NA, KV 2/1255, KF to Christel, 6.5.1950.

314 **her family had paid a price:** Stephen Heinemann, interview with author, Sept. 2013.

314 **every day was the same:** NA, KV 2/1255, KF to Christel, 6.5.1950; FAM, Catchpool to EF, 5.23.1950.

314 **officials moved him to HM Prison Stafford:** NA, KV 2/1255, Skardon note, 6.29.1950.

314 **Fuchs was held in maximum security:** NA, PCOM 9/2377/4, 1950 reports from Stafford prison.

314 **Letters were fewer:** NA, KV 2/2030, H. Skinner to KF, 12.20.1950; KV 2/1257, E. Skinner to KF, 2.20.1951.

315 **Klaus decided to forgo physics:** NA, PCOM 9/2377/2, letter to Paice, 2.26.1953.

315 **Ursula claimed never:** Werner, *Sonya's Report*, 285–88; VENONA, Vassiliev yellow notebook no. 1, 86.

316 **MI5 realized that their approach:** NA, KV 4/472, Liddell diary, 4.21.1950.

316 **reverse naturalization as a punishment:** NA, KV 2/1255, KF to Under Secretary of State, 6.28.1950.

316 **"There is no doubt":** NA, KV 2/1255, Skardon memo, 7.14.1950.

316 **The Deprivation of Citizenship Committee:** VENONA, Vassiliev yellow notebook no. 1, 95.

316 **read parts of Fuchs's letter:** NA, KV 2/1265, "British Nationality of Fuchs," *Times* (London), Dec. 21, 1950.

316–17 **the Home Office canceled his citizenship:** NA, KV 2/1265, Home Office, 2.12.1952.

317 **Emil visited Gerhard:** NA, KV 2/1257, EF to KF, 2.18.1951.

318 **ended the letter with good wishes:** NA, KV 2/1257, KF to EF, 5.12.1951.

318 **two governments had established talks:** NA, CAB 126/338, 6.16.1950.

319 **MI5 took an opportunity:** NA, KV 2/1257, Prison Commission to Sillitoe, 3.7.1951.

319 **"anti-Communist propaganda":** NA, PCOM 9/377, note on Sillitoe visit, 3.7.1951.

319 **Moorehead proceeded without meeting Fuchs:** CHURCH, Moorehead to Born, 10.27.1951, and Born to Moorehead, 11.2.1950.

319 **Skardon was Moorehead's minder:** Moorehead, *Traitors*, 143.

320 **featured Fuchs and two other atomic spies:** Horst Brasch, 9.1.1986; NA, PCOM 9/2377/4, reports from Wakefield prison.

320 **"How that conscience was formed":** Moorehead, *Traitors*, 66.

320 **reminded him of the martyrs:** Raymond Mortimer, "Three Traitors," *Times* (London), July 1950.

320 **Emil Fuchs had his own unique response:** Fuchs, *Mein Leben*, 2:128.

320 **stories of Fuchs sold newspapers:** NA, CAB 21/4320, memo to Frank Newsam, 7.17.1952, and PREM 11/2079, DMF to PM, 7.16.1952.

321 **Fuchs continued to do research:** NA, CAB 126/339, Washington, D.C., to Cabinet office, 4.24.1951.

321 **MI5's Guy Liddell was:** NA, ES 1/493, Liddell to Morgan, 6.10.1952.

321 **Penney, Skardon, and an MI6 officer:** NA, ES 1/493, Morgan to Penney, 2.9.1953.

322 **the prison system had moved Fuchs:** NA, PCOM 9/2377/4, 1954 reports from Wakefield prison.

323 **the distance from Harwell increased:** NA, PCOM 9/337/2, letter to Paice, 2.26.53.

323 **twenty-one-year-old nephew, Klaus Kittowski:** NA, PREM 11/2079, CR to PM, 5.17.1957.

324 **Finally, father and son reunited:** NA, PREM 11/2079, CR to PM, 5.17.1957.

324 **Fuchs's good behavior:** VENONA, Vassiliev yellow notebook no. 1, 57.

324 **more than a model prisoner:** NA, PCOM 9/2377, W. F. Roper, 1.31.1958.

324 **He shared his cigarettes:** BA, NY/4301, KF to

CHAPTER 25: EAST GERMANY, BERLIN 1959

332 **ensure Klaus's safe arrival:** VENONA, Vassiliev yellow notebook no. 1, 59.

332 **reporters, who jumped into their cars:** Klaus Fuchs-Kittowski, interview with author, March 2012.

332 **Johnson called at Wandlitz:** Johnson, *Reuter Reporter Among the Communists*, 158–63.

334 **"I could not have embraced":** Mott, *Life in Science*, 51.

334 **Other requests were equally tied:** FAM, A. W. Miles to KF, 1.7.1960.

334 **He relived memories with old friends:** STASI, MfS AIM no. 8234/73, Teil P/1, Nitschke, 8.13.1959 and 9.12.1959.

335 **Nitschke, impressed with Klaus's humble:** STASI, MfS AIM no. 8234/73, Teil P/1, Nitschke, 7.29.1959.

335 **the cloud over Fuchs's reputation:** STASI, MfS AIM no. 8234/73, Teil P/1, Nitschke, 7.29.1959; VENONA, Vassiliev yellow notebook no. 1, 63.

324 **began to contemplate Fuchs's release:** NA, PCOM 9/2377, Cunningham and Hoyer-Millar, 12.13.1957 and 1.6.1958.

325 **Fuchs went to East Germany:** NA, CAB 128/33/32, 5.28.1959, 5; VENONA, Vassiliev yellow notebook no. 1, 64.

325 **Emil could still draw on:** FAM, EF to Ministry of the Interior, East Germany, 2.12.1959, and EF to Stephen Thorne, 3.2.1959.

325 **As the KGB wrote:** VENONA, Vassiliev yellow notebook no. 1, 58.

325 **Arrangements for him to leave:** NA, CAB 301/108, 6.11.1959, 1176.

326 **"Dear Klaus":** FAM, RP to KF, 6.15.1959.

326 **The one person Fuchs did trust:** NA, PCOM 9/2377, J.H.W. memo, 4.29.1958.

326 **"I'll be glad enough":** Lang, "Letter from Harwell," 154.

326 **"I can't call him a friend":** Moss, *Klaus Fuchs*, 127.

327 **They were driving to London Airport:** London Airport is now Heathrow Airport.

327 **he sat in a private room:** Feklisov, *Man Behind the Rosenbergs*, 225.

327 **Mixed feelings accompanied his departure:** NA, PCOM 9/2377, newspaper reports, 6.23–24.1959.

327 **he expressed some regret:** NA, PCOM 9/2377, Hugh McLeave, "Fuchs: No Resentment," 6.23.1959.

335 **extended an invitation from the KGB:** Feklisov, *Man Behind the Rosenbergs*, 226.

336 **Barwich wanted Fuchs to create:** STASI, MfS AIM no. 8234/73, Teil P/1, n.d.

336 **Fuchs's positions as deputy director:** STASI, MfS AIM no. 8234/73, Teil P/1, signature illegible, approx. 1.9.1959; BA DY30 7970, form.

336 **Klaus had been enamored:** Heidi Holzer and Marianna Holzer, interviews with author.

336 **he had sent her amusing letters:** Feklisov, *Man Behind the Rosenbergs*, 224.

337 **Klaus and Grete were opposites:** Heidi Holzer, interview with author, Sept. 2013.

337 **Klaus took a short break:** FAM, Hermann Scherzich (?) to KF, 7.22.1959.

338 **"Fuchs is an outstanding":** Hoffmann, "Fritz Lange, Klaus Fuchs, and the Remigration of Scientists to East Germany," 418.

338 **He struggled with this:** FAM, KF, interview with Sonntag, 1.8.1987.

338 **there were intrigues:** STASI, MfS

AIM no. 8234/73, Teil P/1, Nitschke report, 9.29.1959.

339 **When he applied for admission:** Klaus Fuchs-Kittowski, interview with author, March 2017.

339 **Klaus acknowledged to the reporter:** STASI, MfS AIM no. 8234/73, Teil P/1, Maye report, 9.9.1962.

339 **Declaring the article:** STASI, MfS AIM no. 8234/73, Teil P/1, Maye report, 9.29.1962.

CHAPTER 26: EXPECTATIONS, DRESDEN 1960

341 **the bureaucracy that Klaus faced:** VENONA, Vassiliev yellow notebook no. 1, 5.15.1960, 61.

342 **how much he told counterintelligence:** VENONA, Vassiliev yellow notebook no. 1, 3.15.1960 and 5.15.1960, 60–61.

342 **Klaus saw breeder reactors:** Klaus Fuchs, "The Promise of Nuclear Power," special issue, *Kernenergie* 7, no. 6/7 (1964): 368.

342 **the peaceful use of atomic energy:** VENONA, Vassiliev yellow notebook no. 1, Kvasnikov memo on 5.28.1960 meeting, 63.

343 **Fuchs canceled his activities:** VENONA, Vassiliev yellow notebook no. 1, May and June 1960, 61–65.

343 **Hans described Klaus:** VENONA, Vassiliev yellow notebook no. 1, 5.28.1960, 61.

343 **A Stasi informant reported:** STASI, "Sonderabt. Ltr.," signature redacted, 7.13.1960; VENONA, Vassiliev yellow notebook no. 1, Starikov memo, 6.2.1960.

344 **Klaus had helped the Chinese:** Communication with Klaus Fuchs-Kittowski and Guenther Flach.

344 **He complained to the SED:** Hoffmann, "Fritz Lange, Klaus Fuchs, and the Remigration of Scientists to East Germany," 419.

344 **a cheap and plentiful supply:** STASI, MfS AIM no. 8234/73, Teil P/1, memo, unsigned, 9.1.1959.

EPILOGUE: REMEMBRANCES, BERLIN, MARCH 1989

351 **Friedrichsfelde Cemetery:** Feklisov, *Man Behind the Rosenbergs,* 227–31. This contains all information on meeting with Grete.

352 **Feklisov recorded in his memoir:** Feklisov, *Man Behind the Rosenbergs,* 232.

352 **he offered a simple moral reckoning:** Feklisov, *Man Behind the Rosenbergs,* 232.

339 **Everyone was a potential informant:** Klaus Fuchs-Kittowski, interview with author, Nov. 2018.

339 **Klaus was ready for another cure:** BA, DY30–9293627.4.60.

339 **He had a hard entry:** There is confusion over whether Fuchs went to Russia immediately after arriving in Berlin.

345 **Klaus informed Werner:** STASI, "Sonderabt. Ltr.," Werner memo, 1.23.1964.

345 **Klaus did add an interesting aside:** STASI, "Sonderabt. Ltr.," Werner memo, 1.23.1964.

345 **a quick political evaluation:** STASI, "Sonderabt. Ltr.," "Schwarzdorn" memo, 4.25.1965; STASI, MfS AIM no. 8234/73, Teil P/1, Maye report, 12.4.1961.

345 **his minder wrote:** STASI, MfS AIM no. 8234/73, Teil P/1, Maye report, 6.1.1973.

346 **Klaus explained that at Harwell:** FAM, Fuchs, interview with Sonntag, 1.8.1987.

346 **he repudiated Stalinism:** STASI, Klaus Fuchs, taped interview, 1983.

347 **Klaus and Grete experienced life:** Heidi Holzer, interview with author, Sept. 2013.

347 **Klaus never used his position:** Klaus Fuchs-Kittowski, interview with author, Nov. 2018.

347 **Released from Westborough Hospital:** Marianna Holzer, interview with author, May 2013.

348 **On weekends, Heidi:** Heidi Holzer, interview with author, Sept .2013.

349 **His funeral, a solemn state affair:** Klaus Fuchs-Kittowski, interview with author, Oct. 2012.

349 **music accompanied every movement:** BA, DY30, 9819, file on funeral of Klaus Fuchs.

350 **The disintegration would:** Klaus Fuchs-Kittowski, interview with author, Nov. 18, 2019.

Bibliography

Albright, Joseph, and Marcia Kunstel. *Bombshell*. New York: Times Books, 1997.

Auger, Martin F. *Prisoners of the Home Front*. Vancouver: UBC Press, 2005.

Behn, Lisa. *Ein Spaziergang war es nicht*. Berlin: Forschung- und Publikationsproject zur Geschichte der Widerstandsgruppen um Herbert Baum, 2002.

Beirat für Geschichte in der Gesellschaft für Politik und Bildung. Schleswig-Holstein e.V, 2012.

Benz, Wolfgang, and Walter H. Pehle, eds. *Encyclopedia of German Resistance to the Nazi Movement*. Translated by Lance W. Garmer. New York: Continuum, 1997.

Bird, Kai, and Martin Sherwin. *American Prometheus: The Triumph and Tragedy of J. Robert Oppenheimer*. New York: Knopf, 2005.

Born, Max. *My Life: Recollections of a Nobel Laureate*. New York: Charles Scribner & Sons, 1978.

Brinson, Charmian, and Richard Dove. *Politics by Other Means*. Middlesex, U.K.: Vallentine Mitchell, 2010.

Brothers, Eric. *Berlin Ghetto*. Gloucestershire: History Press, 1988.

Chappell, Connery. *Island of Barbed Wire*. London: Robert Hale, 1984.

Close, Frank. *Trinity: The Treachery and Pursuit of the Most Dangerous Spy in History*. London: Allen Lane, 2019.

Coleman, Peter, Selwyn Cornish, and Peter Drake. *Arndt's Story: The Life of an Australian Economist*. Canberra: ANU E Press and Asia Pacific Press, 2007.

Conant, Jennet. *109 East Palace*. New York: Simon & Schuster, 2005.

Cornelissen, Christoph, and Carsten Mish, eds. *Wissenschaft an der Grenze*. Essen, Germany: Klartext, 2010.

Cresswell, Yvonne M., ed. *Living with the Wire: Civilian Internment in the Isle of Man During the Two World Wars*. Douglas, Isle of Man: Manx National Heritage, Manx Museum, 2010.

Dohnke, Kay, Renate Dopheide, Tino Jacobs, and Frank Omland, eds. *Schleswig-Holstein und der Nationalsozialismus, 1925–1950*. Kiel: Arbeitskreis zur Erforschung des Nationalsozialismus in Schleswig-Holstein, 2008.

Ehrlich, Kristina. "Der Aufbau und die Aufgaben der RSG an der Berliner Universität in Verbindung mit biographischen Aufgaben zur Person W. Girnus." Unpublished thesis, pp. 12, 14.

Evans, Richard J. *The Coming of the Third Reich*. New York: Penguin Press, 2004.

Farmelo, Graham. *Churchill's Bomb*. New York: Basic Books, 2013.

Feklisov, Alexander. *The Man Behind the Rosenbergs*. With Sergei Kostin. New York: Enigma Books, 2004.

Feller, Ray, and Steve Feller. *Silent Witnesses: Civilian Camp Money of World War II*. Port Clinton, Ohio: BNR Press, 2007.

Flach, Günter, and Klaus Fuchs-Kittowski, eds. *Vom atomaren Patt zu einer von Atomwaffen freien Welt: Zum Gedenken an Klaus Fuchs.* Berlin: Trafo, 2012.

Flowers, Mary. *Atomic Spice.* homepages.inf.ed.ac.uk/opb/atomicspice.

Fuchs, Emil. *Christ in Catastrophe.* London: Pendle Hill, 1949.

———. *Mein Leben.* Vol. 1. Leipzig: Koehler & Amelang, 1957.

———. *Mein Leben.* Vol. 2. Leipzig: Koehler & Amelang, 1959.

Gleick, James. *Genius: The Life and Times of Richard Feynman.* New York: Vintage Books, 1993.

Goltz, Anna von der. *Hindenburg: Power, Myth, and the Rise of the Nazis.* Oxford: Oxford University Press, 2009.

Goodman, Michael S. *Spying on the Nuclear Bear.* Stanford, Calif.: Stanford University Press, 2007.

Greenspan, Nancy. *The End of the Certain World.* New York: Basic Books, 2005.

Hamrick, S. J. *Deceiving the Deceivers.* New Haven, Conn.: Yale University Press, 2004.

Haynes, John Earl, Harvey Klehr, and Alexander Vassiliev. *Spies.* New Haven, Conn.: Yale University Press, 2009.

Hempel, Georg. *Die Kieler Hitlerjugend: Chronik, Geschichten und Aufsätze ihrer Kampfzeit.* Kiel, Germany: Buchdruckerei Max Tandler, 1938. Translated by Randall L. Bytwerk, 2010.

Hett, Benjamin Carter. *Crossing Hitler.* New York: Oxford University Press, 2008.

Hochheim, Dagmar. "Emil Fuchs: Eine Biographie." Institut für Lehrerbildung "Käthe Dunker," Eisenach, 1989.

Hofmann, Erich, Rudolf Jaeger, and F. A. Schmidt-Künsemüller. *Allgemeine Entwicklung der Universität.* Neumünster: Karl Wachholtz, 1965.

Holloway, David. *Stalin and the Bomb.* New Haven, Conn.: Yale University Press, 1994.

Hornblum, Allen M. *The Invisible Harry Gold.* New Haven, Conn.: Yale University Press, 2010.

Hyde, Montgomery. *The Atom Bomb Spies.* London: Hamish Hamilton, 1980.

Igersheimer, Walter S. *Blatant Injustice.* Edited by Ian Darragh. Montreal: McGill-Queen's University Press, 2005.

Jette, Eleanor. *Inside Box 1663.* Los Alamos Historical Society, 2012.

Johnson, Peter B. *Reuter Reporter Among the Communists, 1958–59.* London: Tagman Crown, 2000.

Kellermann, Walter. *A Physicist's Labour in War and Peace: Memoirs, 1933–1999.* Peterborough, U.K.: Stamford House, 2004.

Kellner, Michael. *Karl Hermann, Oh Thüringen, mein Heimatland.* Eisenach, Germany: Michael Kellner, 2005.

Kelly, Cynthia C., ed. *The Manhattan Project.* New York: Black Dog and Leventhal, 2007.

Koch, Eric. *Deemed Suspect.* Toronto: Methuen, 1980.

Koch, H. W. *The Hitler Youth.* New York: Stein & Day, 1976.

Krause, Konrad. *Alma Mater Lipsiensis.* Leipzig: Leipziger Universität Verlag, 2003.

Kuczynski, Jürgen. *Freunde und Gute Bekannte.* Berlin: Schwarzkopf & Schwarzkopf, 1997.

Lamphere, Robert J., and Tom Shachtman. *The FBI-KGB War: A Special Agent's Story.* Macon, Ga.: Mercer University Press, 1995.

Laucht, Christoph. *Elemental Germans.* London: Palgrave Macmillan, 2012.

Leebaert, Derek. *The Fifty-Year Wound.* New York: Little, Brown, 2002.

Leo Baeck Institute. *Year Book XIX.* London: Secker & Warburg, 1974.

Lynton, Mark. *Accidental Journey.* Woodstock, N.Y.: Overlook Press, 1995.

McDonough, Frank. *Opposition and Resistance in Nazi Germany.* New York: Cambridge University Press, 2001.

McKibbin, Dorothy S. "Under a Pinon Tree: Old Santa Fe—New Los Alamos." Unpublished manuscript. Los Alamos Historical Society Archives.

Merson, Allan. *Communist Resistance in Nazi Germany.* London: Lawrence and Wishart, 1985.

Michaelis, Anthony. *The Scientific Temper.* Heidelberg, Germany: C. Winter, 2001.

Moorehead, Alan. *The Traitors.* New York: Dell, 1965.

Moss, Norman. *Klaus Fuchs: The Man Who Stole the Atom Bomb.* London: Grafton Books, 1987.

———. "We Built the Bomb." Audio tape, British Library.

Mott, Sir Nevill. *A Life in Science.* Philadelphia: Taylor & Francis, 1986.

Mühlberger, Detlef. *Hitler's Voice: The Völkischer Beobachter, 1920–1933.* Vol. 1. New York: Peter Lang, 2004.

Panitz, Eberhard. *Treffpunkt Banbury.* Berlin: Das Neue Berlin, 2003.

Peierls, Rudolf. *Bird of Passage.* Princeton, N.J.: Princeton University Press, 1985.

Pieper-Wöhlk, Hannelore, and Dieter Wöhlk. *Kiel: Der dreifache Blick.* Kiel, Germany: Herkules, 2010.

Pikarski, Margot. *Jugend im Berliner Widerstand.* Berlin: Militärverlag der Deutschen Demokratischen Republik, 1978.

Pincher, Chapman. *Treachery.* New York: Random House, 2009.

Rossiter, Mike. *The Spy Who Changed the World*. London: Headline, 2014.

Schumann, Dirk. *Political Violence in the Weimar Republic, 1918–1933*. Translated by Thomas Dunlap. New York: Berghahn Books, 2009.

Sebag Montefiore, Simon. *Stalin: The Court of the Red Tsar*. New York: Knopf, 2004.

Seidler, Harry. *Internment: The Diaries of Harry Seidler, May 1940–October 1941*. Edited by Janis Wilton. Translated by Judith Winternitz. London: Allen & Unwin, 1986.

Stent, Ronald. *A Bespattered Page?* London: Andre Deutsch, 1980.

Szasz, Ferenc Morton. *British Scientists and the Manhattan Project*. New York: St. Martin's Press, 1992.

Taleikis, Horst. *Aktion Funkausstellung*. Berlin: Dietz, 1988.

Teller, Edward. *Memoirs: A Twentieth-Century Journey in Science and Politics*. Cambridge, Mass.: Perseus, 2001.

U.S. Congress, Joint Committee on Atomic Energy. *Soviet Atomic Espionage*. Washington, D.C.: GPO, 1951.

Werner, Ruth. *Sonya's Report*. London: Chatto & Windus, 1991.

Williams, Robert Chadwell. *Klaus Fuchs, Atom Spy*. Cambridge, Mass.: Harvard University Press, 1987.

Wright, Peter. *Spy Catcher*. New York: Dell, 1987.

Index

Aachen, 71
Academy of Arts (Berlin), 350
Academy of Fine Arts (Leipzig), 22, 24
Acheson, Dean, 318
Air Force, U.S., 1
Air Ministry, 130, 132, 133–35
Alamogordo test. *See* Trinity test
"Alexander." *See* Kremer, Simon
Anderson, John, 97, 98, 107, 119, 141, 142
Andes, 143
anti-Semitism, 107, 204
Arandora Star, 111–12, 119
Arlington Hall Station, 3, 5–6, 189–90, 292–93
arms race, 169–71
Army Air Force, U.S., 168
Army Corps of Engineers, U.S., 143–44
Arnold, Henry, 202–6
  background of, 202
  Erna and, 215, 216, 224, 251–53, 254, 261–62,
    279, 337
  Fuchs's relationship with, 204–6, 208–9, 219,
    229–30, 232–33, 238–39, 251–54, 258–59,
    269–70, 323, 326–27
  Fuchs's trial, 289, 295
  at Harwell, 190, 191, 219, 228, 249, 278
  surveillance, 202–6, 208–9, 212, 213, 216,
    221, 229–30, 238–39, 258–59, 261–62,
    269–70, 300
Atlantic Charter, 7, 140–41, 176, 198
atomic bombings of Hiroshima and Nagasaki, 2,
  165, 166, 168, 267, 321

atomic bomb research. *See also* Central Institute
    for Nuclear Physics; Los Alamos; *and specific
    scientists*
  of Chinese, 344
  nuclear fission, 132–34, 136, 137–39, 149
  nuclear weapon design, 157–58, 164, 173
  Quebec Agreement between U.S. and U.K.,
    141–42, 182, 198, 201
  of Soviet Union, 1–2, 169–70, 219, 266,
    267–68, 322
Atomic Energy Act of 1946 (McMahon Act), 169,
    172, 178, 182–83, 262, 318, 324
Atomic Energy Research Establishment (Harwell
    Laboratory), 176, 177–79, 181–85, 189–90,
    193, 202–9, 211–17
attack on Pearl Harbor, 141
Attenberger, Lisa, 42, 56, 66
Attlee, Clement, 2, 4, 175, 182, 247, 300, 301, 304
Austria, 92, 97

Bach, Johann Sebastian, 19, 23, 25
Bad Freienwalde, 69–70
Bad Pyrmont, 93, 186
Barbusse, Henri, 72, 74
Barwich, Heinz, 335–36
Battlefields Park, 120–21
Battle of Dunkirk, 13
Battle of the Atlantic, 125
Battle of the Plains of Abraham, 114
Behrens, Derek, 183–84, 185, 205, 278
Belgian Congo uranium mine, 318

Bell Cinema, 152
Bell for Adano, A (Hersey), 160
Bentley, Elizabeth, 173, 180, 190, 307, 309
Beria, Lavrentiy, 268
Berlin Police, 60, 61
Berlin Wall, 344, 350
Bethe, Hans
 background of, 150
 at Cornell, 178
 Fuchs's loyalties, 152, 280
 at Los Alamos, 150, 152, 157, 158, 160, 178, 350
 at Odenwaldschule, 150
 opposition to use of atomic bomb, 170
 Peierls's letters to, 277–78, 287
Birmingham, 65, 135–36, 139–40, 200. *See also*
  University of Birmingham
Blackett, Patrick, 82
Blitz, the, 2–3, 12–13, 106–7, 124, 125, 131
Blitzkrieg, 94, 106, 119, 124
Bohr, Niels, 237, 277–78
Born, Gustav, 135, 281
Born, Hedwig "Hedi," 88–89, 94, 97, 282, 334
Born, Irene, 88
Born, Max, 158–59
 background of, 87, 88
 Fuchs's and Kellerman's internment, 97, 99, 107,
  119–20
 Fuchs's atomic research, 134–35, 136
 Fuchs's spying, 281, 282
 Fuchs's relationship with, 88–89, 94, 95, 96, 107–8,
  119–20, 129–30, 175, 237, 281, 282, 292, 334
 Goeppert Mayer and, 158, 161
 Mott and, 78, 86
 Teller and, 151, 158–59, 161
 at University of Edinburgh, 86, 87–89, 94, 96,
  129–30, 175, 237, 282
 at University of Göttingen, 78, 86, 87, 88
 Weisskopf and, 161
Bow Street Magistrate's Court, 288–89
Brecht, Bertolt, 41–42
breeder reactors, 342, 344–45, 346
Bristol Evening Post, 85
Bristol. *See* University of Bristol
British Communist Party, 4, 10
British internment, 11–12, 97–99, 101–8
British Overseas Supply Company, 225, 229
British Society of Friends, 68, 78
Brixton Prison, 276, 278–80, 281–82, 288, 290,
  293–94, 297
Brookings Institution, 91
Brooklyn Museum of Art, 152
Buddhist Society of England, 271
Buneman, Mary, 253, 254
 background of, 179
 Fuchs's relationship with, 178–79, 184, 185, 190,
  205, 214, 216, 262–63
Buneman, Micky, 185

Buneman, Oscar
 background of, 179
 at Harwell, 205–6, 253, 278, 287, 303
 at Los Alamos, 178–79, 184
 MI5 investigation of, 278
Burgess, Guy, 284, 301, 319
Burroughs, William S., 157
Burt, Leonard, 271, 273–74, 276–78, 288, 289
Butler, Rab, 325–26

California Institute of Technology, 170
Cambridge Five, 284, 301
Camp L, 75, 114–23, 301–2, 323
Camp N, 123–24, 291, 301, 302, 323
Canada internment, 106–7, 113–24, 301–2
Carnegie Hall, 148
Carnegie Trust, 89, 96, 129
Catchpool, Corder, 279
Central Institute for Nuclear Physics (ZfK),
  335–39, 344
Chadwick, James, 237
Chamberlain, Neville, 60, 92, 94, 96
Chambers, Whittaker, 286
Channel Islands, 106
Chaplin, Charlie, 26
Charles I of England, 180
Charles V, Holy Roman Emperor, 19
Chinese atomic research, 344
Churchill, Winston
 Atlantic Charter, 7, 140–41, 176, 198
 atomic research, 134, 138
 general election of 1945, 175
 Iron Curtain Speech, 4
 Potsdam Conference, 168–69, 175
 Quebec Agreement, 141–42, 182, 198, 201
 war leadership of, 94, 96, 97, 98, 134, 138,
  140–41, 165
Cimperman, John, 293, 304
Clarendon Laboratory, 134
Clegg, Hugh, 305–6, 308, 310–11
Cockcroft, John, 237, 342
 Fuchs and Royal Society, 184
 Fuchs's resignation, 248–50, 251–52
 Fuchs's arrest, 274
 Fuchs's interrogation and confession, 238, 242,
  258, 259, 260, 264, 271
 at Harwell, 176, 177–78, 184, 216, 234
Collard, John, 206, 208
Columbia University, 144, 150, 158, 161, 236
Communist International, 61, 72
Communist Party of Germany (KPD)
 election of 1930, 25
 election of 1932, 28–29, 39, 40, 43, 47
 election of 1933, 62–64
 Nazi era, 60, 61, 66, 67, 71–72, 78, 91, 140
 Weimar Republic years, 25, 27, 32, 40–41, 42,
  45–46

"Conscience Without Reason!" (editorial), 320
Corpus Christi College, 111
Cove Fields, 114
Cuba, 145, 347
Cuno, Wilhelm, 29
Curtis-Bennett, Derek, 295, 296–98

Dachau concentration camp, 335
Davis, Bette, 91
Decline and Fall of the Roman Empire (Gibbon), 314
Denmark, 44, 84–85
Department of Scientific and Industrial Research (DSIR), 13, 152
Deprivation of Citizenship Committee, 316–17
Deutsch, Martin, 168
Deutschtum, 44, 47
Dickens, Charles, 295
Didcot Station, 212, 216, 221, 254
Diels, Rudolf, 61
Dimitrov, Georgi, 72, 81, 336–37
Disraeli, Benjamin, 213
Donaldson's School, 99
Dresden, 27–28, 84, 336, 337–38, 348, 352
Dunworth, John, 224

East Berlin, 331–33
East Germany, 325, 331–39, 344, 346–48
Eden, Anthony, 82
Edinburgh Sheriff Court, 95
"Effect of Fluctuation in the Flow of Nitrogen," 5–7, 198, 199, 201
Einstein, Albert, 72, 119
Eisenach, 19–20, 22, 23–25, 27–28, 30, 31, 68, 333
Elbe River, 90
electrical conductivity, 78–79, 83
XI International Brigade, 102, 116–17, 235
"enemy aliens," 11–12, 95–96, 97, 130, 134, 205
Engels, Friedrich, 25, 42
Essmann, Walther, 46, 51–52
Ettrick, SS, 108–12, 115
"Eugene" (Alexander Feklisov), 180–81, 184–85, 188–89, 282–83, 290
Evangelical Community Newsletter, 12, 19

Federal Bureau of Investigation (FBI)
   Fuchs case, 7–8, 197, 198, 218–19, 225–27, 232, 236–37, 242, 264–65, 275, 286, 287, 290, 298, 299, 303–9
   Gold case, 173, 306–9
   Heinemann case, 202, 217–18, 232
   Peierls case, 217–19, 225
   "Raymond" interrogation, 190
Feklisov, Alexander ("Eugene"), 351–52
Feynman, Richard, 157–58, 161, 168, 280
Flowers, Brian, 184
Folkestone, 11, 77

Forster, E. M., 82
For Whom the Bell Tolls (Hemingway), 117, 132
Fraenkel, Abraham, 52, 57
Free German League of Culture, 131, 140, 294, 334
Free Socialist Student Group, 32–36, 40–41, 47, 49–52, 55–56, 65–66, 349
French and Indian War, 114, 120–21
Friedrichsfelde Cemetery, 349–50, 351
Frisch, Otto, 132–34, 136, 137
Fuchs, Elisabeth. *See* Kittowski, Elisabeth Fuchs
Fuchs, Else Wagner, 24, 30, 31
   death of, 35–36
Fuchs, Emil, 19–24, 78, 225
   arrest and imprisonment of, 68–69
   in Bad Freienwalde, 69–70
   in Berlin, 79–80, 85, 90–91, 186–87
   in East Germany with son Klaus, 321, 324, 325, 332, 337
   death of, 346
   death of daughter Elisabeth, 93–94
   death of son Gerhard, 317–18
   death of wife Else, 35–36
   Harwell visit to son Klaus, 190–91, 283
   at Kiel Pedagogical Academy, 30, 31–32, 36, 56–57, 65
   pacifist beliefs of, 21, 37, 41, 62, 65, 346
   political activities of, 20–24, 25, 30, 35, 36–37, 56–57, 65, 68–70, 186, 320
   Quakerism of, 37, 41, 63–64, 65, 68, 78, 84, 89, 92, 93, 186
   Reichstag fire, 55, 68
   trial of, 69, 72–73
   at University of Leipzig, 186, 188, 190, 191, 228, 229, 232, 238, 269, 317, 324
   von Bardeleben incident, 68, 73
   at Woodbrooke Quaker Centre, 65, 68
   during World War I, 19–20, 21
   during World War II, 186–88
Fuchs, Gerhard
   arrest and release of, 84
   in Berlin, 29, 30, 31, 47–48, 54, 61–62, 64, 65–66, 69, 84
   death of, 317–18
   "Kaspar" report on, 12, 196
   at Odenwaldschule, 20, 21, 22
   political activities of, 26–27, 32, 34–35, 36–37, 40–41, 43–48, 65–68, 79–80, 84–85
   in Prague, 79, 84, 89–92
   in Switzerland, 12, 20, 92–93, 186, 187–88, 317
   tuberculosis (TB) of, 84, 89, 93, 186, 187–88
   at University of Kiel, 44–47
   at University of Leipzig, 24, 26–27, 34–35, 36–37, 43
Fuchs, Karin, 48, 65, 84, 85, 317

Fuchs, Klaus
  at Air Ministry, 130, 132, 133–35
  arrest of, 272–84
  atomic research of, 132–35, 138–39, 143–44,
    146–50, 342, 344–45, 346
    Los Alamos, 155–57, 160, 161–62, 167, 173, 176,
      178, 265–66, 322
    ZfK, 335–39
  in Berlin, 58–62, 64, 66–68, 69
  confession of, 254–55, 257–67
    inducement, 229–30, 260, 261, 264, 268, 271,
      289, 295, 296
  death of, 346, 348–49
  denaturalization of, 316–17
  early life of, 19–24
  in East Germany, 325, 331–39, 344, 346–48
  education of, 23, 24–27, 29–30, 31, 36–37, 66–68
  "enemy alien" status of, 11–12, 95–96, 97, 130, 132
  Erna and, 189, 208, 214–17, 222–23, 239, 240–41,
    249–54, 261–63, 269, 289, 311, 319, 326
  espionage and meetings
    "Alexander," 131, 136–37, 139, 281–82, 290, 294
    "Eugene," 180–81, 184–85, 188–89, 282–83, 290
    "Raymond," 145–49, 152–53, 160–61, 163–64,
      166, 169, 170, 171–73, 180, 190, 265–66, 291,
      305–11, 343
    "Sonya," 139–40, 315, 350
  evil, question of, 352–53
  funeral of, 349–50, 351
  Grete and, 72, 337–38, 339, 349, 350, 351–52
  as "Margot" (Margarete), 323, 325, 336
  at Harwell, 176, 177–79, 181–85, 189–90, 202–9,
    211–17, 247, 253, 269, 271–72, 281, 321, 346
    forced resignation, 247–50, 254
  imprisonment of
    at Brixton, 276, 278–80, 281–82, 288, 290,
      293–94, 297
    release, 324–28
    at Stafford, 314–15, 321
    at Wakefield, 323–25, 327
    at Wormwood Scrubs, 303–4, 305–6, 313–14
  internment of
    in Britain, 97–99, 101–8
    in Canada, 113–24
    Ettrick crossing, 108–12
  in London, 77–78
  MI5 file, 8–15, 140, 300–301
  MI5 interrogations, 231–32, 237–43, 247–48,
    250–51
  MI5 security investigation, 195–209
  MI5 security review, 179–80, 181–82
  MI5 surveillance, 198–209, 211–17, 221–22,
    224–25, 227–30, 233, 234–35, 237, 239, 240–41,
    258–59
  Moorehead interview, 319–20
  naturalization, 9, 129–30, 140, 179, 234
  in Paris, 71–74

  registration card of, 80–81
  student political activities of, 27–28, 29–30,
    34–37, 39–43, 47, 49–56, 66–68
    death sentence, 53–54
  trial of, 285–86, 288–90, 295–98
  at University of Birmingham, 130, 132, 133, 135,
    139, 201, 207–8, 263
  at University of Bristol, 9–10, 74, 77, 78–79,
    81–86, 215–16
  at University of Edinburgh, 86, 87–89, 91–92,
    94–95, 129–30, 282
  work permit of, 9, 12–13, 132, 137
Fuchs, Kristel. *See* Heinemann, Kristel Fuchs
  "Christel"
Fuller Lodge, 162, 172, 177
Furry, Wendell, 291–92

gaseous diffusion, 138–39, 151, 198
Geheeb, Paul, 20, 31, 41, 48, 58, 90
General Electric Company, 213
General Post Office (GPO), 211–12
Geneva Conventions, 104
German Communist Party. *See* Communist Party
  of Germany
German federal election of 1930, 25, 28
German federal election of 1932, 28–29, 39, 40, 43, 47
German federal election of 1933, 53, 62–64
German National People's Party, 63
German POWs, internment of, 12, 104, 106–7, 109,
  112, 114, 115, 117–18
German-Soviet Nonaggression Pact, 94–95, 137, 301
Germany
  during Cold War, 331–39
  Nazi era. *See* Nazis
  Weimar Republic. *See* Weimar Republic
  during World War I, 19–20, 21
Goddard, Rayner, 296–98
Goebbels, Joseph, 28, 60
Gold, Harry (a.k.a. "Raymond" a.k.a. "Goose"), 180,
  190, 291, 306–10
  arrest and interview of, 305–10, 343
  background of, 306–7
  Bentley and, 190, 307, 309
  Fuchs's meetings with, 145–49, 152–53, 163–64,
    166, 169, 170, 265–66, 308–9, 311
  Heinemann's meetings with, 153, 160–61,
    163–64, 172–73, 291, 308–9
Göring, Hermann, 28, 53, 59–60, 63
Gortipohl, 187
Gouzenko, Igor, 173, 180, 218, 309
Government Communications Headquarters
  (GCHQ), 3
Graf Zeppelin, 28
Grand Central Terminal, 280
Great Depression, 4, 25–26, 27, 307
Great Rollright, 315
Greenglass, David, 308

Groves, Leslie, 142, 143–44, 155–56, 159–60
GRU (G.U.), 131, 147
Gunn, Jessie, 74, 78, 79, 279
Gunn, Ronald, 74, 78, 79, 81–82, 234–35, 279
gun-type diffusion, 157–58
Gurney, Ronald, 81

Hager, Kurt, 338
Hahn, Otto, 132–33
Halperin, Israel, 218, 291–92
Hamburger, Ursula. See Kuczynski, Ursula
Hanfstaengl, Putzi, 61
Harper, Russell, 223
Harvard University, 145
Harwell Laboratory, 176, 177–79, 181–85, 189–90,
    193, 202–9, 211–17. See also specific scientists
Haupt, Joachim, 33–34, 36, 57–58
Heinemann, Kristel Fuchs "Christel," 31–32, 336,
    347–48
  brother Klaus at Wormwood, 313–14
  in Cambridge, MA, 92, 144–45, 152, 178, 188, 202
  early life of, 20, 22
  FBI investigation of, 217–19, 232, 248, 251,
    290–91, 305–6
  marriage to Albert Holzer, 347–48
  nervous breakdown and hospitalization of, 188,
    269, 290–91, 314, 317, 347
  at Odenwaldschule, 28, 31, 35, 36, 58
  "Raymond" and, 153, 160–61, 163–64, 172–73,
    291, 308–9
  at Swarthmore, 83–84, 145
Heinemann, Robert "Bob," 145, 188, 217–19, 232,
    290–92, 314
Heinemann, Stephen, 314
Heisenberg, Werner, 27, 87, 139, 159
Hellwig, Joachim, 348, 351–52
Hemingway, Ernest, 117, 132
Herweg, Ludwig, 11
Hill, B. A., 271–74
Hindenburg, Paul von, 39–40, 43, 44, 52–53, 55, 59, 63
Hiss, Alger, 286–87
Hitler, Adolf
  appointment as chancellor, 52–53
  death of, 165
  election of 1932, 28–29, 40, 43
  election of 1933, 53, 62–64
  Kiel rally, 46
  Reichstag fire, 55–56
  Reichswehr trial, 28–29
  rise to power, 23, 26, 28–29, 32, 40, 43, 46
  during World War II, 13, 81, 90, 92, 94, 96,
    118, 121
Hitler Youth, 41
Hodder, Hartley, 11
Hoepner, 45, 49–50, 51
Hollis, Roger, 207, 208, 303
Hollywood Ten, 286

Holzer, Heidi, 347, 348
Holzer, Marianna, 347
Hoover, J. Edgar
  Fuchs case, 265, 285–86, 287, 298, 299, 310, 311
  McCarthyism and, 287
  Venona project, 292–93
Hornig, Don, 167
Horst-Wessel-Haus, 60
Hotel Fürstenhof, 23
House Un-American Activities Committee
    (HUAC), 286–87
Howse, Philip, 292–93
Humphreys, Christmas, 271, 274, 288–89, 295–98
Huxley, Aldous, 82
Huxley, Julian, 82
Huyton, 101–4, 125
Hyde Park, 2–3
hydrogen bomb, 321–22, 322

IG Farben, 79
Immigration Act of 1924, 145
Imperial Naval Station, 32
Imperial Tobacco Company, 78, 234
implosion bomb, 157–58, 164, 173, 267–68
International Brigade, 102, 116–17, 235
internment
  in Britain, 11–12, 97–99, 101–8
  in Canada, 106–7, 113–24, 301–2
  of Japanese-Americans, 156
invasion of Poland, 94, 106
invisible ink, 211–12, 218
Irish Republican Army, 324
Isle of Man, 104–6
Italian declaration of war, 103
Italians, internment of, 11–12, 109, 112, 156

Japan, during World War II
  atomic bombings of Hiroshima and Nagasaki, 2,
    165, 166, 168, 267, 321
  attack on Pearl Harbor, 141
  Soviet invasion of Manchuria, 169
  surrender, 171
Japanese-American internment camps, 156
Jewish internment in Canada, 121–23
Johnson, Peter, 332–33
Joint Institute on Nuclear Research, 341–44
Joint Intelligence Committee (JIC), 1–2
Journal of George Fox, 68

Kadena Air Base, 312
Kahle, Hans, 11–12, 131–32, 180, 224, 235, 350
  British internment of, 102–3, 108, 111, 179, 300
  Canada internment of, 116–19, 122–25
  Fuchs's relationship with, 131–32, 137, 179, 196,
    200, 207–8, 301, 302, 303
  as inspiration for Hemingway, 117, 132
  Kremer and, 131, 137

Karl Marx Medal, 349
"Kaspar," 12, 196, 200
Kearton, Frank, 143, 144, 150, 201–2, 225–26, 235–36, 278
Keilson, Grete
  in East Germany, 323, 325, 331, 336–38, 347, 351–52
  Fuchs's relationship with, 337–38, 339, 349, 350, 351–52
  in Paris, 72, 336–37
Keilson, Max, 72
Kellermann, Walter, 88, 92, 94, 96, 255, 282
  British internment of, 98, 99, 103–8
  Canada internment of, 116, 124–25
  Ettrick crossing, 108–12
  at Southampton College, 130
  at University of Edinburgh, 88, 89, 91, 129–30
Kellex Corporation, 144, 151
Kew Gardens, 185, 294, 314
Keynes, John Maynard, 82
KGB, 147, 153, 173, 189–90, 307, 309, 325, 332, 341–43, 352
Khrushchev, Nikita, 333
Kiel, 31–34, 41–48, 52–53, 58. See also University of Kiel
Kiel Daily News, 32
Kieler Zeitung, 43, 55
Kiel Pedagogical Academy, 30, 31, 36, 56–57
Kittowski, Elisabeth Fuchs, 69
  at Academy of Fine Arts, 22, 24
  arrest and imprisonment of, 69
  in Berlin, 79, 80, 84–85, 90–91
  death of, 93–94
  death of mother, 35
  in Kiel, 30, 31–32, 65
  political activities of, 26, 34, 54, 58, 69, 90–91
Kittowski, Guschi, 93, 145
  arrest and imprisonment of, 69, 84, 85, 90–91
  in Berlin, 79, 80, 90–91
  political activities of, 69, 84–85, 90–91
Kittowski, Klaus, 84, 145, 181, 321, 346, 347
  in East Germany, 331, 337, 339
  education of, 190–91, 339
  visits with uncle Klaus, 190–91, 228, 323
  during World War II, 186, 187–88
  at Young Friends Work Camp, 323
Klaus Fuchs: History of Atomic Treachery (movie), 345
Klopstech, Johanna, 180, 294–95
Koch, Erich, 23–24, 334
Korda, Alexander, 320
Korean War, 311–12, 354
KPD. See Communist Party of Germany
Kremer, Simon (a.k.a. "Alexander"), 131, 136–37, 139, 281–82, 290, 294
Kristallnacht, 145
Krugmann, Werner, 49, 50, 51

Kuczynski, Jürgen, 130–31, 180, 294–95, 335
  background of, 131, 294
  Fuchs's relationship with, 91, 103, 130–31, 139, 140, 294–95, 350
  internment and release of, 96, 98
Kuczynski, Ursula (a.k.a. "Sonya"), 139–40, 315, 350
kulaks, 83
Kurchatov, Igor, 268

Lamphere, Bob, 305–6, 308–11
Leconfield House, 3, 212. See also MI5
Left Book Club, 91, 92, 294
Leipzig, 24–25, 28. See also University of Leipzig
Lend Lease program, 140–41
Lenin, Vladimir, 42, 81, 82
Lichtenfeld, Karl, 44–45
Liddell, Guy, 300–301, 304–5
  Fuchs case, 236, 247–48, 286, 293, 304–5, 316, 321–22
    arrest, 272, 274, 280, 285
    confession, 259, 260, 264, 268
    interrogation, 231–32, 233, 239–42, 247, 248
    German communist activities, 60–61, 64
    Gold's arrest, 310
    MI5 purge, 287–88
Liebknecht, Karl, 25, 349
Lingen, Count (Prince Friedrich of Prussia), 111, 116, 117, 122, 123
Liverpool, 108, 125, 208, 215, 275, 315
London Airport, 327
London School of Economics, 294, 301
Los Alamos, 149–50, 155–72, 353. See also specific scientists
  Fuchs's arrival at, 155–57
  Fuchs's espionage at, 160–61, 163–64, 166, 169, 171–73, 251, 265–66
  Trinity test, 165–69, 178, 266, 268
Los Alamos Main Gate, 127, 156, 163, 166
Los Alamos Ranch School, 157
Luther, Martin, 19, 23, 28
Lutheranism, 19, 22–23, 37, 41
Luxemburg, Rosa, 25, 349

McCarthy, Joseph (McCarthyism), 287
McKibbin, Dorothy, 156, 167
Maclean, Donald, 318–19
McMahon, Brien, 169, 172
McMahon Act, 169, 172, 178, 182–83, 262, 318, 324
MacMaster, Gilbert, 68, 69
Mahnruf (newsletter), 48, 72
Makins, Roger, 272, 274–75
Malleson, Tatiana, 224, 238, 279
Manhattan Project, 4, 5, 7, 143–44, 146–52. See also Los Alamos
Marriott, John, 236, 249

Martin, Arthur
    Fuchs case, 5–15, 195–209, 218–19, 225–28,
        235–38, 241, 242, 250, 251, 282
    forced resignation, 249
    interrogation, 237–38, 264–65
    memo, 2–3, 5–7, 196–97
    MI5 file, 8–15, 195–97
    surveillance, 198–209, 227–28
    Peierls surveillance, 217–18
Martin, Joan, 6
Marx, Karl, 25, 42, 81, 346
Mathew, Theobald, 271, 272–73
MAUD Committee, 134, 137–38
May, Alan Nunn, 180, 320
Mayer, Maria Goeppert, 150–51, 158, 161
May-Johnson Bill, 169, 172
Meitner, Lise, 132–33
Mendeleev Congress, 82–83
Meusel, Alfred, 35, 131
MI5. *See also specific persons*
    bugging of British Communist Party, 4, 10
    covert "purge system" of, 287–88
    Fuchs's arrest, 271–84
    Fuchs's confession, 254–55, 257–67, 286, 289
    Fuchs's interrogations, 231–32, 237–43, 247–48,
        250–51
    Fuchs's postmortem of case, 299–303
    Fuchs's security file, 3, 8–15, 81, 131, 140,
        300–301
    Fuchs's security investigation, 152, 195–209
    Fuchs's security review, 179–80, 181–82, 299–301
    Fuchs's surveillance, 198–209, 211–17, 221–22,
        224–25, 227–30, 233, 234–35, 237, 239, 240–41,
        258–59
    SCR and, 82
MI6, 7, 200–201, 225
Molotov–Ribbentrop Pact, 94–95, 137, 301
Montcalm, Louis-Joseph de, 121
Moorehead, Alan, 319–20
Moorlager, 69
Mortimer, Raymond, 320
Moscow Trials, 85–86
Mott, Nevill, 78–79, 81–83, 86, 89, 130, 281, 334
Münzenberg, Willi, 72, 82
Mussolini, Benito, 81, 165

Nash, John, 334
Nazis (Nazi Germany)
    anti-Jewish legislation, 46, 55, 57
    election of 1930, 25, 28
    election of 1932, 28–29, 39, 40, 43, 47
    election of 1933, 53, 62–64
    Hitler's appointment as chancellor, 52–53
    internment of POWs in Canada, 12, 104, 106–7,
        109, 112, 114, 115, 117–18, 122, 207
    Kristallnacht, 145
    military build-up, 96, 97, 98–99

Operation Barbarossa, 137
Reichstag fire, 55–56, 59, 72, 73
seizure of power, 23, 26–30, 31–34, 36–37, 39–40,
    43–50, 52–53, 59–65, 79
Netherlands, 96, 98
Neukölln, 62, 63
New York Times, 134, 275, 280
"Night of the Long Knives," 58
Nitschke, 334–37, 339
Nobel Prize, 27, 79, 89
Normandy landings, 150
North Korea, 311–12
nuclear fission, 132–34, 136, 137–39, 149
Nuremberg Laws, 121

Oak Ridge National Laboratory, 8, 92, 144, 195,
    198, 265
Odenwaldschule, 20, 21, 22, 28, 31, 35, 36, 58,
    190–91
Official Secrets Act, 137, 139, 140, 229, 267, 272
OGPU (Joint State Political Directorate),
    207, 294
Old Bailey, 295–96
Operation Barbarossa, 137
Oppenheimer, Robert
    Fuchs's arrest, 280
    at Los Alamos, 149–50, 152, 157–61, 165, 182,
        184, 291
    opposition to use of atomic bomb, 170

Paddington Station, 221, 237, 238, 263, 321
Pajarito Plateau, 156
Papen, Franz von, 44, 46–47, 52, 53, 61
Paris, 71–74, 103
Paterson, Alexander, 124
Patterson, Geoffrey
    Fuchs case, 226–28, 242, 310
    interrogation, 232, 233, 237–38, 303–4
    Heinemann investigation, 218–19
Peierls, Genia
    background of, 136
    in Birmingham, 135–36, 282
    Fuchs's imprisonment, 278, 279–80, 294
    Fuchs's investigation, 214, 224
    Fuchs's relationship with, 162, 282–83
    Fuchs's release, 326
    Mott's visit, 83
Peierls, Rudolf "Rudi"
    atomic research of, 132–37, 139, 143–44, 149–52,
        157–58, 161–62, 167, 184, 207–8
    Fuchs's arrest, 275–78, 279
    Fuchs's imprisonment, 294
    Fuchs's investigation, 13, 201–2, 214, 235–36,
        263, 287
    Fuchs's release, 326
    Fuchs's return to Germany, 346
    at Los Alamos, 157–62, 167, 172

Peierls, Rudolf "Rudi" (*cont.*)
    MI5 investigation and surveillance of, 13, 179,
        201–2, 211, 217–18, 237
    Mott's visit, 83
    at University of Birmingham, 130, 132, 133,
        135–36, 139, 177, 184, 201, 207–8
Peierls-Frisch Memo, 132–34, 136, 137
Penney, William, 321–22
Pentland Hills, 91–92
Perrin, Michael
    background of, 197
    Fuchs case, 13–14, 197–98, 201–2, 292, 293, 300,
        303, 309, 322
    arrest, 272–73, 274
    confession, 258, 259–61, 263, 265, 266, 268–70
    forced resignation, 248–49, 251, 252
    interrogation, 238, 241–42
    trial, 289
    Kearton and, 201–2, 226
    Russian atomic bomb test, 1–2
Perutz, Max, 120
Philby, Kim, 284
Plains of Abraham, 114
plutonium, 149, 152
Pohle, Vera, 223–24, 279
Poland, invasion of, 94, 106
Polish Airlines, 328, 331
Pontecorvo, Bruno, 318, 320
Portal, Charles, 233, 234, 242, 249, 264, 272, 274–75,
        292, 293
Potsdam Conference, 168–69, 175
Preussenschlag, 46–47, 53
Proceedings of the Royal Society, 79, 83
Putin, Vladimir, 349

Quakers, 21, 37, 41, 63–64, 65, 68, 78, 84, 89, 92, 93
"Quantum Mechanical Investigation of the
        Cohesive Forces of Metallic Copper Metals"
        (Fuchs), 78–79, 83
Quebec Agreement, 141–42, 182, 198, 201
Queen Mary, 178
Queen's University, 218

Rackwitz, Arthur, 29, 62, 63, 69, 90–91, 334–35
Radomysler, Asik, 301–3
Railway House Hotel, 253–54
Rantzau, Otto Graf zu, 53
"Raymond." *See* Gold, Harry
"Red Scare," 286–87
Red Shock Squad, 66
Red Spark, 41–42
Red Student Group (RSG), 46, 65–66
Red Students (newsletter), 36
Reichsbanner, 27, 41, 44, 56–57
Reichstag fire, 55–56, 59, 68, 72, 73, 81, 336
Religious Socialists, 37, 62
Religious Society of Friends. *See* Quakers

Revolutionary Student Group, 32
Ribbentrop, Joachim von, 61
Richmond Park, 180
Riesengebirge, 65
Rio Grande, 156
Robbins, Joseph Arnold, 304, 307–8
Robertson, James, 217–18, 274
    Fuchs and Arnold, 206, 208, 221, 228–29, 238–39,
        253, 254, 258–59
    Fuchs's confession, 260, 261, 263, 269–70
    Fuchs's surveillance, 198–203, 206, 208, 211–12,
        221, 223, 224–25, 234–35, 238–39, 250
Rockefeller Foundation, 159
Röhm, Ernst, 58
Rolland, Romain, 72
Roosevelt, Franklin D., 138, 140–41, 165
    Atlantic Charter, 7, 140–41, 176, 198
    Quebec Agreement, 141–42, 182, 198, 201
Rosenberg, Ethel, 287, 308, 334
Rosenberg, Julius, 287, 308, 334
Rotblat, Joseph, 168
Rote Burg, 68–69
Rowlands, Archibald, 233, 234
Royal Society, 120, 184, 206
Russell, Bertrand, 82
Rüsselsheim, 19–20, 200
Russian Revolution, 25, 40, 41, 82, 95, 286
Rust, Bernhard, 58

Sakharov, Andrei, 322
Sangre de Cristo Mountains, 162
Saturday Evening Post, 320
Sawyer Hill, 162
Schönefeld Airport, 325, 331
Schücking, Walther, 32–33, 57
Scottish Enlightenment, 95
Scottish Refugee Committee, 96
Secret Intelligence Service. *See* MI6
Security Service. *See* MI5
SED. *See* Socialist Unity Party of Germany
Seeburg, 43, 45, 52, 53
Serpell, Michael, 206–8, 300, 301–3
Seven Years' War, 114, 120–21
Shady Hill School, 190–91
Shawcross, Hartley, 295–98, 316–17
Shell Mex House, 198, 201, 216, 242
Signal Intelligence Service, U.S. Army (SIS),
        7, 195–96. *See also* Venona project
signals intelligence (SIGINT), 287–88
Sillitoe, Percy
    background of, 231
    Fuchs and FBI, 286, 292–93, 304, 311
    Fuchs's interrogation, 231–34
    Fuchs's postmortem of case, 299–301
    Fuchs's surveillance, 248–49
    Halperin and, 218
    Moorehead book, 319

Simon, Francis, 134, 138–39, 281
Sinclair, Upton, 72
Skalweit, August, 39, 52, 53, 54, 57
Skardon, William James "Jim," 334
    Fuchs's arrest, 281–82, 283
    Fuchs's confession, 254–55, 257–64, 265, 271
    Fuchs's interrogations, 238–40, 241–42, 250–51,
        270, 294–95, 300, 303–4, 305, 311, 313–16,
        321–22
    Fuchs's surveillance, 202–3, 212
    Fuchs's trial, 289–90
    Moorehead interview, 319
Skinner, Elaine, 215, 240, 250
Skinner, Erna
    background of, 215
    death of, 315
    Fuchs's arrest, 273, 276, 277, 279, 283–84
    Fuchs's imprisonment, 293–94, 314–15
    Fuchs's relationship with, 189, 208, 214–17,
        222–23, 239, 240–41, 249–54, 261–63, 269, 289,
        311, 319, 326, 337
    Fuchs's surveillance, 211, 213, 215, 217, 222–23,
        224, 240–41
    Moorehead book, 319
Skinner, Herbert
    background of, 215
    death of, 315
    Fuchs's arrest, 275–76, 277
    Fuchs's imprisonment, 293–94, 314–15
    Fuchs's relationship with, 189, 208, 215–16, 238,
        251–53, 264, 281
    Fuchs's resignation, 248
    Fuchs's surveillance, 211, 213, 215, 217, 224
    at University of Bristol, 215–16
    at University of Liverpool, 208, 238, 248, 249, 250
Skyrme, Tony, 144, 150, 151, 160, 161, 201–2, 225, 236
Smith, Officer, 276–77
Social Democratic Party of Germany (SPD), 25,
        26–27, 32–33, 36, 66
    election of 1930, 25, 28
    election of 1932, 40–41, 43, 47
    election of 1933, 62, 63
    Emil's joining of, 22, 25, 346
Socialist Student Union, 26–27, 29–30, 32
Socialist Unity Party of Germany (SED), 332, 335,
        336, 337, 344, 345, 349
Society for Cultural Relations between the Peoples
        of the British Commonwealth and the USSR
        (SCR), 81–82, 85–86
Some of My Best Friends Are Soldiers (Halsey), 160
Southampton College, 130
South Korea, 311–12
Soviet Union
    arms race, 169–71
    atomic bomb project, 1–2, 169–70, 219, 266,
        267–68, 322
    invasion of Manchuria, 169

Molotov–Ribbentrop Pact, 94–95, 137, 301
    Mott's visit, 82–83
    Operation Barbarossa, 137
    post-war period, 2, 4, 176
Spanish Civil War, 85, 92, 102, 103, 116–17
SPD. See Social Democratic Party of Germany
Stafford Prison, 314–15, 321
Stalin, Joseph, 40, 94, 333
    Potsdam Conference, 168–69, 175
    during World War II, 137, 267
Stasi, 334, 339, 343
Steenbeck, Max, 347
Strategic Bombing Survey, 295
Sturge, Paul, 95
Sturmabteilung (SA), 41, 42, 44, 46–47, 53, 54, 58, 60,
        68, 73
Sudetenland, 90, 92
Sunkel, Reinhard, 33–34, 36, 46, 57–58
Swarthmore, 83–84, 145

Tale of Two Cities (Dickens), 295
TASS Russian News Agency, 296, 298
Technische Hochschule, Berlin, 66–68, 336
Technische Hochschule, Dresden, 336
Tel Aviv University, 57
Teller, Edward, 150–51, 158–59, 164, 267, 322
Teller, Mici, 164, 172, 214
Thälmann, Ernst, 40–41, 43, 64, 72
Thomson, G. P., 134–35
Thysville, 125
Trafalgar Square, 237
Traitors, The (Moorehead), 320
Trinity test, 165–69, 178, 266, 268
Truman, Harry S., 2, 219
    atomic bombings of Hiroshima and Nagasaki,
        165, 168
    Korean War, 312
    Potsdam Conference, 168–69, 175
Turnip Winter of 1916–17, 21

Uffington White Horse, 177
Ulam, Stan, 322
Ulbricht, Walter, 332, 335, 337, 338, 342, 343, 345
United Kingdom general elections of 1945, 175
United Nations, 170–71, 176
United Nations Atomic Energy Commission,
        170–71
University of Adelaide, 249
University of Berlin, 48, 66

University of Birmingham, 200
    Fuchs at, 130, 132, 133, 135, 139, 201, 207–8, 263
    Peierls at, 130, 132, 133, 135–36, 139, 177, 184,
        201, 207–8
University of Bristol, 9–10, 74, 77, 78–79, 81–86,
        215–16
University of Cambridge, 87, 116, 216

University of Edinburgh, 86, 87–89, 91–92, 94–95,
    129–30, 282
  Born at, 86, 87–89, 94, 96, 129–30, 175,
    237, 282
  Fuchs at, 86, 87–89, 91–92, 94–95, 129–30, 282
University of Frankfurt, 57
University of Göttingen, 78, 86, 87, 88
University of Kiel, 17, 32–37, 39, 40–42, 44–54
  fee increase protests, 34–35, 36
University of Leipzig, 24–27, 29–30, 159, 317,
    339, 348
  Emil Fuchs at, 186, 188, 190, 191, 228, 229, 232,
    238, 269, 317, 324
University of Liverpool, 208, 238, 248, 249, 250
University of Pennsylvania, 307
uranium U-235, 133–34, 136, 138, 141, 149, 151, 158,
    165, 169, 172, 265
uranium U-238, 133, 138, 149

van der Lubbe, Marinus, 55
Väter der tausend Sonnen (documentary), 350
Venona project, 7, 189–90, 197, 198, 292–93
  Fuchs case, 195–96, 199, 201, 217, 226–27, 233,
    238, 241, 242–43, 251, 257, 283, 284
Versailles Treaty, 32, 43, 46
Victoria, Queen, 116
Victory in Europe Day (V-E Day), 165
Vidal, Gore, 157
Vishinsky, Andrei, 85–86
Vivian, Valentine, 200
von Bardeleben, Frau, 68, 73
von Neumann, John, 119–20, 161, 292, 322

Wagner, Gisela, 225
Wakefield Prison, 323–25, 327
Wall Street Crash of 1929, 25–26
Wartburg Castle, 28
Washington Post, 285
Weimar Republic, 21–22
  election of 1930, 25, 28
  election of 1932, 28–29, 39, 40, 43, 47
Weisband, William, 189–90

Weisskopf, Victor Frederick "Viki," 161
Weiz, Herbert, 349
Wells, H. G., 82
West, Rebecca, 320–21
West Berlin, 331, 333
Westborough Hospital, 290–91, 347
Westemigranten, 336
White, Dick, 6, 196
  Fuchs's arrest, 272, 280, 290
  Fuchs's interrogation and confession, 230, 231,
    238, 242, 251, 310
  Fuchs's surveillance, 198, 199, 200
Whitson, Lish, 285, 286, 292, 293, 299
Wiggs, C. W., 116, 117, 118, 120–21, 122–23
Wilhelm II, 20, 25, 32, 111
Wills, Henry H., 78
Wills, Henry Overton, I, 78
Winchell, Walter, 292, 293
Windscale Piles, 183, 266
Wolf, Karl, 57
Wolf, Markus, 348
Wolfe, James, 121
Wood, Arthur, 157
Woodbrooke Quaker Centre, 65, 68
Woolf, Virginia, 82
Woolworth Building, 144
World Committee Against War and Fascism (1933),
    72, 336–37
World Congress of Youth Against War and Fascism
    (1933), 71, 72, 73–74, 336–37
World War I, 19–20, 21, 39–40
Wormwood Scrubs Prison, 245, 303–4, 305–6,
    313–14

Yapou, Edith, 223
Yapou, Eliezer, 223–24, 238
Young Friends Work Camp, 323

Zehlendorf, 61, 65, 85
ZfK (Central Institute for Nuclear Physics),
    335–39, 344
Zorn, Johanna, 349